Family History
of
Western North Carolina

Second Edition

Joyce Justus Parris

CLEARFIELD

First Edition, containing a collection of
newspaper columns published in the
Asheville-Citizen Times between 1983 and 1994,
originally published in book form in 1994.

Second Edition, improved and augmented,
printed for Clearfield Company, Inc., by
Genealogical Publishing Co., Inc.
Baltimore, Maryland
1998

Reprinted for
Clearfield Company, Inc. by
Genealogical Publishing Co., Inc.
Baltimore, Maryland
2000

International Standard Book Number: 0-8063-4825-9

Made in the United States of America

PREFACE

Family History of Western North Carolina is a compilation of eleven years of special columns included in the *Asheville Citizen-Times*, Asheville, North Carolina. These columns have been edited and divided into subjects rather than arranged by dates.

Thanks to the editors of the *Asheville Citizen-Times*, thousands of inquiries have been published over these years. Many people have received help from readers in Western North Carolina and across the United States that would not have been possible by any other method.

Thanks to the readers of "Family History," for without them the column would have never endured for eleven years. These pages are dedicated to the readers who understand this quest for ancestors and relatives.

Hopefully, these pages will remind you of steps that you could retrace to try to find one of those elusive thirty-two great-great-great grandparents.

TABLE OF CONTENTS

INTRODUCTION

Why do some people search for their ancestors? One common misconception, held by people who do not search, is that most genealogists look for ancestors to brag about a king or a duke or to join some society or to boast about wealth. Reasons, however, are much more complicated, and most people who diligently search give you a blank stare if you ask them "why." They seem to feel that if you don't know, you won't understand anyway.

Some look at family history as a challenge to put the pieces all together into one solid family. Some family searchers run backwards hoping to understand themselves better. Some even look for an ancestor born the exact day they were and then study that ancestor in detail, trying to predict their own futures. Family searchers, gazing at old pictures, look for their own faces.

Graveyards hold no fear; most searchers feel at home there because family members are there. If they can find a graveyard where a 4-great grandfather along with a 3-great grandfather plus multitudes of kin lie, they feel secure. The family searchers sit and "talk" to ancestors, feel and see the ones who buried the kin. You might picture the horse-drawn wagon, bringing the body. You might feel the sadness with which the person was buried. You are not only in the place where ancestors are buried but also where the living ones walked.

The family searchers know they are part of a big family of many kinds of people before them. They see in their own families, if they look deeply and honestly enough, heroes, murderers, sheriffs, extortionists, legislators, anarchists, ministers -- good and bad all mixed up. They find an eight great-grandmother who was beheaded after the attempted overthrow of James II of England. They feel shame that a great-great grandfather really did help take the Cherokees to Oklahoma. History in general becomes more important as people look for the "whys."

The true awfulness of the Civil War becomes apparent when searchers read of the four great-great-great uncles; three joined the Confederacy; one died at Fredricksburg; another died in Virginia; one was killed by "bushwackers" on his way home. The fourth joined the Union army and was a survivor, came back home, accepted still as family. A great-great-great grandfather left for the Civil War but never came home.

1

His wife never knew what had happened to him; she never remarried, just waited, and reared the six children. The family searcher finds him. He was captured in Cocke County, Tennessee, and died March 7, 1864. He's number 755 in the prisoners' graveyard in Rock Island, Illinois.

The family searchers become humble one day, proud one day, shamed one day, sad one day, all because of ancestors. They read a letter that says a great-great grandfather is "poverty-stricken." They're sorry, even though they never had much sympathy for him because they'd seen his stern, unfeeling face in pictures with one thin, turned-down line for a mouth.

They will perhaps gain strength by understanding the survival of the family in the past. They may remember three households of family members all under the same roof during the depression years in the 1930s or mothers and children living with parents during the war years in the 1940s.

Family searchers also find optimistic hope. They see that a son died at two years of age on Christmas Day, and they know that Mother's and Father's Christmases will never be truly happy again. However, they know the parents survived and even smiled again. They read the memoirs of a great-great-great grandfather: "In the year 1849 my Greatest affliction took place. The Lord had in much mercy kept my Dear Companion and self in reasonable health and much harmoney and love, within a few short weeks of forty-nine years together when she was snatched away by Death. . . My fate seemed to be sealed and the world became a perfect chaos to me, and I a lonely wanderer in it. And my future course is veiled in total darkness at this time." However, he remarried in 1853; in 1862, he stated, "The many ups and downs of life can scarcely fail to leave some happy moments for reflection and profit . . ."

Most people who are not interested in learning more than they already know about family cannot imagine why a million people in America are doing research or why they want to.

Working on family history is often a frustrating experience. First, often no one else in your family understands why you are so obsessed with finding out about the old ancestors. Your motives are questioned: What trouble are you trying to "dig up"?

Another frustration is the fury that is heaped upon you if you question

2

Aunt Lillie's story, handed down through the family, that great-great grandfather John was a Confederate general in the Civil War; but you cannot find any proof and see in a Bible that he died in 1858.

An additional frustration is trying to explain by official records that a county historian was not accurate about your family. The printed page is powerful. Who are you to question it? Your family says that it makes no difference that censuses, marriage records and other documents "don't fit."

The final frustration for you is to work for fifteen years on one family, spend hundreds of dollars and uncountable hours; then, you proudly and freely present members of this family with your carefully documented and typed history, and you are told, "Well, when I have time, I'll read that."

Perhaps these frustrations are why you enjoy writing and hearing from "far-flung" cousins who are as interested as you are on finding the family. You may never meet them, but writing long letters about your searching problems to one who understands helps.

You'll never find out all you want to know. If you were born in the 1930s, you have 128 direct ancestors (parents, grandparents, great-grandparents) since the mid-1700s. Working backwards from your parents, you will have quite a puzzle trying to put all the kin in their proper places. There is no telling whom or what you will find during that sorting.

Once you get started, you can spend as little or as much time on your searching as you wish. The records of the ancestors will just sit there and wait for you someplace.

Sometimes when your frustrations are becoming too much for you, you need to relieve your fatigue by having a laugh at your own obsession. Two books by Laverne Galeener-Moore, *Collecting Dead Relatives* and *Further Undertakings*, are sure to make you at least smile. [Genealogical Publishing Company, Inc.,: Baltimore, 1987, 1989] The author takes you with her on her jaunts to visit the national archives and county courthouses, with descriptions about other patrons but mostly about the staff members who thwart the onward investigation by their rules and regulations. She describes the "sure-fire genealogist repellant" from a county courthouse as "sent the records some place else."

She understands the anticipation of discovery in your hearts and the importance of your search; only a fellow historian would call a library "the hottest hangout in town." You'll recognize yourself when mail mania strikes. The author often beats the mailman to the box and hides behind the bushes to pounce out as soon as he drives on. "Who besides a genealogist burst forth into song when they discover a death certificate in their mailbox?"

Her hints for research are interspersed with her humorous memoirs of doing research. No personal letters to the national archives, of course: "You must list whatever form you are attempting to pry out of them by its official government printing number, or they won't play." The main message of the books is that you are not alone in your frustrations.

When you become somewhat "jaded" by looking at too many ancestor charts, you may want to take a little break and do some wandering back in time for inspiration. In Western North Carolina, there are museums to visit that may instill a renewed spirit within you. Some of these are the Carson House at Pleasant Gardens, the Mountain Gateway Museum in Old Fort, the Swannanoa Valley Museum in Black Mountain, the Smith-McDowell House on Victoria Road in Asheville, and the Museum of North Carolina Handicrafts in Waynesville.

At the Carson House, you can ramble around in the three-story house, dating back to 1783, study family histories stored there, listen to history from the "Bard of Buck Creek." The Carson House is impressive from its roofing shingles of hewn white oak to its 1800s furnishings and eight original hand-carved mantles. Col. John Carson, originally from Pennsylvania, built an 18 by 20-foot, two-story house of 12-inch walnut logs on the banks of Buck Creek.

Carson was an agent for William Blount, helping him to buy hundreds of thousands of acres of land. Carson first married Rachel McDowell, who was a daughter of "Hunting" John McDowell, one of the first settlers in this present area of McDowell County (then Burke). In 1758, "Hunting" John McDowell and his friend Henry Wiedner had a wrestling match to see which one of them would claim present Pleasant Gardens. McDowell won.

Col. John Carson and his wife Rachel had six children. He built another 18 by 20-foot, two-story walnut log house about ten feet from the other one and had a tavern and stage coach stop. After the death of Rachel, he married his wife's sister-in-law, Mary Moffitt McDowell, widow of Joseph McDowell. They had six children before Col. Carson's death in 1841. About 1842, his son Jonathon Logan Carson remodeled the two log structures, covering the logs with white clapboards, adding a third story, and putting it all under one roof. This was McDowell's County Court House from 1843-1845.

Another of Col. John's sons was Samuel Price Carson (1798-1838), who in a duel in 1827 killed Dr. Robert Brank Vance over politics. Samuel went to Texas and became its first Secretary of State.

A library room has been set aside in the house to store family histories, church histories, newspaper clippings, Civil War letters, and research books. The family histories include, of course, the early settlers of McDowell/Burke County such as the Carsons, Birds, Browns, Burgins, Davidsons, Alexanders, Elliotts, Greenlees, Hemphills, Ledbetters, McDowells, Pattons, Stepps, Tates, plus about one hundred more. Being in historical surroundings makes you want to study as many of these as possible.

Scott Swanton, the curator and gifted guide, makes history real as he relates the days back to the late 1700s. The Carson House on Highway 70 is located four miles west of Marion, N. C., and is open from May 1 through Oct. 31: Tuesday - Saturday 10 a.m.-5 p.m. and Sunday 2-5 p.m. There is a small admission price. The Carson House is managed by its Restoration, Inc., and the McDowell Historical Society. Instrumental in the house's preservation were Mary and Ruth Greenlee.

Going westward from the Carson House to Old Fort is the Mountain Gateway Museum. Although the native-rock museum building itself was built by the Work Projects Agency in 1937, it is constructed on the site of the old stockade, then called Davidson's Fort.

Sitting at the edge of the Blue Ridge Mountains, up from the Piedmont, this fort was the western outpost from 1756-1776. The early settlers would rush to this stockade during Indian attacks.

On the grounds of this museum on Mill Creek, two log cabins have been authentically reconstructed by chinking the old notched logs with mud and straw and adding wooden shingles. One of these is called the Morgan cabin, dated 1880. The other cabin was the home of John Stepp, originally located on Cane Creek, dated 1851.

5

Inside the museum are a collection of household antiques and a series of excellent pictures depicting life in this area in the late 1800s. While at the museum, don't miss the short historical movie depicting the settlement of Old Fort, recounting General Rutherford's march from that site into the Indian territory and the coming of the railroad.

The museum is located three blocks from the Old Fort exit on I-40, right in the town itself at the corner of Catawba Avenue and Water Street. The hours are 9a.m.-5p.m., Monday - Saturday, and 2-5p.m. Sunday. It's free and well worth a visit.

Going west on I-40, you come to Black Mountain where the Swannanoa Valley Museum is on State Street. The collections of pictures and memorabilia are impressive. Harriet Styles and Bill McMurray and others have helped in this preservation of the past. The pictures recapture earlier times, such as one of a tree on the Patton Farm in Swannanoa "under which Davey Crockett and Elizabeth Patton were married;" horse-drawn taxis at the Black Mountain Depot; Vaughn Academy, established 1891 on Riceville Road in Swannanoa; an aerial view of the Grovemont community in 1925; the mountain residence, "Gombroon," home of Governor Zebulon Vance in the North Fork area near Black Mountain; and the 1915 passenger cars which Perley and Crockett Lumber Company used to take tourists as far as Camp Alice, one mile from Mount Mitchell by its logging railroad.

The information on the Rafael Gustavina Estate, which was located south of Black Mountain, includes not only a picture of the "Spanish Castle" built in the late 1800s but also garments worn by Mrs. Gustavina. Other artifacts range from Indian arrowheads to an old knitting machine, dating about 1920, from an early Black Mountain company, to a doctor's bag belonging to Dr. Eugene Knoefel, Sr.

There is no charge for a visit to the earliest times of the Swannanoa Valley. The Museum is open from May through September from 10 a.m. to 5 p.m., Tuesday through Saturday, 2 to 5 p.m. on Sunday.

The Smith-McDowell House on Victoria Road in Asheville was built by James McConnell Smith, (born June 14, 1787), the son of Daniel and Mary Davidson Smith. He married Mary "Polly" Patton. He ran the Buck Hotel and was in the mercantile business. He and his wife had nine children. Their child, Sarah Lucinda, married William McDowell in 1848, and they and their nine children lived at the house on Victoria Road.

This is one of the oldest buildings in the county, and it has authentically been restored by the Asheville-Buncombe County Historic Preservation Society. This visit is well worth the modest admission price.

For another trip back in time, you should visit the Museum of North Carolina Handicrafts located in the 1878-1880 Shelton House on Shelton Street (Hwy. 276) in Waynesville.

This museum features the handicrafts of the mountains, including spinning wheels, Victorian beds and shaving stands, a plantation desk, and other early furniture. Pottery exhibits are numerous, plus the Indian artifacts - baskets, wood carvings, dolls. There are also needle craft and quilts.

The Shelton House was built by Stephen Jehu Shelton, who was born about 1835 and died in 1913. Stephen and his brother William Perry Shelton married sisters Mahala Conley and Ingabo Drucilla Conley. Stephen Shelton was a Confederate Lieutenant in the Volunteer Co., C, 25th Regiment on May 1, 1861.

For a small admission price, you can visit the museum which is open from May 15 through September, Wednesday - Saturday 10 a.m. to 5 p.m., Sunday 2 to 5 p.m.

After steeping yourself in these earlier times, get back to your research for those ancestors. Good luck!

CHAPTER 1. THE BASICS

For a clarification in terminology, family history is taking your own parents, grandparents, and on back through your earliest known direct ancestors. (This is the way to start regardless of how you plan to organize the information at a later time.) A genealogy starts with the oldest known ancestor and branches out through all the known kin. For example, John (1792-1865) is your earliest known kin. Your first material covers him and his wife and probably lists his known children. In your continuation, each of the next sections would concentrate on everything you know on each of the children and all of their descendants that you have researched. You research family history and compile genealogy from the research.

The basics of how to get started are covered in this chapter, including the following topics: keeping records, observing cautions, discovering "how to" books, adding to the family history, using computers, using inquiries.

Getting Started

The number of people who are just starting their family histories seems to be growing each year. The first question the beginners want to know is how to get started. The answer basically is to get what you can from your own memories, your relatives, visit county courthouses, and then join a genealogical/historical society where the ancestor you are searching lived. Also, it is usually better to concentrate on one surname at a time. Many people do not agree with this, since you may have to go back to some of the same places again; however, getting too many various records at once makes your compilation very difficult.

One caution at the very start is to keep records of where you get all your information. You may think this does not matter since you are only doing it for yourself. Later, however, you can find information from others who are working on the same family, but most of the information that you get from others' research is a sharing-type exchange. No one is interested in your research unless you can tell where you got it. These exchangers of information are not really doubting your words, but experienced family historians know that chasing an error could cost years of going in the wrong direction. Family stories are interesting and should be saved, but you need to say that this is where the information came from. [Eugene A. Stratton in *Applied Genealogy*, Ancestry, Inc.: Salt Lake City, 1989, stated, "Good genealogists are good companions. They take you with them. They show you the way. They document their facts, and they put you in a position to analyze the facts and reach your own conclusions."]

A loose-leaf notebook and plenty of paper and pens are the only supplies you need. If you want family charts and group sheets for ease of organization and helps to carry in your notebook as you research, these are available locally at the Old Buncombe County Genealogical Society, Innsbruck Mall, Tunnel Road, Asheville.

In talking with relatives, be sure to include the oldest ones that you can find. You need to ask names, where ancestors lived, where they are buried, whom they married, what wars they were in, and known children. Take time to listen to stories, even if you are not sure what they are all about. Always ask if they know of a family Bible with family information included. If you find a Bible, notice when the Bible was published and put it down with the information. It is important to note if the Bible were kept while the events were going on or if they were added later. Many times a later descendant will put in only the names of the children that he remembers and, unintentionally, leave out one or more who moved on westward. If the listings were made after the events occurred, you will later want to check the federal census listings for verification if possible.

If possible, visiting relatives in person usually seems to get the best results. One of the most fruitful hours you may spend is to take an elderly relative to a cemetery where some of your family members are buried. Many people remember more, as if literally seeing the names on the gravemarkers take them "back." If visiting is not possible, you may want to write at least before you call to give them time to think about what you are interested in. After talking with kin, you may be given old letters that refer to people you do not know. Make copies and save these; you may know later and understand much information from these. (In the 1800s, letters were more of a luxury than an everyday event and many were saved.)

10

<u>Observing Cautions</u>

In finding your family's history, no set rules will always produce results, but one rule not to break to save you money and time is not to make expensive jumps backwards.

For example, an ancestor you are wanting to know more about was on the 1790 Rowan County census. Then, all the purchasing of wills, deeds, marriage bonds, searching the state records for military service gives you nothing to go further backwards to.

Some researchers become desperate enough that when they see that the same last name was in Pennsylvania in the late 1600s and early 1700s, they start a deluge of letters to historical societies and court houses, purchasing wills, deeds, books, anything with the same last name, thinking that these will lead to the ancestor in Rowan County.

There's only a remote possibility that this jumping will leave you anything but mind-boggled and poorer with all these documents on people you cannot connect as kin. Plus, an even worse mistake is to "latch on" to the family name that had similar first names as yours and just decide that these must be kin. (Even if your ancestor was listed as "Jr." does not necessarily mean that his father had the same first name. Many of the earlier name patterns were to name a son "Jr." to distinguish him from an uncle for whom he was named.) Much of this type research is done by people who are convinced that if the last name is the same, then the people are kin. This is just not true; for example, a Smyth could have come from Germany about the same time a Smith, named earlier from his being a blacksmith, came from England. They both could live near each other in Pennsylvania and be listed as Smiths, but this does not make these men kin.

No substitute exists for the necessary step-by-step backwards. The steps may end before you want them to, but at least you haven't spent time and money researching a family that is not yours. Have patience. That very record you need may be waiting for you someplace.

<u>Researching "How To" Books</u>

There are many, many very good "How To" books for researching genealogy. Only two are discussed here because of their depth of information on searching in the United States. (Specialized books will be discussed later.)

For the person seriously interested in finding out more about ancestors, a 1984 book, *The Source: A Guidebook of American Genealogy*, is correctly entitled. This 750-page was compiled by sixteen genealogists and edited by Arlene Eakle and Johni Cerny [Ancestry: Salt Lake City]. This book discusses where records are and how to find and use them.

The book can help you know where to go next for information on the ancestor you've "despaired" over. Excellent appendixes give addresses of federal records centers, state archives and historical societies, genealogical societies, vital records centers.

Even people with a good knowledge of existing records will find new ideas. Keep paper and pencil handy as you read through the book to jot down places to check that you had never thought of. The introduction to the book discusses general types of materials that may be found in libraries, court houses, historical societies, plus ideas for keeping your records, and a list of "how to" books for each state.

The book is organized into three sections: major records sources, published genealogical sources, special resources.

Section I, major record sources, includes marriage and divorce records, land and tax records, church records, court records, military records and the unusual prison records, mortuary records, coroners' records, and employment records. [Caution: Don't expect to be able to find all of these in all areas.] A typical chapter such as the one on court records includes a discussion of the American court system, an inclusion of legal terms to help understand the court system, court procedures with sample cases, then a discussion of each specific type of court record with what can be found in each.

Section II, published genealogical sources, discusses city directories, newspapers, indexes and biographies, telling what can be found in these as well as where they are. Much material is discussed concerning the records of the Church of Jesus Christ of Latter-Day Saints. [The local access to these LDS records will be discussed under archives.]

Section III, special resources, starts with tracking down immigrant origins. After a discussion of general patterns, dates of immigration, process of Americanization, Ms. Eakle gives specific suggestions for people who have tried in the standardized ways and failed.

Section III is a help to people searching for Indian, Spanish, Afro-American, Asian, and Jewish ancestors since a separate chapter is devoted to each, discussing the special problems attached to their research.

The Source is a book you will want to study in a library and probably get for yourself as a handy reference.

Another "How To" genealogical book that has been very helpful to many people is Val Greenwood's *Researcher's Guide to American Genealogy*. [Genealogical Publishing Co., Inc.,: Baltimore, 1990.] The strength of Mr. Greenwood's book lies not only in how to search for records across the United States but also in how to interpret what you find.

Mr. Greenwood explains that while genealogists identify past ancestors and put them into charts, the family historian also adds an understanding of the ancestors' lives and studies the whole family. He agrees with most researchers that "the most difficult problems in American genealogy is to find the specific place of your ancestor's origin in the old World." However, he feels the "ancestor hunters" spend too much time on this instead of being complete on understanding what ancestors experienced and what they valued. His inclusion of questions you should answer on your own parents and grandparents illustrates what you should be preserving for an understanding of family. He reminds us that "family" is within everyone, and everyone takes with him "large chunks" of ingrained ideas, beliefs, and values. He states that you have to learn how to do the research.

Mr. Greenwood's book is available at most large libraries for a study to see if this is the resource book you need.

Adding to the Family History

When you start putting information together, you may want to already start thinking about making your family history more than a list of charts and descendants. Even though the family historian may have spent years finding the names of the children of great-grandparents, these lists are not interesting to everyone. But people who are not much interested in lists do find pictures interesting. Most people like looking into the faces of ancestors, perhaps to see if they can find a resemblance. It's not too soon to start finding and saving plus taking family pictures of people, homes, businesses, and even cars and quilts.

A 1988 publication, *Photographing Your Heritage*, Wilma Shull, Ancestry Inc.: Salt Lake City, explains what and whom to take pictures of and how to do it. In language that is understandable, she discusses the types of cameras, lenses, filters, and films that give best results.

Photography is relatively new when thinking as a family historian does. Most "old" pictures you find will be cabinet photographs which were made from 1859 - 1914. Daguerreotypes were started about 1839 and taken until 1857; ambrotypes 1852-1863; collotypes and tintypes from 1856-1938. (She points out that if a revenue stamp is on the back of a photograph, it was taken during the time of the Civil War, since it was a special tax to help finance the military.) Different methods are used for copying these types of pictures. One illustration shows a badly bent and discolored tintype made clearer and without distortion by using a dark blue filter.

The range of material covered in the book is from how to clean dirty pictures to how to use lighting. One suggestion is to photograph people while they are involved with their hobbies or work. Hints are included for taking gravestone pictures that turn out more clearly than the stones themselves. If you want a picture to last a long time, she suggests using black and white film.

Not everybody can own the family ancestors' pictures; and most who get them are not willing to part with them, even for copying. So, Mrs. Shull gives detailed instructions on how to copy pictures of these for yourself. If properly taken, your picture can often be better than the original.

Spend a little of the patience you practice in gathering your written family history in photographing it. It will make a difference in the results of what you have.

Another addition that would make your family history interesting is to know more about what the lives of the carefully documented people were like. Everyone who tries to find out more about ancestors does not study local history books on the areas that he is researching. You may feel, usually correctly, that his is a "scattered" approach. If you are looking for a specific ancestor, you can search indexes of official records and find or not find that ancestor quickly. But in studying local history books, you could read many and not find an ancestor listed.

However, it's not a waste of time since you probably won't understand much about your ancestors if you don't understand what was going on where and when they lived. People have to adjust to what is happening in their worlds. You need to understand the local culture, religion, politics, economic conditions if you want to understand your family.

Local history books are plentiful. These can be checked out of libraries and read at your leisure. You may want to start with reading history about your area, such as the South. Some general ones are *The Southern Highlander and His Homeland* by Campbell, *The Southern Appalachians* by Ogburn, *The Southern Country Store* by Clark, who explains that the country store was the "hub of the local universe" since it was the market place, a banking and credit source, a recreation center, public forum, and news exchange. At the country store, ancestors could buy postage stamps, school books, coffins, axle grease, cheese, opium, camphor, asafetida, whiskey. (Sometimes the country store owner had to read the mail to his customers since they were illiterate.)

You may then want to study histories of North Carolina such as the two volumes by Ashe, covering from 1584-1925. Two books which have recently been republished are interesting: *Historical Sketches of North Carolina* and *Reminiscences and Memoirs* by John Hill Wheeler. These books, written in 1851 and in 1881, contain over a thousand pages about the history of North Carolina and its people.

In *Historical Sketches* Wheeler's account starts with the earliest English settlers in America. In 1584, Sir Walter Raleigh's two ships landed on the shores of present North Carolina. After the visit, two native Indians, Manteo and Manchese, returned to England with the crew. A year later over a hundred colonists came but arrived in August and went back to England the next year. Queen Elizabeth called this present area of N. C., "Virginia."

A detailed account is given of the 1587 "Lost" Roanoke Colony that contained 89 men, 17 women, and 2 children. In 1590, only the word "Croatan" was found carved on a tree. These colonists were never found.

Finally, in July of 1653, a colony from Virginia, led by Roger Green, "settled on the banks of the Roanoke." However, Wheeler stated that Quakers and other religious groups who had sought "refuge" were already in N. C.

Wheeler's book contains information that does not seem to be compiled in other books. A discussion is given about the first governor in 1663, William Drummond from Scotland, and is followed by accounts of all the governors. Indian attacks, which started in 1711, are detailed as well as an account of the pirate "Blackbeard," Edward Teach, whose head was hung to the "bowsprit" of Lieutenant Maynard's vessel on November 17, 1718. Even the graduates from the University of North Carolina are listed from 1798-1851. After the history of the state, a history of each county follows.

The history of Buncombe shows that the population in 1850 was 12,738 and that products sold included $18,127 worth of ginseng. Some prominent citizens are discussed, and the elected officials to the General Assembly from 1792-1850 are listed. This format for Buncombe County is similar to the one followed for each county.

While the emphasis is on history of the state and counties in *Historical Sketches*, the focus is on the people in each county in *Reminiscences and Memoirs of North Carolina*. In fact, if your family is included, the genealogy is extraordinary.

Buncombe was named for Revolutionary Colonel Edward Buncombe, who lived in a home called "Buncombe Hall," in Tyrrell County. At his own expense there, he trained and kept about seven hundred men of the 5th Regiment, awaiting Washington's call. Col. Buncombe was wounded at Germantown in 1777 and died at the age of 30 in Philadelphia.

From the Buncombe history, information is included about David Swain, Elisha Mitchell, Zebulon B. Vance and family, James Love Henry (editor of the Asheville *Spectator* at age 19), Merrimon, Clingman, Gudger, Robert M. Furman (editor of the *Asheville Citizen* in 1872). From Rutherford County, Wheeler relates the Felix Walker's "talking for Buncombe" story, and from Watauga, the stories of Daniel Boone and John Sevier.

With the politics, the duels, Governor Vance's letters to Mr. Wheeler while Vance was in prison in Washington before his pardon by President Andrew Johnson, the reader feels he is living in the mid-1800s.

Both of these were republished by Clearfield Company, 200 East Eager St., Baltimore, MD 21202, in 1993.

After this, you may want to read historical books about Western

North Carolina, such as Arthur's *Western North Carolina: A History, 1730-1913*, written in 1914, with much information from old diaries. Arthur started with the history of the Cherokees and Catawbas, the earliest settlers of the counties, the earliest trails into the mountains, and the early arguments with South Carolina, Georgia, and Tennessee over where the state lines were and how the boundaries were finally established. He further explained what the first settlers brought with them, what they did when they first arrived, plus early manners and customs. His writings include early "tales," duels, extraordinary events, "notable" resorts, schools and colleges, and the Civil War period.

You may also want to look for county histories, such as Sondley's *A History of Buncombe County*, Allen's *The Annals of Haywood County*, Patton's *The Story of Henderson County* and/or Fitzsimons' *From the Banks of the Oklawaha*, which also is on Henderson County.

If you wish to visit Madison County, N.C., and know its happenings 100 years ago, you should read *The Season of Dorland-Bell, History of an Appalachian Mission School* by Jacqueline Burgin Painter. This book is more than just a history of the school itself. Mrs. Painter shows insight into the feelings and the problems of the mountain people since she is from Madison.

Western North Carolinians have long resented Northern visitors showing the Appalachian people as the epitome of poverty and ignorance. However, the Northern Presbyterian missionaries who came to WNC and established mission schools did a great service to thousands of poor and unschooled. The influence through the education the Presbyterians made possible has extended through our generation.

When Dr. Luke Dorland came to Hot Springs in 1886, he saw a contrast between the wealthy visitors who stayed at the luxurious Mountain Park Hotel with its 160 gas-lighted rooms, French chef, New York band, and golf course and the "poorest mountain families with numbers of hungry, ill-clad, unschooled children." Dr. Dorland wrote friends in the North of the situation, saying that the local people had "no hope and they need light." He and his wife started teaching the local children in their home.

With monetary help from the Presbyterian Board of Home Missions for books and supplies, Dr. Dorland added to his house. By the third year nearly 90 children enrolled, with some living in the Dorland home.

By 1890, Dr. Dorland wrote the Board, "The children have poured in from the mountains and valleys; many walking a distance of from two to six miles until the roll counts one hundred of ages from six to nineteen years."

By 1894, the now Dorland Institute had a new girls' dormitory, a five-story Victorian style house with crystal chandeliers, detailed woodwork, and beveled glass doors. An 1895 picture shows the prestigious-looking school campus building. Children coming from a two-room cabin must have felt these buildings looked like castles.

Boys had attended the school as day students, but for the ones who were too poor to pay for their board in town and lived too far away for "commuting," the school rented a house. By 1903, a farm of 235 acres was purchased for the boys.

Julia Phillips, who was the principal of the school after the Dorlands, would visit the mountain homes to let people know about the school and to encourage parents to send their children. The "well-to-do to the poverty-stricken came." Clothes sent from donors in the North were traded for produce. This exchange would cause women to walk eight or ten miles carrying a half bushel of beans in order to get clothing. Produce also paid many children's tuition, such as a "dressed sheep, five bushels of apples, six candy roasters, two pounds of black walnuts."

Along with the usual academics, the students had industrial training in cooking, cleaning, home nursing, sewing, food preparation, farming.

By 1918, the Bell School in Walnut, established in 1897 by the Presbyterians, was combined with Dorland to cut expenses. The campus in Hot Springs was seven acres with boarding facilities for one hundred girls, and the three-hundred acre farm a little over two miles down the river had housing for forty boys.

The faculty encouraged their students to complete their education at the Asheville Normal for girls or the Farm School for boys in Swannanoa. But in 1926, the boys' school was moved to Farm School. Then, in 1937, the *Asheville Citizen* stated that "The Board expects to merge the Asheville Farm School near Swannanoa and the Dorland-Bell School at Hot Springs into a co-educational institution." By May of 1942, the final graduation of the Dorland-Bell School was held; the school that had the purpose "to train leaders who will carry a light to their communities to give a vision of Christianity that serves in daily living."

18

[Book published by Mrs. Arthur Painter, 12 Jones St., Sylva, NC 28779.]
A history of a town is mainly focused on the people of the town. This was the purpose of the 1992, *A History of Black Mountain, North Carolina and Its People.* It is not officially a family history, but most of the people who resided in this eastern area of Buncombe from the late 1700s and many to the present are profiled and documented along with their way of life and the town's interesting "outsider" inhabitants.

The town of Black Mountain was not an incorporated town until 1893, but the people were there, driving their stock down to Charleston, S. C., once a year, watching the stage coaches go through along the dusty roads, or hunting and fishing in mountainous areas, a way of life continuing until the railroad came up the mountains from the east in the late 1870s. Then, the travelers started pouring in, causing the creation of boarding houses, hotels, sanitariums for tuberculosis, and an interest for assembly places in the scenic mountains. The people of Black Mountain decided they needed a real town.

For its physical size and population size, Black Mountain is an unusual town that has attracted many interesting people and happenings. The town of Black Mountain still has a year-round residency of just close to seven thousand people, but in the summer the swarms of assembly attendees make it a moving population of about 100,000. The current conference centers include the Presbyterian Montreat Assembly, established in 1905; the Southern Baptist Assembly, 1906; the YMCA Blue Ridge Assembly, 1908; Christmount Assembly, 1948; Camp Dorothy Walls A. M. E. Zion, 1958; "In the Oaks" Episcopal Center, 1957; Cragmont Baptist Assembly, 1979.

Interesting people built homes in the Black Mountain area. North Carolina governor and then United States senator, Zebulon Vance, built a three-story mountain retreat in the North Fork area in 1883, where the current Asheville watershed is. Rafael Gustavino, Spanish-born, world-famous architect built in the late 1890s what the local people called the "Spanish Castle" one mile south of the town. From a 1928 interview, one learns that Mr. Gustavino thought this a great joke since he intended for this to be his barn after he built his real house. Franklin Terry, vice-president of General Electric, built his estate, "In the Oaks," just west of Black Mountain in the early 1920s.

More interesting people came with the creation of Black Mountain

19

College. It's hard to imagine more educated professors in one school than the ones who congregated there. Although the professors' children attended the public schools in Black Mountain and were well-received, the situation with the college and the town people was more or less "live and let live."

The stories are included of how the people hated to leave their mountainous North Fork valley when the City of Asheville decided this area was to be its watershed. A church, first established in 1898, was destroyed, and its 250 grave occupants had to be moved with some unmarked remains placed in the new area where the plaque says, "Known only to God."

Mainly it is a history of the varied people who make up the day-by-day "goings on" in any small town. People were born, people achieved, and people died as in all places. This was a tribute to the people who called Black Mountain their home.

A long-time family resident became sheriff of Buncombe County and served for 34 years. A newspaper owner and editor became a state congressman for 20 years. A former local school teacher became a U. S. Representative and served for 16 years. Being born in Black Mountain and living to be 105 years old, a former slave had told his memories of the early valley. An early settler built a house in 1832, which still stands, where eight generations of the same family lived.

A History of Black Mountain was written by Joyce Parris, published by the Black Mountain Centennial Commission. Information about this book should be addressed to Swannanoa Valley Museum, P.O. Box 726, Black Mountain, NC 28711.

Buncombe County did not have any plantations in the usual sense of large slaveholdings. When the term "plantation" is seen in WNC's deeds, the meaning is the man planted and had a dwelling house on the land.

Jane Turner Censer's *North Carolina Planters and Their Children, 1800-1860*, [Louisiana State University Press: Baton Rouge, 1985], discusses 124 planters who did have plantations based upon large slaveholdings in 1830.

Not many ancestors were as prosperous as these planters, but since the ideas and life-styles of the elite are often copied by the less prosperous, these planters' attitudes toward life, marriage, children, religion give insight into what many ancestors in North Carolina felt was "success." The closest "rich and famous" to Buncombe were in Burke County: Issac T. Avery, William W. Erwin, and James Murphy.

The basic cash crops were cotton and tobacco. The planters who practiced self-reliance, industriousness, and thrift, also profited by owning sawmills, gristmills, cotton gins, tanneries, brandy stills. Several, including Issac Avery and William Davidson, added cash by gold mining.

The planters' households were child-centered; therefore, their wives were valuable in producing heirs. However, from letters and diaries, wives were also treated as valuable partners. Plus planters' emphasis on education, achievement, independence, and material success seemed equally bestowed upon their daughters and sons.

Both were expected to get an education in order to be prepared for life. While the sons went to colleges, the daughters went to academies, studying grammar, geography, math, history, literature, and French. Sons and daughters shared equally in estate settlements except that married daughters were more likely to get money and slaves rather than land.

Both sons and daughters were encouraged toward marrying the well-to-do, preferably in their local communities, even if it meant cousins. (At least one-tenth married first or second cousins.)

The basic religious belief was that of a personal God who "held them strictly accountable. He was a jealous taskmaster who demanded intense commitment and who directly intervened in human affairs to aid, reward, or chastise."

The planters' families had an average of seven children, and at least one child in four did not live to be five years old. Mary Henderson, who had five children die, wrote in her diary: "We must not love her too much, the Lord might take her . . . but God doeth all things well. I feel so unhappy about the two remaining ones thinking it may be God's good pleasure to recall them and shuddering at the bare idea."

The planters' families were important to them, but a paradox is illustrated by their treatment of their slaves. To them slaves were material property. Most slave-owners feared them and would not hesitate to separate slave families if it were a matter of "setting an example" for disciplinary purposes.

Ms. Censer used public documents and private records for her extensively researched book. It is enlightening for the reader who wants to know the facts.

Regardless of whether you find your family's name in history books, your understanding of your ancestors will increase since you'll know the history, customs, rituals, of where your family lived.

Using Computers

Many people like to keep their records in looseleaf notebooks, divided by families, but the method for recording family history has gone modern for many people. Nearly everyone has heard about using computers in genealogy, but many people wonder what a computer could do that their volumes of notebooks couldn't do.

Paul Andereck and Richard A. Pence in the 1985 book, *Computer Genealogy: A Guide to Research through High Technology*, [Ancestry: Salt Lake City] say, "nothing .. if you have the time." Many tasks take so much time without a computer that they don't get done. This book is an excellent background discussion concerning computers since they do not take for granted that you already know everything such as many of the more recent books do.

The authors continue that if the computer is used only as a word processor, you probably aren't really doing much different than you could with your notebooks, a typewriter, and a copying machine except saving space with floppy disks and saving time when you want to mail out information.

However, the new programs which can be purchased and used with a computer give you a retrieval system. Imagine looking for an ancestor born between 1820 and 1830, who died in Maryland, and entering these specifications. "The program will display in family group sheet form any records matching these specifications." (If you have entered this previously, of course.)

Information in this book is clear on features that a "genealogically adequate" computer would need: two disk drives, data entry or support function keys, a printer. The first software purchases would be a word processing program, and the authors discuss pointers on what type you need.

Questions that you need answers on for your family history or genealogical application programs are discussed, such as how many files will it hold, does it print a family group sheet on an 80-character line printout (a 8 1/2 inch wide sheet) or does it require a 132-character line printout, what do the pedigree charts look like, can you easily locate records for an individual. These questions are still important; however, there have many new programs developed since 1984.

You will need to check an up-to-date book, such as *Guide to Genealogy Software*, by Donna Przechna and Joan Lowrey. [Genealogical Publishing: Baltimore, 1993] This book gives numerous samples of what each reviewed program would do, such as charts, generation sheets, etc.

Of course, no program will do the research for you, but the program would help you to organize the material after you get it.

Using Inquiries and Writing Letters

Probably nobody supports the United States Post Office any better than the family searcher. These are your contacts with others who are interested in the same family that you are. Some correspondences go on for decades without the people ever meeting each other in person. Many times only an answer to an inquiry from a stranger can help when all your official records have just run out.

All family historians think that they have a hard time when searching for records. However, some have an added handicap: They don't know for sure the surname they are looking for.

A social security card in whatever name one chose was not hard to obtain in the mid-1900s. Some people left home, perhaps after a disagreement at home and simply changed their names to whatever they pleased. The only hope for the family-searching children of these people is for some member of the family to have a good memory for anything that father "whatever" said.

Direct questions were probably not answered. However, thinking back to conversations, did he mention a state often, a Grandma Smith, hunting in the mountains, brothers or sisters. Most usually kept their first names and often adopted the mothers' maiden names, as if not completely to cut off family. Sometimes the first names they chose for their own children are the same as remembered brothers and sisters. Sometimes, none of this fits.

If you can determine the state, county, and at least one correct name, you may have a chance through other people.

A real case of a lost surname involved a man who took the name William Lee Lambert. He was born from 1912-1916 in North Carolina in a place called Bandana. [In checking, there was a Bandana in Mitchell County.] His father was Charles Lafayette _____ born February 10, 1888 and his mother was Della Winna Grindstaff born 13 May 1889. After serving in the Navy in the 1930s, William went home but soon left for California and never again had contact with his family. His family members in California wanted to know more about their ancestors after Mr. Lambert had died in 1975.

This inquiry was put in the "Family History" column [*Asheville Citizen -Times*] in 1986. Within a week, the family in California had heard from family members in Mitchell County who always wondered what had happened to him.

Of course, most inquiries sent to newspapers or genealogical newsletters and journals are not this dramatic, but often you do get results that you can find no place else.

[An alphabetized list by surnames and the addresses of people who have written to the "Family History" column for the past eleven years are included in the Appendix.]

When answering other people's inquiries, you do not need to enclose a pre-addressed, stamped envelope unless you want information from them. In all other cases, except for the National Archives, you need to send this if you expect an answer. Many courthouses don't bother to answer unless you do.

Also, in addition to sending the stamped, addressed envelope, be sure that you do not ask so many questions that the person would need to take hours to answer you. Keep your requests simple and be sure to include the full name, a date of birth or an approximate one, where the person lived, and what your interest is in the person. Most court houses and archives will not answer over one question at a time about one person.

Another thing that keeps people from helping others is that after they spend much time in looking up material and even spending money on a copying machine, they do not get even a simple "thank you." Another common thing that sometimes happens is that the person who wrote for information uses the helpful person's information, sometimes in printed books, without ever giving the person credit for his or her help. Most family history people try to help others, hoping for help in return, but too many bad experiences make them wonder if it is worth helping others.

Don't be one to help mess up this essential family "pipeline." Plus, read the inquiries wherever you find them. Help the ones you can; you never know what you'll get in return.

CHAPTER 2. OFFICIAL RECORDS

When "official" records are mentioned, you get the idea that every piece of information you find from one would be absolutely a fact. On the whole, these are reliable, but a local marriage register application showed the following on one: the woman's first nor last name was "official." She used a nickname and the last name of her step-father, listing her step-father as her father. She used her correct age of 21. (This is not always true for "underaged" females or females marrying a younger male.) The man's age was boosted by three years to 21. He used the correct first name, but his mother's maiden name as his last name; therefore, on parents, he listed his mother's name correctly (although he had her living when she was dead) and his grandfather as his father (and he had him dead when he was living). Perhaps this could all be pre-wedding nervousness; however, what is listed on these records is exactly what the people at the court house were told at the time and these cannot be changed.

Remember too that information for a death certificate is taken immediately following the death. The informant may not be able to recall everything correctly at this time.

Official records are a great help to family historians, but keep an open-mind if other records do not agree.

After this caution, still the first records you'll probably want to check after you get what information you can from relatives are the various court records. Since archives also have official records, these will be discussed after the ones at the court house.

The courthouse records are indexed and easy to search and use; plus, these do contain some of the most valuable information you can find, such as marriage, birth, death, deeds, wills. When visiting the court houses, don't be afraid to admit that you are new at this and ask for help. However, be considerate of the employees. If you spend much time there, you'll know they are the ones who are constantly indexing, filing, retrieving these records.

If writing, send a pre-addressed, stamped envelope when you ask if the record is available and the cost. For a small fee, some clerks will send a copy of the indexes for a family's name if you request it and if you are specific, such as wills for the Sorrell family from 1790-1820.

There is really no comparison to what you can find by going to the court house for yourself rather than having to write. Plus, by studying indexes, you may find much that you would not have known to ask for. For example, by reading through the whole surname death index for the name you are searching, you find the name you are looking for, Davis, Alfred, father, Davis, James. You then notice there are two other Davises who have James Davis listed as father. You can quickly put down the reference numbers and check these death certificates for possible kinship. This court house trip may be just what you need to add to your records.

<u>Register of Deeds</u>

Marriage records, starting in 1851 in North Carolina, are older than birth or death records. (Some state archives have earlier marriage bonds and these will be discussed under archives.) As with these basic records, the marriages are indexed. There are two indexes, one for females and one for males in Buncombe County. This is very helpful when you know a woman's maiden name but not whom she married. Once you find the name you are searching for, you just ask for a copy. The standard information are the names, ages, place of residence, and date of marriage. However, in <u>some</u> counties, there are marriage registers you can check. These are the marriage applications that the people filled out and include the parents' names. These usually cannot be copied by machines since these are the original records and in somewhat fragile condition in most places. If you ask about these and are told that the marriage record is all there is, the records probably have not been saved.

Death certificates were not required to be registered until 1913 in North Carolina and in most southern states. The indexes for death certificates give the date, name, and father's name with the reference number beside the entry. The reference number is for the document itself. These have much information.

(The death certificate will be in the county where the person died, not necessarily where the person is buried.) These give the birth date and place, age and date of death, husband's or wife's name, names of parents and birthplaces, place of death and burial, funeral home, cause of death, how long been ill if applicable, doctor's or coroner's name, and the name of the person who gave the information. A copy of this death certificate costs $3-$5 if you want it certified, but if you just want a copy, it is usually under a dollar. In some cities, such as Asheville, you may find some earlier death records. Asheville has records for the city from August 1, 1892-1898. Even though you may not find your own family, the reading is fascinating for the curious who learn not only what was causing deaths in the city but also what was causing deaths in other areas. As you read these causes, you wonder how babies died of teething, are not really surprised about one's dying of malnutrition, are puzzled over what "military" tuberculosis or summer "diahrrea" could be. You see typhoid fever, meninjitis, cholera, pneumonia, apoplexy, consumption (duration 1-2 years), inanition (?), diptheria, convulsions, nervous exhaustion, constipation, shock. You also see the same scourges of society existed in the 1890s: deaths attributed to cigarette smoking, alcoholism, a pistol shot to the head (duration of illness was "instantaneous"), herpes, syphillis, cancer, boiler explosion, drowning, even opium poisoning. Of course, no car accident victims were listed and, surprisingly, very few listed as death by heart failure. In 1892, Asheville had a population of about 12,000. A study of the records shows there were 34 deaths in August, 1892, with 12 of these being babies under two years of age.

Even though **birth certificates** were not required to be registered until October of 1913, you will find many from the late 1800s to early 1900s which are **delayed birth certificates**.

Since everyone who files for social security benefits, which started in 1937, must have a birth certificate, people who never had their births registered did. They went to the Registrar of Deeds' offices where they were born with family Bibles, school records, military discharges, baptismal records, relatives or notarized relatives' statements, to establish their dates of birth. At some court houses, these have been indexed into the regular birth indexes, such as in Buncombe; however, in some court houses you must ask about these delayed births, since they may be separately indexed. A birth certificate normally gives name, when born, where born, name of parents and address.

Generally, birth certificates for adopted children are not accessible in most counties in North Carolina. This is usually a case where you'll be told that the records have been sent someplace else. You could try writing to the Office of Vital Statistics, Box 2091, Raleigh, NC 27602. For early "adoptions," you may want to check the Apprentice Bonds (Indenture Book) 1795-1882, 1890-1919, on microfilm at Asheville-Buncombe Technical Community College Library or at the Buncombe County Archives, Valley Street, Asheville. (More about these two source places will be discussed in the archives section of this chapter.) Just because these records say "orphan," do not automatically put down the child's parents died before that date.

From Apprentice Bonds, Buncombe County, Book C, p. 166: "October, 1842, John J. Cogburn an orphan to Joseph Lance." This is John Jefferson Cogburn, son of James and Polly Lance Cogburn. John, who was nine years old at this time, was not really an orphan since both his parents were alive but separated. Joseph Lance was a brother to Polly Cogburn. John Jefferson Cogburn was later apprenticed to John Frady, Polly's second husband.

Deeds are some of the earliest records available in most counties. Before knowing where to check for deeds for the person you are searching, you need to determine what county the land was in at the time of purchase. For example, Buncombe County was formed from Burke and Rutherford Counties in 1791. If you think your ancestor was in the present Buncombe County area earlier than this, you would check Burke County if the land were north of the Swannanoa River; however, if the land were south of Swannanoa River, you would check Rutherford County. Land deeds were not moved from the original county when the new county was formed. In 1791, Buncombe was all of Western North Carolina. Haywood County was formed in 1808 and comprised the western deeds; then, Macon County was established in 1828. The other counties first covered by Buncombe included Henderson, established 1838; Cherokee, 1838; Yancey, 1833; Madison, 1851; Jackson, 1851; Clay, 1861; Polk, 1855; Transylvania, 1861; Graham, 1872; Swain, 1871. [A basic book which is valuable in North Carolina, not only for county formations but also for the location of towns, creeks, mountains, etc., is *The North Carolina Gazetteer, A Dictionary of Tar Heel Places*, by William S.

Powell, University of North Carolina Press: Chapel Hill.]

The first land transactions in America are often confusing. Terms are frequently interchanged, but probably the biggest concept that is hard to understand is that land, never before owned, was claimed and granted to early settlers. Individual land ownership was an accomplishment for many of the immigrants who never had owned land and believed it impossible.

The English wanted settlers badly enough to award or to sell very cheaply the "new" lands, vast unsettled wildernesses that are now cities, suburbia, and resort areas. England wanted the trade possible from its new country.

Land granting started in present North Carolina in 1669 by eight Lord Proprietors from England who were given this power by King Charles II. Basically, the land the Carolina proprietors could grant was between the Virginia line through Northern Florida and west to the Pacific Ocean. However, the lands had to be bought from the Indians or to be obtained by treaties before the granting to early settlers took place.

As early as February 19, 1678, the papers from the State Office in London recorded that Sir George Carteret, and other Lord Proprietors, gave a "commission to Robert Holden to proceed on an expedition of discovery, either on this side, or beyond the Apalatian mountains." The records did not show if the Indians were approached at that time for this area.

Overall, the Indians may not have understood what they were selling since they had never owned land but instead had used areas of land as common tribal property. The Indians did not understand that they would no longer be able to use the lands for hunting and "camping" rights. By the time they did realize what they had sold, it was usually too late.

Even if isolated settlers were killed, the land would be re-granted to more white settlers. From the North Carolina Land Grant Office, Book I, it seems one group of Indians themselves decided to be granted some land: Page 136, File #64, "To the King and Nation of the Yawpim Indians 10,240 acres. (No county or precinct given.) Northeast side of southwest side of North River adjoining Henry Creech land" on October 2, 1704.

The land under the Proprietors could be granted under two terms:

31

sold outright and rent free or sold with quitrent stipulations. Quitrent was similar to the present property tax and was required on land so that the governing officials would have income. Quitrent could be a nominal one ear of Indian corn per acre when demanded, could be half-penny or penny per acre, or 10 shillings (120 pennies) per 1,000 acres per year.

Since the land grant system was to attract settlers, the "grantee" was to clear, plant, and generally settle himself upon the land. A "lapsed" grant meant that the terms had not been fulfilled and the land could be regranted.

Starting in 1777, after the American Revolution, definite steps were necessary to obtain land through grants. From start to finish the procedure could take two years. (The land grants could be made in North Carolina for land not previously owned until 1959.)

The first item of business for the yearning settler was to determine the type of grant given in the chosen area. For the first land grants, there were two distinct types: state land grants and public domain (federal) grants.

North Carolina, as well as the surrounding states of Virginia, Kentucky, Tennessee, Georgia, was a state-land state, having received the land from the federal government. If the land had not been granted by the Lord Proprietors before July 4, 1776, the land belonged to these states. The states appointed an entry taker and a surveyor for each county.

The prospective settler's next step was to go by the county land office to get a general idea of where land was available. He would asked to purchase a state grant. He could receive it for military service, which will be discussed later.

With his permission from the county land office, he would go into the unclaimed wilderness, pick out his land, notch the trees around the boundary, and go back to the county land office, with his rough description, to file his claim to be granted land. The entry taker put down the description into the land entry books. If no one claimed the land after several months, the next step could take place. The settler was awarded a land warrant, which was an order to the county surveyor to map out the land entered. The land was surveyed, and a plat/map was drawn and sent to the secretary of state.

The next step occurred when the secretary of state wrote out a patent or land grant for the settler, sending the plat. The last step was paying the fees. Then, the land grant was filed in the state land grant office, and the settler was sent his grant. (By this time the settler had often planted his crops and built a shelter on the land.)

Additionally, the settler was encouraged to have his grant registered in the county where the land lay. However, many saw no reason to register the land; they had the treasured piece of paper from the state. Many times this would not be registered until the owner decided to sell it, and then, hopefully, that piece of paper was still in hand.

Many times descendants wonder if the North Carolina land grants they see listed for their ancestors were military bounty grants. Only two types of land grants existed in North Carolina: the regularly purchased grants and the military bounty grants.

However, no land in present North Carolina was awarded as military bounty grants. North Carolina owned and gave its land from present Tennessee. (Similarly, Virginia gave land in Kentucky and Ohio while Georgia and South Carolina gave land within their own boundaries.)

From 1778-1797, North Carolina issued about 6,500 warrants for grants of bounty land in what became Davidson and Sumner Counties in Tennessee. These grants were made as late as 1841 but made by Tennessee after 1800.

North Carolina only gave military grants for soldiers who were in the N. C. Line of the Continental in the Revolution, not the State or "home guard" militia. Privates could request 7.6 acres for each month of service, a possible 640 acres for seven years' service. A brigadier general could request 12,000 acres. To obtain these lands, the former soldier had to send his proof of service claims to the Secretary of State checked the register of the Continental Line before he issued the warrant to the surveyor to lay off the specified number of acres.

These warrants could be sold to anyone else who wished to purchase them from the former soldiers. The buyers were the assignees. Many times these warrants were sold to another assignee. The last assignee would turn in the warrant and the surveyor's plat to get the granted title to the land. In North Carolina many of the records show the last assingnee on the indexes for these registers in the Secretary of State's Land Grant Office in Raleigh; so these are not proof of military service.

In determining if your ancestor received a military grant, you first may want to study the book. *North Carolina Land Grants in Tennessee, 1778-1791*, compiled by Betty Cartwright and Lillian Garniner in 1958, copy at Pack Library in Asheville. In using this book, you first need to turn to Appendix A to see if the name you are searching for is listed. If the name is only listed in this alphabetized appendix, the Revolutionary soldier or his heirs sold his warrant for military service to someone else, and the grant is in the purchaser's name.

The North Carolina State Archives has a "Military Land Warrant Book, 1783-1841" with 6,554 Revolutionary War bounty warrants. Write to N. C. Archives, 109 E. Jones St., Raleigh, NC 27611, for the name you want checked.

Many family historians want to know the exact location where their ancestors originally lived. Deeds give property descriptions which include white oaks, corners of fences, maples by springs, and often even a specific place, such as Laurel Branch. Then, you find out there are twenty-five Laurel Branches in Western North Carolina, so it's not much more specific than a spring. The deed may, however, give you a more valuable key: a plat map number and page.

First, go to the county court house to find the deed for the original property your ancestor bought. Look up his name in the Grantee (buyer) Indexes to find the deed book and the page number. Next, check the deed book and read the deed itself. If there are references to plat maps, put down the number of the map and the page. In Buncombe County, you can see a copy of the plat map on microfiche in the downstairs office of the deeds where the indexes are kept. A copy of the plat map can be made in the main floor office of the deeds for a small fee. By studying the deed with the plat map, you can probably find an exact location for your ancestor's property.

(A caution in reading deeds: Many times people suppose that if a deed says, along with the acreage "all buildings, structures, orchards," that these existed on the property at that time. They may not have since this was standard deed writing.)

If no plat map is mentioned on the deed, your search will become more complicated and, perhaps, impossible. The earliest land had to be surveyed before it was granted to individuals and a plat map made, but all plat maps were not registered at the county court house.

Your steps in trying to locate a plat map would start as you did before by finding your ancestor's original deed copy. Then, check for his name in the Grantor (seller) Index. Find the deed to see if it matches the property deed you have, and again look for a plat map mentioned. If one is not mentioned, you check the Grantee Index to see when that person sold it. You are basically checking for one piece of property, often through numerous owners until a plat map exists. This is a painstaking search that requires perseverance since often property started with 500 acres and had many buyers of several acres or less throughout the years.

To complicate your search further in Buncombe, you may suddenly "lose" any record of the grantee or grantor. You need to remember that early Buncombe County covered all of Western North Carolina; therefore, when new counties were formed, deed activity after that formation would be in the new county. Plus, if taxes for land were not paid, there would often be a sale by the sheriff of the county and the land "grantor" would be the sheriff.

In 1887, a tourist came from New York City and stayed at the old Battery Park Hotel in Asheville. The hill where the old hotel sat was much higher at that date than the present Battery Park. E. W. Grove, a wealthy tonic entrepreneur, who arrived in Asheville in the early 1900s, cut down the hill and built the new hotel in 1920. Perhaps the previous height gave the visiting tourist a view he couldn't resist. Regardless of why, George W. Vanderbilt decided he must own the sight he saw from south Asheville to the Pisgah Mountains.

Starting in the late 1700s when Western North Carolina was "opened up" for settlement, others perhaps had noticed the beauty but probably had decided the rich valleys of the French Broad River would make provident farms. These owners' mansions were mainly log cabins, and instead of eyes turned to the view of the Pisgah Mountain range, they tramped the woods to furnish deer, turkeys, bears, and squirrels for their tables.

However, these lands along the French Broad River also had been bought by land speculators. Land could be bought from the state for 50 shillings (about $7 in 1860) for every hundred acres. Through state grants numbered 251, 252 and 253, which all mentioned the French Broad River, John Gray Blount and William Cathcart bought 846,880 acres in 1796. Other owners of land along the French Broad in the late

35

1700s included Thomas Arnold, Moses Ashbrook, James and Waightsell Avery (over 3,000 acres), James Clemons, John Bradley, Elijah Williamson, William Wilson, William Stewart, Josiah English, Ebenezer Fain, William Forester, Joseph Henry (2,000 acres), Richard Hightower (1,600 acres), Samuel King, Spruce McCoy, Lambert Clayton, Thomas Hemphill, Benjamin Cochran, Abraham and Archibald Reed, John Craig, Benjamin and William Davidson (over 1,500 acres), John Davis, Charles and James McDowell, John and Robert Patton, Burdit Sams, William Mills, William Sharpe, and Andrew, David, and James Miller.

Mr. Vanderbilt started buying the land piece by piece through his attorney, Charles McNamee in May of 1888. He found sellers because good land was still available, and many of the sellers had never even dreamed of so much money as they were offered. Some of the earliest sellers were George W. Britt, who received $2,400 for 43 acres, and Henry Bynam, who received $1888 for 24 acres. Other early sellers were the Reeds, Pattons, and Lances.

By 1890, Mr. Vanderbilt was buying the land in his own name: June 13, 1890, from Philetus M. Jones, who sold 45 acres for $10 in the township of Lower Hominey; June 16, from Henry Allen White and Lawiaita, his wife, from Madison County, hiers of Charles Hemphill, 134 plus acres for $10,056; June 18, from Samuel H. Reed and Jessie M. Reed, his wife, $10,000 for 42 plus acres in the township of Asheville on the "southerly bank of the Swannanoa River directly under the middle line of the bridge crossing said River at the Hendersonville Road." (Buncombe County Deed Book 71, p. 393). Over six hundred deed transactions were required before the original Vanderbilt land was acquired.

Regardless that descendants may marvel that their ancestors sold the beautiful land, fate goes in "ups and down." Vanderbilt's acquisitions kept the land more or less unspoiled so that we still have a remembrance of the grandeur our early ancestors lived and survived on.

Indexes for deeds are often found in libraries. One local book for study is *Buncombe County, North Carolina, Index to Deeds, 1783-1850*, compiled by James M. Wooley 1983, [Southern Historical Press: Easley, S. C.]

Macon County, North Carolina, located in the western section of the state was formed in 1828 from Haywood County, which was formed from Buncombe County in 1808. Barbara S. McRae has compiled *Records of Old Macon County, N. C.*, 1829-1850, [Clearfield Publishing: Baltimore, MD, 1991]. The book is based on abstracts of original documents in the Macon County Register of Deeds' Office.

Ms. McRae stated that the region of old Macon went to the boundaries of South Carolina, Georgia, and Tennessee, covering all or parts of seven western N. C. counties and half of the Great Smoky Mountains National Park. This region was opened for settlement by treaties of 1817 and 1819 with the Cherokee Indians.

Captain Robert Love, leading the surveyors, mapped the new territory in 1820 in 50 to 300 acre sections which sold for $4 per acre to 50 cents an acre. (The deeds were registered in Haywood County until 1828.) The treaty excluded a number of 640-acre reservations granted to individual Cherokee Indians. These were later sold by the Cherokees. There are lists dated March 1830 of the Cherokees who sold their 640-acre reservations and the price paid to them by the state of North Carolina.

Buncombe County's issuing land grants in this area as early as 1797 caused some problems for the new settlers who had filed according to Captain Love's sections of acreage, such as 200,960 acres then in Buncombe on the Tennessee, Tuckasegee, and Nantahala Rivers granted in 1797 to John Holdeman and Jacob Eshleman, which was registered in Macon in 1832.

These records also include a few slave transactions. Patents are also listed, such as, "James Barnes of Lawrence County, Tennessee, obtained a patent on October 14, 1830, for an improvement in washing, the Revolving Steam Washer. Benjamin Demmane patented a machine to destroy bed bugs, June 22, 1832. Matthew Hughs and Company purchased exclusive rights to making, using and selling these machines in Macon, Haywood, and Buncombe Counties from the patentees."

In Ms. McRae's book many transactions are listed under the surnames of Ammons, Angel, Bryson, Cockerham, Enloe, Gray, Hall, Howard, Ledford, Love, McDowell, Moore, Siler, Welch, and Wilson.

In the counties of Bladen, Anson, Mecklenburg, and Tryon, land was granted to pioneers in the 1740s through the early 1770s. There was nothing unusual about this other than North Carolina was granting South Carolina's land in about 1,000 cases.

After the survey in 1772, west of the Catawba River, these people's lands were in Craven or Berkeley Counties and St. Mark's or St. David's Parish, S. C., (now Spartanburg, Greenville, Laurens, Newberry, etc.)

Brent Holcomb has compiled abstracts of these land grants plus the file numbers in *North Carolina Land Grants in South Carolina*, 1986, [Brent Holcombe, P. O. Box 21766, Columbia, SC 29221]. The grantees' names are alphabetized in the four counties from which the grants were made. Some of these people were later in Western North Carolina, such as Abraham Kuykendal and brothers James and Peter 1763, John and Robert Love 1764, Samuel and William McBrayer 1767, James Miller 1768, plus Pattons, Moores, and Davidsons.

File numbers for these grants were included so that you could write to the Land Grant Clerk, Secretary of State, Raleigh, NC 27603, to ask about abstracts for these deeds.

Clerk of Court Records

Probably the official document family historians prize finding, second only to an ancestor's Revolutionary War pension papers, is an ancestor's will. Wills give very reliable family history; however, they are somewhat elusive and are not always available.

Just as today, many people didn't bother to make wills and the court house fires seemed to have wiped out many estate settlements that existed. In reality, it seems wills and estate records were not so carefully preserved by making copies as the all-important deeds were.

Everyone who dies is declared as died intestate, without a will, or testate, with a will. Regardless in which situation your ancestor was declared, various court procedures were followed for estate settlements.

If you can find **estate records** for an ancestor, you will find valuable family history, such as all the children of the deceased, wife's or husband's name, where the person owned property, his or her lifestyle by the list of personal possessions. Four types of estate records exist.

About twenty percent of people make a witnessed official will (testate). These will and probate records are usually easy to find at the county court house where the person died or in the state archives. Probate, by law, normally occurs within 30 to 90 days after the person's death.

Similarly, a holographic will, or one written in the deceased's handwriting and filed with other valuable documents, can be valid in most states. A nuncupative will, or oral death-bed wish, if properly witnessed, can be valid for personal property but not usually for real property.

By far, most people die without a will (intestate). These records normally show the surviving spouse as getting one-third of the estate and the children two-thirds, if the records exist since North Carolina did not require their filing. An inventory of all the deceased's property must be made whether testate or intestate. Often ancestors disposed of all property before their deaths, so there may be no estate records.

The official estate records tell basically what happened to a dead person's property and include records such as inventories, accounts of sale, petitions, land records, special proceedings, and settlements.

For example, in the Buncombe County Probate Court on January 15, 1879, "J. A. Lance, being sworn, doth say that Joseph Lance late of said county is dead, without leaving any will and testament." (Joseph's tombstone states he died January 7, 1879.) Joseph's sons, J. A. Lance and F. A. Lance, were declared by the Court to be Administrators for their father's estimated $1,500 estate. These sons at this time had to agree to make a "True and perfect inventory" of Joseph's personal property. On May 8, 1879, they submitted an inventory such as two mules worth $200, seven hogs worth $20, and 1,500 pounds of bacon worth $90.

Just as today, though, what may start out as a simple estate settlement may become more complex. This case was complicated when a storeowner/blacksmith said the deceased Joseph owed him $108.32. The summons for the sons from the Superior Court on August 3, 1879, is included in the estate records plus a copy of the court settlement in September of 1879.

The evidence was an interesting inclusion since it consisted of nine pages of Joseph's accounts with the storeowner. This account ledger showed that a typical Buncombe County farmer in the late 1870s bought only items such as salt, coffee, lead pencils, tobacco, and clothing from the stores. It also showed that a mule could be shoed for fifty cents, a chisel made for ten cents, coffee purchased for fifty cents per pound and a half, twenty yards of cloth for $2.80, and a pair of shoes for $2.25.

Joseph must have been in the sawmill business as well as into farming since his account showed credits when he sold such lumber materials as 40 feet, sheeting planks, 31 inches, for twelve cents.

These various credits and debits were what made the amount owed in question. Joseph did have debits of $108.32, but he also had credits of $76.54; however the Court awarded the storeowner $64.49; perhaps interest was included.

Normally, widows received a year's provisions until the estate was settled. A widow's dower equaled one-third part of all lands and goods. A widow was normally appointed as the administrator of the estate as shown in Joseph Lance's estate records by his second wife, Emelia Lance, signing a statement, "I relinkish my right as administrator . . and request you to appoint F. A. Lance in my stead."

To check for estate settlements or records for someone who died without a will but had property, you may want to go to the Clerk of Superior Court's Offices in the county where the person died. In Buncombe, the Administrators' Records are available from October 5, 1896, in bound volumes as are the Cross Index to Administrators. The Cross Index is alphabetized by the names of the people who received from the estate.

The Administrators' Books 1 - 3 are in the North Carolina State Archives on microfilm. To see if an earlier estate settlement is available for your ancestor, write to N. C. State Archives, 109 East Jones Street, Raleigh, N.C. 27601-2807, and include the name and county where the person died, approximate date, and a pre-addressed, stamped envelope. The Buncombe County Archives on Valley Street has the indexes to settlements from 1831 and records of settlements from 1869.

There are several ways to try to track down a will for the few people who made these.

The earliest North Carolina wills from 1663-1760 were filed with the Secretary of the Province of North Carolina. From 1760, the individual counties started keeping the wills; some kept them in the Registrar of Deed's offices and some kept them in the Clerk of Court's offices. In Buncombe County, the Clerk of Superior Court has "Will Indexes 1831-current" and "Records of Wills 1831-current."

One of the easiest ways to check for wills without traveling to every court house is to go to a library, such as Pack in Asheville. Some of the books available are discussed briefly.

An Abstract of North Carolina Wills from about 1760-1800, compiled by Fred A. Olds, reprinted from 1925 publication [Clearfield: Baltimore], includes 7,500 abstracts.

North Carolina Wills: A Testator Index, 1665-1900, by Thorton W. Mitchell [Genealogical Publishing: Baltimore, 1992], lists indexes for 75,000 wills found in county courthouses and in the North Carolina State Archives. This book does not have the abstracts such as in Olds, but it is more complete and explains how a copy of the will may be obtained.

Each entry contains the name of the person who wrote the will, the county where the will was recorded, the date of the probate, the location of the will by book and page number in each of the counties, and where the original will is, if available.

Only a few of the original wills proved before 1700 have survived. Some wills probated during the colonial period do not have a county identification and were proved by the governor. Whether in the county court houses or in the State Archive records, the location of the original will is given if it still exists. In Buncombe County, some wills are missing before 1865 because of fires and losses. Will books for wills probated after 1830 appear to be complete in the index, but many original wills are missing. A typical listing in Mitchell's index shows "Garren, John 013 [Buncombe] probate 1843, will book WB A/90."

Henderson County, formed from Buncombe in 1838, did not list wills until 1841. A typical listing shows Lyda, Anna 050 [Henderson] probate 1894, will book WB 2/194, with the original at the Henderson County Court House. Registers or recorded wills started in 1782 in Rutherford County. The wills of former Tryon County, from which Rutherford was formed in 1779, are in the records of Lincoln County or in the State Archives.

After finding the listing for a will, you may obtain a copy by writing to the clerk of court in the county where the will was listed or to the State Archives. (The cost for the copy will depend upon the length of the will.)

When writing to the N. C. State Archives, 109 East Jones Street, Raleigh, NC 27601-2807, include a pre-addressed, stamped envelope. (Out-of-state correspondents must include $8 with the request for a search).

A step you may want to try is to see if the county you are interested in has a book of will abstracts. The abstracts are informative, usually listing everyone and relationship mentioned in the will itself. If the abstract exists, it would probably determine for you if this is really the ancestor's will you had hoped to find. Among the books of abstracts for counties in North Carolina, Pack Library in Asheville has Currituck, Dare, Halifax, Tryon, Sampson, Anson, Camden, Pasquotank, Granville, Edgecombe, Nash, Orange, and Bladen. Check in the North Carolina reference card catalog under the county you are searching. (Out-of-state will abstract books are discussed in the library chapter.)

A caution when using books containing will indexes or abstracts: Don't take it for granted there is no will or estate records available if they are not listed. The compiler could have, inadvertently, missed some or some estate record could exist. If you know the county and the approximate date of death, check with the clerks of court and the state archives, asking them to check their wills and estate records.

Other records you may want to check for at the Clerk of Court's office are Cross Index to Civil Judgements which would include divorce records and Guardianship papers from 1902.

Researching Official Records at Archives

Archives basically store copies of records. At state archives, the state records are stored. At the National archives, the federal records are stored. Getting these records without visiting the archives in person can be done by mail, but it is a one-at-a-time procedure. In this section, the Buncombe County Archives will be discussed, followed by the North Carolina State Archives, the National Archives, and, even though their records cover more than official records, the Latter-Day Saints of Jesus Christ's records (LDS).

Buncombe County Archives

Buncombe County has an asset for family historians that no other county in North Carolina has. While most counties have sent all their older official records to the State Archives, Buncombe has made the records also available for local study at the Buncombe County Archives on Valley Street in Asheville.

Not many places exist that you can just browse through to see what old records you want to check. The first step is to check the index for all the microfilmed holdings. The headings include general county court, historical, list of confederate pensioners, naturalization records 1889-1904, special proceedings 1798-1812.

An interesting microfilm listed under historical is one compiled by Geo. A. Digges, Jr., "Historical Facts Concerning Buncombe County." Specific items such as the building of Beaucatcher Tunnel and a general history of Buncombe are included.

A roster of county officials starting 1872 has some comprehensive biographies: Col. Samuel Bell Gudger, who was chairman of the Board of County Commissioners from 1874-76, was born February 7, 1808, at Cross Roads, Leicester Township, to James and Annie Love Gudger. His eight brothers are listed. His father James was born January 6, 1782, to William and Martha Young Gudger in a house on the present site of the Municipal Golf Course. James Gudger was probably the first white child born to early Buncombe settlers.

The start of the government of Buncombe was recorded by Col. David Vance, the first Clerk of Court, at the first county court meeting on April 16, 1792, at the home of Col. William Davidson.

The minutes of the January term in 1862 included "Ordered by court that the following amounts be appropriated out of the taxes for the next year, to wit: for volunteers' wifes and family (confederate), $2,100; for the poor, $1,300; for the county, $700."

In April 1862 the court was to send someone to the "Sea Coast where salt is manufactured and purchase salt as contemplated in an order the 15 Jany 1862."

In February 1868 a public ferry was to be established by N. W. Woodfin on the French Broad River at the mouth of Glenn's Creek. The charges were set at five cents for a footman, ten cents for man and horse, three cents each for cattle, two cents for hogs and sheep, sixty cents for every six-horse wagon and cart.

A superior court judge while presiding over the August 1925 term "Severely arraigned the county for its inadequate court house; crowded conditions at the jail and failure to construct a building in keeping with Buncombe County's taxable wealth." Details are soon included for building the new court house to replace the 1903 one. The figures were given as $490,347 for land, $134,703 for furniture and fixtures, $1,968,646 for the building. The formal opening was held December 1, 1928.

The births, marriages, and deaths are on microfilm there. Also, on microfilm are indenture bonds 1870-1919, special proceedings 1798-1970, wills 1831-1970, settlements 1869-1970, minutes, pleas, and quarter sessions 1791-1985, voters 1902-1908, Buncombe County Confederate Pensions.

There are brief abstracts of court actions and judgments of the court clerk for criminal and civil proceedings and records of court minutes. (Records of felonies which were not major are usually destroyed after 30 to 60 years.) Criminal records are different from the civil ones in several ways. The criminal records cover cases that involve the State against someone being tried for a misdemeanor or felony. This is the state trying to protect society.

The civil records cover charges that one individual has brought against another. Civil records also cover name changes, naturalizations, indebtedness, lunacy, coroners' records. The early equity records, such as the ones available in the Buncombe County Archives from 1809-1832, film #89 covered land disputes, disputes of estates, contracts, and other appeals for "wrongs" on property rights. This court was abolished in 1868 and was sometimes called "special proceedings" court.

Civil and criminal actions are indexed by the court term when the case or action was completed, not when it started. The procedure for studying these records is to know the name, the approximate date of the offense, and whether the offense was civil or criminal. For example, for criminal trials if you think an ancestor was involved in stealing (larceny), get the microfilm for the approximate date, such as "1931-1933, Criminal Trials Minute Docket." This microfilm starts with an alphabetized list and page numbers in the film which contains a brief description of the offense, how the defendant pleaded, and if the arrested defendant was found guilty, not guilty, or case dismissed. On these pages will be a court case number. Write down the name, date, title of microfilm, plus the court case number if you wish to order a copy of the complete proceedings from the North Carolina Archives.

Not well-indexed but, in general, interesting reading on everything from notches on cows' ears to public whippings are the "Minutes of the

Buncombe County Courts and Pleas and Quarter Sessions." You may find in these that your great-great grandfather was arrested for illegal distillery and retailing, a four-great uncle was declared a lunatic, or a three great-grandmother was arrested for a misdemeanor. Of course, in these early times, one could be arrested for not keeping up the road in front of his house. One could be declared a lunatic for "overindulgence" of the homemade wine.

As mentioned previously, the Clerk of Court's office has the cross index to judgments, including divorces from 1915-present. The County Archives has divorce files from 1868. Divorce files before 1868 are in the State Archives. However, divorce records do not give family history. They include only the names and the date the divorce was granted.

Some tax scrolls for Buncombe County are available at the Buncombe County Archives. The ones for 1858-1861 often give river-name descriptions since all the present townships were not formed, such as "Upper Swannanoa" for present Black Mountain. Information on these listings include acres, valuation, white poll, black poll, gold watches, silver watches, interest, total valuation.

Information on the listings for 1905 include age, poll, number of acres, value of land, number of town lots, value, real property value, horses, value, mules, value. Landless men, usually between the ages of 21 through 50 were listed because they had to pay a poll tax. In reading these, you may be surprised to find a town lot valued at $25 but a horse valued at $40-$60. The valuation for acreage varied since residences were listed with the acreage and the value or non-value of mountain land had to be considered. For example, one acre in 1905 could be valued at $5, $40, $250, or $500.

Also at this archives are volumes of Buncombe censuses from 1800-1880, some cemetery listings, and deed indexes from 1791-1923. Buncombe County Archives is open Monday through Friday, 8:30-4:45.

Many microfilms of court records, including some for Burke, Yancey, Madison, and Rutherford Counties are available at Asheville-Buncombe Technical Community College Library and will be discussed in the chapter on libraries.

North Carolina State Archives

Basically the North Carolina State Archives has all the older records all the county court houses have. If you are searching in several different counties for records, it may be easier to visit this one place than to travel from county to county. Many times it is possible to borrow microfilms from the state archives through a local library. In addition, the state archives is a place to search for military and pension records that may not be available on the county level.

Most libraries have a copy of the "Guide to Research Materials in the N. C. State Archives." A visit to the Archives allows you the opportunity to search all the records, but some are available by mail. As mentioned before, wills can be checked by mail.

Also checked by mail are pension papers for 98 veterans of the Revolution as well as all the Confederate pension papers for North Carolina. You would again need the county of residence for the person.

Copies of marriage bonds, which go back to 1741, are available by mail. These bonds were "statements of intent" and were filed by the prospective groom in the bride's county of residence. The bond fee was not paid if the couple married but was "pledged" in case it was found that one of these was underage, already married, or not a "free" person. A typical marriage bond gave the following information:

"Know all men by these present that we Benjamin Burgin and Daniel Little are held and firmly bound unto our Sovereign Lord the King, His heirs and Successors in the just and full sum of fifty pounds proc. for the true payment of which we bind ourselves, our Heirs, Executors, and Admrs. jointly and severally, firmly by these presents; sealed with out seals and dated this eighteenth day of November 1772.

"The condition of the above obligation is such that whereas the above Benjamin Burgin hath made application for a license for a marriage to be celebrated between him and Lear Man of the County of Rowan. .."

This matter, as seen from the price of the bond, was not to be taken lightly. The indexes for these bonds in North Carolina are available at Pack Library in Asheville on microfiche, giving the same information except for all the wording.

Also in the same building as the archives is the State Library which has books including family histories and Bible records organized by surnames. To check if the name you are searching for is available, write Genealogical Services Branch, N. C. State Library, 109 E. Jones Street, Raleigh, NC 27601-2807.

As a reminder when writing for records to be checked, ask only one question per letter.

Mark Sumner visited the Archives to check for estate records for his great-great grandfather, Jesse Sumner, who had died in 1878 without a will. Since there was no will, he checked Buncombe County Estate Records (1815-1924). After finding information there that Jesse was in lawsuits over the office of Sheriff of Buncombe, he went to the Buncombe Election Records of 1871-1900 and found a story he never knew anything about. (This incident shows politics were just as complicated over a hundred years ago as they are now.)

Jesse, born 1814, was a farmer along the French Broad River until 1868 when he went into politics. He was elected as Sheriff of Buncombe County in the general election on April 21 and 22, 1868. However, Jesse's term was cut short, when on September 5, 1870, the county commissioners refused to accept his bond. (Bonds were posted annually.) The Commissioners instead appointed James M. Young as Sheriff.

Not giving up, Jesse tried in October to be reinstated but was not; so he took his case to state court, Jesse Sumner vs. James M. Young. On January 9, 1871, a North Carolina judge ordered the Buncombe County Coroner to summon James M. Young and bring him to trial.

Later, at the trial Young said Jesse did not post bond regularly and did not account for tax monies collected. Young also stated that at the end of April or the first of May, 1871, Jesse left North Carolina and did not intend to return. Young stated that another general election was held and that Jesse lost. It is not clear how this case was resolved, but it was appealed to the N. C. Supreme Court which charged each party with the cost of court. Apparently, Young continued as Sheriff, and Jesse did leave the state since he was in Nebraska in February 1873. However, he later returned and is buried at Mt. Zion Cemetery, Skyland, beside his wife Rozilla Sorrells Sumner.

You never know what you'll find in old records to make you know more about your ancestors.

The growth of materials prove more and more records are being preserved, bought, and used. More genealogy books are being published each year. More computer programs are being created for genealogists. More people (about three thousand every day) are using the Morman Research Library in Salt Lake City, Utah. The Mormons, who already have over a billion names recorded from various sources, are listing all the American people and their kin.

Second to the Mormon records for research are the records in the Washington, D. C., National Archives and its branches preserved by the federal government.

National Archives

The National Archives records of most interest to genealogists start with Revolutionary War records and continue through the federal censuses from 1790 through 1920. There are also passenger lists, naturalization and pension records, and any other individual's records with the federal government.

Occasionally, something unusual ends up in the National Archives. Joe Hill was a songwriter and a member of the Industrial Workers of the World (IWW). After being convicted of murder in Utah, he asked that he be cremated and that his ashes be scattered in every state with the exception of Utah. On November 19, 1915, he was executed, and his ashes were placed in envelopes to be sent to the different states.

However, a little mishap occurred at the U. S. Post Office in Chicago. One envelope of his ashes was damaged. The postal authority seized the envelope and its contents, sending these to the P. O. Department in Washington, D. C. The envelope was eventually placed in a case file among records relating to the Espionage Act of World War I. These were saved by the National Archives and "catalogued" in 1944. On November 18, 1988, after Frederick Lee, chair of the IWW, requested the ashes, the National Archives turned over a vial with the ashes but retained the original envelope.

Don't expect to find ancestors' ashes, but the National Archives does have millions of records of individuals who were involved with the Federal government through census records, military service, immigration, and land grant documents. However, to obtain these documents, certain steps must be followed carefully. The National Archives has a free catalog, "Aid for Genealogical Research." This catalogue gives instructions for obtaining copies of the Archives' records and the addresses of the eleven regional archives. (Write: "Aids for Genealogical Research," National Archives Trust Fund Board, Publications Services, Room 1W1, Washington, DC 20408.)

The National Archives has records of births, marriages, and deaths at U. S. Army facilities, 1884-1912. It will search these records if provided with the following: birth records - name of child, names of parents, place of birth, and date; marriage records - names of people; death records - name, date, place, and rank of deceased. The National Archives also has some records of births and marriages, through 1941, and reports of some deaths, through 1949, of American citizens abroad, registered at Foreign Service posts. Address these later requests to Civil Archives Division, National Archives (GSA), Washington, DC 20408.

The Archives also has all the federal census information, arranged by state and alphabetically by surname. The information depends upon what was taken in the particular year you ask for. This census information will be discussed in the library chapter. The National Archives does have the microfilm records for sale.

You may wonder how, when you read your latest census forms in 1990, this information may later become available as public records. Very little is considered private after many years regardless of what you are told. The first federal census taken in 1790, Don W. Wilson, archivist of the United States, explained in *Forum* magazine, a publication of the Federation of Genealogical Societies, was for political reasons to allocate representation in Congress. These records were considered private and only for governmental usage. The 1880 Census Act for privacy demanded the census takers to swear they would "not disclose any information contained in the schedules, lists, or statements obtained by me -- except to my superior officers." In an act of June 1929, the Census Office was further told that no information or publication could be supplied that furnished information on an individual.

Then, in 1952, the Bureau of Census agreed to transfer census schedules to the National Archives with the provision that they remain closed for 72 years after the enumeration date for each census. (It's hard to imagine what family historians did without them as research tools.)

49

While the 1790 census of the United States could be printed in thin books for each state, the 1920 census, (the last one released in 1992), consisted of 2,076 rolls of microfilm.

There are in the National Archives many records relating to Indians who kept their tribal status. (The Indians had to register as Indians.) The records, arranged by tribes, are dated chiefly 1830-1940. They include lists of Indians, mainly Cherokee, Chickasaw, Choctaw, and Creek, who moved west during the period 1830-1846; annuity pay rolls, 1841-1949; annual census rolls, 1885-1940 (available on microfilm); and Eastern Cherokee claim files, 1902-1910. Some of these records are available locally and will be discussed in a later chapter. Most people state that these records from the National Archives are only available by a personal visit and not by mail.

Naturalization records will be searched by mail if the naturalization occurred before September 27, 1906, if you send the full name of the person and the approximate date of naturalization.

Incomplete series of customs passenger lists from 1820 and immigration passenger lists of ships arriving from abroad at Atlantic and Gulf of Mexico ports are available by mail. A customs passenger list normally contains the following information for each passenger: his name, age, sex, and occupation; the country from which he came. (The records less than 50 years old are not available for research.) However, the National Archives will search the customs passenger lists if in addition to the name of the passenger and the name of the port of entry, an inquirer can supply the following information: the name of the vessel and the approximate date of its arrival or the name of the port of embarkation and the exact date of arrival. (Perhaps if you knew all of this, you would not need their services!) Plus, you must write to get the correct form to request information. Ask for order and billing for copies of passenger lists at the address below.

The service the National Archives is most noted for is to obtain military papers and pensions for service since the Revolutionary War until World War I. The National Archives has bounty land warrant application files based on service in wartime between 1775 and 1855 and pension application files based on service between 1775 and 1916. (These include only the servicemen from the Union during the Civil War since the individual states have the records for the Confederate soldiers.) For these records, you must first write for NATF Form 80 at General Reference Branch, National Archives, Records Administration, 7th and Pennsylvania Avenue, N. W., Washington, D. C. 20408. After you send in your completed form, you will receive a reply telling you if the record was found. If found, you are to send $10 within 45 days or fill out a new form. Have a little patience since this is not immediate, but should you wait about three months after you send in your money and the check was cashed, you might have to write Tod J. Butler, Chief, General Reference Branch, National Archives, etc. The problem arises because while you are notified by the Washington branch that your record was found, the payment you send is to Atlanta. Atlanta sends a printout of who paid before the record is mailed. If your name was omitted from this printout, well . . . .

In obtaining copies of records for World War I or II, write National Personnel Records Center, NARA, 9700 Page Blvd., St. Louis, MO 63132.

Some people are not aware of the eleven branches of the National Archives nor of the records kept in these. These branches document regional and local activities plus have a large percentage of microfilm from the Washington agency.

Archives, other than the Buncombe County one discussed, are not the browsing places libraries are. For the most part, you have to tell the archivist what record you want to see. Therefore, to make your visit profitable, you need to have a plan of search.

The Atlanta Branch in East Point, GA, (south of Atlanta), has records from Alabama, Florida, Georgia, Kentucky, Mississippi, North Carolina, South Carolina, and Tennessee. The "paper" records maintained and available for research equal 41,000 cubic feet, dating back from 1716 through the present.

Files and photographs of Cherokee and Seminole Indian agencies, maps of the U. S. Army Corps of Engineers, and World War I draft registration cards for all men in the United States born between 1873 and 1900 are just a few of the historical documents to be found at the Atlanta Branch.

The federal court naturalization documents here should help the family historian. (Records are most complete after 1906.) North Carolina U. S. District Court records are available from 1789 - 1958. Papers are also available concerning the relocation of families from areas of the Tennessee River Valley where the dams were built including lifestyles of the people, family structure, cash crops, etc. (These are arranged by which dam, county, and family.)

Some of the available microfilm holdings in Atlanta include "Index to Passengers of Vessels Arriving at Ports in Alabama, Florida, Georgia, South Carolina, 1890-1924," "Final Rolls of Citizens and Freedmen of Five Civilized Tribes in Indian Territory," "Records of the Cherokee Indian Agency in Tennessee, 1801-1835," "Index to Compiled Service Records of Volunteer Soldiers who served during the War of 1812 in organizations from North Carolina," "Records of Admissions to Citizenship, District of South Carolina, from 1790."

If you know the records you want to see, you'll spend a day of research instead of a day just getting acquainted with the holdings. A 1988 publication, The Archives: *A Guide to the National Field Branches*, [Ancestry: Salt Lake City] should be a helpful study before visiting the branch services.

The Church of Jesus Christ of Latterday Saints, LDS

Although not an archives in name, imagine finding access to family history books, immigration records (after 1820), property and probate records, tax and church records, and more, all in one place - plus not only for the United States but also for many foreign countries. These records are found weekly by thousands of people who flock to Salt Lake City, Utah, and the largest genealogical library in the world: the Church of Jesus Christ of Latterday Saints (LDS). More families' histories are residing there than anyplace else in the world. You may be surprised to find your Methodist great-grandfather's name listed among the billions there.

Moreover, you do not have to go to Utah to "tap into" their records. There are family history libraries across the United States and one locally on Sweeten Creek Road in Skyland, N. C., where you can get much information immediately and can order more.

At the LDS Library, first check the Accelerated Index Systems (AIS) on microfiche. These indexes are divided into Searches I-VIII: the Colonial Period from 1600-1819, 1820-29, 1840-49, Southern states 1850,

New England and North 1865, United States 1850-1906, mortality schedules 1850-1885. These nationwide searches include compiled information from jury lists, tax lists, census listings, and will give you an idea of what locations your ancestors were in. Be sure to check for varied spellings. Write down the names you are interested in. For example, "Nicholas Justason, 1761 jury list, Gloucester County, N. J." You now have a start on what state you'd need to check for more information.

Next, one of the most useful sources, the International Genealogical Index (IGI), with over 80 million names, has names listed under states and countries. This index included information on birth listings, christening dates, marriages from vital records and church records. An example from New Jersey is "Justason, Elizabeth, father Justa Justason, christened 05 November 1741, Gloucester." After the name, county, date, type of record, there will be a microfilm number so that you can see the complete document. If this microfilm is not available at the library, it can be ordered for your use for $2.75.

You may also want to check the Family Registry, looking up the family names in which you are interested. Put down the FR number to see the addresses of the people who have registered information if you wish to share information on a family name. You are also invited to register the ancestors you are searching. Ask a librarian for the necessary forms.

Another helpful index is the surname Family History Library Catalog (FHLC), which lists 30,000 titles of printed family histories, manuscript genealogies, and family history periodicals. Most of these are on microfilm which can be ordered through the library.

Much more information is on microfilm. Check the microfilm card catalog which is divided into world locality catalogs such as county histories and gazeteers, subject catalogs such as pension application files, immigration records, and religious affiliations, and surname catalogs. The library on Sweeten Creek Road in Skyland also has some area research books. The use of this library is free, but donations are accepted. You may want to call (828) 684-6646 to check for current times opened before going.

Archives are not the easiest places to do research in because of the plethora of records stored at these, but a little study of research books before you go and a careful listing of the people you are searching for should make it worth your while.

CHAPTER 3. LIBRARIES

Libraries should be looked upon as a place where you are going on an adventure since you never know what you will find. Of course, there are books, but in larger city libraries, there are microfilms, microfiche, vertical files, a whole world of places to search for your family members. Plus, libraries are so relaxing that you will find hours have gone by before you realize you still have a stack of books before you. Mainly non-book sources at different local libraries will be covered before books that will be found at various libraries.

Newspapers

Have you ever thought to ask to read old newspapers on microfilm at libraries. You may find more than you you imagined.

Is there gold in the hills of Western North Carolina? Many ancestors had good reason to search for gold since successful gold mining was very much in the news in the early 1830s, particularly in Burke and Rutherford Counties.

When finding gold is mentioned, most people think of California, 1848, and of wild west "boom" towns. A few people speak of the Georgia gold land since they've heard some of their kin rushed out of Western North Carolina to go for the quick fortune in the 1830s and 1840s. The gold region of Georgia started in Habersham County across the Chattahoochee River and ran west through the Indian Nation into Alabama; the width was only about twenty miles. The ones who did go off for the Georgia gold could not just start panning the best gold without the wrath of the Cherokee Indians and the federal troops upon them. However, the prospects of finding gold in north Georgia caused many to invade the "Nation." In the early 1830s, periodically, the United States troops would go out from the forts and expel the whites. Thousands were practicing illicit prospecting from Georgia, North Carolina, South Carolina.

However, by a vote of 102 to 97, on May 26, 1830, the United States Government passed the Indian Bill for the removal and settlement of the Indians west of the Mississippi. (Needless to say, the Indians were not allowed to vote.) The land was still not free to prospect. In 1832 "gold lots" were being lottered in the Cherokee Nation of Georgia. Only residents of Georgia for three years could participate in the "draw" for the 40-acre gold lots.

The North Carolinians who rushed off to Georgia for gold might have been better off heading to their neighborhood creeks. Perhaps they weren't reading *The North Carolina Spectator and Western Advertiser*, published in Rutherford in 1830-1831 and Western North Carolina's only weekly newspaper. (No daily papers existed at that time in Western North Carolina.)

The March 26, 1830, edition showed much excitement over local gold-mining finds. Gold had been discovered on Second Broad River in Burke County on the lands of James Jeans. From this mine developed "amounts of $2 per day has been washed with a pan." The mine sold immediately to General Bryant for $4,500. Another mine in Burke was on the land of John Logan, Esq., near the junction of Cane Creek and Second Broad, "which is very thick set with particles of gold large enough to be plainly seen with the eye."

By May 12, 1830, the *Raleigh Register* stated that 42 pounds of the precious metal was paid to the State Bank from the mines in Burke County. The Brindle Mine in Burke and the mines on the Second Broad River in Rutherford were said to surpass the gold found in Georgia.

The October papers of the North Carolina Spectator showed individuals searching for gold had gone beyond the creek-panning method. On October 13, Mr. Thomas Allison was killed in one of the pits of his gold mine: "the rope attached to the tub in which the dirt is drawn up broke while the tub was ascending and precipitated it with its contents upon his head. The weight of the loaded tub was about 200 pounds."

Mr. John Woody from Jeanstown warned gold miners against "building or using a machine lately invented by me, called the Gold Cradle, for washing or separating alluvial gold from earth, streams, etc., or constructin such upon my plan and invention," since he intended to apply for a patent on it.

By July 1831, Mr. Christopher Bechtler at his establishment near Rutherford was assaying and stamping ingots "20 carots fine." Much of the gold he used was from nearby gold sources.

Perhaps all the gold miners left for California in 1848, but even through the early 1900s, mountain land was advertised for sale with the added lure of "possibly gold on this land."

Many microfilms from the State Archives can be ordered from local libraries for your viewing. Ask at city and college libraries for the procedures.

One of the best local libraries is Pack Library, Haywood Street, Asheville, which has a North Carolina research room. The information seems endless there.

Newspaper microfilms are fascinating. Even though "projector fatigue" may set in after several hours, to microfilm through the old local newspapers is fun. While browsing, you never know what you may find. You may find great-great uncle Jesse's name in the headlines as being tried for shooting two people on April 5, 1895. This item, which was never mentioned to you when talking to family members, gives you the incentive to keep rolling the microfilm. The holding for trial, the change of court to Henderson County because family members are turning the county against him, and the pleadings are like an ongoing "soap opera" through October of 1895.

These early newspapers do not just present the facts. These describe the family feuds, what the neighbors and everybody else and their brothers think about the murder case. Even though the newspapers were short, it take hours to search the headlines and to read the interesting stories.

The microfilm for local newspapers at Pack Library in Asheville affords months of reading, starting with the 1870s. Since there are no indexes, it is a "hit or miss" situation that isn't for people who are in a hurry to "hone" in on one person. But you learn much about the people of an area in general, and you never know what the next page will bring. One old family story in the Whitaker family was that the Whitaker family had a fortune coming to them in England from their ancestor John Whitaker. The tale went that John from Pennsylvania had loaned all his money to Majesty George III of England in the beginning of the Revolutionary War trouble between the years of 1764-1774.

About 1884 a Reverend William G. Whitaker, a direct descendant of John, decided he would try to reclaim what he said had grown to $96 million or 20 million pounds; he further said that he had gone to Liverpool, England, and that in his research he found the descendants were also heirs to the Bannister Estate, the Townley Estate, and the Clayton Estate. He said the Bank of England told him to get a list of the heirs in order to make the claim.

In searching for heirs, he found that William Whitaker, supposedly an uncle to John, had left for North Carolina in 1752 according to a letter from the Friends in Bradford, Pennsylvania, who recommended that this family was "in good degree orderly." ("True" copy from Ruth Whitaker, Ann Arbor, Mich.) In 1800 James Whitaker, a grandson of William, moved from Rowan County "to the wilds of Buncombe County. Then a new settlement and rather a wilderness. My first settlement was upon Cane Creek where two of my brothers were then living having moved there years before." (From James Whitaker's Memoirs). Many Whitakers from this line remained in Buncombe County.

Therefore, the Reverend Whitaker had come to the Asheville area for Whitaker family history proofs and to get contributions for his search. He had also written letters asking for donations to help him collect this fortune. While in Asheville, February 1908, he was arrested and tried for mail fraud. (The *Asheville Citizen* gave accounts of this case from July 11, 1908-November 14, 1909.)

A Harold W. Vessey came from the Bank of England and said that although there were unclaimed funds, a fund did not match the claim of Mr. Whitaker. (By this time the Reverent Whitaker calculated that the money had grown to $300-600 million.) The July 16, 1908, newspaper account described Reverend Whitaker as "the main star witness, the great mongul of millions, the raven locked and oil annointed, silk-hatted magnate who needs to wrestle catch as catch can with the Bank of England for his assorted million. . .."

He was convicted and sentenced to 18 months in the Atlanta Federal Prison for mail fraud on September 8, 1908. The paper accounts "The Reverend will depart with regret and the many heirs in this vicinity who chipped in $10 or more each to help recover the treasure from the avaricious bank will also regret his departure because many of them still believe in the existance of the fund . . .."

The last account in the *Asheville Citizen* was on November 14, 1909, when the Reverend was described as "looking pale from so much indoor life, but otherwise in good physical condition, was released from prison Friday and came promptly back to Asheville despite the fact that it was here that he was convicted. What is still stranger, he at once domiciled himself as close to the jail as he could get, being the guest of Deputy Sheriff. . ." Some expressed the opinion that Mr. Whitaker should prefer to get as far away from prison as possible.

"There was hardly one [heir] who expressed disbelief in the defendant. Mr. Whitaker will not be deterred by his experience but will resume his efforts to establish the claims of the heirs."

To study Asheville newspapers, go to the North Carolina section of the Pack Library. Since no indexes exist for these, you pick a date and search for what you want.

The earliest copies are the *Highland Messenger* from 1840-1951, but not all copies are available. (These may be worth a search since some records at the Buncombe County Court House were destroyed by fire during this period.) Also earlier but incomplete copies include the *Asheville Weekly Pioneer*, 1867-1874 and the *Asheville News*, 1851-1874.

The *North Carolina Citizen* starts March 8, 1877, various dates, but practically none in the 1880s. Starting with the 1890s is the film with the *Weekly Citizen* and *Asheville Citizen*, incomplete. The *Asheville Daily Citizen* and the *Asheville Citizen* are continuous from the 1900s through the present. The *Asheville Gazette News* is from 1904 through 1916 at which time the *Asheville Times* picks up.

Since the older newspapers are interesting to read not only for the news and features but also for the advertisements, a day-by-day newspaper study of a certain period can give you an understanding of the area and the people.

Books may also be found in libraries about what is in the newspapers. Newspapers have always had a profound impact on their readers. Many historians feel the American Revolution would have never been successfully supported without the newspapers in the mid-1700s. Even though North Carolina was one of the last colonies to get a printing press, there were newspapers. *An Index to North Carolina Newspapers, 1784-1789*, by Alan D. Watson, [Historical Publications, North Carolina Archives: Raleigh] discusses the newspapers from New Bern, Hillsborough, Edenton, Wilmington, Fayetteville with the index including names, places, and events which were in these papers.

The first was the *North Carolina Gazette*, published in 1751 by James Davis in New Bern. The next pre-Revolutionary paper, *North Carolina*

Gazette and Weekly Post Boy, was in 1764 in Wilmington.

Many problems existed for successful newspaper publications. The newspapers came slowly and went quickly. First, North Carolina was a rural state with no city having more than a thousand people. Readership was hard to reach. Next, the venture was expensive. The printing presses and the paper were scarce and expensive since they had to be imported. Also, New York and Philadelphia were the main distributors of the news.

Therefore, even though the North Carolina Declaration of Rights stated "That the freedom of the press is one of the greatest bulwarks of liberty; and therefore ought never to be restrained," the state was a "vast burial ground of dead newspapers" even through the 1850s.

Basically, the early newspapers favored international and national information over local news except for marriages and death notices. However, the indexes focus on the local aspects.

Robert K. Headley's publication, *Genealogical Abstracts from 18th Century Newspapers,* 1987, [Genealogical Publishing: Baltimore], should help with Virginia research. Even Virginia did not keep official marriage and death records until 1853. Plus, Virginia had perhaps more than its share of "burned out court houses" during the Civil War.

From over seven thousand issues of eighty-one 1700s newspapers from Virginia, he has abstracted marriage and death notices, estate sales and settlements, advertisements for runaway slaves, servants, apprentices, and military deserters, and court cases. Also, he had included from the *Maryland Gazette,* the *American Weekly Mercury,* the *New York Post Boy,* the *Pennsylvania Chronicle,* and New Bern's *North Carolina Gazette* information that related to Virginians.

The information is arranged by family names rather than by newspapers or dates with a few exceptions, such as nine pages of deserters from the Virginia Regiments, a large number of runaway convict servants, convicts, sailors, and slaves, and a large number of people killed by Indians. "Deserted from John Posey's Company of the Virginia Regt. in Fredsbrg. seven recruits including: John Barry, from Alexandria, seen to cross over to Md. with his wife; James Devine from Loudon Co., b. in Dublin, married since he enlisted to a freckled, red-headed girl [?];James Fitzpatrick from Westmoreland Co., b. in Dublin, was a soldier in Posey's Co. in 1758 and 1760, gardener and ditcher by trade. (*Maryland Gazette,* June 24, 1762.)

"Killed by Indians on the Cumberland Path in Tennessee near the Crab Orchard on 13 Aug: Paul Cunningham, Daniel Hitchcock, William Fennikin, Stephen Renfro." (The *Virginia Gazette and General Advertiser*, Sept. 10, 1794.)

Just as today, the newspapers carried various news stories and advertisements. "Thomas Coldwell of Prince Edward County on January 21, 1775, advertised that his wife, Delphia, "has been a naughty and furious housewife for some years and has threatened to ruin him; he will no longer pay any of her debts."

James Tracey was captured by Shawnee Indians in 1763 on Stinking Creek, New River. He escaped in 1773 and went to his former home "to learn that his father and family had removed to Fredsbrg., Virginia," and was seeking information on them.

James M'Clannahan said on April 4, 1798, that his marriage in Westmoreland County to Miss Fanny Pierce, as announced in the March 21 paper, was a "maliciious and notorious lie." "John Fowler, son of John Fowler late of Wapping St., London, sandman, went from Eng. as a servant six or seven years ago to some part of North America; if he will apply to Captain David Ross, commander of the ship *Betsey* at Norfolk, Ross will inform him of matters greatly to his advantage."

Microfiche

Microfiche with early records is often available at libraries. Pack Library has on microfiche the North Carolina marriage bonds' index; there are 170,000 of these from 1741-1868. These marriage bond indexes are actually like abstracts in that they have the same information as the marriage bonds. A typical entry shows Benjamin Justice on 24 Jan. 1803 intended to marry Elizabeth Hemphill. The number after this, 081 01 143 shows this was in Randolph County. (The codes are explained in the booklet that accompanies the microfiche.) This number along with 000112628 which follows would be the information sent to the N. C. State Archives if you wanted an actual copy of this record.

Federal Censuses

Even if you have found family material which you think is written correctly by someone else, you may want to check census information to make sure that all the children have been accounted for. Perhaps someone forgot about that son Josiah who left for Arkansas at 16 and was never seen again, but as a child, he would be on the census with the family.

On the recent censuses, you'll have to check the microfilm itself, but for many there are at least indexes that will help you. Pack Library has indexes for most of the Buncombe County censuses through 1880.

The 1790 federal census only lists head of household by name plus number of males over 16 and number of males under 16, numbers of females, number of free persons and slaves. Usually the districts are included.

The 1800 and 1810 censuses give the head of household plus five age brackets for males and females. By this limited information though, you can tell the number of children and the birth date range. However, without names, you do need to be cautious since some other children could be with the family or a young couple. Keep going with the later censuses to be sure.

The 1820 adds the town of residence, and slaves by age brackets. The 1830 goes to twelve age categories for whites, six for slaves and free Blacks.

The 1840 is similar to the 1830 in age categories but adds more total information such as deaf, blind, etc.; however, the 1840 added a feature that some researchers overlook. On the second page of the enumerations, there is a category for the name and age of pensioners for Revolutionary or military services. For example, the 1840 census for Haywood County includes Elijah Henson 77, Leonard Hice 77, Andrew Shook 85, Absalem Hooper 80, William Underwood 80, Robert Love 80, Lewis Smith 77 as Revolutionary pensioners.

The 1850 census starts becoming a real help. It listed free inhabitants by name plus birthplace, occupation, age, sex, color married within the year, attended school, ones over 20 who cannot read and write, even noted if any were paupers. No relationship of the people listed is shown; for example, under a name John Smith 50, Lucy 19 could either be a daughter, a wife of John, or a wife of the William listed who is 20. Just put down all the information and hope to straighten it out eventually, perhaps by a later census.

For 1850 and 1860 a slave listing was made separately, but no names of slaves were listed, just the owner, number, description by age. The 1860 census added value of property.

For 1870, all Blacks, Chinese, and Indians were listed by name. Also, occupation and if father/mother were of foreign birth were added. The 1880 census added relationships of each person in the household to the head of the household, such as daughter, mother-in-law, grandson, etc. Also added were marital status of each and the parents' place of birth. (This adding of where parents were born is a real clue into going backwards.)

The 1890 census listings for North Carolina except for a few scattered districts and none for Western North Carolina were destroyed by fire -- as were the rest of the nation's. Only 6,160 persons listed out of 63 million people in the United States at this time were saved. These were burned in a fire in 1921 in the Commerce Building in Washington before copies were made since at that time the census listings were still secret. Although not widely available, there is an 1890 special census of Union veterans and widows.

The 1900 and 1910 include month and year of birth, number of years married, number of children born to each female and number living. The 1920 schedules include name, address, relationship of each listed to the family head, sex, race, age, marital status, year of immigration to the U. S. if foreign born, whether naturalized and if so year, school attendance, literacy, birthplace of person and parents, mother-tongue of foreign-born, ability to speak English, occupation, home owned or rented, (if owned whether mortgaged plus market value, balance due, and interest rate.)

From 1900, you basically have to just read the microfilms. Before you start your census research, you may want to just write down for yourself all the possible spellings of the name you are interested in, such as Lance, Lants, Lints, Lins, Lince, Lintz, Lentz. If you have looked at any deeds in the county you are searching, you may see that the spellings are varied, depending upon how the person pronounced his name or how the census taker heard it.

The easiest way to keep from having to recheck periodically is to copy down all the people and all the information with the last name, or close to it, in the county you know was a residence. Usually this is not difficult with the early censuses from 1790-1840. If John is listed on the 1810 but not on the 1820, perhaps Mary is his widow. Older children in this ten year span could have died or could become listed on the census themselves. If a family stays in one area, through four censuses, you may see one last name listed in 1790 grow to fourteen or fifteen of the same last name. By studying the age brackets, you can make a guess on whether more with the same name moved into the area or if this man had sons with families. Before the 1850 census, it is very difficult to keep up with the female children.

Censuses are organized by states and then counties. A book available at Pack's library, *State Census of North Carolina, 1784-1787*, published by the North Carolina Department of Archives, would include any early settlers of Western North Carolina under Burke or Rutherford Counties. Burke and Rutherford Counties would also be the ones to study for the first federal census since Buncombe County was formed after the 1790 census. Of course, the first census of Buncombe County would cover present areas of not only Buncombe but also Haywood (first census 1810), Macon (from Haywood, first census 1830), Cherokee (from Macon, first census 1840), Henderson (from Buncombe, first census 1840), Yancey (from Buncombe and Burke, first census 1840), Jackson (from Haywood and Macon, first census 1860), Madison (from Buncombe and Yancey, 1860), Transylvania (from Henderson and Jackson, 1870), Clay (from Cherokee, 1870), Graham (from Cherokee, 1880), Swain (from Jackson and Macon. 1880).

For the study of nearby counties, McDowell County was formed from Rutherford and Burke, first census 1850; Polk was formed from Henderson and Rutherford, first census 1860.

The census information at Asheville's Pack has not only all North Carolina's census information on microfilm by county for 1800-1920 (no 1890) but also has indexes for North Carolina from 1790-1870. Asheville-Buncombe Technical Community College has the Buncombe County censuses from 1800-1920 plus the slave census of 1850 and 1860.

Toe River Valley Genealogical Society published the *1880 Federal Census , Mitchell County, N. C.* [Toe River Valley Society, 491 Beaver Creek Road, Spruce Pine, NC 28777] In 1861, Mitchell County was created from parts of Yancey, Watauga, Caldwell, Burke, and McDowell Counties. If you've "lost" an ancestor who was in one of these counties in 1860 or 1870, you may want to check Mitchell County, 1880, where 1,665 heads of households were listed.

As mentioned previously, much information is given on the 1880 census. For example, among the many Garlands listed was Christopher Garland, who was white, 36 years old, a farmer, living in Red Hill Township, born in N. C., as were his parents. His wife was Naomi, and also in his household were Pollie Peterson, his 80-year-old mother-in-law; Landon Webb, 24, a laborer; Jane Crowder, 18, a house servant.

In Herrell's Township, Sarah Cox, 25, wife of Aaron Cox, was born in Tennessee. Her father was born in Ireland and her mother in N. C. In Snow Creek Township, David Silver, 49, a farmer, had his father, Jacob, who was 89 and a minister, born in Maryland, living with him. Jacob's parents were born in Russia.

In Linville Township, Wesley McKerson, who was 56 and a mulatto farmer, was born in N. C. His father was born in Pennsylvania and his mother born in Africa.

Most were farmers in Mitchell County, but quite a few in Bakersville Township were mining for mica. Along with occupations and birth places are "details of health," which very few commented on, but there are additions of headache, maimed, pneumonia, insane, blind, rheumatism, epilepsy, consumption, idiotic.

The *Map Guide to the U. S. Federal Census, 1790-1920* by Thorndale and Dollarhide [Genealogical Publishing: Baltimore, 1987] gives detailed help for searching census records throughout the United States.

As mentioned earlier concerning counties, to find your ancestor in the census schedules, you must not only know the present name of the state or territory where he or she lived but also the name of the location at the time he or she lived there. The maps in this book show, in relationship to the United States today, what the states' territories included. For example, in 1790, Georgia included present Georgia plus most of present Mississippi and Alabama. Virginia included present Virginia plus present West Virginia and Kentucky.

In 1810, the Louisiana Territory covered most of the midwest, such as the present states of Montana, Iowa, the Dakotas, Missouri, while the present Louisiana was the Orleans Territory. Present Oklahoma was the Indian Territory until it was made a state in 1907.

65

After the national maps in the book, individual state maps are included for every ten years showing county changes. The book points out that the first Walton County, Georgia, from 1803-1812 was in present Transylvania County, N. C. In Western North Carolina all the present counties were not established until 1920, since even for 1910, residents of Avery County were in Mitchell, Caldwell, or Watauga Counties.

The book shows counties that no longer exist. In northwest Iowa a county named Buncombe existed in 1860 but was renamed Lyon in 1862. The compilers stated that middle and eastern Tennessee were the most difficult of all sections of the states for accuracy since early maps showed many variances.

General census information is given such as the warning that age is the most unreliable listing and that the 1870 census in the South has perhaps as many as 1.2 million people missing from it because of the unsettled populations after the Civil War.

Census records showed that the population grew from 3.9 million people in 1790 to 23.2 million in 1850 and to 92.2 million in 1910.

Sometimes when you study census records, particularly the ones starting with 1850, which give more information, you often come across some information that puzzles you. You may see that a relative is checked off as insane or idiotic. You just have to wonder if that was the opinion of the census taker or the idea of the person who gave the information. (You hope it wasn't a next-door neighbor.) Then, there are cases where elderly people were declared "lunatics" just as they are declared "incompetent" today. Old court papers just have they are declared "lunatics" but not what caused someone to say so. People had to be categorized to fit the census.

In 1790, the first census takers in the area where Tennessee, Kentucky, Virginia, and North Carolina join ran into a problem when they found people who did not fit into their enumerating categories. They found bronze-skinned people. The men wore beards, had straight, black hair and often had dark blue eyes: These were the Melungeons.

The Gowen Research Foundation is gathering data to find the origin of these people. There are many theories. Mary Sue Going of the Watauga Association of Genealogists of Jonesboro, Tennessee, stated that John Sevier first encountered the Melungeons in 1774 when his expedition crossed the Appalachians in Lord Dunsmore's War. (Sevier's report is in the N. C. Archives.) Louise Davis in the "Mystery of the Melungeons" concluded they were descended from Portuguese sailors shipwrecked off Cape Hatteras in the mid-1500s. Henry Price in "Melungeons: The Vanishing Colony of Newman's Ridge" felt they were descendants of Sir Walter Raleigh's "Lost Colony" of Roanoke, established July 23, 1687.

Mary Sue Goings suggests that they were descendants of deserters from a Spanish expedition, under Captain Juan Pardo, who explored eastern Tennessee in 1567. Ms. Going's research from Spanish Archives shows that Spain "impressed" Portuguese men into Spanish regiments. Goings says that Pardo's report stated that early in 1566, he with 250 men established his headquarters on present Parris Island and moved inland, establishing a fort at Joara (present-day Newport, Tennessee). One hundred men were left there under the command of Sgt. Hernando Moyano de Morales.

Genealogists nation-wide who have Melungeon data or who would like to participate in the Melungeon probe are invited to join the Gowen Foundation's research team by contacting Evelyn L. Orr, Chairperson, 8310 Emmet Street, Omaha, Nebraska 68134. (This was in 1990.)

Microfilm of Official Records

While searching for official records, family historians drive many miles to visit court houses. However, to study early records from Madison, Yancey, Burke, and Rutherford Counties, you may not need to visit each court house.

Asheville-Buncombe Technical Community College, Victoria Road, Asheville, has many records from the State Archives on microfilm for these counties.

For Madison County, which was formed from Buncombe and Yancey in 1851, the records are the marriage bonds from 1851-1868 and the marriage register from 1851-1969, cross index to wills from 1851-1969 and the records of wills from 1851-1952 plus the inventory docket from 1852-1862. Also, there are the indexes to real estate and the records of deeds from 1851-1903. Minute dockets of the court are from 1851-1874.

For Yancey County, which was formed in 1833 from Burke and Buncombe, the records are the appointments of administrators, executors, and guardians from 1870-1928, the record of wills from 1838-1935, the probate minute docket of county court from 1834-1868, cross index to deeds from 1831-1925, and records of deeds from 1831-1862.

Since Buncombe County was created in 1791 from Burke and Rutherford and many of the earliest settlers to Buncombe moved from these counties, these records may be good ones to study.

For Burke County, which was formed in 1777 from Rowan County, the records include land entries from 1778-1795. (Land entries were applications to get land which may or may not have been granted). Also for Burke are records of wills from 1793-1905, inventories of sales and estates from 1832-1899, and minutes of the county court from 1791-1834.

For Rutherford County, which was formed in 1799 from Tryon County, the records are marriage bond abstracts from 1782-1868 plus the marriage register from 1784-1833, an index to wills from 1782-1971. Also, there are land entry indexes from 1778-1803, index of real estate conveances from 1779-1916, and records of deeds from 1779-1793. The minutes of the county court are from 1779-1798.

The Buncombe County records on microfilm are more extensive and have the federal censuses from 1800-1920, with the exception of 1890, and a portion of the 1790 for North Carolina, including Burke, Lincoln, and Rutherford Counties. The slave censuses of 1850 and 1860 cover the alphabetized counties from Alamance through Cumberland. (These slave censuses do not list the slaves by name but only the owners' names with the ages and sex of slaves.) Indexes and records of deeds from 1789-1889 are at this Library plus the land entries from 1795-1832. The marriage registers from 1851-1937, the cross index of wills from 1831-1964, records of wills from 1831-1897, plus an incomplete series of inventories from 1822-1929, and minutes of the county court from 1792-1855 are included in the holdings. The Buncombe County claims for the War of 1812 are in the Minutes, Courts of Please from 1798-1832 and include the names of Robert Baldwin, Robert Brittain, and David Hughey. (These are very faded and hard to read.)

You may want to call the college for variations in the hours; however, the normal hours are Monday-Thursday 8 a.m. -10 p.m., Friday 8 a.m.-4:30 p.m.

<u>Vertical Files</u>

In libraries, you sometimes do not realize there is file material from other people, from old newspaper columns, brochures, etc., which may contain information that you need or at least would find interesting. Suppose you see in old papers that an ancestor attended the Asheville Female Academy. You have never heard about this school. Go to the library in the area, such as Pack in Asheville, and you will be surprised what information the vertical files have about this school in the late 1800s. Sometimes this old information has been gleaned from attic boxes and trunks.

If anyone in your family has an old trunk put away in a garage or an attic, go through it carefully. Small notepads, usually advertising tonics, were where some ancestors commonly kept crop information and expenses. Frances Freeman Honeycutt of Edneyville, N. C., found a "sketch" of one of her ancestors, Major Benjamin Burgin, in a notepad written by Jacob Lyda.

Major Benjamin Burgin (1779-1874), wife Elizabeth Branon) was a lawyer, the surveyor for the boundary line between Burke and Yancey Counties in 1838, and in the N. C. House of Commons in 1844, representing McDowell County.

"A Short Sketch of Benjamin Burgin." "He settled on Crooked Creek in McDowell County. When young, he formed the habit of early rising and kept it up. That he was never drunk. He refused to drink with Governor Graham when a legislature member. In entering the Church door would take off his hat and keep it off till he came out. That he would never eat just as much as he wanted. But was soon satisfied after he quit eating. He would keep his own secrets. That at one time he had 21 law suits and gained them all. He would ride from home to Morganton to see his lawyer, gather and never tell anyone his business. That in riding he would keep himself in his saddle and keep his position, not hanging on this side or that. That in traveling he would not drink water but coffee. That he would keep his feet of an even temperature and not bake them."

Old letters, pictures, lists of family members may be found in vertical files at local libraries. These are filed by family names. You must ask the librarian for access to these files. At Pack are records such as the

Confederate dead in Buncombe County cemeteries, general articles concerning Potter's Field, Buncombe County's graveyard in the Erwin section where residents were buried from the late 1800s. There is an index at Pack to scan to see the areas that may interest you.

City Directories

City directories are actually books but more like official records. These are often near the telephone books and really somewhat like them. Ask in libraries if they are available. Hendersonville Public Library has Hendersonville City Directories starting with 1915, then 1926-1971. Pack has them for Asheville from 1883-1884, 1887, 1890, 1896-97, 1899-1900, then yearly. Since the 1890 federal census is missing, city directories there could be helpful.

In addition to listing businesses, even blacksmiths and coopers, apartments, attorneys, colleges and schools, ministers, churches, "The Asheville City Directory and Buncombe County Gazetteer," edited by J. P. Davison, 1883-1884, has alphabetized listings for who lived where in Asheville. There were 2,408 white residents and 1,466 black residents.

A typical listing shows "E. S. Carpenter, wks (works) T. L. Clayton, res (lives at) Spruce St." This directory separates the whites and blacks.

Asheville farmers are listed. You read that Mrs. M. A. Hildebrand farms 145 acres, two miles east of the court house square.

An excellent addition to this earliest one only is a suburban directory for all of Buncombe, such as Chunn's Cove, Woodfin, Arden, Shufordsville, Black Mountain, and others. Busbee is described as "a farmers post office 7 miles S. of Asheville, on Hendersonville Stage Road. On Squire Murray's farm are found three distinct varieties of mineral waters - chalybeate, yellow sulfur, and a mixture of both."

In the suburban section, all of the residents are not listed, but the churches, magistrates, principal farmers with their amount of acreage, and occupations of some, such as M. L. Burnett had a saw and grist mill, 4 m. N. of Black Mountain, while S. F. Daugherty had a general merchandise and a boarding place.

There are other interesting additions to this 1883-1884 directory since it describes organizations, including "The Asheville Light Infantry is a military company composed of about fifty young men of the city and was

70

organized in the present year [1883]. It is well equipped with arms and handsome uniforms and presents a brilliant and warlike appearance on parade."

Historical sketches also are included on "To Asheville by Stage"; improvements are suggested "Asheville is at present lighted with the old-fashioned kerosene lamp; but the march of progress demands its speedy abolition." The need for an ice factory is mentioned. Eighteen leaf-tobacco dealers existed with 500,000 pounds of tobacco raised in 1882, with prices sometimes of over a dollar a pound.

The population for Asheville jumped from 2,610 in 1880 to 11,913 in 1890. The fast-growing town had a new Opera House on Patton Avenue; it opened August 1889, with a seating capacity of 1,200 and was described: "Three hundred gas and electric lights shine forth with beauty and incantation. The center chandelier, which is of hammered brass . .. has 150 additional lights."

In 1890, a boarding and day school "for young ladies and little girls" was run by Mrs. Burgwyn Maitland on 40 French Broad Avenue. The course of study included the usual English branches (normally included grammar, geography, bookkeeping, and arithmetic), with Latin, French, German, instrumental and vocal music, drawing and art embroidery. "The school offers special advantages to delicate girls who wish to pursue their studies while benefiting by the salubrious climate of Asheville." The later ones do not include the county information, but if you had an ancestor who lived in Asheville, the information is priceless.

Books

Of course, libraries have books. Pack Library has three sections of books you will be interested in for research. Most of the research books are marked REF, meaning you must research these at the library; however, many background history books are listed and available for "checking out" too. Also, there is the North Carolina research section.

The North Carolina book section at Pack includes many family history books. These are referenced in the North Carolina card catalog by the families' last names, but many times you may want to browse through the indexes in the books to see if someone in your family married into this specific family. Also, with the individual family history books are the many North Carolina heritage books which have been published by genealogical societies. Check all the indexes in any counties you suspect ancestors could have resided. These are interesting as well as helpful since most have a history of the county before the individual families' histories. Some of the local ones are discussed in the Genealogical Societies, Chapter 4.

County history books are also available and may contain names you are searching for, particularly if a member of your family started a business, became a sheriff, a member of the legislature, or even if he were a very early settler in that particular county. Some books are indexed better than others; and if you know your ancestors was in a cer-tain county, you would probably enjoy reading the whole book.

The following books discussed are valuable for genealogical research and are found in various libraries and genealogical societies. The complete addresses of the publishing companies mentioned in this book will be included in Appendix B.

Over three hundred and seventy years ago, 104 settlers looked across the harbor into the wilderness of Massachusetts. William Bradford, later Governor of the Plymouth Colony, wrote, "If they looked behind them, there was this mighty ocean which they had passed . . . to separate them from all the civil parts of the world." Not one of his people aboard the Mayflower died on the long crossing except for a youth, William Butten, servant to Samuel Fuller, died when they neared the coast. Then, while at anchor, Dorothy Bradford, wife of William, either fell or jumped overboard and drowned.

Bradford wrote, ". . . brought safe to land, they fell upon their knees and blessed the God of heaven, who had brought them over the vast and furious ocean, and delivered them from all the periles and miseries thereof . . . they now had no friends to wellcome them, nor inns to entertain or refresh their weather beaten bodies . . .."

About half of these farmers and artisans, their wives and children, died that first winter, basically from malnutrition. Not many individual accounts about the passengers are known, other than the John Alden, Miles Standish, and Priscilla Mullins story.

However, the names of all the passengers are known, and fifty of these survivors had descendants -- possibly twenty to thirty million by 1986. Many of you may be descended from one or more of these people who made the journey on the "Mayflower."

These ancestors were John Alden, Issac and Mary Allerton and daughters Mary and Remember, John and Eleanor Billington and son Francis, William Bradford, William and Mary Brewster and son Love, Peter Brown, James Chilton and wife and daughter Mary, Francis Cooke and son John, Edward Doty, Francis and Sarah Eaton and son Samuel, Edward Fuller and wife and son Samuel.

Also were Dr. Samuel Fuller, Stephen and Elizabeth Hopkins with his son Giles and daughter Constance, Richard More, William and Alice Mullins and daughter Priscilla, Degory Priest, Thomas Rogers and son Joseph, Henry Sampson, George Soule, Miles Standish, John Tilley and wife and daughter Elizabeth, Richard Warren, William and Susanna White and sons Resolved and Peregrine, and Edward Winslow.

To join the General Society of Mayflower Descendants, you must have official documents such as wills, birth and death certificates, family Bibles, to prove ancestry to the above listed fifty. For more information, write the General Society of Mayflower Descendants, 4 Winslow Street, Box 297, Plymouth, MA 02361.

Books available on Mayflower ancestors and their family histories at Pack include *The Mayflower Descendant*, a genealogy of the Jonathon Brewster family, son of William Brewster, and *English Ancestry and Homes of the Pilgrim Fathers Who Came to Plymouth*, which contains biographical sketches of the 102.

Also, there are *Mayflower Descendants and Their Marriages for Two Generations after the Landing*, a genealogy from the early 1600s through the early 1700s, and Volumes 1 and 2 of *Mayflower Families through Five Generations*, which covers the families of Francis Eaton, Samuel Fuller, William White, James Chilton, Richard More, and Thomas Rogers.

The oldest printed official North Carolina records you can search for family history are the 26 volumes of *Colonial and State Records*. The earliest volumes, which started being printed in 1887, were edited by William Saunders, who was the Secretary of State. He compiled these from the papers of the state offices and received others from the British Public Record Office in London. Later volumes were compiled by Walter Clark,

Chief Justice of the Supreme Court of North Carolina.

Volume I basically covers from 1662-1712, with a few scattered Virginia records from 1622. North Carolina started being settled in the 1650s by settlers purchasing land grants from the Governor of Virginia or purchasing land from the Indians. The earliest complete copy of a grant is from the "King of the Yeopim Indians on 1st of March 1662 to George Durant on the Perquimans River and Roenoke Sound."

By 1681, and free persons who wanted to be planters "in Carolina before the 25th day of December 1684" and were at least sixteen could be granted sixty acres of land. From early British papers it seems many whales were off the Carolina coast since "inhabitants may have free lease for the space of seaven yeares to take what whales they can and convert them to their owne use."

If you want to know precisely what was "going on" in North Carolina from 1735 through 1754, Volume VIII will tell you. The inhabitants of N. C., their problems, and life styles are discussed in letters, petitions, orders, warrants, patents for land. During these years the counties westward established were Granville, Orange, Anson, and Rowan. The steady immigration stream, which filled up these empty lands, basically came overland from colonies to the north, especially Virginia, Maryland, Pennsylvania, and Jersey. These people were mainly English with some modest numbers of Lowland Scots, Welsh, French, and Swiss, Ulster Scots, and Germans. The highland Scots came directly to the colony, pausing only briefly at Wilmington or Brunswick.

North Carolina became known as "the best poor man's country." Land was easy to acquire and servitude was "shortlived." By 1744, N. C. land had only about 30,000 whites, but from 1748-1763, almost two million acres were sold, mainly in tracts of 300 to 500 acres.

Corn was the most important field crop, with enough hogs and cattle to export to the West Indies and even in overland drives to Pennsylvania, but tar, pitch, and turpentine, were the "chief contribution to colonial commerce." A place was considered a town if sixty families lived in it. (Charlotte had five or six houses in 1772.) A town was important because many had a court house, jail stocks, were religious centers, had an inn or tavern, and sometimes a billiard house and a course for horseracing.

Old Buncombe County was, of course, not mentioned since this area was recognized as Cherokee Indian territory until the 1790s. However, the names mentioned often in the book later show up in the mountains: Adams, Allen, Campbell, Clark, Clayton, Goodman, Hawkins, Hill, Moore, Taylor, Thomas, White, Williams.

The information recorded in these books was varied. In April of 1761, a complaint was filed to the Speaker of the State Assembly that "Mr. Charles Cogdell hath been guilty of a contempt and indignity of the House by throwing a cat upon Mr. Charles Robinson one of the members of the House" (during a session.) Mr. Cogdell was taken into custody for contempt but said the cat leaped upon his shoulders from a staircase and he just threw the cat that could have fallen accidentally upon Mr. Robinson.

Many name changes are recorded, such as James Rousom became James Long, and James Lytle became James Nichols. Land was returned to Thomas Lacey; property was confiscated from John Lancaster; elections were held at the house of John Larkins; John Shelton was given a land grant.

Volume 16, on July 12, 1783, contains a letter written from Governor Alex Martin that people had moved near Indian towns on the "eastward of the French Broad River" and wanted the settlers removed. He later directed General McDowell and Colonel Sevier to "drive off all our people who have settled " on the lands of the French Broad River since it was the agreed upon boundary line for Indian property. This volume also contains a roster of the Continental Line from North Carolina, showing the names alphabetically, rank, dates of commissions and enlistments, "periods of service and occurrences, taken from the original and muster pay rolls of the N. C. Line of the late Army of the U. S."

Volume 26 includes the 1790 census of North Carolina except for the counties of Caswell, Granville, and Orange. For these three, lists of taxpayers are recorded for each township. The four additional volumes are a big help for researchers since they are indexed for all names and places in the 26 volumes. All you need to do is search the indexes for the ancestors' names. The first number after the name gives the volume number; other numbers are page numbers to refer to in that specific volume. These volumes are at Pack Library.

For other early records of North Carolina, Margaret M. Hofmann's books are helpful for land transactions: *Province of N. C., 1663-1729, Abstracts of Land Patents* and *Colony of N. C.*, Volumes 1 and 2, which cover from 1735-1775. An example of the details in these books is one from the Crown to Mounce Justice, 19 May 1772, for 640 acres in Mecklenburg County on the long branch of Coldwater Creek, including Justice's own improvements, joining the land of Samuel Sewil.

All "how to" books advise checking tax payers' listings to account for places of suspected residence earlier than the 1790 census, but finding these old lists of tax payers is another matter.

Two volumes of *North Carolina Taxpayers, 1679-1790*, compiled by Clarence E. Radcliff, should help. This information was taken from the N. C. State Archives' microfilm and photocopies plus lists found in early genealogical magazines. These two cover the complete known taxpayers in N. C. before 1790. [Genealogical Publishing: Baltimore, 1988] If you can find the county where your ancestor lived, you will have better luck finding deeds for this person.

A 1992 publication of Jo Linn's *Surry County, N. C. Wills, 1771-1827*, lists the wills, inventories, bonds, bills of sale.

Surry County, bordered by Virginia to the north, was fromed in 1771 from Rowan County from where many Western North Carolina settlers came. (By 1777, part of Surry County became Wilkes County.) Ms. Linn points out that there are "loose estate papers" in the North Carolina Archives that can be searched by mail if you know the county where the person died. [Search Room, N. C, Dept. of Cultural Resources, 109 E. Jones Street, Raleigh, NC 27601-2807]

Over 547 estate records are abstracted plus a list of several unrecorded wills. [Genealogical Publishing: Baltimore]

Voter registrations for 1902-1904 may not sound like a good source since these records seem too recent to be of value in ancestor research. However, in North Carolina a law, which became effective on July 1, 1902, stated that all voters should be able to read or write and to have paid a poll tax. But there was an exception: the potential voter could vote if he were a voter in 1867 or if he had a grandfather who voted in 1867.

Carolyn Aslund compiled this registration from North Carolina's Archives microfilm in *Buncombe County, North Carolina Voter Registration 1902-1904*. For your ancestors in Buncombe, this may be an important first search since the voter registration included precinct, name, age, "from who descended unless a voter himself January 1, 1867, or prior," "in what state he or ancestor was a voter January 1, 1867, or prior," and date registered.

In the Asheville precinct, Lewis Maddox was 81 (born about 1786), was a voter in Ohio in 1867. Family groups are often obvious. In the French Broad precinct, for example, Mont Sluder is listed as the voter-ancestor in 1867 for Gaston Sluder 27, J. M. Sluder 22, J. W. Sluder 53, L. A. Sluder 25, W. C. Sluder 31, W. J. Sluder 51. (Mont Sluder was probably the grandfather for the younger men and the father of the older two men.)

Over 4,320 voters registered in Buncombe County between 1902-1904 are listed in this book. [Carolyn Aslund, 315 Fairfax Ave., Asheville, NC 28806]

After reading a book in a library or borrowing one from a neighbor, you may find you'd like to have a copy, particularly if an ancestor is mentioned in it. You probably won't find these on regular bookstore shelves since these old books are not "best sellers." You also know they are not always accurate, but with burned down court houses, no early death records or birth records, you study whatever you can. Looking at lists of books for sale by reprint companies is one place to try since they republish old county histories, old newspaper notices of marriages and deaths, censuses, some family histories. One reprint company that emphasizes the southeastern states for books of an historical or genealogical nature is the Reprint Publishers, P. O. Box 5401, Spartanburg, SC 29304.

Some books this company has sold concerning Western North Carolina are Allen's *The Annals of Haywood County*, Griffin's *History of Old Tryon and Rutherford Counties*, Patton's *The Story of Henderson County*, Sondley's *A History of Buncombe County*, Topkins's *Marriages and Death Notices from Extant Asheville, N.C., Newspapers, 1840-1870*.

This company also publishes indexes of North Carolina ancestors, with each index listing about ten thousand North Carolina ancestors with biographical information. This company is the distributor of the back issues in yearly volumes of the *North Carolina Genealogical Society Journal.*

Wherever family members go, they leave a "trail in the form of deeds, tax records, census enumerations, court records, probates; the content of those records sometimes is all that remains of the fabric of millions of lives." *Red Book* [Ancestry: Salt Lake City, 1989] tells you about the records in existence and how you can get them, plus a brief history of the settlement of each section of America with maps, showing counties and county seats.

Significant information for family historians is first given by the different areas of the United States. In the New England states, the town form of government is the essential unit. Immigration dates and migration patterns for areas are discussed. "From the early 1660s to the present more immigrants have come to and through the Mid-Atlantic region than any other." Dutch, Swedes, and Finns were in the Delaware River area from 1638-1655.

The Old South's record-keeping system left much to be desired on early immigrants. "Europeans were already aboard in the lush lands bordering the Gulf Coast eleven decades before the Pilgrims got their first glimpse of Plymouth Rock." The Ordinance of 1787 caused an impact on the areas of the Midwest; since there was a population requirement for statehood, many areas recruited immigrants. By 1867 the land was still only $1.25 per acre. For each district, additional reading material is suggested so that you can understand the histories of the areas.

The overall history section for each state includes church records, military records, newspapers, immigration records, and county resources in each state.

The information for each county's resources gives the name and address of each county seat, the date the county was formed and from what county, the dates from which birth, marriage, death, land, probates, and court records are available. You'll know when you are wasting your time and your postage writing to certain places for early records. Some people say they have trouble getting records from Texas, for example. One of the differences in Texas is that statewide recordings of marriages did not begin until January 1966, and certified copies are still not available through the state office, but the counties' addresses are given. Also, Texas marriage records prior to 1836, if they exist, are in the custody of the Catholic Church, and the address is given. A book of history and addresses for the United States may not sound exciting to everyone, but this information gives "searching power" to the family historian to follow ancestors' trails.

When thinking of passports, you picture going to a foreign country. You probably don't think of people in the United States needing passports to travel to North Carolina, South Carolina, Georgia, Louisiana, or Florida. However, passports were necessary for Americans in the late 1700s and early 1800s to travel to or across "foreign" lands of the Indian Nations or the Spanish-held territories.

The book *Passports of Southeastern Pioneers, 1770-1823*, by Dorothy Potter [Genealogical Publishing, Inc.: Baltimore, 1990], gives a little-known history lesson plus over five thousand names of travelers or settlers going through Spanish and Cherokee, Creek, or Chickawaw Indian lands.

According to a federal law of 1790, passports were supposed to be issued only to people who would not cause trouble. Everyone needed a "certificate of good conduct" before the passport was issued. A study of Ms. Potter's records shows that people wanted to go into these lands to trade, collect debts, recover stolen property, just to pass through Indian lands for a "shortcut," or to contemplate settlement in the Spanish lands.

Passports could be issued by state governors, officers of U. S. troops "at the nearest military post on the frontiers, or such person as the President of the United States may authorize," according to the 1790 federal law.

A history of the Spanish Colony in Louisiana is included from 1765. The Spanish tried to prevent westward expansion of the United States and required their commanders to issue passports before anyone could enter. Plus, shipping vessels could not enter the Mississippi without paying port duties. (River transportation played a large role in settlers' transportation.)

Ms. Potter stated, "Between the thin line of Spanish posts and the clusters of American frontier settlements lay four formidable Indian tribes . . . Creeks, Cherokee, Chickasaw, Chocktaw." If an American wanted to go across the Indian territory, he would need a U. S. passport; then he would need a Spanish passport to journey onto their lands.

People from Pennsylvania, Kentucky, Virginia, Connecticut, New York, Ohio, Tennessee, went down the Mississippi River in flatboats to trade or to settle. Many settlers with their household possessions would go down the river on a flatboat and then dismantle it to build their houses. By 1805, there were well-established boat schedules between Nashville and New Orleans, a trip which took about ninety days.

Travelers to present west Florida, which included large areas of Alabama and Mississippi, needed passports in this area by 1770. By 1781, Spain took over this area.

In Tennessee, many passports from the Cherokee Indian Agency were for people to pass through the Cherokee Nations into Jackson and Franklin Counties of Georgia. Plus, many passports were issued by Governor John Sevier in 1798 to people in Tennessee who had settled on Indian territory south of the French Broad and Holston Rivers. These "intruders" forcibly were removed and were supposed to lose all their property plus be fined, but Sevier's passports gave them a right "to gather their crops, livestock, and other provisions." From reading the passports, it seems many whites were living in the Cherokee lands in this area until 1820.

Sometimes amazing stories can be imagined from the few words on a passport. From the Cherokee Agency, South West Point, 1803: "Samuel Crosley hath permission to go into the Cherokee Nation to the Lookout Mountain or the Muscle Shoals to look for Mrs. Ann Roach, a relation of his family who was left sick in the Chickasaw Nation when traveling towards Tombigbee River about four years ago and is now supposed to be at one of the places above mentioned." Happenings of less than two hundred years ago seem to be ancient history. [Genealogical Publishing: Baltimore, 1990]

For most people, searching for ancestors in **South Carolina** is difficult because of its unusual system for record keeping. Land and probate records were kept in Charleston until the 1780s regardless of where the people lived.

Before record-keeping counties were created in 1785, South Carolina had three sections established in 1682: Colleton, Berkeley, Craven. Granville was established in 1710, but these were just locations. District circuit courts were established in 1781 and took over the probate records. These districts were Ninety-Six, Camden, Cheraw, Orangeburgh, Charleston, Georgetown, and Beaufort.

Before searching for records in South Carolina, you will probably be interested in studying Brent Holcomb's *A Guide to South Carolina Genealogy and Records.* [Brent Holcomb, Box 21766, Columbia, SC 29221]

This guide tells you not only where records are found but also tells about printed volumes you may search for these records: probate, land, equity, county court minutes, military, marriage, birth, death church, census. Nine maps show the changes of counties. These start with the original counties, the parishes, the circuit court districts after 1785, and lead to the present counties.

The formations of all counties, including the border problems with North Carolina, are discussed along with which counties keep which records and which ones are in the South Carolina Archives. While the Archives is the main research area, the main library for genealogical purpose is the South Caroliniana Library in Columbia.

You may want to write the South Carolina Archives to check for information. Even though state records for deaths, births, and marriages were not recorded until 1915, indexes of the following records will be searched by mail: Wills to 1853, Land Grants and Plats, Memorials of Land Titles 1732-1775, Audited Accounts for Revolutionary Service.

Land transactions are important since you can find out when someone sold and bought land. Sometimes a copy of the deed when he bought land will tell where he was from. The personnel at the S. C. Archives requests you furnish full name, approximate dates of residence in South Carolina, and the location of the residence. They also request you asked about only one person in each letter and send a pre-addressed, stamped envelope for their reply. Address: South Carolina Department of Archives, P. O. Box 11669, Capitol Station, Columbia, SC 29211.

There were also twenty-one parishes of the Church of England established from 1706-1768. Some early marriage, birth, and death records may be found in the parish records that still exists.

Over three hundred years ago, a few English families settled on the banks of the Cooper and Wando Rivers in South Carolina. French Hugenot families, raising grapes for wine, olive trees for oil, and mulberries to entice worms to make silk, settled in the interior from French Quarter Creek to Cooper River. Churches were built in these areas, and some parish records for these survived. In 1884, Robert F. Clute collected and published *The Annals and Parish Register of St. Thomas and St. Denis Parish in South Carolina from 1680-1884.* [Clearfield: Baltimore, 1990] The Church of England in the St. Thomas Parish, which included the river areas of Charleston, built Pompion Hill Chapel in 1703. St. Denis, where Brick Church was finished in 1708, was made a different parish for the French-speaking people. Their Episcopal minister gave their sermons in French. Rev. Clute stated that by 1728, there were "1600 hundred souls" in St. Thomas Parish. He recorded seven hundred marriage records from these parishes from the early 1700s to the late 1800s. He also recorded one thousand births and baptismal records which often gave whole family histories, such as the children of Vincent Guerin and Judith Guerin, who were married July 12, 1703, had seven children, including Issac born April 10, 1704. By 1731, the records show Issac and Martha Mouzon Geurin were the parents of an Issac born March 5, 1731.

Five hundred deaths and burials are included, usually with the name of the church or the name of a plantation. For example, Rev. John Tissott was buried May 28, 1763, on Pagett's old plantation.

Perhaps your early ancestor was a protestant refugee from Europe who came into South Carolina with about 4,000 others from 1763-1773. To find out, check the book, *A Compilation of the Original Lists of Protestant Immigrants to South Carolina*, compiled by Janie Revill. [Genealogical Publishing: Baltimore, 1988] This book is more than just a list of names of protestants since it included the countries they came from, including Ireland, Great Britain, Germany, France, Scotland. The date each group arrived is included plus often their ages and the names of the ships. Copies of documents from the "Council Journal" discussed where to place the people, how to provide for them until crops were harvested, and how the townships were to be divided. The immigrants were granted 100 acres of land for every person over 15 years of age and 50 acres of land for ones under 15. Plus, the ones from 1763-1768 were granted a bounty of about 20 shillings to pay their passage fees.

Provisions included wheat flour, Indian corn, a cow and a calf for every five persons. After 1768, only the 100 acres was provided, so some had to indenture themselves for passage costs for three years. The areas granted for settlements for these immigrants were the townships of Boonesborough, Belfast, Londonborough, Orangburg, Hillsborough, and the counties of Berkley, Granville, and Craven. These areas were unsettled and the people were warned that they were "to build houses for their towns and a fort in it not less than 120 feet square of palisades for their common security to which they may retire at any alarm."

The first entry of arrivals was February 19, 1753, when a vessel arrived in the "Port of Charles Towne with about seventy persons from Ireland." Two new townships, Boonesborough and Belfast, were formed for these people who had "certificates of their being Protestants." On March 2, 1764, a group from Germany arrived and were followed in April by a group from the southern part of France. The colonists leaders felt the 183 French could be very useful to the colony because of their "culture of silk and vines" and requested a 20,000 acre township be started for them on the "Savanna" River. In January of 1765, Germans from the ship "Dragon" were given by names and ages, such as Elizabeth Krabin's being 91 while Maria Strum was 1. Family groups can be seen such as in December 1765 from Great Britain: Catherine Moore 33, Ann 13, Hugh 13, James 10, William 2. Most of these immigrants were from Ireland, and in 1767, the Irish names of Watts, Ross, Lindsey, Patterson, Reid, Pressley, Cunningham, Montgomery, Alexander, Doharty, Walker, were numerous. A thorough search of printed material that others have put together from various records deposited in various places is sometimes the only way to find South Carolina ancestors. Another book that shows early settlers in S. C. is *The Jury Lists of South Carolina, 1778-1779* [Clearfield: Baltimore, 1991]. On January 5, 1778, the South Carolina General Assembly felt it necessary to establish an act for a new list of "jury men" who would be "deemed and declared to be qualified and and obliged to serve as Jury men" for their disticts. The locations of where the men were from as well as maps are included. This list was to be for all men that could serve on a jury, not just for one court session. The General Assembly said the 1778 list was not complete for Ninety Six District, so it was redone in 1779.

Another book that is helpful if you are researching ancestors in South Carolina is *South Carolina Provincial Troops* by A. S. Salley [Clearfield: Baltimore, 1990]. This is a record of the papers of the first Council of Safety of the Revolutionary Party in South Carolina from June through November of 1775. The Council of Safety governed the Patriots' war efforts in S. C. This group was made up of citizens who decided to resist "British oppression" and provide for three regiments of troops.

Mr. Salley has recorded the details of the provisions of the men in the regiments, including how much beef, rice, vinegar, salt, and pepper "if it can be procured" and, of course, rifles, cannons, and gun powder. One group of men from Charleston wrote to the Council to ask permission to establish a volunteer "Company of Foot." It seems this group was mainly concerned about what its soldiers would wear since 64 men "strongly recommended that the uniform be; Scarlet French Frock coats - with white buttons lappels collars and cuffs with white buttons and white waistcoats and breeches; to wear Buskins and black Garters . ... The privates to wear military cocked hats with Cockades."

The letters to the Council showed that all the people did not agree with the Patriots. There are copies of letters from the Ninety Six District telling of problems with deserters plus a story of 200 "disaffected people from over the river" coming armed and robbing Fort Charlotte of powder and supplies and declaring "themselves entirely in favour of Government [the English]." The men, their rank, and how much was paid to the troops were listed. Plus, many states or countries of birth are included for the soldiers. If you ever wondered how the Patriots managed their affairs to organize for the Revolutionary War, this will be interesting.

Sara Ervin compiled *South Carolinians in the Revolution* [Clearfield: Baltimore, 1991] from records in various repositories, such as clerk of court offices, booklets and documents published by the South Carolina General Assembly and the Daughters of the American Revolution in the 1800s, librarians in various states. South Carolina had many men involved in this was because, as Ms. Ervin pointed out, there were 146 battles fought in this state during the Revolution. This book includes pension rolls by districts, names, ages, dates and where served, officers of South Carolina regiments, medical men, Sumter's brigade, fifty-eight genealogies of families descended from S. C. soldiers. Also included are lists of S. C. Revolutionary soldiers who are buried in fourteen other states, and an abstract of wills from Laurens County, 1775-1855. There are also records of S. C. War prisoners who were captured by the British and placed in prisons and in ships. General Griffith Rutherford of North Carolina was captured on November 15, 1 780, and put on the ship "Sandwich," which took the prisoners to St. Augustine.

Brent Holcomb in l986 compiled records from Greenville newspapers, 1826-1863, *Marriages and Death Notices from the Up-Country of South Carolina.* [SCMAR, P. O. Box 21766, Columbia, SC 29221. These marriage and deaths concern many already in Western North Carolina: Dr. Robert B. Vance "Departed this life at Whittedsville in Buncombe County," on October 6, 1827, "in the 30th year of his age, formerly a member of congress from Morgan District, N. C. This gentlemen's death was caused by a wound received in a duel with the Hon. Samuel P. Carson, the present member of congress from the same distict. Died at White Oak, Rutherford County, April 15, 1840, of a protracted and distressing illness, Miss Mary Salena, youngest daughter of Marvil Mills, Esq., aged 16 years. Died very suddenly on Friday the 12th of May, 1843, at his residence on White Oak, Rutherford County, Mr. George Jones, aged 70 years. The deceased was a native of Orange County, Virginia, but came with his father at an early age to Wilkes County, N. C., where he was raised. Soon after he grew up, he commenced the mercantile business as a clerk with Messrs. Patton and Erwin in Wilkesboro." Later they moved to Buncombe County and married in Buncombe in 1806, the daughter of William Mills, Sen'r, and had nine children.

The obituaries include some information on Revolutionary soldiers: "Died at the residence of Mr. Silas Woody, on Spring Creek, Buncombe County," on November 17, 1849, "William Woody, Sr., aged 114 years. He was a soldier in the War of Independence, and for a great many years an orderly and acceptable member of the Baptist Church."

Many times the deaths were from bilious fever, cholera, typhoid fever, consumption. One T. J. Spencer from Marion, S. C., age 25, had "gone from home to plant two kinds of Palma Christie seeds - white and red - the latter a poison. On his return he eat some of the poisonous sort which caused his death a short time afterwards."

Another helpful publication from South Carolina was compiled by Caroline T. Moore, *Abstracts of Wills of South Carolina* (available at Pack Library, three volumes). These cover wills from 1697-1784. An example of an abstract from Volume I is "Alexander Parris, Charles Town, Esq., sons Alexander and John; daughters Jane DeLa Bere, Anne Davis; grandsons James, John, Alexander, under 21 years of age, sons of son Alexander; George, son of son-in-law John DeLa Bere; granddaughter Sarah, daughter of Mr. John DeLa Bere; sons-in-law John Davis, John DeLa Bere, and Mr. Peter Boynton. The will mentions if bequests of money are not paid to grandsons James and John Parris in allotted time, they may enter into rents of "one half my island in Granville County, called Archers Island near Port Royal." Also listed are witnesses, executors, and dates: this will was written 6 February 1735, proved 17 March 1735, recorded 29 April 1736. As illustrated from this abstract, quite a bit of family material can be gathered. The will itself probably would not give more.

Many "how to" genealogy books tell you to check church records, but in the South, you know that most are nonexistant. However, George F. Jones and Sheryl Exley found in the Library of Congress the 1754-1781 German records for Jerusalem Evangelical Lutheran Church (called Ebenezer) in Effingham County, **Georgia.** [If you've tried to ask a question of the Georgia Archives lately, you know that each out-of-state question must be accompanied by a $25 fee, regardless if anything is found.]

The translation of the *Ebenezer Record Book* [Genealogical Publishing: Baltimore, 1991] has numerous records to search. In 1734 religious exiles came from Salzburg, Austria, and settled in Georgia. This group was joined by 1754 by Swiss and Palatines plus Swabians from the territory of Ulm on the Danube River in Germany.

The records show about two thousand names. A few indicate the native land: "Anna Catherine Fischer, a native of Langenau, died after a protracted sickness in Bethany, March 15, 1758 . . . 30 years and 1 month." The causes of deaths for adults were usually "consumptive disease." Children's deaths outnumbered adult deaths, such as out of twenty deaths in 1756, eleven were children. Over fifty black children were baptized in the church with the typical entry, "Salome, a Negro girl belonging to the estate of Urban Bunz, was born March 10, 1776, and baptized April 12th. Sponsors were Widow Bunz and Anna Barbara Bunz."

The naming customs of the Germans is clearly illustrated by observing entries: "Christian, son of Joh. Justus Gravenstein and his wife Catharina, was born February 3, 1764 . . Christian Gravenstein, a child of 9 days died in the night before February 13, 1764, and was buried on that day in Bethany. Christian, son Johann Justus Gravenstein and his wife Catharina, was born on May 7, 1773." In addition to naming a child after another child who had died, parents often named all male children Johann and female children Maria or Anna. These children would be known by their middle names.

Starting in the 1760s, many family members from North Carolina went to present **Tennessee**. The state of Tennessee was not admitted to the Union until 1796. Present eastern Tennessee, when it was first settled in the winter of 1768, was part of North Carolina and settled before present West-ern North Carolina. The Watauga Settlement began about 1769 on the Watauga and Nolichucky rivers. This area was where Daniel Boone would sneak to out of Wilkes County for hunting among the tremendous herds of buffalo and deer and, of course, bear.

Others started fleeing to the wilderness from the more civilized but "misgoverned province" of eastern and pied-mont North Carolina where they had fought very high fees and unreasonable taxes (to their way of thinking) as Regulators against the English rulers. (In the battle of the Alamance on May 16, 1771, two hundred Regulators were killed while others were captured and hanged by Royalist forces.)

Delegates from the Watauga Settlement attended the Provincial Congress at Halifax, N. C., in 1776. Honoring George Washington, it became the District of Washington by 1777. Many settlers moved into this area from Virginia and North Carolina. After the Revolution, North Carolina ceded this area, which was roughly east to present Asheville and west to Knoxville, to the federal government (territory of U. S., south of Ohio), but the people of the area created their own State of Franklin in 1785. North Carolina re-annexed it, but both governments had their own sets of officials and chaos resulted until North Carolina won out in 1787.

If you are looking for a preacher ancestor from 1775-1875 living in Western North Carolina or Tennessee, you may find a family history in *Sketches of Tennessee's Pioneer Baptist Preachers*. This 1919 book by J. J. Burnett has been reprinted in 1985 [Dan Crowe, 2361 Hiwassee Drive, Kingsport, TN 37664]. It contains 211 biographies, 60 photographs, church histories, and some general history of eastern Tennessee.

One biography rich in family history is about Tidence Lane. He was the son of Richard and Sarah Lane, born in Maryland on August 31, 1724, grandson of Dutton Lane and Pretitia Tidings, and a great-grandson of Major Samuel Lane, an officer in the King's service in Maryland in 1680. Tidence was the father of Lieut. Issac Lane who was under Col. Sevier in the Battle of King's Mountain. Tidence moved from Maryland to

Virginia and then to the Yadkin River in North Carolina where he married Esther Bibbin/Bibber on May 9, 1743. He was "the first pastor of the first permanent church organization of any denomination" in Tennessee. This was at Buffalo Ridge, Washington County, in 1779, then North Carolina in the area of Boone's Creek.

One early 1800s preacher, Joel Aldridge, is described as "the best revivalist . . . he swept Clinch Valley by his wonderful power in protracted meeting efforts. From Powder Spring Gap to Puncheon Camp, where there were not churches between these points, he swept the valley clean of sinners, leaving no heads of families in the ranks of the enemy, except a hard knot or two - snarly cases, on which the devil had the first mortgage."

Sketches are included of J. M. L. Burnett, born in Buncombe in 1829, son of Swan P. and Frances Bell Burnett. This family made its way down the French Broad River to Cocke County, Tennessee in 1835 for better land. Richard Knight, son of William Knight, was born in Buncombe in 1800, married Elizabeth Burke and moved to Cocke County in 1827.

Edythe R. Whitley's *Tennessee Genealogical Records* [Genealogical Publishing: Baltimore, 1989] includes copies of Revolutionary warrants, original grants, abstracts of pension reports, will abstracts, tombstone inscriptions, deed abstracts, court minutes (with divorce records), and marriage bonds. The dates for these records vary but are from 1785 through 1846.

Revolutionary warrants in Tennessee granted land to the men who fought with the North Carolina Continental Line. The records illustrate privates received 640 acres, musicians and sergeants 1000 acres, captains 1371. ensigns and lieutenants 2560; "General Jethro Sumner, a brigadier-general in the N. C. Line. 12,000 acres; issued 27 April 1793." However, much of this land was sold numerous times before any settlement took place. Many land entries were made by locating warrants for N. C. Revolutionary soldiers which were often bought by speculators who made money by reselling these to people who wanted to settle in Tennessee. John and Thomas Bount located land warrants for 20,000 acres in Henry County alone. The University of North Carolina also used this practice. "Richard Ward, sergeant; 1000 acres; issued 1 August 1821 to William Polk, attorney of the President and Trustees of the University of N. C., transferred the warrant to Thomas

Henderson on 4 October 1821. On the same day Henderson assigned the warrant to Allen Wilkins. The said Wilkins assigned the same to Thomas Jones on 30 Oct. 1821. Thomas Jones assigned it to Samuel Polk on the 8th of Nov. 1821." With thousands of land warrants going through this procedure, lawyers much have stayed busy.

Another research book reprinted in 1989 is Worth S. Ray's *Tennessee Cousins, A History of Tennessee People.* He tells of the people who came from Virginia, Maryland, the Carolinas, and Georgia who "played important roles in Tennessee history." His book is divided by counties with extensive histories of the people who lived in each.

He called the Watauga settlement, settled in 1766, "the most remarkable free government ever instituted by white men, after civilization." Since this land was not surveyed, no one knew at this time what state Watauga was in. The settlers bought their lands from the Indians and set up their own government. In 1776, in order to receive help from Indian attacks, they petitioned the legislature of North Carolina for annexation. When it became Washington County, N. C., in 1777, North Carolina had taken in all of present Tennessee. However, even after the people were taxed, they received no protection. Because of the people's dissatisfaction, they organized the State of Franklin in 1785; then in 1790 the federal government decided this area was the "Territory of the United States south of Ohio."

This book is full of names of the early settlers of each county with complete transcriptions of wills, marriages, and much genealogical information for over 3,000 different family names. Extensive family histories with the beginnings for some in Maryland, Virginia, N. C., etc., are given for the Morrows, Wallaces, Henleys, Howards, Calloways, Hendersons, Harrisons, and Armstrongs.

When you think of progress in a town, you picture renovation or building of stores and industries. You don't think of progress as putting a whole town under water. Butler, Tennessee, was the only incorporated town ever purchased and inundated by the Tennessee Valley Authority. *Old Butler and Watauga Academy* by Dan Crowe [1984, Crowe, 2361 Hiawassee Drive, Kingsport, TN 37664] tells the story and included 80 photographs and illustrations.

Mr. Crowe tells the early history of Watauga County including how Daniel Boone named Roan Creek. Much of the book tells about the founding, building, and progress of a school from 1860, which became the Watauga Academy. Butler was located on the Watauga River at the forks of Roan Creek, and the people did contend with numerous floods. However, they seemed to tolerate these and would "scrape the mud from their floors and replant their crops." A 1939 rumor of a dam to control flooding became a reality in 1941. The people of Butler did not want it, but they could not stop it. The dam was built after nearly "12,000 acres of land had been acquired. Seven hundred and sixty families had been relocated. After the gate closure of December 1, 1948, these families began a lonely vigil beside the Watauga. Coming from far and near they gathered to watch one final flood." Mr. Crowe has compiled a fitting tribute to this eastern Tennessee town of Butler where the former residents truly can't go home again.

You may have early family in Tennessee that you can find out more about from the Tennessee Library and Archives. As in most southern states, birth and death records were not registered statewide until 1914. The staff at the Archives will answer specific questions whenever possible concerning births and deaths and check indexed county records for marriages, deeds, court minutes, and probate records. You may also want copies of family names from the Tennessee census schedules which are indexed for 1820-1860. The military records of Tennessee are housed at the Archives. The indexes for N. C. Revolutionary War service records, including the pension and bounty land material can be searched. Indexes are also available for the War of 1812, the Seminole Wars of 1818 and 1836, the Cherokee removal 1836-1838, the Mexican War of 1846-1848, Tennessee Confederate and Union soldiers, Confederate and widows' pensions, Spanish-American War, 1898.

A particularly helpful source for some families at the Archives is the large collection of family records copied from Bibles and indexed by principal families listed. For more information, write Department of State Library and Archives, Public Service Section, 403 7th Avenue, North, Nashville, TN 37219-5041. Send a pre-addressed, stamped envelope for a reply. Send no money; if the records you want are located, you will be told the charges.

Because of the lack of safe harbors, the first permanent settlers into North Carolina came not from the ocean but from Virginia. First to come out of Virginia in the mid-1600s were the English immigrants who always searched for more and better land. Many Scotch-Irish came into the North Carolina Piedmont by the early 1700s.

Virginian John Fiske in 1897 stated that North Carolina was settled by people who could not "maintain a respectable existence" in Virginia and by "outlaws who fled (from Va.) into N. C. to escape the hangman." Others, such as George Davis in 1855, stated the settlers were "all gentlemen of birth and education." The truth probably lies someplace in between, but the earliest settlers, good or bad, were from **Virginia**.

Since the earliest settlers came into N. C. from Virginia, you may want to search the earliest official records of Virginia for ancestors.

Virginia Colonial Abstracts, researched by Beverly Fleet from 1837 to 1949, includes 2, 087 pages of births, marriages, deaths, tax lists, court orders, militia lists, wills, and deeds. In 1988, it had been published in three volumes [Genealogical Publishing: Baltimore].

Volume I contains records from the following counties: Accomack 1632-1640, Lancaster 1652-1666, Richmond 1692-1724, Northumberland 1650-1749 with birth records from 1661-1810, Westmoreland 1653-1657. Typical birth listings give the following information: Samuel Daughity son to James and Elizabeth Daughity was June 16, 1766."

Volume II contains records for Essex County from 1703-1717 and general records for the 1700s from King and Queen Counties such as wills and tax listings, many from family collections.

Volume III contains records from the counties of York 1633-1657, Charles City 1655-1696, Henrico 1736, and Norfolk 1651-1654, Washington County Marriage Register 1782-1820, and the list of extensive holdings concerning Virginia from 1607 through 1850 at the Huntingdon Library in San Marino, California. Each volume is indexed by the names included.

In reading old records, you find that what you may think is modern is not. The records from Charles City County in 1661 show Mrs. Sarah Debdall, widow, was "to be soleminzed" in marriage to Thomas Marston of Chickhomely, but she desired her estate left to her by her former marriage "should be made sure to her as remayning to her proper use, as if no such marriage had beene."

Since many family historians who live in North Carolina had ancestors who came in from Virginia, many people research Virginia's records.

However, so much has been published and so many research areas are available, one is never sure if he or she has checked every possible source. Finally, a 1993 publication, *Virginia Genealogy, Sources, and Resources*, by Carol McGinnis will probably tell you. [Genealogical Publishing: Baltimore]

This book starts with a brief history of Virginia, the immigration and migration, then leads into where vital records, censuses, and court records can be found. Also included are the origins of its people, county and city records, a listing of genealogical collections and societies. Ms. McGinnis quotes from Colonial leader William Byrd that "In the beginning, all America was Virginia" and mentions that one colony created from it was North Carolina. Virginia until 1820 was the most populated state, with one million in 1800.

All the early settlers' origins are briefly described. Settlers in addition to the English during the 1600s included Germans, Poles, French, Africans, Italians, Scots. The main motive for migrating to America was economic, but, of course, many indigent children, prisoners, and (after 1660) slaves were just sent.

In the immigration and migration chapter, the roads are described, including the "Great Wagon Road" from Pennsylvania through Virginia. This road branched into the Carolina Road and the Wilderness Road, which was extended by Daniel Boone into Tennessee and Kentucky. The people traveling these primitive roads had no way to carry provisions to get from Pennsylvania to Kentucky in a non-stop trip. These trips often took years with the families stopping to settle temporarily to raise some food before moving on. Plus, often some family members stayed on the homestead instead of pushing onward with the family to the unknown.

The book includes detailed sources to check for each item mentioned plus an explanation of the laws at various dates. When the vital records (births, deaths, marriages) are discussed, the marriage bond laws of Virginia are explained. Alternatives to the vital records are detailed, such as church records with each early denomination listed: the Brethren/Dunkards, who were usually of German descent; the Jewish synagogue established in 1789; the Church of England records at the state archives.

Court records are discussed. During the Revolution, many land and court records were destroyed, but the ones which exist are shown. Land was granted to individuals by 1616, and an account of how land was acquired by the "headright" system is included. Ms. McGinnis points out that since primogeniture existed in Virginia until 1786, which made real property automatically pass on to the widow for the "dower" share of one-third and the eldest son two-thirds, no will was needed, and the will, if in existence, did not need to name these two. More details on this system are explained in the cases of no widow or eldest son. After 1786, real property generally was divided equally among the children with the widow still receiving her "dower."

A separate chapter is devoted to African-American research. Africans were in Jamestown in the early 1600s since they had been brought in by the Dutch and traded for supplies. These were treated as indentured servants, and when their indentureship had been served, they were free. Ms. McGinnis stated that Anthony Johnson, owning 250 acres, was the first African landowner. Free African-Americans were the most numerous in Virginia. By 1860, Accomac and Northampton Counties had 4,380.

Specific ways to find more information are explained by Ms. McGinnis throughout this and all chapters. She even includes a brief history of each county before detailing the available resources. You are an unusual researcher if you cannot learn more from this book.

Many people proudly announce that their ancestors were among the first settlers of Virginia, and many people have an image of these ladies and gentlemen stepping off the ship, grandly dressed, and moving into plantation homes. Hotten's famous book, written over 100 years ago, *The Original Lists of Persons of Quality* may have led to a belief that only cultured people from England settled in the New World.

If this is the view you want to keep, you will not appreciate *The Complete Book of Emigrants, 1607-1660* by Peter Coldham.

A basic premise of the English rulers and parliament was that settlers were needed in the new colonies and that there were types of people they'd just as soon get off their mainland. Therefore, vagrants, orphans, thieves, "night walkers," political and religious dissenters were sent to America.

The English writers of the 1600s thought of Virginia as a "penal colony" and of New England as "a hotbed of schismatics and separationists." In the "Calendar of State Papers" of August 17, 1610, Sir Thomas Dales's report stated "that the 300 disorderly persons he took with him to Virginia are mutinous and unchristian and are so disordered that only 60 of them are employable." Many prisoners were sent from prisons such as Newgate. In October 1618, a report presented a project for the voyage to Virginia: "The city of London is to ship to Virginia 100 young boys and girls who lie starving in the streets." By 1620, constables were to walk the streets and "apprehend vagrant children" and to ask people who had too many children, ages 12 and up, to let them be sent to Virginia.

Coldham has researched English official documents for every mention of people connected to the English colonies in these early years. His research included probate of wills in England that referred to the colonies, such as in January 1658, "Probate of will of Joseph Holland, citizen and clothworker of London, whose daughter Elizabeth was wife of Richard Bessy in Virginia, whose son Nathaniel Holland was in New England, and whose son Samuel Holland was in Virginia."

The documents are presented on a year-by-year basis, starting in 1606 as the ships left from England for the Chesapeake Bay. Although no story-line is given, the facts illustrate the hardships of passage and living in an unsettled country and the diverse makeup of the people who became Americans.

Hardships started on the ocean crossing with people crowded together, spreading diseases, fighting, often lacking food and water. On September 24, 1636, "Mr. John Hogg, bound for Virginia with 50 men and boys and 7 women, was taken by a Salle man-of-war and all on board were sold for slaves including the examinant's son aged 9." In 1637, the Spaniards captured 120 passengers off the Virginia Coast.

After reaching land, these emigrants suffered Indian captures and massacres plus starvation and murder. Lists of living and dead, divided by location. showed in 1623 that more were dead than still alive at Martinis' Hundred of Virginia.

The diversity of backgrounds is reflected in the passenger lists. The tradesmen and their families were going to the colonies along with the "gents" and also the "dangerous persons, vagabonds, and other idle persons." Many wanted to go the colonies enough to indenture themselves for three to seven years to pay for their passages. The

Carillons are first mentioned in March 1630 where French Protestants wished to settle and were given permission if they had certificates from their pastors in France. No matter what background these ancestors had; after a study of this book, you will wonder how so many did survive.

Since the United States did not keep immigration records until 1820, you may find your earlier ancestors from England in these records. In this book, there are about 150,000 names and records of these settlers. [Genealogical Publishing: Baltimore, 1990].

Peter Wilson Coldham again searched British archival records for the emigrants who came to American in the 1600s. The result was the 1990 publication, *The Complete Book of Emigrants, 1661-1699*, with 30,000 emigrant entries. [Genealogical Publishing: Baltimore]

As mentioned, the English coming to America basically were in one of two categories: the ones trying to better their lives and the ones England wanted rid of. Most of the emigrants were indentured servants and were expected to work for as little as three years or as many as eleven years before they repaid their passage. The most common apprenticeships were for four years to not only the mainland America but also Barbados, Jamaica, Nevis (a small island in the Caribbean near Puerto Rico).

A petition on July 12, 1664, showed that English citizens wanted stricter rules to combat the "wicked custom to seduce or spirit away young persons to go as servants to the plantations." In April, 1668, it was reported that "the child John Brookes had been freed again. Several other children enticed from their parents are embarked in the *Seven Brothers* which is already at Gravesend with two other ships carrying children bound for Virginia."

Typical entries are "The following apprentices in Bristol: Roger Phillips to William Flowers, 4 years, Virginia; Elizabeth Fletcher, aged 22, daughter of John Fletcher of Drury Lane, St. Giles, Middlesex to Nathaniel Jones of Deptford, Kent, mariner, 4 years, Jamaica."

With the restoration of the English monarchy in 1660, the undesirables were shipped across the sea to work the plantations. These undesirables included Quakers, political "troublemakers," and many felons from prisons. The Quakers were not wanted in the New England colony either. On February 11, 1661, Governor John Endecott wrote a letter to the King "praying the King's protection" and making reference to the banishment of Quakers. A report to the King on May 17, 1661, stated that Quakers in New England were being imprisoned or banished. Prisoners were "reprieved to be transported" and tried to survive however they could in the new country. The Americans protested that they did not want "gaol birds or others who, for notorious offences, have deserved to dye in England." But the prisoners were sent, and the entries list their names, sometimes their ages and/or occupations and townships. In January 1665, "Ann Hayley of St. Sepulchre, widow, was sentenced at Middlesex Sessions to be transported to Jamaica for attendance at unlawful religious assembly." James Ward in April 1667 petitioned "for the transportation to the plantations of his wife who was convicted for stealing." Other entries give a realization of the hardships emigrants suffered. Edward Godfrey, former Governor of Maine, wrote to the King in 1661 saying he'd "spent 30 years abroad as an original planter, had lost a vast estate, his only son had been ruined and his nearest relatives killed by the Indians." In January 1665, "the Governors of Virginia and Maryland are instructed that ships returning to England are to go in convoy because of the shortage of seamen and the risk of capture by the Dutch." In 1672, Mr. William How from James River, Virginia, was captured in his ship by the Spanish and some of the crew was set adrift with Mr. How and the others in the crew put in prison in Havana and Cadiz. In 1699, it was established that "Ephraim Stocker went from Bristol to Virginia before 1694, but he and his ship were never heard of again."

Also included in this book are estate settlements that were probated in England with heirs in America. The individual researcher looking for ancestors to America would have a difficult search in studying the manuscript sources Coldham has compiled.

As mentioned before, in reading "how to" genealogy books, you would think that everyone had a will or estate settlement. Some did not. For example, you read that an ancestor here in the early 1800s bought several hundred acres of land, disappeared in the 1810 census. Of course, there is no death certificate since these weren't consistently kept until 1913. Not finding a marked grave is also common. You think that the person would have to have an estate settlement because of the land. However, the land could have been sold and the ancestor living with the relatives, so no estate. Therefore, when you are at the Clerk of Court's office searching for the estate settlement that may not be there, check the deed books to see if all the property was sold and when. In the South, there are relatively few wills. In North Carolina there are only about 75,000 wills from 1665-1900.

If you are searching in Virginia, there has now been a republication of *Virginia Will Records*, which is composed of articles dealing with Virginia wills, inventories and administration accounts from various sources. [Genealogical Publishing: Baltimore, 1994] These records cover from the 1600s through about the 1850s. There are will indexes, will abstracts, and complete wills with an index of 27,000 names. Even a couple of lines from June 8, 1646, can be a big help, such as "John Brock's deed of gift of 'a stocke of Beds' to his god sons Joseph and Benjamin Croshaw, sons of Joseph Croshaw."

Many early wills, such as one in 1768, included ideas the devisee had about after life. Francis Fauquier wanted his body to be "deposited in the earth or sea, as I shall happen to fall, without any vain Funeral Pomp and as little expense as decency can possibly permit, Funeral Obsequies, as it has long appeared to me being contrary to the Spirit of Religion of our blessed Savior, who on a proper occasion said, Let the Dead bury their dead, follow thou me." His will continues for four pages with minute instructions about his property.

People who don't study old court records may not understand their fascination to family historians. However, not only are they primary sources for ancestor research but also are interesting in themselves for the stories they tell of earlier times. *Chronicles of the Scotch-Irish Settlement in Virginia* by Lyman Chalkley was first published in 1912 and now republished. The three volumes have over 50,000 names in their 2,000 pages. [Genealogical Publishing, Inc.: Baltimore, 1989]. These Chalkley records cover Augusta County, Virginia, from 1745-1800, but this was not your ordinary county since it extended from the Alleghenies to the Mississippi River and from the northern part of Tennessee and North Carolina to the Great Lakes. The court records are the basic sources for these early settlers, including court cases, marriage bonds, licenses, guardian books, land entries, records of military service in the colonial wars and the Revolution, abstracts of wills.

The court cases include trials for horse stealing, murder, drunkenness, vagrancy, stealing deer skins, and one person's being "sentenced to stocks and fined for damning the court and swearing four oaths in their presence." On June 1, 1751, the verdict in the case of Shields vs. Watson and Gilmore was "stayed because jurors, Walter Davis and Malcolm Campbell, the one ran out of the Court House, the other jumped out of the Court House window." On Saturday, February 6, 1748, it was recorded in the minutes as "the coldest day yet known in America."

The abstracts of wills have much family history. For example, "28th February, 1761. John Lewis' will: Wife, Margaret; son, William, tract with the mills . . . grandson, John, son of Andrew; daughter, Margaret Crow; to son Charles . . . to purchase a watch on which the testator's name shall be engraved in testimony of esteem ." William Patton's will, dated 31st March 1793; proved 5th April 1793. About 1740 he was married to Mary Beaty, daughter of Alex. Beaty, of the parish of Donnagh, County Dunnigall, Ireland, by whom he had one son John. The names sound familiar in Western North Carolina from James Patton as the Sheriff in December 1745 to the justices, with names of Buchanan, Lewis, Woods, Anderson, Robinson, Bell, Thompson. Also, all the people did not seem to be Scotch-Irish since many wills were noted as signed in German.

As mentioned previously, the 1880 census gave where parents of the individuals were born. If you find parents of ancestors born in Virginia, your next step backwards would be to learn where in Virginia. The 12 volumes of *Heads of Families at the First Census of the U. S., 1790* are available at Pack Library. The Virginia volume, which is not the regular census schedule since those have never been found, was compiled from state enumerations and tax lists from 1782-1785. These listed only the heads of the families but did tell the county of residence. By listing the family name with counties, you have a start. Instead of writing to Virginia first, trying to get documents, do as much study in the library as possible. Numerous publications are available at Pack such as ones with colonial, immigration, and militia records, early settlers of specific counties, *Wills of Rappahannock County, 1656-1692, Rockingham County Marriages from 1778-1816, Births and Deaths, 1717-1778, Albemarle Parish Register of Surry and Sussex Counties.*

Records can be checked by mail if you can give the specific document, such as deed, will, marriage bond, the full name, approximate date, and the name of the county. The procedure is to ask the information for no more than two names per letter and to enclose a pre-addressed, stamped envelope so that you can be notified if the document is available and the cost. Write: Archives Branch, Virginia State Library, Richmond, VA 23219-3491.

Early births and death records are practically non-existent. The ones from 1853-1896 are available from the Bureau of Vital Records, James Madison Building, P. O. Box 1000, Richmond, VA 23208.

Most of the time, family researchers who have been told that their earliest family members came from Virginia don't think of **West Virginia.** The state of West Virginia was not formed until 1863 when the residents objected to withdrawing from the Union with their eastern cousins who had prosperous tobacco plantations. Being separated by the Allegheny Mountains and the resulting topography caused a true division of interests for the western Virginia farmers and livestock growers.

However, the area now known as West Virginia was settled, on and off, in the 1700s. As early as 1671, an English scouting party made a month's long trip across the Alleghenies into present West Virginia to see if the "south sea" were on the other side. From 1725, many Ulsters from Northern Ireland started moving in, including Porters, Lewises, Kincaids, Blantons, Meeks. (The earliest permanent settler was supposedly Morgan Morgan, a Welshman). The Pennsylvania Germans and other Scotch-Irish quickly followed. Most of these entered by the Virginia headright law which permitted each adult male immigrant to 50 acres of land in the public domain.

In the 1750s, the French who wanted the territory tactfully worked with the Indians, particularly the Shawnees; and the French and Indian War of 1754 compelled many settlers to flee eastward across the Alleghenies. In 1758, a treaty with the Indians gave them perpetual hunting grounds in this area; furthermore, by 1763, settlers were forbidden by King George III to live west of the Alleghenies. The settlers ignored this, and many deadly skirmishes from Indian raiding parties resulted. By 1774, Ohio was designated as the boundary of Indian Country, and more settlers flooded into present West Virginia. By the American Revolution, 30,000 settlers were in western Virginia.

Three publications may help you to see if the early ancestors were in western Virginia in the 1700s. One, *West Virginia Estate Settlements: An*

Index to Wills, Inventories, Appraisements, Land Grants, and Surveys to 1850, covers 25,000 names. The records are alphabetized by the thirteen earliest counties before 1800: Hampshire (1753), Greenbrier, Berkley, Pendleton, Hardy, Monroe, Wood, Brooke, Kanawha, Randolph, Mongahalia, Ohio, and Harrison. [Genealogical Publishing: Baltimore]
   Second is *West Virginia Genealogical Sources and Resources* by Carol McGinnis. This is very comprehensive on where to search for genealogical collections, with addresses for historical and genealogical societies and vital records. [Genealogical Publishing: Baltimore, 1988]
   Third is *History of Monroe County, West Virginia,* by Oren F. Morton, reissued in 1988, originally published in 1916. [Genealogical Publishing: Baltimore] This book contains much history of all of West Virginia, and for Monroe County genealogical biographies for about three hundred and fifty families, resident lists for 1782-1799, pensioners of the Revolution, plus land surveys and patents, naturalization records for the 1800s, and lists of the soldiers in the various wars.

   If your background research of census schedules and published sources leads you to **Maryland**, you are lucky. Maryland has the most complete colonial records of any of the other colonies since it established a repository in 1729 in Annapolis.
   Pack Library has Brumbaugh's *Maryland Land Records,* giving colonial marriages, Revolutionary service lists, baptisms, census of 1776. It also has Skordas's *Early Settlers of Maryland,* listing the index of immigrants from land patents 1633-1680, and the *Archives of Maryland,* such as Volume 18 which gives the Maryland troops during the Revolution, 1775-1783.
   The Maryland State Archives may be of some help. For a $5 fee, a staff member will check indexed material by mail. You must sent the following information with the fee: full name of individual, county of residence, type of information sought, and the approximate date of the record. The $5 fee pays for a one-hour search, and photocopy fees would be extra. Basically, there are no birth or death certificates before 1898, but there are many earlier religious records that can be searched if you know, in addition to the above four items, the name of the church or parish and the denomination. For requests or more information, write: Maryland State Archives, Hall of Records, Box 828, Annapolis, MD 21404.

Most family historians in some way want to learn more about themselves; and most would like to discover the country from which their ancestors came. And then, of course, to find more ancestors in the **mother country**.

Eugene A Stratton in *Applied Genealogy* [Ancestry: Salt Lake City, 1989] states that "We also learn about history in a most immediate way . . .. In a sense, we were there back in history as part of our ancestors." And, your ancestors are more numerous than you may think. In ten generations, you would have 2,046 ancestors; forty generations would take you back about A. D. 800 with about one trillion ancestors. Of course, you have duplicates, triplicates, etc., in ancestors, as most of you already know by going back only three or four generations, but no wonder family historians never finish with their family histories.

Stratton has written a thought-provoking and different book which would be particularly interesting to the family historian who is ready for a study of **English ancestors.** However, he states, "It is absolutely impossible for anyone to trace back generation by generation to an eleventh-century peasant. The records just do not exist." Perhaps this is why people are fascinated with royal genealogy. The records exist. Therefore, many people jump on "the name's the same" when studying for the across-the-Atlantic connection. He does tell the ways to research royal genealogy including the titles of specific books and background sources to study and the types of records available.

He also evaluates the genealogical journals, standards and documentation, discusses hereditary societies and gives the standards used by the authorities for acceptance into these organizations. In his discussion of name patterns, he includes the general patterns used, the usage of Sr. and Jr., and the naming of children after a deceased spouse or sibling. Also included are the uses of computers in genealogy and a discussion of medieval English land tenure, which helps explain why many younger English sons came to America. Stratton feels, in addition to a "greater appreciation of what the generations of the earth have accomplished before us," that much of the fun of genealogy is the "thrill of the chase, the satisfaction of solving puzzles, the delight in making new discoveries, and the association with many fine people."

Do"s and Don"ts for Ancestor Hunters [Genealogical Publishing:

Baltimore, 1988] may inspire some people to get started on their family history adventure or some to get across the ocean for research in the old homeland. Angus Baxter has done several books on research in Europe, and in this book, he summarizes his research methods for the United States, Canada, England and Wales, Scotland, Ireland, France, and Germany. He first points out that you must start with yourself and work backwards, not find a famous person who shares your name down to you. He feels that the main point to doing family history at all is that it is fun; plus most people do have a natural curiosity about their origins. After studying your family, "You will realize that the word family encompasses many hundreds of people over the past centuries whose blood you share, however diluted it has become with the passing of the years. You will feel close to the hitherto unknown men and women who helped form your character and your physical appearance."

Mr. Baxter points out that one of the cheapest ways to get started on your ancestors is to study the records at The Church of Jesus Christ of Latter Day Saints; a branch library is located in most communities. (Near Asheville on Sweeten Creek Road in this area)

Where the repositories are for the vital records, wills, censuses is covered for the various counties plus available records from church registers. For example, these church registers are available for the Church of England since September 5, 1538. A special chapter is included for Jewish sources.

Coats-of-Arms are discussed, and Mr. Baxter explains why he says, "Let me say at once there is little chance that you or your family have any right to a coat-of-arms." However, he does tell you the procedure to receive an authentic coat-of-arms from the College of Arms in England, Scotland, and Ireland. You will have to prove your direct descent from an arms-bearing family plus pay about three thousand dollars. He emphasizes that it is more important to "put leaves on the bare branches of the family tree" by finding out the details of the lives of your family, such as where they lived, crops and livestock they raised, the food they ate, the clothes they wore. "If your ancestors were immigrants to this country, and you discover the date, then by delving into the history of the place from which they came you can find out why they came."

People who even declare they are not interested in family history would probably like to know their countries of origin. Finding more than just a vague family story, "Three brothers came from England," is difficult. The earliest records do not always exist, or people are not sure where to look.

A 1988 publication *American Passenger Arrival Records* by Michael Tepper [Genealogical Publishing: Baltimore] discusses what records do document the arrival of millions of immigrants from Europe to America, where the records are, and what the various records contain. This book is divided into four parts: the colonial period, the beginning of the federal passenger arrival records, customs passenger lists, and immigration passenger lists.

The people who arrived in the colonial period had no rules of immigration to follow, so the fewest official records exist. The object was to colonize the country. However, Mr. Tepper points out, "So much attention has centered on the immigrants of this period (1620-1820), in fact, that practically every known record of migration, every passenger list - original or synthetic - has appeared in print." [If anything ever existed.] "Original" refers to the passenger lists themselves while "synthetic" refers to records kept for other purposes that prove immigration, such as the land patent books in the Virginia State Library in Richmond which include the planters as well as the individuals brought over as "headrights." "Headrights" refers to a sponsor's receiving fifty acres of land for every person he brought to the Virginia Colony. The patents and grants from 1623 to 1732 have been compiled by Nell Nugent in the book *Cavaliers and Pioneers*. Over thirty publications that prove immigration in the colonial period are described for the various states, including Janie Revill's *A Compilation of the Original Lists of Protestant Immigrants to South Carolina, 1763-1773*. These settlers had to prove to the South Carolina Council they were Protestants before they could receive land, and the records were kept.

By 1800, some federal passenger arrival records were kept in the form of "baggage lists" which incidentally listed the colonists whose baggage was exempt from taxes. It was not until 1820 that arrival records were kept consistently at United States ports of entry. These were the customs passenger lists, started to try to prevent overcrowding which caused disease and death. "On one ship setting out from a European port, more that 700 of the 1,267 persons aboard perished . . . with `ship fever.'" The main and minor ports of entry are discussed as well as what

103

was included in the official records, denoting the additional information added over the years. By the 1890s, the Immigration Passenger lists give the most information. If you are serious about "leaving no stone unturned" while searching back to the place of origin for your ancestors, this book guides you in the steps to take.

John P. Colletta wrote a book *They Came in Ships* that also explains how to find and to use the publications about ship passenger lists to locate a particular individual. He discussed the preparation you need to undertake your search. [Ancestry: Salt Lake City, 1990]

Seeing in records that an ancestor came from Barbados is usually a puzzle to a family historian. You're never quite sure if it was just the ship's "stopover" or whether someone stayed several years. And why did someone stay in **Barbados** since it is over 3,000 miles from London and a West Indies island only 21 miles by 14 miles.

Barbados started being colonized in 1627 by the English after Captain John Powell found the deserted island in 1625. The King of England granted lord proprietors, sponsored by merchants, the rights of feudal lords. These lords established a plantation system for growing sugar cane to produce rum and molasses. To protect themselves from foreign sailors' attacks, the settlers built 21 forts spaced along the coastline. By 1640, Barbados had 1,000 proprietors and 30,000 people. The people were basically English and mostly indentured servants, either former prisoners from England or people who voluntarily chose to be indentured for 3-7 years. Slaves were imported from Africa. Also, after an unsuccessful rebellion against James II of England, Scotsmen were sold into slavery to the lords of Barbados. Documents show that the death rate for indentured servants was higher than those for slaves. Slaves were possessions to be kept so were not as ill-fed, ill-housed, and overworked as the temporary servants. Not being adaptable to a variety of products, the land was overworked from the sugar cane crop. Many settlers then made their way to the American mainland for a new start.

Finding emigration records from the beginning of colonization through 1820 from any country is difficult. In addition to Coldham's *The Complete Book of Emigrants* (only England, 1602-1660), P. William Filby's *Passenger and Immigration Index: A Guide to Published Arrival Records* is a source available at Pack Library and is a guide to published lists of early immigrants to North America.

If your ancestor intended to travel abroad, the National Archives has some passport applications which start in 1791. However, you would need to have the name, the place and approximate date of application. The National Archives is a bigger help if you are interested in immigrants who arrived in 1820 and later. However, the staff will not search the customs' or passengers' lists unless in addition to the names of the passenger, you have the port of entry, the name of the vessel and the approximate date of its arrival or the name of the port of embarkation and the exact date of arrival. To send a request to the Archives, you must first have the correct form. These forms are available from Reference Service Branch, National Archives and Records Service, 8th and Pennsylvania Ave., NW, Washington, DC 20408.

Piecing together what country an ancestor came from is a tedious, and sometimes an impossible, task. You may find an ancestor in Buncombe in 1800. You find in census records that his children listed their birthplace as Virginia. You could find in the 1790 reconstructed census in Virginia someone with the same last name that "could be" the father of your ancestor. You could find someone with the same name as the one in Virginia as an emigrant to Virginia in 1740. Don't adopt this ancestor as yours until you have proof for this "could be." Many carelessly written genealogies have "could be" factors as facts. It's better not to know where your early ancestor came from than to hamper your research and others' research by guesses listed as truths.

However, if you have worked step-by-step backwards, have a letter from kin in the old country to your ancestor, or have the immigration records for your ancestor with the country and the date, it is possible to do some exact tracing in some countries.

A 1985 publication, *In Search of Your European Roots*, by Angus Baxter is a "how-to by mail" guide. [Genealogical Publishing: Baltimore] Baxter advises using the LDS sources before becoming involved in overseas correspondence. (The LDS Branch on Sweeten Creek Road in Arden has records for Austria, Belgium, Denmark, Finland, France, Germany, Hungary, Iceland, Netherlands, Norway, Poland, Sweden, and Switzerland; plus, more are being added all the time.) Since a knowledge of the history of an area is always needed for research, Baxter starts with an introduction to major events in Europe that changed the boundaries of countries. His guide to records available make this book an aid which

105

will save time, money, and frustration.

The chapters are discussions of how to search each different country. Don't assume if you know the country of origin, you can find the information needed. This would be like knowing someone was in America thinking you could write to one place and find out where. Baxter never makes going back across the ocean for ancestors look like an easy trip, but he makes a guide available for the ones who know the country and area they are searching for.

A book mentioned briefly above, *Passenger and Immigration Lists Index*, edited by Fliby and Meyer in 1981, four volumes, is available at Pack Library. These lists contain 500,000 immigrants' names to show where the complete information may be found.

For example, "Gustafsson, Gustaf 31, NY, NY, 1849, 641l, p. 167" is a typical entry. (The Gustafsson name went from Justusson to Justis, not something given in the book but must be learned from background information.) The last two numbers are references to the source book and page number in it. Upon looking up number 641l at the first of the Index book, you'll find it refers to "Swedish Passenger Arrivals in NY, 1820-1850," by Nils Olsson. Finding the book and turning to p. 167, the following information is included: "Gustaf Gustafsson, farmer from Boda in Hagerstad Parish b. in Yxsmedshult in Vastra Eneby Parish January 28, 1818, s. Carl Gustaf Jonsson, farmer and Anna Stina Gustafsdotter, [Notice that his father did not have the last name Gustafsson. The son listed who came to America was the son of Carl, who must have gone by the middle name Gustaf, so his last name was created from son of Gustaf. Carl was the son of Jon, and Anna Stina was a daughter of a Gustaf also.] He was married to Anna Lovisa Zachrisdotter, born in Skalhamra, Hagerstad Parish April 13, 1821, daughter Zacharias Andersson, farmer and Lena Maja Pehrsdotter. They had three children, the oldest born in Vastra Eneby, the younger two in Hagerstad; Anna Maria b. June 2, 1842; Emelia Charlotta b. September 18, 1844, and Carl Gustaf, born January 27, 1847. The family received papers in Linkoping May 5, 1849, and emigrated to Andover, Ill. Here the husband and children soon died, all of cholera. The wife survived, bought a farm near Andover and married a German, Otto Lobeck. Later she moved to Nebraska and died in Fremont March 30, 1903."

Not all of the books in the index are in Pack Library, but it is a start.

And by reading just the titles of the books, often a nationality is given, such as *18th Century Palatine Emigrants, Ulster Emigration, A list of Ye French Refugees.*

You may have heard or found in Bibles or public documents that you had an ancestor born in **Ireland**. Deeds often state where the grantee was from, sometimes wills, often military records, and the federal censuses. A few Irish, but only four percent of immigrants, were in the United States by 1790, but a potato blight, resulting in widespread famine resulted in the greatest group of immigrants between 1820 and 1860 coming from Ireland. The largest number came in 1847. If you are curious to know where in Ireland your ancestor came from, there are basically three research steps you may try.

First, check the *Passenger and Immigration List Indexes* and its supplements by P. William Filby. Pack Library has nine volumes of these in all. If Pack Library does not have the source you are referred to, such as *Some Irish Immigrants*, check with the reference librarian to see if they can get a copy of the page you need. (There is a small fee for this service.)

Second, a 1988 compilation by Brian Mitchell, *Irish Passenger Lists, 1847-1871*, gives information from the business records of two large shipping companies. These Irish ship owners, J. J. Cooke and William McCorkell, kept lists of the people emigrating, the place of Irish residence and the ages and family groups in most cases, plus the name of the ship and its destination and year of sailing. The passengers, 27,495, were mostly from counties Donegal, Londonderry, and Tyrone. [Genealogical Publishing: Baltimore]

To receive official immigration papers, the third step is to check with the National Archives as mentioned before.

Many Americans have heard that their ancestors had fortunes in England which they never recovered after emigrating to America. Now there is a simple way to see if any of your family fortune stories were true. You don't even have to go to England or Wales to search for personal estates which your ancestors should have received from 1610 through 1857.

The perogative court of Canterbury had jurisdiction over these personal estates when the person died abroad, and the records are now in print. Peter W. Coldham has compiled American Wills, *Administrations in the Prerogative Court of Canterbury, 1610-1857*. There are 6,000 abstracts of wills which contain references to over 5,000 more names. [Genea-logical Publishing, Inc.: Baltimore, 1989].

These wills are alphabetized and contain much family history. "Adams, James, of North Carolina, clerk, bachelor, Administration to Alexander Junes, attorney for the sisters and next of kin Jannett and Elizabeth Adams, now in Aberdeen, Scotland" (Sept. 1711). "Love, William, formerly of South Carolina but late of London, whose daughter, Elinor, wife of Harmer Powell, was in Ninety Six, South Carolina. Probate to Thomas Shivers" (Aug. 1789).

"Lane, John, of North Carolina, bachelor. Administration to the sister Elizabeth, wife of Rev. Rodney Croxall; the mother Bridget Lane, widow, renouncing (Aug. 1748)." "Atkins, John, of Virginia, Bachelor. Administration with will to the brother, William Atkins (Oct. 1624). Revoked on his death and granted to the brother Richard Atkins, guardian of the children, Elizabeth, George, Ann, and Lee Atkins, during their minority (Aug. 1626). Revolked on his death and granted to the brother, Humphrey Atkins (June 1627)."

The records seemed to have been well kept; so there is a good probability that if your ancestor didn't receive any money, there was none to be loaded on the "ship" from England. Mr. Coldham also pointed out that "during the eighteenth century and earlier fewer than one person in ten in England died testate or had a personal estate of a sufficient value to warrant attention by one or other of the probate courts."

One booklet of only 30 pages but packed with information and interesting reading is "Records of Emigrants from England and Scotland to North Carolina, 1774-1775," edited by A. R. Newsome, and available in 1984 from the Division of Archives and History, Historical Publications, Raleigh. This booklet gives names, ages, quality, occupation, employment, former residence, reason for emigrating, and the name of the vessel and master of 500 from Scotland and 100 from England.

Several of the English, with occupations such as a baker, a leather dresser, a clock maker, a printer, were coming as indentured servants for two to four years. The "reasons for emigrating" such as "going to settle" were not surprising, but to see that quite a few men and women were "going for pleasure" was. Since one reads in history books of the unpleasant crossings on these early ships, this type of vacation in 1774 is incredible.

The Scottish gave their "reasons for emigrating" as "in hopes of good employment, for a better way of doing, in hopes of better bread," and one "to get a husband." However, most Scottish, particularly from Glenurcha and Intyre, gave "high rents and oppression." The booklet's introduction points out that mass movement of Scotch Highlanders came specifically to North Carolina because many of their kinsmen had settled on the Cape Fear River since 1739. Friends in America had told them "that people who are temperate and laborious have every chance of bettering their circumstances."

Many of these Scottish settlers had never imagined the price they would have to pay for "bettering their circumstances." They did have better living conditions on the Cape Fear River where they joined other Highlands near Cross Creek. According to Lefler and Powell in *Colonial North Carolina*, they had "substantial homes, more furniture than they could ever have dreamed of enjoying in Scotland." (North Carolina had the largest number of Highland Scots than any other colony.) They produced naval stores from the long-leafed pine which they sold to England; they had a printing press in Fayetteville in the late 1700s in their native Gaelic; they had been denied their kilts at home but could wear them in America.

In addition to holding their lands directly from the English, they had also taken an oath of allegiance to England before they came to America. These who arrived in 1774-1775 just arrived at the wrong time. By 1776 during the Revolution, many died because of this loyalty to England. In February, sixteen hundred Highlanders met at Cross Creek and were led by Donald McDonald toward Wilmington to fight for the English against the Patriots. Eighteen miles from Wilmington at Moore's Creek Bridge, eleven hundred men, under the Patriot Colonel James Moore's directions, reached the bridge across the swamp first. The Patriots removed many of the bridge planks and greased the logs with "soft soap and tallow." At least fifty Loyalists were shot and wounded or killed as they stumbled across the bridge while only one Patriot was killed. This battle of Moore's Creek Bridge resulted in a drawing card for more patriotism. The British forces could be defeated. By April 12, 1776, the Halifax Resolution stated the majorities' belief in freedom from England.

By 1777, many of the Scottish Highlanders, who came to America for "a better way of doing," had their estates taken by the Patriot-dominated legislature and many had to flee from North Carolina.

The background information for finding out if you had an ancestor from **Scotland** could start with a study of David Dobson's *Directory of Scots in the Carolinas, 1680-1830.* [Genealogical Publishing: Baltimore, 1986] In this book he has listings and various information on 6,000 Scots in North Carolina and South Carolina, giving birthplace, often wife or husband, children, first settlement in the Carolinas and often where he or she died. Included in the ones who settled in Western North Carolina are "William Gudger, born in Scotland during 1752. Married Martha Patsy Young in Maryland during 1775. Settled in Surry County, NC. Died in Buncombe during 1833."; "Benjamin Kimsey, born in Scotland about 1725. Married in Scotland Agnes Lamb. Settled in Buncombe. Died in Burke County, 1827."; "John A. Hall. Born in Scotland about 1803. Married Elizabeth Young in Rutherford County during 1828. Died in Cherokee County about 1880."

Another of Dobson's books is *The Original Scots Colonists of Early America, 1612-1783*, with over 7,000 listings. (Dobson states that over 150,000 Scots emigrated by the American Revolution and that the Carolinas had one of the greatest concentration of these Scots.) In this book, he states whether the men and women came voluntarily or were involuntarily transported as thieves, vagrants, rioters, Jacobites, etc. From British records, he has listed for each his or her places of residence in Scotland.

If you can find an ancestor listed with his or her place of residence, your next step could be to check for the county of the residence. Check *A Topigraphical Dictionary of Scotland* by Samuel Lewis, first printed in 1846. A complete description if given. For example, Dundee is "a seaport town and parish, in the county of Forfar," 47 miles N. E. of Edinburgh. The detailed descriptions include early history, how named, principal trade, religions, churches, schools, and castles.

Your next step could be to visit the local stake of the Latter Day Saints of Jesus Christ (LDS) to check the International Genealogical Index for the county in Scotland you are interested in. LDS has copied the available parish registers for births, marriages, deaths, from the earliest dates to 1855.

If you still think that Scotland is the correct country, you need to do more background study for the records available there. David Moody has written two guides discussing how to write for or how to search in person for official information. *Scottish Local History* and *Scottish Family History* discuss sources available from the local public libraries to the archives offices. Most records are at the Scottish Record Office in Edinburgh. Also, in Edinburgh are the General Register Office, the Roman Catholic Church's Archives, and the Register House. The Register House has a genealogical listing of the families entitled to display arms. Moody states that one in every forty-five Scots were entitled to display arms in 1672 when the register was started. (Moody gives the usual warning that one should not assume that "sharing a surname with a Scottish aristocrat constitutes a degree of affinity with him.") In his complete discussion of the clan system, he points out that much of the "clan system" relating to Scotland now is a myth created by businessmen to sell tartans. [Genealogical Publishing: Baltimore, 1990]

In Moody's *Scottish Family History*, he stresses getting a deeper understanding of early ancestors. Moody's suggestions include getting the usual biographical information of ancestors and then studying the local historical books to find how the ancestors lived and to even find what sermons were preached by the ministers in the area. Moody feels that "The feelings and ideas with which your ancestors grappled did not die with them but were transmitted to their successors." He feels that we should find more than ancestors' names and dates since descendants also inherit their ideas and character. Therefore, for a real family history, you need to try to find out more than the usual material for a pedigree chart. You need to search for physical characteristics, medical history, and family life. He suggested that you asked your oldest kin about courting rituals, punishment and authority in the home, funeral customs, a detailed description of the household and the household chores. For example, how were clothes washed, soap made, livestock killed and preserved.

Moody then suggested you move from the lives of individuals to what the local community was like, such as schools and local pursuits and then to the state and nation with what historical events could have affected the lives of the individuals.

He included detailed instructions in searching for records and the

111

dates these are available in Scotland. The General Register's Office in Edinburgh is the major depository for Scottish archival records. He gave reminders that surnames were not "fixed" until the end of the 16th century and the 18th century in the highlands. He also warned of the "pitfall" in assuming that individuals "sharing a surname have, or ever have had, any blood relationship." He pointed out that only a minority of the population owned land in Scotland before the 19th century and that if a researcher is looking for an ancestor of "humble origin" in Scotland before 1855 (the date of the introduction of civil registration), there is a possibility that no records can be found. Scotland was different from America in the 1800s; for example, in 1878, only sixty-eight people owned nearly half of Scotland's land. Moody gave many ideas for discovering how the minds of one's Scottish ancestors "worked" from the customs and traditions to what songs they sang and what tales they related.

In 1790, a federal census estimate was made that 240,309 English people and 32,388 Scottish people were in North Carolina. How many from each group fell under the term **Scotch-Irish** is hard to know. The Scotch-Irish were Scots and mainly Presbyterians who came to America from northern Ireland where they had emigrated starting in 1610. By the mid-1600s there were Scotch-Irish in Maryland. From the early 1700s, these people were coming, for economic reasons, by the thousands to America.

People who are seriously interested in knowing more about the Scotch-Irish will learn much by studying the book, *The Scotch-Irish in America*, by Henry Jones Ford, written in 1915 and reprinted. [Clearfield: Baltimore, 1992]

In 1729, there was alarm in Ireland over the population "drain." The "run to America" was attributed to bad seasons for three years, high prices on land and rent. These conditions led to families' "leaving their houses and lands desolate." In the first two weeks of August in 1729, three thousand and five hundred people arrived in Pennsylvania from Ireland, and five hundred arrived in North Carolina. (These were Scots-Irish since Irish migration did not start until the 1800s.)

Ford stated that by 1779 in Carolina large tracts of the best land was unoccupied, and a thousand families of Scotch-Irish in one year drove their cattle, hogs, and horses overland before them. They received small tracts on one to three hundred acres in the "back settlements."

This book includes a complete history of the Ulster settlements by the English and the Scottish in Ireland, listing people who received one to three thousand acres. Over five hundred thousand acres of land had been granted in northern Ireland by 1611 to the English and Scottish. A background history of the Irish people is included. However, most of the book is devoted to the migration to America and the various settlements on the eastern seaboard plus a detailed history of the growth of American Presbyterianism, its pioneer preachers, and the contributions of the Scotch-Irish to America.

Since estimates are that 200,000 **Germans** immigrated to North America in the 1700s and more than three million in the 1800s, chances are good that at least one of your ancestors was from Germany.

Angus Baxter wrote *In Search of Your German Roots* [Genealogical Publishing: Baltimore, 1991] to help you trace your ancestors back to the "old country" whether they were from Germany, Austria, or any of the other European countries which had German settlements. Plus, the book has helpful guides for starting your search for ancestors regardless of where they were from. Baxter also included "cautions" to keep you from making time-consuming errors in your search.

Since you need to understand your ancestry, a brief history of the Germans and Germany is included. There were various reasons for the mass entries of Germans into North America starting as early as 1683. Baxter stated "poor crops, bad winters, heavy taxes, religious persecution." Plus, "The winter of 1708-09 was the worst in Europe in more than a century" with the intense cold destroying crops, trees, vines. By 1709, about 30,000 Germans arrived in London wanting to go to Pennsylvania and the Carolinas.

In starting your search, Baxter suggested starting back from yourself and not assuming that everyone with the last surname is kin. [How many times have you heard that advise now; guess people learned the hard way.] "Do not take someone with your surname who was famous two centuries ago and try to trace his or her descendants down to you." He stressed checking at your local stake/branch of the Church of Jesus Christ of Latter-day Saints (LDS) to see what research already had been done on your family. A chapter is included on LDS, explaining their IGI

113

records which have names listed from church registers such as baptisms, births, marriages, deaths, burials, and Family Group Records (FGRA). He also includes the addresses of German Genealogical Associations in the United States and Canada. A chapter was included on Jewish records plus organizations' addresses in different countries to contact for help in your search.

Even though your ancestor had a German name and was said to be from Germany, he or she could have come from Austria, Belgium, Czechoslovakia, Denmark, France, Italy, Russia, etc. Probably Baxter's most encouraging news is "You can do all your searching by correspondence by using the resources" of libraries, archives, church and government records, historical organizations, newspapers. He gave suggestions for not only where to write letters abroad but also for writing successful letters.

Germans started coming into Rowan County by 1745. Many came into Buncombe in the late 1700s, and many more followed these from their homeland. *The Wuerttemberg Emigration Index*, Vol. I [Ancestry: Salt Lake City, 1986] contains 11,500 names of Germans from Wuerttemberg who made application to leave Germany basically from 1817-1910. Compilers Schenk, Froelke, and Bork studied the original emigration records which are on microfilm at Ludwigsburg. They alphabetized the names, spelling them in the most common German way, included the date and place of birth, residence at the time of application, application date, destination, plus microfilm number.

A typical entry showed Wagner, Michael, born 29 December 1837, in Schoenaich, now in Boeblingen in September 1854 and applying to go to North America, film number 560439. Most were on their way to North America, but some were going to other countries, such as Hungary, Poland, Austria, Switzerland, Russia. Thousands of these Germans who emigrated to Russia came to America in the 1870s to avoid serving in the Czar's army.

Occasionally, unexpected results come from "doing" family history. When an Afro-American woman from Denver, Colorado, and a white woman from Black Mountain, N. C., started tracing their ancestors, they did not know their paths would cross when tracing a Rev. William Fullwood.

As Black historians know, they often have to go back to the owner's name to research their families. Janice Little-Siebert from Denver was searching for her three great-grandfather, London Fullwood, in McDowell County, N. C. Betty Austin from Black Mountain had found her four great-grandfather's will, dated October 27, 1851, in which he bequeathed "slave" London to his son. Until then, Ms. Austin had no idea anyone in her family had owned slaves, but she was told by a genealogist that Ms. Little-Siebert was researching the same family.

Even though Ms. Austin and Ms. Little-Siebert were both apprehensive, they contacted each other and met in Asheville. Together they went on a rural dirt road to the black and white cemeteries where their ancestors were buried. The anticipated apprehension of one perhaps being bitter and angry and the other perhaps feeling guilty and defensive disappeared as the two women became acquainted in their common search for the past. Family history research can have unexpected and pleasant rewards for individuals who choose to make it a learning experience.

Until you get back to 1865, searching for **Afro-American** ancestors is done the same way as searching for white ancestors. Start by talking with relatives, searching for old family Bibles and personal papers. Get all the full names, dates, and residences you possibly can. Try to think of all the ways the name could possibly be spelled before checking the records, for example, Pertiller, Pittillo, Patillo, Potilla.

For lists of children, your next step could be to study the federal census for the residence county. Pack Library has the N. C. census for all counties from 1790 through 1920 (no 1890). The first census for Buncombe was 1800. Although Western North Carolina was a minor slave-holding area in the South, in 1800 there were 347 slaves out of 5,815 people. Depending upon the information you need, you may want to start with the most recent census and work backwards. The first census to list Afro-Americans, unless freed earlier, was the 1870, which includes the head of household, wife, children plus ages and where each was born. The 1880 picks up where the parents were born. There are slave listings for 1850 and 1860, but there are no names, just the owner and the description by age.

While you are at Pack Library, you may want to check the earliest Asheville City Directories. The first is "The Asheville City Directory and

Gazetter" 1883-1884. This lists the names, street addresses, and occupations of 3,874 Ashevillians plus a suburban directory of some of the county residents, such as principal farmers and store owners. The book uses parentheses with "col." to denote Blacks, which is a help for researchers. For example, listed at the Black Mountain Station is "Daugherty, Nelson (col.), blksmith, 1 mile west."

Another place to check would be at the county court house. Births and deaths are listed from October 1913 - present. The indexes are in the Register of Deed's offices and easy to use. If you find a listing in the indexes you want, ask to see the certificate itself since it would give parents' names and other information. Marriage records were kept from 1851 and the race was given in the indexes.

Before the Civil War and 1865, Afro-American ancestors are much harder to trace. A standard "how to" genealogy book will tell you to use "plantation books"; however, not one seems to be available for Western North Carolina. Most owners used only first names for their slaves; then after the Civil War, of course Afro-Americans could choose any name they wished. Sometimes they chose the name of the former slave owner, sometimes a previous owner, often an admired famous person, such as Lincoln, sometimes the given name of the father. If the slave owner can be determined, his family records will be the key to your early information. Since the changing of ownership was recorded in deeds and in wills, these books can be checked at the court house. In these documents first names of the slaves and age descriptions are usually all that was given. Without reading all the deeds for a family, you can tell by the deed indexes which ones need to be searched by looking to the last column under "description." A slave transaction will say "deed of gift," or "bill of sale," or just be left blank with no location or acreage.

Early estate records are very scant in Western North Carolina; plus the indexes are only from 1831. Some earlier ones are scattered through early county court records but without indexes and hard to find. The Buncombe County Archives on Valley Street is the best place to search for estate records.

Searching for Afro-American ancestors is difficult, but with all the problems, Charles Blockson's book, *Black Genealogy*, [Black Classic Press: P. O. Box 13414, Baltimore, MD 21203] should make the searching for ancestors easier. Mr. Blockson's advice is first to check with your family,

116

putting down all you and any family members know. Check family Bibles, papers, and "consider every attic a potential treasure trove of information."

He gives a step-by-step plan of what to keep and how to organize records. Blockson suggests that you study your gathered family information for "gaps" that you want more about and divide your needs into geographical areas before going to the court houses. He also suggests you check the youngest people first for births, deaths, marriages, since they'll be easier to find.

He advises when writing a courthouse for records, ask for a copy of the index with all names beginning with the same letter so that you can search for various spellings to see what specific wills or other records you may want to order. Quoted prices for copies come back faster with a pre-addressed, stamped envelope. Some archives have manumission records, or formal freedom papers. You may also want to check the 1790 "List of Free Black Heads of Families," which is available from the national archives with names alphabetized under each state.

The appendixes contain a directory with addresses of research sources, such as state and country archives, historical societies, newspapers.

Mr. Blockson's book is worth reading since he has written an interesting American and African history book along with his helpful genealogical ideas. He adds, "The vast majority of us will never be able to add that important piece -- to trace our ancestors back to Africa. But the challenge still exists, the chance you will find that final fragment." He also stated that your main reason is to find out not just who but "how they lived and a feel for the world and society they inhabited."

Was the French Broad River once called Agiqua? That's a detail in an old book, "As the day dawned he came to the bank of a river which he supposed to be the river the **Cherokees** called Agiqua but which we know as the French Broad."

The Wild Rose of Cherokee, Nancy Ward, by E. Sterling King, first published in 1895, takes the reader back to the Western North Carolina and Eastern Tennessee mountains over 200 years ago. A love story is told of Nancy, part Cherokee and part English, and Sir Francis Ward, an Englishman stationed at Fort Loudon, an east Tennessee garrison built in 1756 on the south bank of the Little Tennessee River.

Nancy's father was Oconostota, and her mother was Lady Lucy Ward. To strengthen the English ties with the Indians, in 1730, Sir Alexander Cuming came to the Cherokees as an envoy for King George II and took six Cherokee envoys with him back to the English Court. Oconostota was with them, and Lady Ward agreed to marry him. They were married in Westminster Abbey and returned to live at Chota, an Indian town on the south bank of the Tennessee River. Along with the history of the Cherokee Nation in north Georgia, Eastern Tennessee, and Western North Carolina from 1758 to 1769, the book conveys the mountains as our early ancestors must have seen them. Near an area where Agiqua and Cootla (Little Tenn.) Rivers meet, the narrator described what a thundering troop of buffalo looked like to one who'd never seen them: "Some of them looked like huge lions, with great shaggy manes, but their feet were shod with hoofs like oxen, and their heads were armed with long horns." The number in the herd was so numerous it sounded as if an earthquake were taking place.

Old style adventure is included when Sir Francis necessarily flees to Kentucky. On his way in the Watauga Valley of North Carolina, he meets Daniel Boone, Captain William Bean, Mrs. Bean, and Andrew Greer. How much is fact and how much is fiction doesn't matter, for the book has you living in another time in these mountains. [Reprinted by Dan Crowe, Tennessee, 1984]

People who are interested in Cherokee Indian history and research can find a microfilmed copy of *The Cherokee Phoenix*, 1828-1834, at Pack Library. This unusual weekly newspaper, published by the Cherokee Nation in New Echota, Georgia, and edited by Elias Boudinott, had the English and the Cherokee languages parallel in the columns. This paper included the Constitution of the Cherokee Nation, written July 1827, local news, scripture translations, poetry. World news was printed such as a discussion of the seven types of churches of Asia and of an earthquake in the Netherlands.

Household hints included such items as to put "camphor in the bottom of a trunk to protect woolen gooden . . . to sew in small bags and fasten to the inner corners of bedsteads since no insects can long endure it." Included also was a reprint of a speech given in Philadelphia by George Washington, August 29, 1796, "to his beloved men of the Cherokee Nation" mainly concerning how the game was becoming scarce and his suggesting their raising cattle and hogs.

Basically, searching for your Cherokee Indian ancestors can be relatively simple or impossible. Finding from a complete compiled family history or nothing usually depends upon if your ancestor filed a claim with the United States government for benefits resulting from the 1835 treaty for payments.

Before starting to do Indian research, you should get all the information possible so that you'll know the correct name or names you are looking for. The more information you know about parents, brothers, sisters, the surer you will be to find the correct family. Don't count on family stories to give you enough information for research.

Pack Library has the census of Jackson County, N. C., of 1870 which lists many Indian families in Western North Carolina. Check locations to see if others would be helpful.

Numerous research records are available at two area libraries. Hunter Library, Western Carolina University, Cullowhee, N. C., has several microfilms for study. The "Old Settler Cherokee Census" (film number 279 at Hunter) lists Indians who were beneficiaries back to 1835.

Another census that may be helpful is the 1835 "Henderson Roll," (film number 275) of the Cherokee Indians East of the Mississippi," which lists the whole Cherokee Nation of 1,959 people in this area.

In 1851, David W. Silar was appointed to take a census of the Cherokees east of the Mississippi for payment based upon the 1835 treaty. Silar's book *The Eastern Cherokee. A Census of the Cherokee Nations in N. C., Tenn., Ala., Georgia in 1851,* is available at Hunter Library.

There was also a Mullay roll taken in 1848 of the Cherokees still in North Carolina who were born before 1836. In this roll 1,557 Cherokees were listed. Even though this one is not available locally, these records should show up in the 1910 rolls of Guion Miller.

The Miller roll was compiled from earlier records and new claims added. Hunter Library has two important sources related to these rolls. "Records Relating to Enrollment of the Eastern Cherokee by Guion Miller, 1908-1910," is on film number 427. Plus, there are the seven printed volumes *Cherokee by Blood: Records of Eastern Cherokee Ancestry in the United States Court of Claims, 1906-1910,* compiled by Jerry Wright Jordan. About half of the 46,000 entries have been included from the federal government's 348 rolls of microfilm. Pack Library in Asheville also has

Jordan's volumes.

Before anyone could receive benefits, affidavits had to be verified; therefore, many people testified concerning their ancestry. Even though many of these claims were rejected for lack of evidence, they were filed, and much family history if included.

Also, at Hunter Library is a Special Collections Department, which, along with manuscript collections and items concerning regional history, has the only microfilm set (800 reels) of "Cherokee Documents in Foreign Archives." These contain copies of primary records concerning the Cherokees from Great Britain, France, Spain, Mexico, and Canada. The Special Collections Department is open from 9 a.m. to 12 noon or by appointment. George Frizzell is the archivist and the one to notify for further information concerning this information. (Mailing address: Hunter Library, WCU, Cullowhee, NC 28723-9002)

Both Hunter and Pack Libraries have numerous historical books on the Cherokees for background reading.

CHAPTER 4. PEOPLE SOURCES

Books are great for your leads to "positive proofs" in the official records, but the background in knowing if you have the right person and learning more about that person normally comes from other people.

The popularity of researching family history has grown in the last ten years to one of the most widespread hobbies in the United States, but the researchers have been around for decades. They have saved the letters, remembered the stories, gathered the records, seen the Bibles. Somebody who has searched for forty years or more into your family probably has some clues that you need, if only you knew where he or she could be located. You'll have to write some letters to newspapers, genealogical societies, family societies, and nationality societies.

Newspapers

The people who can help you may be found by your writing inquiries to columns such as this one which was compiled from the *Asheville Citizen-Times*. (Appendix A contains eleven years of inquiries.) Most researchers enjoy sharing with kin, no matter how "far-flung."

Only about ninety newspapers across the United States have columns in which genealogical queries can be placed. When available, these are normally free of charge. There are usually specifications that the person you are asking about has a "local" connection and that you limit the length of your inquiry from fifty to one hundred words. You will get the best results if you give the most specific place you can on where the person lived, at least an approximate date, and some connections with someone else, such as parents, brothers and sisters, wife, a child or children.

The most up-to-date list of these columns (published yearly) is from Merle Ganier, 2108 Grace Avenue, Fort Worth, TX 76lll-2816 and available for $8. (Ms. Ganier also includes lists of family periodicals in this publication.)

Genealogical and Historical Societies

Another way to contact people who are interested the same families you are is to write to genealogical organizations in the geographical location of your ancestor. Genealogical societies have newsletters where inquiries can be placed and files on family names. (A list of genealogical societies in North Carolina, with addresses, are included at the end of this chapter.)

There are many genealogical societies in Western North Carolina. Visiting in person may be your best introduction to these.

Wander into the Innsbruck Mall, Tunnel Road, in Asheville, between the hours of 9 to 5, Mondays through Friday, and you'll find an association that has one basic purpose: to help you search for your ancestors who lived in Western North Carolina. It is the Old Buncombe County Genealogical Society.

When there, your first step is to tell the last name you are looking for and to request a check of the charts of members. You may find a "cousin" who is already a member and has done much work on the name. Plan to stay awhile to check the library of genealogical materials, including family histories, N. C. counties' histories of families, Buncombe County grantor/grantee indexes, Buncombe County birth records, back copies of the society's newsletter, Asheville city directories, a family history file, many research books from out-of-state.

Helpful books are for sale at the office. Also, to organize the family history you are acquiring, forms for ancestor charts, family group sheets, and census work sheets are available.

Their newsletter, "A Lot of Bunkum," includes sections on early Buncombe families submitted by researchers, census listings, wills, new books in the research library, inquiries on ancestors, announcements of meetings and workshops you may find helpful in Western North Carolina.

This society has on-going projects to help you in searching for ancestors. For example, a project completed in 1988 is a booklet "Poll Books of 1835," edited by Charles Biddix. The listing containing 7,845 names are for the 12th Congressional District in North Carolina for the counties of Burke (McDowell included), Haywood, Yancey, Macon, Rutherford, and Buncombe. This was all of Western North Carolina at that time. Other information in the publication discusses "bad" votes, mainly by people who had voted in the wrong place, such as Barney Bowman who voted in Yancey but lived in Tennessee. The names of voters are divided by counties plus where they voted. A gazetteer is included to denote the locations of the various precincts. Some interesting spellings occurred, such as Swaneno for Swannanoa and names, Davice for Davis.

The benefits to joining an organization such as this one, besides receiving a quarterly newsletter are that you'll be associated with people who have the same hobby as you plus know about informative monthly meetings and valuable workshops.

Most family historians work years searching and piecing together their information. Their findings are very important to them, and they often wish they knew whom to share them with. Somebody "out there" would be interested in their knowledge of ancestors. One of the best opportunities for sharing family history if through books sponsored by genealogical societies.

If you are not familiar with *The Heritage of Old Buncombe*, published 1981, [Volume I], you don't know what you are missing. Not only is the book general historical reading but also a "mine" of individual family histories, both covering Western North Carolina.

The first 132 pages cover "Our Heritage," which includes numerous pictures such as the 1920s Buncombe County Court House, the digging of the Beaucatcher Tunnel, early Pack Square, the 1916 flood; histories and current detailed maps of what was old Buncombe: Haywood, Macon, Henderson, McDowell, Jackson, Transylvania, Swain-all of Western North Carolina; the 1800 census, church histories.

One historical article from papers in the State Archives reproduces John Brown's diary. John Brown was from Pennsylvania and visited Western North Carolina in 1795 to buy land. He described his visit as "we rode down to the Seat of Justice for Said County and Lodged at Mr. Streets we had very poor intertainment this town is but two days walk from the Cherokee Nation they keep a near Sixty men out about 7 miles distant from town in small garisons to Prevent the Indians from coming in on them. This town stands a mile distant from French Broad and a mile below where the Swanno River empties into French Broad the settlement is very thin and they live but very indifferently." Mr. Brown "calculated" land in Buncombe to amount to 299 thousand acres. A section on early prices tells that land, which still abounded with wolves and panthers, went from fifty shillings per hundred to $10 per hundred acres by 1854.

From Alexanders through Youngs, the individual family histories were written by family members and cover 240 pages. There are 358 photographs in this heritage book.

In 1987, over six hundred people shared their families' stories and genealogy and over four hundred pictures for *The Heritage of Old Buncombe County, Volume II*. The time and effort of the contributors and the editors, Doris Ward, Charles Biddix, and Roberta Hall, were well spent for this worth-while publication.

You can read about George Aden Burgin's trip in 1885 as he proceeded from Crooked Creek across the mountains on Broad River to Cooper's Station, now Swannanoa. In his travels, he described the Broad River Township settlement, the early settlers of Black Mountain and where they lived, including the Stepps, Doughertys, Walkers, and Burnetts.

Dorothy Rumbough Hussey delved into the history of Warm Springs/Hot Springs from the late 1700s where visitors drank the 98-102 degree mineral water to cure "gout, stiff joints, spinal disease, sciatica, lumbage." Bean Parsley Warren wrote the history of the Turnpike Hotel on the Buncombe-Haywood line, built by Smathers in 1866. Also included are church, hospital, and school histories.

The family histories start with Abbot and end with Young, including many references to the following families: Allen, Allison, Bailey, Brown, Buckner, Byrd, Carter, Clark, Cole, Davis, Edwards, Fisher, Freeman, Green, Hall, Hampton, Henderson, Holcombe, Honeycutt, Howell, Hunter, Jackson, Johnson, Jones, Lance, Miller, Moore, Morgan, Murray, Owenby, Parker, Patton, Penland, Ray, Reynolds, Roberts, Robinson, Rogers, Rutherford, Shepherd, Smith, Taylor, Thomas, Vance, Walker, Warren, Watts, West, Williams, Wilson.

The family histories are interesting even if they are not your own. Bruce Whitaker had researched the life of Elizabeth Patton, born in 1788, who married David Crockett, famous soldier who died at the Alamo. He told how David in 1816 did not care for the toll charge at Black Mountain on the road to get from Asheville to Old Fort. Therefore, David cleared his own path, once known as David Crockett's Bridle Trail, now Old Fort Road from Fairview to Broad River and then Old Fort. In Fairview in 1826, the Cooper family felt it important to add in their family Bible that "at age 15 Elizabeth (daughter of Adam Cooper) played the fiddle while David Crockett danced at the Cooper Home."

Sarah Beatty included a list made by Charles Mackey from Burke, now McDowell, County in April of 1865 of "things taken from him in Stoneman's raid" which included "two lively mares and bridles, one stack of fodder, one stack hay, 75 lbs. bacon, 40 bushels of corn, 20 gal. molasses, 30 chickens, robbed 4 stands of honey. ..."

The life of Robert Rice Reynolds, United States Senator from North Carolina, 1933-1945, Asheville lawyer, was written by Ruth C. Reynolds. Senator Bob was a colorful figure who "circled the globe more than a dozen times." His fifth wife was Evalyn W. McLean, owner of the famous Hope diamond.

If you have family from Old Buncombe, you are sure to learn more from these two volumes.

Many explanations have been suggested concerning why more people are becoming interested in their families histories, estimated as third largest hobby in the United States. Social scientists tell you that all people have a need to "belong" with a group for establishment of a sense of security. Medical scientists tell you that certain diseases have hereditary patterns and that you need to know your physical weaknesses so that you can guard against them. Regardless of scientific explanations, interest is growing, but most people who research their families seem to think it is just interesting and fun. These people, however, do try to preserve what they have worked so hard to discover.

Sometimes individuals do an enormous amount of collecting and preserving. It is hard to imagine what knowledge of early Buncombe County would have survived without Dr. Foster A. Sondley, born August 13, 1857 and died April 17, 1931. His collection of 100,000 books went to Pack Library, and his *The History of Buncombe County* has never been surpassed

Many organizations have been established in Western North Carolina for this preserving purpose. One is the Big Ivy Historical Society which was established in 1980. (Big Ivy is in the northwest section of Buncombe County.) Its members' goals include not only preserving early written records but also the early artifacts. Two of their initial project were completed by 1985: the pre-Civil War log cabin of Henry S. Carson was restored, and the compilation of local cemetery listings was published.

The cemetery book is not only a listing of over seven hundred tombstone inscriptions but also family identifications added. These members have researched for you, such as in the Morgan Hill Cemetery, "Fitzgerald, Minnie C., 1883-1954, wife of Fate L. Fitzgerald, daughter of James A. Carson." Most graves are from the mid-1800s to 1983. A few of the older ones are "Buckner, Benjamin, 1794-18 April 1845; He was a soldier in Jackson's War 1812; Carter, Solomon, 16 February 1791-27 July 1873, married Alvira Hopper March 6, 1817, son of Edward and Mary (Brown) Carter; Greenwood, Madison, 11 June 1812-8 July 1871, son of John and Mary (Hurst) Greenwood."

A detailed map of the Barnardsville area is included. Plus, with each cemetery, complete directions are given. The family names of Allen, Anders, Buckner, Burleson, Carson, Carter, Hensley, Maney, Morgan, Rice, Ray, Williams, and particularly Dillingham, abound.

For more information on this society or ordering this book, *Ivy Township Cemeteries*, write: Big Ivy Historical Society, Barnardsville, NC 28709.

Many of you waited for *The Heritage of Henderson County*, which was published in 1984. Although there was no county named **Henderson** until 1838, the people were in the coves and fields and on Mills River, Clear Creek, Mud Creek, Davidson River, Hooper's Creek (then Buncombe) by the late 1700s.

Early pictures are included such as one of the first county courthouse built in 1842, looking somewhat like a fort. A history of the schools and twenty-eight of the churches with pictures are depicted along with Civil War rosters of the Union and Confederate men of Henderson County. However, the focus of the book is on the people rather than the history of Henderson County. Over 500 family histories have been written and contributed by descendants of the early settlers.

J. Roland Freeman wrote about Ambrose Mills who was born in England in 1722, went to Virginia then to the frontiers of South Carolina with his wife Mourning Stone and children, including William Mills, born 1746. Here Ambrose's wife and all the children except William were killed by Indians. Amborse remarried and moved to Green River, which became Mills Spring, N. C. William Mills married Eleanor Morris and lived near his father. When Ambrose and William decided to remain loyal to the King of England during the Revolutionary War, Ambrose was made a colonel and William a major. In the Battle of King's Mountain, Ambrose and William were captured. William, even though severely wounded, escaped to a cave on Sugar Loaf Mountain, in present Henderson County; however, Ambrose was hanged near Rutherford. Going back to Mills Spring, William learned of this father's death and of their lands' being confiscated. He and his family went back toward his place of hiding and settled in what became Fruitland.

Another first family nearby on Clear Creek was the Edneys from Pasquotank County. Asa Edney, born 1772, and his brother, Samuel Edney, Jr., born 1768, were both circuit riding Methodist preachers and both married daughters of William Mills. Mrs. Joseph Guarding described Samuel, who first came in 1792, as riding a big horse, carrying a Bible, a Watts hymnal, and a pistol in his saddle bag.

Anne Clarke told of another early settler connected to the Mills: Merrimon Featherstone. He had served under the Mills in the Revolution and married Amborse Mill's daughter Amelia. They made their way to Clear Creek in the early 1800s.

The account of Robert Thomas, who was the first sheriff of Henderson County and who served until 1865 when he was killed by outlaws as he tried to extinguish the fire they had set to his home, was told by Bette Wilke.

The history of Henderson County is well related by the people who wrote of their ancestors. Numerous accounts are given for the earliest settlers. Included are Daniel Allen who settled in Mills River in 1803; Thomas Allison, Jr., in the Boylston area; Gordon Anderson, born 1783, an early Mills River settler; the Brittains in Mills River from the late 1700s; William Capps, Revolutionary soldier who was on Green River by 1799; the Drakes who settled in 1800 near the fort on Point Lookout; Nathaniel Robinson Freemen, 1775-1831, of Bearwallow, Gerton, and Hickory Nut Gorge; the Garrens of Hooper's Creek; the descendants of Ephraim Hart, 1787-1853, of Second Broad River; John Jones, Sr., who came with his brother Thomas to the Blue Ridge section in 1790; John Justis, 1741-1829, on Clear Creek by 1800; the Birds, the Cases, the Davises, the Hills, the Greers, Hamiltons, Hendersons, Jacksons,

Johnsons, Kings, Maxwells, McCalls, McCrarys, Merrells, Moores, Orrs, Paces, Pattersons, Reeces and Reeses, Shipmans, Stepps, Statons, Taylors, Williams, Youngs, and hundreds more. The address of the Genealogical Society of Henderson County is P. O. Box 2616, Hendersonville, NC 28739-2616.

Interest in family history keeps growing with more societies, more publications, and more available records. You hope the records are someplace to solve your "lost" ancestor problem, but the search does take perseverance and, often, the help of others.

Two genealogical societies were established in 1992: Jackson County, N. C., and Newberry County, S. C. Both of these are of interest to many people in Western North Carolina.

Jackson County was created in 1851 from Haywood and Macon Counties, which were both part of Buncombe County until the formation of Haywood in 1808. The newsletter "Journey through Jackson," January 1992, included cemetery listings, continued lists for death certificates, delayed birth certificates, and voter registration lists for 1902. The address for Jackson County Genealogical Society is P. O. Box 2108, Cullowhee, NC 28723.

The "Up Country" and the Ninety-Six District of South Carolina are very familiar to many family historians who had ancestors that came into Western North Carolina during the early formation of Buncombe County. **Newberry County** which was formed in 1808 has the land, probate, and court records from that area of Ninety-Six from 1776. The address is Old Newberry District Chapter, SCGS, Inc., P. O. Box 154, Newberry, SC 29108-0154.

The mountainous area that is now **Graham County** was remote and part of the Indian Nation until after 1838. Graham County Historical Society published its history in 1992.

The Heritage of Graham County relates much Indian history. President Andrew Jackson ordered the removal of the Indians to the West, although many of the Cherokee residents had aided him at the Battle of Horseshoe Bend in 1814. Even Chief Junaluska, who had saved Jackson's life, was taken to Oklahoma but walked back and was granted 337 acres of land around present Robbinsville. Fort Montgomery was built near Robbinsville to hold the Indians as they were rounded up by General Winfield Scott's 7,000 soldiers. About 13,000 Cherokees were placed in stockades. Other stockades in Western North Carolina were Fort Lindsey, Fort Scott, and Fort Hembree. The old Tatham Gap Road was built from Fort Montgomery to Fort Delaney as the first twelve miles of the "Trail of Tears."

The Snowbird Indians of Cheoah hid out, as did the Qualla Indians, and never left. Their descendants still live in Graham County. An account of Nancy Ward (about 1738-1824), Cherokee princess, who befriended the captured Mrs. William Bean and who warned the east Tennessee settlers that Indians were going to attack, is presented in the families' section. Many histories are included for the families of Adams, Aldridge, Carver, Crisp (descended from William, settling in 1835), Denton (descended from John, settling in 1879), Farr, Garland, Hooper (including Dr. Enos Hooper, first medical doctor in Cheoah), Hyde (descended from John, settling in 1838), Jenkins (moving into Stecoah about 1849), Millsaps, Orr, Phillips, Wiggins, Williams.

A detailed account of William Holland Thomas (1805-1893), who had been adopted into the Cherokee tribe and who tried to help the Cherokees receive payment for their land taken in 1835, is included. Thomas bought property for the Indians. He was also a colonel of a Cherokee brigade during the Civil War, known as Thomas's Legion. The last battles of the Civil War took place in Western North Carolina, and Bill Millsaps related that the "last surrender of the Civil War, east of the Mississippi, took place at Col. William H. Thomas's store at Cheoah on May 14, 1865." Confederate Major Stephen Whitaker in command of the First Battalion of Thomas's Legion came with Union soldiers to issue paroles.

Graham County was established in 1872 from Cherokee County. James Whitaker, Sr., (1779-1871) is credited as the one who persuaded the State Legislature to grant Cherokee's charter. Whitaker was a former Buncombe County State Representative before moving from Swannanoa by ox-cart in 1825 to the Little Tennessee into the Indian Nation.

The churches' and schools' histories are included. Church histories have two of the oldest as the Old Mother Church, formerly Cheoah Baptist Church organized in 1848, and Stecoah Baptist Church organized in 1849. Cemetery listings are included for the entire county. The one-room schools abounded in this mountainous section from the early 1800s; plus in 1876, one of Peabody Institutes was opened in the

Robbinsville Court House. Changes stated for this remote area in 1916 with the construction of the Cheoah Dam by the Tallasee Power Company. From 1916 to 1931, railroads were the only real transportation. The town of Robbinsville did not have electricity until 1927. The address for Graham County Historical Society is P. O. Box 985, Robbinsville, NC 28771.

To preserve the history of Macon, the **Macon County** Historical Society has republished two books. In 1987, the society published its 630-page *The Heritage of Macon County, North Carolina*, which consists of 82 pages of history and 732 family histories.

The historical section discusses the beginnings of the area in Western North Carolina which was later named Macon County. Before 1819, this territory had Indian towns with hundreds of people residing in them. These were not nomadic hunter-gatherers. Two of the larger towns were Nikwasi, now the site of Franklin, and Cowee.

Military expeditions from 1760-1781 created many hardships and deaths for many Indians, but their lives changed completely when settlers were allowed by the treaty of 1819. The historical section continues with accounts of the earliest settlers, using Captain Robert Love's survey map of 1820 to indicate their home sites. Histories for the towns include Highlands, Horse Cove, Nantahala, Brush Creek. Pictures date back to the late 1800s. Detailed accounts of Macon during the Civil War are discussed.

The families of Allen, Angel, Bryson, Cable, Conley, Crawford, Fouts, Gibson, Hall Higdon, Ledford, McConnell, McClure, McCoy, Moore, Patton, Penland, Shepherd, Siler, Slagle, Tallent, Waldroop, Welch, Wilson are referred to numerous times.

The Macon County Historical Society also republished the 1938 *Cherokee Indian Lore and Smoky Mountain Stories* by Margaret R. Siler. These stories of the past were told by earlier settlers with most of the happenings taking place before the mid-1800s. One story tells of Jacob Siler and William Britain, who in 1818 left Sandy Mush in Buncombe and went to explore a valley near the headwaters of the Little Tennessee River. They were confronted by Chief Santeela who ordered them to leave. However, the treaty for white settlers had been signed and more came. Later, Jacob Siler's brother William helped the Indians who sneaked away and back to their homeland while enroute to Oklahoma.

Siler deeded them several hundred acres, which became Sand Town. The "hunted" and the "hunting" tales are included about the Indians and the early settlers.

Both of these books are available from Macon County Historical Society, P. O. Box 822, Franklin, NC 28734.

Organized in 1975, the Macon County Historical Society publishes a newsletter, "Macon County Echoes." Letters from soldiers in the Civil War and travelers to "the West," official records, cemetery surveys, church records, plus early photographs are featured.

A genealogical and historical society was organized in **Swain County** in 1984. The Swain County Genealogical Society puts out a quality publication four times a year. "The Bone Rattler" is packed with what family historians are looking for in the western part of the state, particularly from Swain, Macon, Jackson, and Graham Counties.

The January 1987 edition, for example, contained the family history of George Addison Brooks, born 1844, and Matilda Herren Brooks, both from Pole Creek in southwest Buncombe, who moved to Swain in 1880. Other family histories include James Johnson and Sallie Ann McBryant, Joseph Alexander Wiggins who was a Methodist circuit rider from 1859-1861, and Benjamin Hyde. Public records in this edition are the 1850 Macon County census, Graham County marriages, Swain County marriages for 1889, and the delayed births of Swain before 1900.

Members of the Swain County Genealogical Society published *The Heritage of Swain County* in 1989. The purpose of the book was to record and preserve the early local history of communities, schools, churches, and families. The result of their work gives an interesting study of this far western North Carolina county.

Swain was not formed until 1871, but land was sold in sections from the Oconalufty River to near the mouth of Soco Creek by 1798. The land was then part of Buncombe, and much of it was bought by land speculators such as Waightstill Avery and Felix Walker. Most of the white settlers started moving in from 1802 through 1810. The deeds from 1808 would be in Haywood County when it was formed from Buncombe. Some of the earliest settlers were Robert Reed, Robert Turner, Jacob Mingus, John Beck, Thomas Dillard, Samuel and George Sherrill, John and Benjamin Hide, Michael Wikle, William Welch, Sr., Jesse Cornwell, Jeremiah Stillwell, James and Hugh Davidson, Jesse McFarland, George

Gunter, Robert Cain, Doras Felmet, William Wiggins.

The local history starts with the Cherokee Indian history when the tribe controlled 135,000 square miles of territory in 1721. By 1800, diseases, particularly smallpox, had caused the Indian population to dwindle and to reduce their strength. The Cherokees were removed to Oklahoma, and only because of the efforts of William H. Thomas, who established the Qualla Boundary, were there about 1,000 Cherokees left in Western North Carolina after 1838.

History is also included concerning how hundreds of Swain County residents lost their homelands to the Great Smoky Mountains National Park (which makes up sixty-five percent of Swain County) and to the Fontana Dam site. In the 1940s over 600 families had to be removed, and communities such as Bushnell, Judson, and Proctor disappeared. Fourteen churches were lost.

Stories are included of how early settlers had to be self-sufficient by making soap, running sawmills, building houses, running gristmills. From Abbott to Wyatt, 446 family histories are included, filled with numerous early pictures of people and of places, such as the Bushnell Hotel and Store, the Mingus House, Proctor High School.

Much family history is found for the following families: Burchfield, DeHart, Hall, Hughes, Leatherwood, Parris, Sherrill, Thomas, Thomasson, Welch, Wiggins, Woody. The address for the Swain County Genealogical Society is P. O. Box 267, Bryson City, NC 28713.

Buncombe County was formed in 1791 and included most of what is now Western North Carolina. As you are searching for family members in the federal censuses after the 1800 Buncombe one, the family may seem to have disappeared. Don't take it for granted that they moved at all. They may be exactly where they were but in a newly created county, such as Haywood County by the 1810 census, Henderson or Yancey by the 1840. Check closer to home before deciding these members ventured into Georgia for the gold rush or into Tennessee for cheap land. To the northeast from Asheville, Yancey County was formed in 1833 from Burke and Buncombe. Mitchell was formed in 1861 from Yancey, Watauga (formed 1849), Caldwell (formed 1841), Burke (formed 1777), and McDowell (formed 1842).

Then, Avery was not formed until 1911 from Mitchell, Caldwell, and Watauga. The census takers themselves seemed to have had a hard time keeping up with the county lines since in the 1870 census of Mitchell County, many people who were previously listed as living in Watauga County but who then lived in Mitchell were omitted.

The **Toe Valley** Genealogical Society was formed in August, 1989, to aid the people searching for ancestors and kin who lived in present Mitchell, Avery, and Yancey Counties. It publishes newsletters from March through November and meets in Spruce Pine.

This genealogical society has recently published the "1870 Federal Census, Mitchell County, North Carolina," which includes the listings for all ten existing townships. Part of Toe River and all of "Lynville" and Cranberry are now in Avery County.

The listings under each township include over eight hundred names of the "heads of Households," plus each person in the household, their ages, whether male or female, color where born, and occupation. The "where born" lists the states in all cases and for about one-third the exact county. For example, William Buchanan of Bakersville Township, who was 61 in 1870, a farmer, was born in Burke County; Margaret 56 was born in Greenville, S. C.; Barbery 36, Jasper N. 28, and Lurany 23 were all born in Yancey County. From studying the index, you can easily see numerous Averys in Tow River, McKinneys, Youngs, and Gouges maily in Bakersville, and Buchanans, Garlands, and Hughs all over the county. For more information, write to the Toe Valley Genealogical Society 491 Beaver Creek Road, Spruce Pine, NC 28777.

If you are doing research in North Carolina, one of the most valuable journals you can read for early information is the *North Carolina Genealogical Journal.* The emphasis in the journal is on primary source documents of N. C. which would be of interest to family historians. Other features are current book reviews and inquiries.

The primary source document information includes lists of such items as legal name changes, apprentice indentures, wills and administrations granted in N. C., divorce petitions, Revolutionary War service records and settlements. Articles include background information such as an explanation of the headright system in North Carolina. The material covered in the journals gives state-wide information, such as one in 1991 which covered cemetery inscription from the Methodist Church Cemetery at Mills River, the Britton Cemetery in Henderson County, and the Valley River Cemetery in Andrews. The book reviews are divided by

133

county publications, general genealogy, and family histories which have recently been published. The inquiries are indexed in each journal. Subscription to the journal, which is published four times a year, is available by becoming a member of the N. C. Genealogical Society. Copies of this journal since its start in January 1975 are available at Pack Library. The journals have been bound into volumes with a separate index included for each year. The former journal, *North Carolina Genealogy*, is also available in bound volumes.

Below are some addresses for genealogical societies in North Carolina. These are from "A Lot of Bunkum," Vol. XIII, #11, November 1992.

Alamance Co. Gen. Soc., P. O. Box 3052, Burlington, NC 27215-3052
Alexander Co. Gen. Soc., P. O. Box 241, Hiddenite, NC 28636
Alleghany His./Gen. Soc., P. O. Box 817, Sparta, NC 28675
Broad River Gen. Soc., P. O. Box 2261, Shelby, NC 28150
Burke County Gen. Soc., P. O. Box 661, Morganton, NC 28655
Caldwell Co. Gen. Soc., P. O. Box 2476, Lenior, NC 28645 Carolinas
Gen. Soc., % B. Small, 605 Craig St., Monroe, NC 28110
Coastal Gen. Soc., P. O. Box 1421, Swansboro, NC 28584
Cumberland Co. Gen. Soc., P. O. Box 53299, Fayetteville, NC 28305
Duplin Co. Hist. Soc., P. O. Box 130, Rose Hill, NC 28458
Guilford Co. Gen. Soc., P. O. Box 9693, Greensboro, NC 27429
Haywood Co. Gen. Soc., P. O. Box 1331, Waynesville, NC 28786
Henderson Co. Gen. Soc., P. O. Box 2616, Hendersonville, NC 28739-2616
Jackson Co. Gen. Soc., P. O. Box 2108, Cullowhee, NC 28723
Lee Co. Hist. Soc., P. O. Box 3216, Sanford, NC 27330-3216
Macon Co. Hist. Soc., P. O. Box 822, Franklin, NC 28734
Mecklenberg Co. Gen. Soc., P. O. 32453, Charlotte, NC 28232
Old Buncombe Co. Gen. Soc., P. O. Box 2122, Asheville, NC 28802
Old Tryon Gen. Soc., P. O. Box 938, Forest City, NC 28043
Rockingham Hist. Soc., P. O. Box 84, Wentworth, NC 27375
Southwestern NC Gen. Soc., 101 Blumethal, Murphy, NC 28906-3095
Stanly Co., Gen. Soc., P. O. Box 31, Albemarle, NC 28002-0031
Surry Co. Gen. Soc., P. O. Box 997, Dodson, NC 27017
Swain Co. Gen. Soc., P. O. Box 267, Bryson City, NC 28713

Wake County, Heritage, P. O. Box 17713, Raleigh, NC 27619
Wilkes Gen. Soc., P. O. Box 1629, North Wilkesboro, NC 28659

National Genealogical Society, 4527 Seventeenth St., North, Arlington, VA 22207
North Carolina Genealogical Society, P. O. Box 1492, Raleigh, NC 27602

Family Societies" Newsletters

Many family societies exist for surnames. These may just be for family reunion purposes, but many publish news- letters which have family information and inquiries.

Family historians are always searching for more information and do not mind spending money for new resources; however, sometimes it is hard to tell authentic helps from the ones put out by greedy opportunists. There are a few bogus family newsletters, quarterlies you can order supposedly devoted to your family. These are centered around a last name, but the information is all general from easily obtained information about names in books. The material on history is so general that it could fit most names.

Since there are also authentic family newsletters, it is hard to tell the difference from the notices. The best advice is for you to write to the publishers before subscribing, asking what particular person or persons the family is descended from, the nationality, what state or states are involved for these earlier ancestors. Finally, ask for a free copy of the cost for one of the latest copies. If you don't receive an answer, you'll know you have saved yourself some money. Prices vary from a high of $27 per year to a low of the publisher just taking donations. Most are about $10 per year.

A comprehensive listings of about 660 of these family associations are compiled yearly by Merle Ganier, 2108 Grace St., Fort Worth, TX 76111-2816, and is available for $8. This compilation includes the family name, address of periodical, how often published, and cost per year. (This booklet also contains lists of newspaper columnists who write genealogical columns.)

Elizabeth Bentley also has compiled a *Directory of Family Associations*, 1993-1994. [Genealogical Publishing: Baltimore] This source gives about 4,000 associations and costs about $30.

Yearly family reunions are growing across the country --in numbers and in attendance. For many it is a journey "back home" to a place that they have never lived. It is a journey rooted in curiosity. For many people who plan reunions, there is no better place than a site where some of the earliest ancestors lived. However, different ideas are being tried. A family reunion takes at least one dedicated person to get the plans started and to get others interested. The biggest problem is getting the "far flung" kin notified of the event. When first getting started, some small groups organize a family association to ensure continuation of their address compiling efforts.

A helpful magazine to study is *Reunions* which offers helpful ideas for the planning of all types of reunions: family, school, military. Reunion retreats are listed, including hotels, resorts, cruises, and ranches, that cater to large groups. Not only does the magazine discuss reunions but also includes genealogical information, lists family reunions, includes much information on adoption searches. The address is Reunions Magazine, Inc., P. O. Box 11727, Milwaukee, WI 53211-0727.

Many authentic and helpful family newsletters do exist. An interesting new one is *Frady Family Archives Newsletter*. People interested in Fradys should write Steve Frady, 4895 Cool Springs Drive, Reno, NV 89509. Don't let the address fool you; the second issue listed Fradys buried in New Salem Cemetery, Skyland, N. C. Plus, the main feature is about Charles and Nancy Frady who left North Carolina for Indiana and gives many Asheville/Buncombe connections.

An excellent local one is *Garren Goodies* concentrating on the Garren family of North Carolina. This is published by the Garren Heritage Association, 380 Corbly Drive #11, Hendersonville, NC 28739. Their publication has been published quarterly for six years.

A quarterly newsletter, "Gilliam Clan, Descendants of Epaphroditus Gilliam," is published by David L. Smith, 2330 Greenglade Rd., NE, Atlanta, GA 30345. This Epaphroditus Gilliam moved into Wilkes County, N. C., before 1790, and before 1800, he moved to Buncombe County. He moved on into Haywood County before moving into Tennessee.

In 1987, Sally Williams, 418 Hwy. 110 North, Whitehouse, TX 75791-1110, was publishing *Families of Yancey County, North Carolina*. She included family histories, marriage license for Mitchell and Yancey Counties, the 1900 Yancey County census, and free inquiries for people seeking information relating to Yancey County.

Nationality Organizations

If you have the nationality of your ancestor, you can join a nationality organization for more contacts with people who share your family name. For example, for the Swedish and Finnish settlers' descendants who landed on the Delaware River 350 years ago and formed the colony of New Sweden, there is the Swenson Swedish Research Center, Box 175, Augustana College, Rock Island, Illinois 61201. (You may be surprised how many Swedish names there are in the United States; for example, Swenson became Swanson and then Swan.) There is also a *Swedish American Genealogist* journal published by Swedish American Genealogist, P.O. Box 2186, Winter Park, FL 32790.

A Western North Carolina organization for the Scottish is the Scottish Tartans Society, P. O. Box 645, Highlands, NC 28741.

The National Archives does not have records of the Hessian soldiers who fought for the British during the Revolution. These records for Hessians are difficult to find, even though family tales are numerous about English-hired Germans who fought, liked America, deserted the English cause, and decided to stay here. Also, some of these Hessian soldiers were captured, and in 1782 were allowed by the American government to purchase their freedom by contracting or indenturing themselves to American citizens for three years upon payment of eighty dollars. Of the approximate 30,000 Hessians who came to America, about 6,000 deserted or were discharged and stayed in America.

Lorenz Schoenbacher, who later became Lawrence Shinpecker/Shinpock, deserted the British command on 25 April 1779, and traveling north from Charleston, S. C., he joined Patriot Thomas Sumter's state troops. He later ended up in North Carolina in 1784 where he bought land in Mecklenburg County and later raised a family in Montgomery County. Profiles of numerous Hession soldiers plus recruit lists are published in the *Journal of the Johannes Schwalm Historical Association*.

For more information, write: Kenneth S. Jones, P. O. Box 732, Worcester, MA 01613.

The more people you find and keep in touch with, the better your chances are of getting the right direction in finding the information you need. You wait for the key items that often will come in the mail for just your enclosing a pre-addressed, stamped envelope. Family history is a hobby that you cannot explain to people, often even to your own family who are not interested, but the strangers you hear from do want to help you. They know how hard it is to find an elusive ancestor, particularly one you may suspect had something to hide. They know you don't care what was hidden and only want to understand the ancestor more and to find his or her parents and where they were born. On and on backwards, it's unending.

CHAPTER 5. A COMPENDIUM OF WESTERN NORTH CAROLINA

Opportunity, desperation, adventure, curiosity -- no one knows all the reasons for the first settlers coming into Western North Carolina, but some of the earliest bid the Catawba neighbors "goodbye" and climbed the Blue Ridge Mountains going through Swannanoa Gap and to Bee Tree Creek into the "Swannanoa Settlement" in 1785.

These settlers saw buckeye and walnut trees measuring 13 feet around, thick cane along the river bands, bears, deer, wolves, buffaloes, at least the footprints of panthers along the sparkling creeks of the valleys.

The People

Most of the earliest settlers in the Swannanoa River section were Davidsons or the Davidson's kin. Along with Major William Davidson and his family came his sister Rachel and her husband John Alexander. John Alexander was an American Revolutionary soldier from Lincoln County. With John and Rachel was their son James Alexander, born December 23, 1756, and his wife Rhoda Cunningham, born October 13, 1763. James had also been a Patriot in the Revolution.

John Alexander, Rachel, and a son Thomas with Thomas's wife Elizabeth Davidson, a daughter of Major William Davidson, moved on to Tennessee about 1800. However, James and Rhoda Alexander stayed on Bee Tree Creek until their deaths in 1844 and 1848 and are buried at Piney Grove Cemetery, Presbyterian Church, Swannanoa. James and Rhoda's son, James Mitchell Alexander born on Bee Tree, May 22, 1793, married Nancy Foster, daughter of Captain Thomas Foster and Orra Sams, and in 1828 established the Alexander's Hotel on the French Broad 10 miles north of Asheville. Another son George C. Alexander, born September 10, 1790, married Elizabeth Foster and established Alexander Inn near the Swannanoa River in the 1820s.

Colonel Daniel Smith, who had organized the search for first settler Samuel Davidson's body, was married to Mary Davidson, daughter of Major William Davidson. They later moved from the "Swannanoa Settlement" to be one of the first settlers in present Asheville. Their son

James McConnell Smith married Polly Patton, daughter of Colonel John Patton, and built the Buck Hotel in Asheville.

A son of Major Davidson, Samuel Winslow Davidson, with wife Martha McRee continued to live on his father's farm on Bee Tree. Their daughter, Margaret Eliza, born 1805, married John Erwin Patton. Their son, Joseph Cruser Davidson, born 1806, married Sarah S. Foster, also a daughter of Thomas Foster, and stayed on at Bee Tree. Captain Thomas Foster, born October 14, 1774, in Virginia moved with his father, William Forster in 1786 to Buncombe. (Thomas did not spell his name with the "r.") Thomas married Orra Sams and lived on Sweeten Creek in what became Biltmore. He built the first bridge across a river in the county, on the Swannanoa near the influx of Sweeten Creek.

His father William Forster's home and farm were north of the Swannanoa River in the present Biltmore Avenue and Kenilworth area, Asheville. (Newton School and cemetery were on his property.) He was among the first settlers of present Asheville. William's sister Mary was the wife of John Burton, founder of Asheville.

Two brothers of Major William Davidson, James and Benjamin, came into Buncombe and settled. By 1790 they were buying land on the French Broad River and other property on what became Davidson River in present Transylvania County.

From the few in 1785 at the "Swannanoa Settlement," by 1800 Western North Carolina settlers numbered 5,815. Many of these settlers liked where they were since descendants of these first families are still here.

[This information was compiled from history and heritage books, deed studies, helpful people such as George Reynolds. You can find much material by local study and other people.]

The early settlers who came into Western North Carolina decided they wanted a county of their own. The settlers south of the Swannanoa River were in Rutherford County, while the settlers north of the Swannanoa River were in Burke County. Since these neighbors were physically isolated together by the mountains, they felt they had more in common with each other than they had with people in their eastern and southern county seats.

On December 17, 1791, Colonel David Vance, living in Reems Creek (present Weaverville) and representing Burke County in the House of

Commons, and Colonel William Davidson, living south of the Swannanoa near present Biltmore and representing Rutherford County in the House of Commons, introduced an act to create a new county. This act was ratified January 14, 1792, and the county became Buncombe. (Colonel William Davidson was a cousin to Major William Davidson of the early "Swannanoa Settlement.") Colonel David Vance, born about 1745 in Virginia, and grandfather of Zebulon Baird Vance, had gone into Reems Creek after the Revolutionary War from the Catawba River where he'd married Priscilla Brank. He'd been a Patriot in the Revolution and in the battles at Brandywine, Valley Forge, Kings Mountain. His son David Vance married Mira M. Baird and was the father of Zebulon Vance. Another of his sons was Dr. Robert Brank Vance who was wounded and died from a duel on November 5, 1827, with political rival Samuel Price Carson, son of Colonel John Carson, builder of the Carson House at Pleasant Gardens. The duel was held at Saluda Gap, South Carolina, since dueling was against the law in North Carolina. Colonel David Vance's daughter Elizabeth married Major Davidson's son William Mitchell Davidson.

On April 16, 1792, Buncombe County Court began and was held either at Colonel William Davidson's house or in his barn. Justices were James Davidson, David Vance (also Clerk of Court), William Whitson, William Davidson, James Alexander, James Brittain, Philip Hoodenpile. Justices of the Peace were Lambert Clayton and William Brittain; Thomas Davidson, entry officer of claims of land; John Patton, surveyor; John Davidson (son of James), registrar; John Dillard, ranger; Edmund Sams, coroner. [Buncombe County Archives' microfilm]

The names from this list of the first officials are still common in Western North Carolina except for Hoodenpyle. Research showed that the Hoodenpiles moved on. In the first federal census of Buncombe in 1800, Philip Hoodenpyle was between 26-45 years of age as was his wife; they had two males under 10, two females under 10, and two females 10-16 in their household.

Buncombe deed records show 18 listings for Philip Hoodenpile/Hoodenpyle from 1796-1812. (He perhaps bought land earlier that 1796, but before 1792 it would have been registered in Burke or Rutherford Counties.) The first listed was on September 15, 1796, for 600 acres on Big Pigeon River; the largest was on December 2, 1807, for

640 acres on the French Broad River. He was on the 1810 Buncombe census and, then in 1812 with the last deed listed as selling, disappeared from Western North Carolina records.

Joy Bryant wrote in *The Heritage of Buncombe County* that his name was Phillip Gijaberti Hoodenpyle, being born 1756 in Amsterdam, Holland, and emigrating to Philadelphia in 1780 with his wife and son. His wife and son later returned to Holland; and after their divorce, he married Jane Ronceville and moved to Buncombe. At Hot Springs he had a pub and ferry on the French Broad River. He and his family went to Pikeville, Tennessee, where he died in 1833.

All settlers in Western North Carolina could not "stay put"; the mountainous sections had limited farming lands. Moreover, the ones who lived on the Buncombe Turnpike heard of vast land waiting for settlers in Tennessee, Arkansas, Texas, as they talked with families on wagons loaded with belongings, moving westward. The restless, adventurers not through searching, moved on from Buncombe.

While searching for family history, you sometimes happen upon old artifacts that give insight about your ancestors.

Daniel Asbury Justus, born 1816, died 1908 in Henderson County, had written his name in an 1876 book by John King. M. D., entitled *American Dispensatory*, published in Cincinnati. Dr. King called himself a liberal and progressive physician of the American Eclectic group who questioned many of the "Old School Practice" ideas from Europe. He encouraged physicians and "pharmaceutists" to study the medicinal value of American plants.

He wrote of the curative powers of aloe plants when the gel was applied to a blistered surface, which many people feel is a new discovery, along with the oldtime uses of leeches. The leech, used as a substitute for general "blood-letting" among children and delicate adults and for drawing bruises, local inflammations, tumors, was described as having three jaws with 69 to 90 sharp teeth in each. The one- to six-inch leech pierced the skin with a "sawing motion, so as to present three incisions meeting at a common center." After the leech became filled with blood in about fifteen minutes, it had drawn "about a drachma and a half" (about one-fifth of an ounce). The leech was made to "let go" by dropping a little salt upon it. How to keep leeches alive was discussed. They should be placed in uncrowded glass jars with loose moss and pebbles and clean rainwater, which should be changed every day.

A weak solution of vinegar was prescribed as a cooling drink for fevers. "Lint" dipped in a solution made from the leaves and flowers of "marygolds," steeped in alcohol or boiling water, was applied to surgery wounds to prevent gangrene and tetanus. The numerous wildflowers in Western North Carolina were valuable. A solution made from the leaves of Trailing Arbutus was drunk for urinary difficulties, and bloodroot was stated to be a "sedative to the heart." (Many warnings were included on the usage of bloodroot, including the signs of a poisonous dose.)

A section in the book included methods for collecting and preserving plants. Another section included the composition of the principal mineral waters in well-known springs. The Chabybeate waters contained iron and were good for people with anemia. "Sulpherted waters are impregnated with sulphureted hydrogen, in consequence of which they have an odor resembling that of rotten eggs." Chronic rheumatism was stated to be helped by drinking from sulfur springs.

Since there was a scarcity of doctors in these remote areas of Western North Carolina, many early settlers relied on their own "means" to treat their families and themselves. Daniel Justus had written in the back of the book notes and page numbers he must have referred to often, such as "wild yams good for colic, page 335." Page 335 has a description of the plant, its history, properties and uses: "an antispasmodic . . . cures bilious colic." The roots were dried, pulverized, dissolved in water or alcohol. Two- to four-fluid ounces of the solution were given every half-hour.

Daniel had also written down several remedies for "chronic affection of the kidneys," including Queen of the Meadow roots. Not only is it inspiring to hold a leather-covered book that a great-great grandfather owned, but also with a medical book and notes, plus feather markers inserted, it can give a clue to the health problems of the family.

By finding artifacts, you can realize that early family members were real people instead of just names on an ancestor chart.

You probably thought you'd heard everything about Zebulon Baird Vance, Jr., (1830-1890), renowned governor of North Carolina and United States senator, but Robert Grayson, a researcher from Illinois, wrote about a Thomas Dula, who is better know by the famous song as Tom

Dooley; and there is another Zebulon Vance tale.

Tom Dula was supposedly in Vance's CSA 16th Regiment of North Carolina during the Civil War. Tom was arrested early in 1866 for the stabbing death of Lira Foster. The trial was set for the May term, 1866, in Wilkesboro, but Tom Dula's lawyer, Zebulon Vance, got a change of venue from Wilkes County to Statesville in Iredell County for the fall term of 1866. Tom Dula was found guilty, but Vance did not give up and appealed the case to the Supreme Court. Even Vance could not save Tom Dula though, and he was hanged in Statesville.

If you recall the song, you'll remember that a Grayson is credited for keeping Tom Dooley from fleeing to Tennessee. The Grayson family says this is Colonel James William Grayson (1833-1901) who was responsible for his capture.

The well-known Davy Crockett has been of continuing interest to people in Western North Carolina because of his pioneer/Alamo fame and because he was in this area as an in-law to the early Patton family. He married as his second wife Elizabeth Patton, daughter of Robert and Rebecca Patton who lived on the Swannanoa River as early as 1780 and owned a thousand acres near present Swannanoa, N. C. A memorial erected by the DAR to Elizabeth Patton on the grounds of the Swannanoa School, within a short distance from where she lived, states, "Elizabeth Patton Crockett wife of Colonel David Crockett, born 5-22-1788 in Swannanoa Valley, Buncombe County, N. C. Died 1-31-1860 in Hood County, Texas."

While in this area as has been mentioned before, David Crockett in 1816 was one who helped blaze a trail from Fairview to Old Fort after a toll charge was put on the road to Old Fort from Black Mountain.

David Crockett who was a congressman from West Tennessee in 1826 was defeated for reelection in 1834. Many said this was because of his unpopular stand against removing the Cherokee Indians to Oklahoma. He "removed" himself to Texas where he and his nephew William Patton died defending Texas against the Mexicans in the Battle of the Alamo on March 6, 1836.

Sometimes you see how small the world really is when it comes to interrelationships of families. On May 4, 1990, at the end of the *20/20* segment of "Whatever Happened to Fess Parker," Hugh Downs mentioned that he was related to Davy Crockett. The family historian must know "How kin?" In a correspondence, Mr. Downs stated: "As I understand it, an ancestor of Davy's and mine, Gabriel Gustave Crocketagni was born in France on a date unknown to me. His son, Antoine Dessaure de Crocketagni, born 10 July 1643 fled France for religious reasons, landed in Ireland and shortened his name to Crockett. His son Robert Watkins Crockett, Jr., had a son, Robert Watkins Crockett, Jr., who was the father of Joseph Lois Crockett.

"This man is an ancestor of mine and the grandfather of Davy Crockett. One of his sons, John Crockett married Rebecca Hawkins and they were the parents of Davy Crockett of Alamo fame. John Crockett's brother, James Crockett married Martha Gay and they were the parents of Jane Crockett from whom I'm descended in the following way: Jane Crockett married Alexander Black who was born 14 October 1765. His son James Black was born 8 February 1798 in Clark County, Kentucky, was the father of Susan Black born 24 October 1835 in Champagne County, Ohio. Susan married John Staub and they were the parents of Emma Staub, my paternal grandmother. Emma was born in Champagne County right at the end of the Civil War and married Sherman Downs, whose son Milton Downs was my father."

In summary, Hugh Down's 5-great grandfather, James Crockett, was a brother to Davy Crockett's father John Crockett. Hugh Downs is a first cousin, five times removed to Davy Crockett.

People ask why you are interested in old, dry genealogy, and you wonder how anyone could not be interested in the woven intricacies of people in families. Your kin are "out there," but you have to find them.

For an interesting book on how to figure out what to call all your different kin, there was a 1990 publication *Kinship: It"s All Relative* by Jackie Arnold [Genealogical Publishing: Baltimore]. She explains that first cousins are relatives who share one set of grandparents; second cousins share one set of great-grandparents; third cousins share one set of great-great grandparents. If your first cousin has children, they are your first cousins, once removed. The term "double first cousins" means brothers or sisters married brothers or sisters; the resulting children have the same two sets of grandparents.

Thomas Wolfe is one of Asheville's most recognizable names because of his fame as an American novelist. By researching, you can find out much about him. Visiting the Wolfe family plot at Riverside Cemetery in Asheville., you can see the markers "Tom Wolfe, s/o W. O. and Julia E. Wolfe b. Oct. 3, 1900 d. Sept. 15, 1938, Beloved American author"; "W. O. Wolfe b. Gettysburg, Pa., Apr. 10, 1851 d. June 20, 1922"; "Julia E. Wolfe b. Feb. 16, 1860 d. Dec. 7, 1945, Mother of five sons and three daughters." The other Wolfe markers are for Frank, Grover, Ben, Leslie, Mabel, Fred.

Visiting the Registrar of Deeds' office in Buncombe County, you can find that on January 14, 1885, W. O. Wolfe, age 33, married Julia E. Westall, age 24. The death indexes say William Oliver Wolfe whose father was Jacob Wolfe died June 20, 1922. To get a copy of Thomas Wolfe's death certificate, you would write the Maryland State Archives since Thomas Wolfe died in Baltimore. Visiting a library, you could read on microfilm the newspapers' coverage of his death. You can read local history books and find out more about his family. In addition with Thomas Wolfe, you can read biographies about him. Bernard DeVoto said, "his attempt [was] to describe the dark and nameless fury of the million-footed life swarming in his dark and unknown soul." John Peale Bishop said his aim "was to set down America." Finally, you can read the books he wrote. When you get through reading, you probably know more about Thomas Wolfe than you know about your own parents.

Have you ever asked or did you ask your parents what they valued more than anything else? What were their earliest memories? What were their greatest disappointments in life? What was the best time, the worst time? What did they want to be when they "grew up"? You search so hard and spend your time and money to find all the names, places, and dates for those ancestors "back there," but you need to make sure you get the inward feelings of the ones who are living. The majority of your great-great-great -grandchildren will find these feelings more fascinating than your pedigree charts that take up more of your time. You need to take time from your "way back" search to start finding the dreams and feelings of your people since these may tell you more about yourself than their nationalities. Thomas Wolfe's "look homeward" advice was good.

The Schools

Many schools were set up in Western North Carolina from the earliest settlements. By December 5, 1889, *The Asheville Democrat* reported that every district in the county had some sort of school house. "Several of these houses are not comfortable, while a large majority if they were furnished with desks and other school furniture, would be considered very good school buildings." The article pointed out that the buildings were 24 feet wide and 40 feet long by 12 feet high and that the entire cost of each building was $330. The article also added that the money for these was hard to get and "that the bolt out of which so many garments must be cut is entirely too small."

Ancestors from Western North Carolina will tell you they don't know how many years of schooling they had. This isn't surprising since even as late as the early 1900s, many communities had a school only the number of months they could afford to pay a teacher, such as three months free plus longer for the ones who could pay tuition of about fifty cents a month. Professor A. C. Reynolds, Superintendent of Buncombe County Schools in 1927 said that in 1825 a fund was set aside for starting a school system in North Carolina, but it was not until 1837 that the system materialized. In 1868 a four months school was established, and in 1918 a six months' course was the standard for many schools. High schools were not established until 1907. [*Asheville Times*, December 11, 1927]

In these early days, the school day was not organized as it is today because all grades were in the same room. A one-room school, called Lance School, was established in the late 1800s in Black Mountain. In 1984, a former student of Lance School, Grace Lance Justus, described what attending a one-teacher school, with about fifty students who ranged in age from 5 to 20 years of age, was like.

"The school was on the top of a hill. The oblong structure had windows on either side and was standing on brick pillars. The steps led up to the front entrance through the big door, with a space on either side for coats and wraps. The girls hung theirs to the right, the boys theirs to the left.

"A wide walk was down the center of the teacher's desk which sat beside the woodstove. On both sides of the walk were long benches with a top for writing and books. About five students sat at each bench. There was a small space between the ends of the benches and the window walls.

"Beginning on the front benches, the youngest children would sit near the teacher and the other students would be in grade order behind them. The youngest children were taught first, but all stayed until 3 o'clock. The teacher always had a long switch to use for discipline.

"Recess was a great time. Hide and seek was played, the brick pillars furnished a good hiding place. Also there was jump rope and a baseball field at the foot of the hill. Only the boys played baseball. A large forked tree furnished the place for a large log used as a seesaw; sometimes one end would hit the ground hard enough to bounce some off the opposite end.

"Friday afternoons were the times for recitation (assigned memory work to recite) and spelling matches. Students were lined up on the area between the benches and the windows. The spelling match was a show-off time or a time to be embarrassed, depending on how well the student studied." In the fall of 1921, consolidation had taken place. The Lance School closed, and a scared bunch of students were bussed to the Black Mountain School. "The first bus for these students was a long-bed truck with an added top and benches built on both sides with an open back."

Who knows how much is handed down indirectly from our parents and grandparents. The influence of their childhoods and adulthoods must make a difference in the expressions we use, the things we value in life. The schools they attended probably made a difference in our lives later.

In the mid-1800s in Western North Carolina, most people only imagine the one-room schools similar to the one previously described. However, there actually was a college for women in Asheville founded in 1842, the one College Street was named for. By 1890, eight thousand young women from twenty-three states had been graduated from this school.

The Asheville Female College was "the first founded of the educational institutions in the western part of the state." [*Asheville Daily Citizen*, 1895, Thanksgiving Day] This college was first started as an academy at the corner of Patton Avenue and Church Streets before moving to Oak Street.

In 1856, its turreted four-story, 58-room dormitory had been built at the corner of Woodfin and Oak Streets. In the summer of 1850, a father kept a diary that was published in the *Asheville Citizen*, November 6, 1927. He described his seven-day carriage journey from Virginia to bring his daughter to the Asheville Female College. They progressed at about twenty miles a day where they went through Bristol, Virginia, and into Bloutville, Tennessee, where he set out early and had to pay a toll of 75 cents to go across a three-mile stretch of road across Paint Rock Mountain before reaching the French Broad River. He thought this "one of the wildest and most picturesque regions" he'd ever seen. "The River itself is unlike any other in the U. S. The entire bed of it leaping and rushing through thin fissures, in an almost continued succession of rapids." As he approached Asheville, three miles away, he could see the "cupola and steeple of the Court House." He described the town as appearing to be "built on a number of short hills in a sort of cove formed by the surrounding mountains." He described the "Toute Ensemble" as a "picture of loveliness."

The main school building was relocated and on Oak Street between Woodfin and College Streets. This four-story building from an 1890 photograph looked like part of a modern college campus. Tuition at the college ranged from $12 to $29 plus $75 for boarding for twenty weeks. John Waldroop shared his mother's report card addressed to Dr. J. M. Lyle on December 1, 1887, while she was taking such courses as World Analysis, Algebra, Physiology, Instrumental Music, Latin. Mary Lyle was a senior with out-of-town students from as far away as Nebraska and New York to as close as the Cherokee Indian reservation.

An historical article in the *Asheville Times* on May 23, 1937, stated that when the students "appeared in public, they were required to wear white Jaconet dresses in the summer, with a plain straw bonnet or hat trimmed with blue lute string ribbon. In winter a Mazarine blue worsted dress. The wearing of jewelry was forbidden."

By 1888, the dormitory was sold and made into the Oake Hotel; by 1908, it was redone for the Cherokee Inn. Briefly in the early 1920s, it was a YMCA before being sold in 1924 to be torn down for the First Baptist Church.

By 1901, the college had closed, and the school building became Asheville High School until it was torn down in 1916 and became the site for David Millard High School.

Much that influenced our ancestors took place in Western North

Carolina. The information you are curious about often is not difficult to find. Check the vertical files for the topic you are interested in at Pack Library.

About a half-mile from the town of Black Mountain, on Hwy. 70 west, the state of North Carolina put up a historical marker about the well-known Black Mountain College. However, exactly where the sign is located was the southern border of the property of an earlier university: Holman Christian University. It was established in March of 1905 and was given the "regular power of a University by a special act of Legislature," according to the 1906 college catalog.

The school was named for Mrs. Sarah A. Holman, a generous benefactor. The courses offered at this University included English, Mathematics, Greek, Latin, German, French, Spanish, Italian, Hebrew, music, art, Bible study, philosophy, law. Plus, there were a primary department and a preparatory school. The twelve faculty members included the president Dr. James Coggins; Honorable Foster A. Sondley, dean of the law school; Yatta Minachuchi, a Japanese scholar from Yale College, who understood eight languages; and Mrs. Lenora Gaskins, teaching languages and elocution, who, according to the college catalog, was "born and reared here in the mountains, surrounded with the rhododendron and ivy, and under a circle of heavens jeweled with the most brilliant stars . . .."

By 1906, the two-and-a-half story 40 by 80 feet Young Ladies' Building was completed for six class rooms. dining room and kitchen, and rooms for over seventy girls. This was the first building on the campus which was to include a main university building and a boys' dormitory with a gymnasium. Cottages were available for the boys in 1906. The campus of fifty acres had views "of the towering blue Mount Mitchell . . . beautiful Black Mountain . . . valley of the charming Swannanoa River." The campus included land to the Asheville Avenue (now Highway 70), north to "Chicago Avenue," and West and East College Streets.

The University, according to the catalog, was also selling 50 residence lots 100 by 200 feet "only to the best people" for $50 and up in the surrounding area. The tuition for college was $40 for nine months with rooms being $1.50 per month and meals $6 to $8 per month.

The aim of Holman Christian University was to "make possible for every ambitious boy and girl, in this part of the country, to get an education, and we believe we have solved the problems! We are in the country, away from the evil influence of the city life . . . no saloon within 12 miles . . . and no young man will be registered who comes with a cigar or cigarette advertising his habits . . . The boys and girls will never under any 0.circumstances be associated together without the presence of a teacher!"

Holman Christian University obviously did not develop the way the founders had imagined. There is a possibility that it went bankrupt since by 1923 the lot where the Black Mountain College sign is located had been sold by the Central Bank and Trust. The only current reminder that the school was ever there is on the street names of West College and East College. A list of students was not found, but if a relative ever mentioned attending this college, it did exist.

Religion

Religious beliefs came with the individual people who entered the area. The Presbyterians, the Methodists, the Baptists built churches early in their communities. However, many families have a story that a great-great-grandfather was a Quaker, but no matter how hard you search, there were no early Quaker meeting houses here. There is a reason. If the story is true, you may be surprised though at what records are available for research. The Quakers were originally "The Religious Society of Friends" and the inspiration of George Fox, an Englishman, who began his preaching in 1644. Fox's belief was that "Christ speaks directly to each human soul who seeks him"; and that since man had an "Inner Light," he did not need a minister to interpret God for him. The term "Quaker" was first a name given by mockers either because Fox told his followers they would "Tremble at the Word of the Lord" or from the Quaker's habit of quivering with religious emotion.

Quakers were persecuted in England and forbidden in New England by the Puritans who decided Quakers worshipped the devil. The Puritans would expel any Quakers, and in 1657 passed a law that any who returned would have an ear cut off and sent off again. When Charles II of England granted a proprietorship in 1681 to William Penn for the present states of Pennsylvania and Delaware, the Quakers had a refuge.

However, from the late 1600s, many Quakers moved from Pennsylvania, south to Virginia, the Carolinas, and Georgia to spread their religion and to buy cheap land. Quakers were widespread in these states, but most left the South from 1795-1820 to go westward or northwestward, particularly into Ohio and Indiana. This exodus from the South was caused by the Quakers' opposition to slavery. The individual members who owned slaves and would not free them were banished from the Quakers.

A 1987 book, *Our Quaker Ancestors*, written by Ellen and David Berry is a "how-to" publication for beginners in Quaker research. [Genealogical Publishing: Baltimore] The book is intended as a guide for searching records from the mid-1600s to 1850. The authors point out that most family history is found in the monthly meeting records and discuss where these are found.

Before 1790, no location such as census records can guide you to find where an ancestor lived; therefore, they suggest you study Hinshaw's *Encyclopedia of American Quaker Genealogy*. (Pack Library has Hinshaw's volumes.)

Basically, you must find the monthly meeting place where your ancestor attended and then search the unindexed original records for yourself in Quaker repositories. The monthly meeting records contain marriages with lists of all present, lists of births and birth dates, records of disowned and why, such as lying, keeping liquor in the home, fighting, marrying outside the faith, and certificates of removal. These certificates of removal are valuable because they tell when a family was leaving the meeting house and where they were going. Sometimes these certificates showed where the immigrant family came from, such as Wales, Ireland, England, and Barbados. The book tells which records are in published form and where the original records may be found. The largest collection is at Swarthmore College in Pennsylvania, but North Carolina has the extensive Guilford College records in Greensboro, which begin in 1680 from the oldest North Carolina records.

In North Carolina, two Quaker Meeting Houses had been established in the late 1600s and at least fifteen more during the 1700s. Four principal centers of Quakerism arose in South Carolina in the mid-1700s, and two in Tennessee in the late 1700s. As mentioned previously, many Quakers left the South and went to the midwest because of their religious beliefs. William Heiss wrote in *Quakers in the South Carolina Back County*, (Indiana

Quaker Records), that the Quakers "soon set their faces against " slavery and declared it was "irreligious." If members who owned slaves did not free them, the members were disowned. He further related that between 1800 and 1804, the Friends at Bush River, S. C., were warned by Zachary Dicks, a traveling Quaker preacher, "to come out from slavery." By 1807, most of this Quaker population moved.

From *Religions of America*, Leo Rosten stated that in the mid-1600s, Quakers in England suffered imprisonment, mob violence, loss of property, and severe persecutions. In Massachusetts, they were banished or put to death by Puritans. (The Puritans wanted religious freedom but only for themselves.) Rhode Island and Pennsylvania were their early sanctuaries -- and, of course, from other records, North Carolina. The Quakers, believing that God can be approached and experienced by the individual directly without priest or preacher, opposed the rituals of the Church of England. The Puritans opposed the early Quakers because of the Quakers' belief that man was born good -- and that they were not Puritans.

William Wade Hinshaw did the most intensive compiling of the Quaker records. His *Encyclopedia of American Quaker Genealogy*, Volume I, covers from 1680-1920s. This volume includes all the existing records for North Carolina, upper South Carolina, and eastern Tennessee. He stated that from Bush River in South Carolina between 1802 and 1807 "more than one hundred certificates of removal were issued, most of them for families" going to Indiana. The membership in Bush River was depleted so that the Meeting House property was sold in 1808.

Since Quakers did not have their vital records recorded in civil offices until 1850., Hinshaw's records are very valuable for researchers. Since serving in the militia or other armed forces was a deviation from the Quaker's belief, from 1776-1882, twenty-one men from Bush River were dismissed for "taking up arms.and going forth in a warlike manner." About a hundred pages are recorded in this volume from the Cane Creek Monthly Meeting which was in the large county of Orange, North Carolina. (Eleven counties in this central area were formed from Orange or parts of it.) These records show many members as being born in Virginia, Pennsylvania, or Maryland. A typical marriage entry is Francis Wilkinson, son of Thomas and Catherine, born March 21, 1736, Entrom County, Ireland, married Elizabeth, daughter of John and Ann Magnume, born March 26, 1739, Dery County, Ireland. A record of their 12 children, born from 1763-1781 in Orange County, are listed.

The Cemeteries

While driving by large corn fields, you may notice a small irregularly shaped grove of trees, usually including some cedars, overgrown with brambles, honeysuckle, and poison oak, sitting in the field. You may be looking at an old abandoned family burial ground.

How many of these are scattered throughout North Carolina is anyone's guess, and perhaps the buried could not find a more peaceful site. However, many people wish they knew where these early ancestors were buried so they could show their "respects." Since these grave sites are by far more different from the more popular, manicured resting places, you should visit these in winter to avoid snakes and yellow jackets hidden in the periwindle. The trip is worth it since you step into another time. In earlier times many families took care of their burials on their own property, not foreseeing the mobility of the next generations in which land quickly passes into lots from one unrelated family to another.

One family burial site is in a corn field on Howard Gap Road, one mile on the right from Fletcher, N. C. The cedar trees are there, but mainly it is a circle of brambles. After crawling in, you see three marked grave sites; there may be more graves there of course. Upon close inspection two markers, overturned on slabs of granite covering the whole graves, have readable names: John Fletcher 1783-187_; Martha Fletcher, death date appears to be 1854. The guide to the nondescript field, George Fletcher Frady, said the old home site of John Fletcher was nearby. [The town is names Fletcher, but an early Fletcher burial place lies in disrepair.]

Another circle of scrubby oak and locust trees covers about one-half acre in a field in the Swannanoa Valley. The Black Mountains overlook it from miles away while Grovestone Company lies between the cemetery and the North Fork River. This is the Ingram Family Cemetery and has been taken better care of by descendants. Stepping from the open field through the brambles and onto a mass of periwinkle-covered ground, you can see numerous rock stones. It is a peaceful environment. In 1983 there were twelve engraved stones in readable condition: Roda M.

154

Walker, March 23, 1852-December 2, 1875; Martha L., daut. of J. W. and S. Walker, Feb. 25, 1862-Oct. 12, 1862; William H. Burnett, Co. K, 60 NC INF CSA; William A. Burnett, Co. K, 11 NC INF CSA; (These two are perhaps memorial stones only.) Nancy S. wife of Wesley Goodson, B. June 1, 1832; Harriet J. Stepp, Sept. 13, 1834-Mar. 28, 1864; Colbey Stepp, Oct. 5, 1804-Apr. 21, 1862; Sarah, wife of Colbey Stepp, Nov. 29, 1808-Feb. 5, 1889; Infant daut. of W. and S. Goodson, b. and d. Feb. 18, 1863; Sarah M. daut. of W. and S. Goodson, July 20, 1861-Jan 20, 1862; S. M. Hemphill, June 12, 1816-Sept. 18, 1873; Sarah, wife of S. M. Hemphill, Mar. 6, 1820-Aug. 23, 1859. You can be sure the Lewis Ingram, an early settler, family is there in unmarked graves.

A family cemetery wasn't a bad choice for our ancestors unless they happened to put it in a place that stood in the way of "progress."

A Lance family cemetery is obscured by numerous houses, yards, and driveways on the south end of Royal Pines Mountain in the Skyland off Sweeten Creek Road. The field stones have been removed with civilized encroachment, and only two old stone pillars off Royal Pines Drive show the general direction. Peter and Flora Lance who first bought land in Buncombe in 1800 and son John Lance and wife Mary who first bought land in 1798 are buried there along with an indeterminable number of early Lances.

Next to Arden Presbyterian Church, Hwy. 25, Skyland, was a peaceful patch of woods that was once known as the Hunter Cemetery. No Hunter graves are marked, but they must be there somewhere among the trees. Pine and leaf-covered woods are contrasted by the vandalized stones of the four marked graves: John M. Frady, Oct. 20, 1841-July, 1906; Alice Frady, 1854-Aug. 3, 1888; George Lindsey, 1850-1913; Martha Lindsey, 1832-1928. Martha and John were the children of Lewis Frady, born 1804.

These must be related to the Hunters in some way. This cemetery stood in the way of progress, and most of it now is a asphalt parking area for the Presbyterian Church. John Hunter, who lived on this property, died in Union County, Georgia, in 1848.

Sometimes an unusual situation occurs concerning even a church cemetery. Mr. R. N. McCray bought a lot on Burge Mountain Road, Henderson County, and discovered an overgrown fenced burial plot on it. Two headstones had decipherable names: Joseph Garren, Aug. 14,

1842-July 3, 1883; Mary Garren, July 6, 1818-June 13, 1892. Mr. McCray found this was once the Brown's Chapel Cemetery and feels there may be unmarked graves on his property also. He explained, "The chapel stood to the west of the plot in the middle of what is now Burge Mountain Road. It was built on land donated by the Featherstone property and reverted back to them when the church was terminated early in this century."

Most cemeteries do tell "tales" to the ones who take the time to meander through the markers. Some are sad tales such as seeing three babies' graves all in a row, all with the same parents, with death dates, 1898, 1899, 1901, telling of a couple who had children only for each to die from three-months to two years old. You see unmarked field stones only telling that someone was buried but now with name and dates lost. You see bare spots among a crowd of gravemarkers and know that some are there even without an unmarked stone. Normally, these are left undisturbed, but sometimes an unusual event forces an unusual marker.

At Mountain View Baptist Church Cemetery near Black Mountain is an engraved stone that states, "Forty Known Only to God, 1884-1950." From this cemetery, you have a view of the North Fork Valley and the Asheville watershed. The watershed was the reason these forty unknowns were uncovered one-by-one and placed in their new communal grave.

The creeks from the Black Mountains halt their flow in the reservoir before the overflow goes into what is still known as the North Fork River until it merges with Flat Creek between the towns of Black Mountain and Swannanoa to become Swannanoa River.

The original Mountain View Baptist Church, which was first named United Baptist Church of Christ, was established in 1838. Its location was called "Wallace Pond" and was on the North Fork River itself beside the wagon road to Mt. Mitchell. The minister in the late 1800s was T. K. Brown. Then, in 1898, the second church was built to the east of the river on a hillside with the name changed to Mountain View. This structure burned in 1940, but the church was rebuilt of native stone on the same site. However, by 1951, the proposed Asheville watershed showed the location of the church and cemetery as underwater.

The Church agreed to a new site overlooking the valley and high above the water, but over 250 graves and markers had to be moved, along with the found unmarked ones. The early settlers of North Fork

Valley included the names Walker, Burnett, Patton, Stepp, Bartlett, Powers; some of these are surely included in the "Forty Known Only to God."

At Montmorenci Methodist Church in Candler is a different type of marker on land donated by W. G. Candler. This marker was erected January 1, 1888, by Confederate soldiers of the Hominy Creek section. Company I of the 25th NC Volunteers was organized at Hominy Creek Baptist Church on July 22, 1861. The monument has a long list of names engraved from the muster roll, including Allens, Alexanders, Gudgers, Curtises, Knights, Luthers, Meaces, Millers, Pendlands, Warrens, Wises, and Youngs. The marker further states that this company's involvements included such battle sites as Whiteoak Swamp, Malvern Hills, Fredricksburg, before surrendering at Appomatox on April 9, 1865. The Captain of this company was Augustus B. Thrash, December 6, 1829-November 20, 1906, whose grave marker in the adjoining cemetery says that he was a Confederate soldier for three years and ten months.

The land for the original Montmorenci Church was deeded in 1857 from Walton Stines to trustees Samuel Gudger, Burton Cathey, and J. Curtis for $5 for one and a half acres.

One of the oldest cemeteries in Western North Carolina, established at least by 1837, is located beside Tabernacle United Methodist Church near Black Mountain. (Tabernacle is across the road from the large Mountain View Cemetery.) The first piece of land for this church was donated by the Kyle family for the Tabernacle Methodist Meeting House and School, and next to the church a cemetery was established.

The largest stone was purchased by Mrs. Vanderbilt for the Walker sisters, Emma Marian, born October 4, 1899, and Charlotte M., born April 4, 1890. These sisters were nursing students and drowned in the flood at Biltmore on July 16, 1916. Another large grave marker in the cemetery is a pink grave-covering stone, marked Robert Edgar Currier, 1884-1927. Mr. Currier was a bookkeeper for the Perley and Crockett Lumber Company in Black Mountain. This company was established in 1912 and built a railroad to Mt. Mitchell to haul out the balsam logs.

Some of the oldest markers have the Walker name, such as Sarah Walker, born 1802, died 1842. There is a very worn stone for Mrs. Lydia Watkins; the death date looks like October 14, 1820, but probably is 1870. Major John Dougherty, born November 17, 1784 and died September 8,

1864, is one of the numerous Dougherty/Daugherty markers. There are also Browns, Stepps, Halls Goodsons, Boones, Byrds, and many other early settlers of the Swannanoa Valley.

Flat Creek Baptist Church in Weaverville was one of the earliest churches in present Buncombe County. Rev. Stephen Morgan had a "meeting house" as early as 1811 on Flat Creek which was the forerunner of this church. Rev. Morgan was its minister until his death in 1859. Growing from a log building with a few members, the church is still active and had 289 members in 1987. Mrs. Norma Morgan transcribed from microfilm the church's minutes from 1833-1931. These minutes, which showed it was usual to have two or three sermons preached by various ministers on Sunday mornings, included membership lists, articles of faith and decorum plus obituaries for members.

These minutes illustrated that the church members, numbering fifty-eight in 1837, tried to be the moral guardians for one another. If one member was "hurt" by another, members would be appointed to talk with the disorderly to try to come to some kind of agreement, usually with success. One female member who was "dancing after the fiddle" changed her ways after members went to "tenderly talk with her."

The obituaries included one for Clem Davis, who died in 1838, at 83 years of age and who was a Revolutionary soldier from 1776 "till Wallace was taken at York by General Washington in 1781." One who died during the Civil War was Oliver Erwin McDaris of the 5th N. C. Cavalry who had volunteered in 1862, was captured in Kentucky, sent to Camp Chase then Fort Delaware, paroled, but died at Winder Hospital in Richmond on October 14, 1864. Another was George Whitfield Morgan who died April 25, 1865. He was killed at Beaverdam in Buncombe while acting as a lieutenant in "A" Company. The obituary for Brother Abraham, a Black belonging to Col. James M. Alexander, died in 1847 at age 72, stated that he had come from Virginia and was an "orderly Member" of the church who died with "Christian patience." The church members 0. believed "that our black brother has gone home . . . and has become God's Free Man . . .."

Many who had ancestors in the Flat Creek area have been influenced by the beliefs of this church. Some of the family names include Allman, Buckner, Burl/Burrell, Davis, Gentry, Lankford, Morgan, Myers, Roberts, Robinson, Sams, Wild, Williams. More information on this book with 2,000 entries may be obtained by writing Morgan, 132 Dogwood Drive, Weaverville, NC 28787.

Visiting the graves of ancestors is important to family historians. If they can stand beside the graves as family members did in years past, their feelings of kinship deepen. But so many cemeteries are scattered throughout Western North Carolina, the searching and finding are difficult.

Ethel Kirkpatrick did the cemetery "leg" work from Troublesome Gap to Doggett Mountain to Mack's Patch and Catpens, for Spring Creek in Madison County. The book *Spring Creek Cemetery Survey* includes an index, detailed map, plus listings for twenty-nine cemeteries: Anderson, Bluff, Brooks, Brown, Davis, Ebbs, Spring Creek, Gap of Mountain, Goforth, Harris, Hurricane View, Keenersville, Kent, Ledford, Lemon's Gap, Meadow Fork, Mt. Pleasant, Plemmons, Popular Gap, Presnell, Reynold, Sexton, Waddell, Woody, Worley, Yates, Zion.

For each cemetery, Ms. Kirkpatrick added road instructions plus notes such as for Old Bluff, "98 stones with no inscriptions"; for Gap of the Mountain, "At the very top of the hill there are about 50 tombstones in one row. Tradition has it that they are graves of Civil War soldiers"; for Harris "sometimes called Ball City Baby Cemetery." Some are well-maintained; some require four-wheel drive even in good weather; some are abandoned with trees and brambles growing where cattle grazing throughout. More Plemmons are listed than any others. There are also numerous listings for the names of Brown, Balding, Cogdill, Duckett, Fowler, Hipps, Keener, Ledford, Woody, Price, and Waldroup.

Ms. Kirkpatrick knows her "home" area and knows who gave the land for many of the cemeteries. For four years she searched and checked with many local people to make this 1985 survey as complete as possible. For more information, write Kirkpatrick, Route 1, Box 140, Spring Creek Rd., Hot Springs, NC 28743.

In 1984, good news started for the family searchers who had a hard time finding, much less visiting, all the cemeteries in Buncombe County. Through 1989, Carolyn Aslund and Billie Ledbetter researched and compiled five volumes of *Cemetery Inscriptions of Buncombe County, NC.* They braved the bees, snakes, and angry bulls for you. What started out as personal research turned into a service.

In Volume I, eighty-four cemeteries, which ranged in size from one-and-two-grave plots to the 2,230 sites at Calvary Episcopal. The ones covered in the Asheville area were Noble Bacchus Westall and Newton Academy; north of Asheville, Faith Baptist, Union Chapel, Whitted, Old Weaverville, Chambers, Capps, Jacob Weaver, Brank, Mundy, Flat Creek, Lankford, Boyd Union Chapel, Ramsey; south of Asheville, Biltmore Estate, West Chapel, Rock Hill, Mt. Zion Baptist, Calvary Episcopal, Chapel Hill Baptist, Taylor, Avery's Creek Methodist, Avery's Creek Christian, New Salem Baptist, Hunter, Roberts Memorial.

Those Northwest of Asheville include Robinson Cove, Jones Valley, Cross-roads Missionary Baptist, Ebenezer Baptist, Alexander Baptist, Elk Mountain, Jarrett, Mt. Sheba Baptist, Alexander Chapel Methodist. Southwest of Asheville includes Joyce, Pole Creek, Hice Hill, Liberty Missionary, Francis Asbury Methodist, Justice, Luther, White Rock Baptist, Penland, Gladys Baptist, Stoney Fork Baptist, Lance, Graham, Avery's Creek Freewill Baptist, Baker, Candler Family, Acton Methodist, Capt. Moore, Sardis, Inanda Baptist, Bent Creek Baptist, Jones, Oak Hill Methodist, Starnes.

Northeast of Asheville includes Greenwood, Vance, Maney, Penland, Ballard, Swan, Honeycutt, Jones, Riceville, Patton. Southeast of Asheville includes Azalea Methodist, Emma's Grove, Sharon Methodist, Tweed's Chapel Methodist, Pleasant Hill 0.Baptist, Spring Mt. Baptist, Pleasant Grove Baptist, Nesbitt's Chapel, Wilkey Baptist, Laurel Springs, Marlow, Broad River Baptist, Gilliam.

A map is included in all of these volumes to help you find these cemeteries. These are well organized and indexed.

Volume II covered fifty-two cemeteries with a concentration on the older ones. You can read that the Clayton Family cemetery is on the Smokies Hilton Golf Course, 10th tee. These Claytons were born in the early 1800s. Other cemetery listings in the Asheville area are Trinity Methodist, Riverview Methodist, family cemeteries of Smith, Jones, Fore.

Eastward are St. Luke's Episcopal, Bathesda, Gashes Creek, Bethel Methodist. On toward Swannanoa are Hughey Family, Warren Wilson, First Presbyterian, and Macedonia A. M. E. Zion. In the Black Mountain area are Oak Grove and Mountain View Baptist. South of Biltmore is Shiloh A. M. E. In Avery's Creek is the Israel Family cemetery where Michael Israel, Sr., 1734-1819 has a marker stating he was a Colonial soldier in Virginia. Arden has the Williams family; Fletcher, New Boilling

Springs Baptist. Fairview has Bethany Methodist; Broad River, Bald Mountain Baptist. Revolutionary soldiers John and Jacob Merrell are among the ones buried at Bearwallow Baptist in Gerton.

Westward on the Asheville School grounds is the Henry Cemetery and Enka, the Edgewood Baptist. Candler cemeteries listed are New Morgan Hill Baptist, Hominy Baptist, Beaverdam Freewill Baptist, Laurel Hill Methodist, Brownsview Methodist, and Samuel B. Gudger where in addition to many of the Gudgers are many early Candlers. Leicester is well represented with Shook, Cole, Daves/Brooks family cemeteries plus Corinth Baptist, Snow Hill Methodist, Zion Hill Baptist, Western Chapel Methodist, South Turkey Creek Baptist, Penland's Chapel, and Brick Church. Big Sandy Mush Methodist has Revolutionary soldiers William Robison, 1760-1837, and Jesse Palmer, 1768-1850. Also buried there is David Palmer, 1801-1881, who gave the church property in 1875. Studying these early gravestone inscriptions, you can see early settlers of Sandy Mush included Lowrys, Swains, Joneses.

Northeast of Asheville are Mount Olive Baptist to Pleasant Grove in Weaverville and on to Barnardsville where Paint Fork, Jay Allen/Pegg, Ballard, Big Ivy, Antioch, Calloway, and Harris cemeteries are included.

Volume III included nineteen cemeteries. Three are in the Sandy Mush area: Chestnut Grove Missionary Baptist, Payne Chapel Methodist, Teague's Chapel Methodist (This one is in Madison County). In the Newfound area is Grace United Methodist. Closer toward Asheville's northwest section are Bethel Baptist, the Rich Family Cemetery, Cedar Hill, the first half of Green Hills, including the Afro-American section of Green Hills, and the Sluder Cemetery. The earliest markers at Sluder include William Sluder, died January 5, 1848, Manervy C. Sluder, died November 6, 1850, and John Sluder, died August 29, 1855.

North of Asheville is the Asbury Methodist. Toward the southwest of Asheville are Oak Forest Presbyterian, Monmorenci Methodist, Pisgah Methodist, and the Reynolds Family Cemetery. The southeast ssection includes the large, old Cane Creek Cemetery, which has been used since 1807. The Broad River area has listings for the Ledbetter Family Cemetery, Old Broad River Baptist, and Mount Pleasant.

Volume IV included the listings from 34 cemeteries throughout the county. The cemeteries in the Barnardsville area are Dillingham and Joel

Brigmon. In the Broad River area are listins for Chestnut Hill Baptist, Gilliam-Ledbetter, Ledbetter, and Stone Mountain Missionary Baptist. In Arden is the Mt. Carmel Baptist, and in Skyland, the Penland. Candler listings include Piney Mountain United Methodist, Reeves Chapel United Methodist, and Trull Cemetery. In Leicester are Dix Creek Chapel United Methodist, Newfound Baptist, Union Baptist, Gudger's Chapel, Highland Baptist.

In Alexander are Alexander Missionary Baptist and Mountain View Freewill Baptist. French Broad Township listings include French Broad Missionary Baptist, Oak Grove Missionary Baptist, Redmon Baptist, Turkey Creek Missionary Baptist. Weaverville listings are Chambers, Long's Chapel Missionary Baptist, and Clark's Chapel United Methodist Church. The Surrett Family and the Worley Family are in Sandy Mush, and over the county line into Madison are Roberts Cemetery and Piney Grove Baptist. New Liberty Missionary Baptist is in Erwin Hills, and the Church of the Redeemer Episcopal is in Woodfin. Asheville's listings are Beaverdam Baptist, the second half of Green Hills, and South Asheville Cemetery.

Volume V lists the markers at a place established in 1885 in Asheville, N. C., should be revered. Few cities of this size in the United States have a cemetery which contains one of the greatest American novelists and one of the greatest American short story writers. Riverside Cemetery has Thomas Wolfe and William Sidney Porter (O'Henry) buried on the eighty-seven acre hillside above the French Broad River. Plus, there are many local notables among the 11,000 at Riverside, which Thomas Wolfe called "the lonely hill of the dead."

Riverside Cemetery and the adjacent Beth Ha-Tephila Cemetery, organized in 1891, a burial place for the Jewish Temple are covered in Volume V.

Many people who are buried in Riverside Cemetery helped develop early Western North Carolina. If the names Vance, Pritchard, Rankin, Merrimon, Woodfin sound familiar to you, the men these places are named for are buried at Riverside: Zebulon Baird Vance, Civil War N. C. Governor, U. S. Senator, born May 1830, died 1894; Brigadier General Robert Brank Vance, awarded this rank after the Battle of Murfreesbora, born April 24, 1828, died November 28, 1899, 29th Reg. N. C. Inf., CSA; Senator Jeter Prichard born 1857, died 1921; J. E. Rankin, banker,

Asheville mayor, born April 27, 1845, died Feb. 12, 1928; James H. Merrimon, attorney and superior court judge, born Dec. 24, 1842, died Dec. 21, 1921; Branch Merrimon died in 1881 (His remains perhaps were moved from an earlier cemetery which closed in Asheville.); Nicholas Woodfin, lawyer and state senator born Jan. 29, 1810, died May 23, 1875.

If the names Jokobi, Denecke, Schlause, Wahnschaffe, sound unfamiliar, these were German prisoners held in Hot Springs during World War I. They and fourteen others died from typhoid fever and are named in Section M of Riverside. Even in the early 1900s, if families owned a few acres, many wanted their kin buried on their own property. Over the years the old family members died out or moved away from the lands of their ancestors, leaving behind the family in the cemeteries. The burial sites of the old family members may be taken over by vines, shrubs, trees, but more likely they are encroached upon by builders of subdivisions, shopping centers, and golf courses. The value of land in these developed areas often causes intended carelessness. One pass of a bulldozer across a site can obliterate the stone markers, some of which were already broken or pushed over by vandals.

In an effort to record what is left at these family plots, the Greenville Chapter of the South Carolina Genealogical Society in 1987 included over forty of these in their *Greenville County, S. C. Cemetery Survey.*

Many of these family plots have the oldest markers in the county, and three are already called "Unknown" family cemeteries, such as one with two marked graves, including Elender Mullinax who died January 25, 1811. The Shockley Family Cemetery is now in the Sugar Creek Subdivision. The Hawkins family members, buried in the early 1800s, now lie beside the parking lot at Eastgate Village Shopping Center. At Brushy Creek Baptist Church in Greenville, there is a memorial to "eleven persons removed in 1972 from the oldest known cemetery in Greenville County, formerly located in the Del Norte Estates Subdivision."

About one hundred cemeteries with 18,020 entries are in this book which has each cemetery marked on a map of Greenville County. For more information, write Brent Holcombe, P. O. Box 21766, Columbia, SC 29221.

CHAPTER 6. FAMILY HISTORY BOOKS

Family historians who find a book that has the "searched for" family name in it are excited. They hope much elusive information that they have been searching for is included. However, be cautious. All family history books are not equal.

Most people spend 20 or more years researching families before they publish a book since they want the book to be as accurate as possible. Their basic goal in publication is to share the research with other family members so it can by enjoyed and added to. The many years of research are necessary because no one piece of information, no matter where they got it, is proof. Every record needs to be checked by another source if possible. Even official documents, such as a death certificate, are only as accurate as the person who gave the information. On parents of the deceased, for example, a son could give his father's mother as Sue Jones if that's what he thought her name was, while her name may have been Sally James. You need a third source if you are unsure. Sometimes there is a difference of opinion by careful researchers on matters such as if someone was a son or grandson of a certain ancestor, but sometimes you may be reading a book that is not carefully researched. These useless and misleading family histories can be divided into two categories.

First, there are family histories that include books written by people who are not really out to make money but who don't realize how misleading it is to publish "facts" that are not carefully researched. These may be your real family, but the inaccuracies may devastate your research forever if you blindly copy it down. These historians usually have good intentions but have become in a hurry to have a "complete" family history with no blanks. There are some guidelines to consider as you read a family history.

One, remember that you cannot tell by the "slickness" of the publication. The accuracy of the researcher is what is important, whether it is a handwritten booklet or a hard-cover book; the writers are the ones responsible for the contents, not the publisher.

Second, study the preface of the book to try to determine if the writer did research and the type of research done, why it was written, how long the writer studied the families. Any admittance of uncertainty in some areas is usually a plus.

Third, in reading the book, be suspicious if every ancestor goes back to someone famous. Look closely at these to see if there could be a real family connection or if this is just a "latch on." Suppose Governor Jones did have a son named John, born in 1780. You have a John Jones, born about 1790 whom you never found a father for. Is this Governor Jones, with no other proof, presumed to be his father? This is a "latch on" and will probably be wrong if careful research is done.

Fourth, is research obvious by inclusion of census records, deed information, military records, specific births and deaths, Bible records?

Fifth, does it logically make sense? If you have seen the tombstone of ancestor Andrew Hawk beside all your later Hawk ancestors that he was born July 11, 1807, you know the book is wrong when it lists his first child as born in 1817.

Enjoy other people's family histories, but always check the official records possible for yourselves. A good family history gives you leads you did not have and enables you to learn more from your own research.

Worse, there are surname books that are published to just make money. These take for granted that every Smith or Smyth in the world is related. Your name is found in the telephone directory, and you are sent a letter from perhaps Ohio telling you that you have a rare name, and that a book has been published with your name in it. The "surname" books are the biggest "rip-offs" since these people do not know anything about your family to begin with. These are businesses which sell information on names throughout the United States. These are not specific family histories.

Normally, these state that your family's history has been published and that you "are already in this book." (Your name and address will be if you order it.) You are usually warned that this edition will never be printed again and that you must "act fast" to reserve your copy. Many times you are told that it will save you from spending thousands of dollars and "months" of searching.

In general an American history on pioneers and immigrants is included along with an "unusual coat of arms," but no specific information on your family line has been researched. Your last name is discussed; something you can easily find in city libraries.

The advertisement will say that the book will "educate you in the fundamentals of genealogical research by describing the history of

American origins, the development of family crests, the origin of family names, the recording and documenting of family heritage." This means that not one person with your family name has been researched. This special information can be found in much more detail that you will get in this book.

The history of American origins is rather simple. The American people came from practically all nations in a short span of time. A book, *American Origins*, by L. G. Fine, in Pack Library, gives the predominant countries Americans came from plus the history of each region as it applies to genealogical records. The origin of family names as discussed in *American Surnames* by Elsdon C. Smith said that the most common name in 1790 was Smith with 33,245 people. By 1969, Smith was still number one with 2,238,400 people. The origin of family names came about in at least four ways.

One, most names in the United States are estimated to be named for places, particularly if the people are from England, Germany, and France, such as Fields, Meadows, Brooks. Two, fathers' names were very popular in Ireland, Scotland, Wales, Spain, such as Edward's son could become Edwards or Edwardson or MacEdwards or O'Edwards. Three, occupational names are also common, such as Smith, Taylor, Miller. Four, descriptive names told size, color of hair or skin, such as Longfellow, Brown, Red/Reed. These "nicknames" were popular surname choices in Italy and Portugal.

The development of "family crests" is discussed under "heraldry" in Pack Library where you can find thousands of crests which were awarded to individuals with thousands of surnames. In Europe, coats of arms were first designed by knights for identification purposes. The background is that in the 1100s in western Europe. The men who fought various types of battles would put on suits of armor with closed helmets. These knights had a hard time telling each other apart. Therefore, to keep from whacking the wrong person, a symbol was painted on each one's shield and embroidered on a cloth and hung over the armor. This was his coat of arms. These were very simple at first, such as an "x" or a star, but there were too many knights; so the coats of arms became more elaborate. Records started being kept so that two people would not have the same symbol, even if they were in the same family. There is no such thing as a family coat of arms. A coat of arms was granted to an individual only.

Crests did not develop until during the Crusades and started as designs on helmets or arm bands. Later these were transferred to the shield. These crests were awarded for personal merit; therefore, you only have a crest if it were awarded to a direct ancestor. It is not surprising that people with the same surnames have different crests. For example, some English Justices had a cat, but Henry Justice, Esquire, had a bird, and Scottish Justices had an upright sword. That all families with the same surname had one crest or coat of arms is not logical.

Researching for your personal family's history takes hard work. Many books will help you, but make sure you don't waste money by buying books that have misleading advertisements and are useless to you.

The family history books included in the following discussion have been carefully reviewed and are authentic.

Many family histories are published, and for future "leads" to the past, you probably should consider the opportunity to learn more from any legitimate books you can find on your family. However, just occasionally, a different type of family history is written, not just a list of descendants but the historical stories of the ancestors and the area where they lived.

Duane Oliver has written *Remembered Lives: A Narrative History of Our Family*, and this is such a family history that all family searchers will wish Mr. Oliver were researching their families. His detailed stories revolve around the Farleys, Cables, Cooks, Olivers, Proctors, Sherrills, and Welches. Their historical significance in the Swain County area does not prevent Mr. Oliver from presenting their "warts and all" histories embedded in the history of the area.

The mountains where these people settled was basically in the area now covered by Fontana Lake or uninhabited because of it. This was once part of the 25 million acres that comprised the Cherokee Nation. The history of Hazel Creek includes how the early settlers lived, from Moses and Patience Proctor and infant son William, who arrived there by 1830, then Macon County. Coming through the Smokies across an old Indian trail from Cades Cove, Tennessee, they settled where there would be no road for fifty years. From investigations, the first Proctor cabin was made of hewn logs one-foot in diameter, no windows, two doors, a fireplace, and a dirt floor. Oliver stated, "Most settlers made, cut, raised, picked, dug, gathered, trapped, or shot almost everything they needed for existence." Powder, shot iron, salt, and needles were obtained by selling a few skins, some herbs, and cattle, and, in Proctor's case, some peach brandy.

Oliver added that this couple had no way of knowing that in a little over one hundred years "no one would be living on the creek and that the fields they had laboriously cleared and tended would be returned to forest, and that all signs except for their gravestones, of their ever having been there would be forever erased."

Samuel Cable, who became a neighbor in the late 1830s, was a descendant of Kasper Goebell/Casper Cable, a Hessian soldier who deserted during the Revolution.

Oliver related many tales of the mid-1800s. When seven men left the creek to go off to the Civil War, the women have a fearful time from roving bushwhackers who came through their area stealing horses, cured pork, even clothing. Their tales of survival are included.

Also, concerning the Civil War, the history of Colonel William Thomas, who created Thomas's Legion for the Confederacy, composed of Cherokee Indians and local whites, is discussed. On February 2, 1864, an Illinois Cavalry went to the mouth of Deep Creek near Bryson City, overrunning about two hundred of Thomas's soldiers. The soldiers fought, but twenty to thirty of them were taken prisoners. The Yankees claimed "they had wiped out Thomas's companies" and promised the Indian soldiers they would have " liberty and five thousand dollars gold if they would bring in the scalp of their chief, Thomas." They agreed but upon release rushed to tell Thomas. This loyalty was not surprising since Thomas had owned 150,000 acres in the mid-1800s, a part of which he gave or sold for the Qualla Boundary on behalf of the over sixteen thousand Cherokees who hid out and did not go to Oklahoma.

During the skirmish, Joseph Welch was taken prisoner and not released. He was sent to Fort Delaware where he remained as a prisoner of war for over a year.

The Welch family account gives a detailed history as they came from Scotland to Pennsylvania and to Rutherford County, North Carolina, in the 1760s, before moving westward about 1820 into the former Cherokee Nation. The original Welch land was still held by the descendants in 1942 when the Tennessee Valley Authority began to buy land for Fontana Lake. The Supreme Court gave the Tennessee Valley Authority power to condemn and buy all of the family's land. Oliver discussed the "Road to Nowhere" built by the government that never went, as promised, to the "ancestral homesites and graveyards that were not engulfed by the lake."

Luckily, Oliver is descended from interesting families, and since he is related to the Sherrills and General John Sevier married Catherine Sherrill, an account of the famous "State of Franklin" is included. Every time settlers went into a new area of the United States, whether it was in the 1600s or the 1800s, their methods for settlement were much the same. To really understand these early settlers in a remote area of Western North Carolina, read Duane Oliver's *Hazel Creek from Then til Now*. This is an account of the people who settled there plus how they lived.

Memories are about all that are left for these Western North Carolina families who cannot go visit a real community of Hazel Creek again. Hazel Creek is now part of the southern boundary of the Great Smoky Mountains National Park, established in 1944. "Over two thousand people once lived on Hazel Creek, but the forest and time have erased most indications of previous tenure on the land. It looks today much as it did when the first settlers arrived."

The pioneers carried all of their belongings, were accompanied by their families and all of their livestock, were "beset by fears at entering a strange place" as they followed the Indian trails into the wilderness.

In 1830, Moses Proctor, his wife Patience, and son William settled on Hazel Creek without neighbors until Samuel and Elizabeth Cable with their seven children settled in 1835. Moses Proctor paid five cents an acre for his land. By 1860, Hazel Creek had at least four families. "Each family had cleared what land it could, but the creek still remained a primeval wilderness with more bears and wolves than people."

After buying land and moving into a new settlement, the settlers had to build a cabin by felling trees, usually tulip poplars. The cabin would have notched logs and wooden pegs, roofs with wooden pine shingles, windows with shutters. Then, the barn, corn cribs, smoke house, and spring house would have to be built. "Once the cabin was built and some land cleared, the pioneers settled down to live in a new land. Although there were contacts with the world beyond the encircling mountains, life centered around the cabin and farm."

Details are included on the types of furnishings in these cabins and how they were made, such as looms, beds, spinning wheels. Life in the mountains just about a hundred and fifty years ago included activities such as tanning leather for shoes, spinning, weaving, sewing, gardening, soap making, drying and pickling food, digging for wild roots. "Everyone had to be basically self-sufficient, and if something extra were needed it could often be gotten by barter or trade."

The customs described will remind you of the tales you've often heard on your grandfather's knee. A time not too long ago when hogs browsed on chestnuts, "hams, middling and shoulders hung in the smokehouse and cured by being rubbed with salt and smoked over a fire made with corn cobs and green hickory chips," when the usual spring tonic was sulfur and molasses, when cows were milked and butter churned. "People sometimes got the itch, and to cure this, pokeberry roots were boiled and a bath taken in the water. When the afflicted stopped screaming from the pain, they were usually cured." In the late 1800s patent medicines were available, strong with opium and alcohol; stores, churches, schools, post offices built. However, by the end of the 1800s, the pioneer period on Hazel Creek was drawing to a close since the land had been claimed and copper mines and timbering had started.

Between 1941 and 1944, the residents of Hazel Creek and the surrounding areas knew they would have to sell their land and move; since when the TVA dam, Fontana, was completed and the lake filled, they would have "no road to the outside world." Most of the land was purchased for about thirty-eight dollars per acre since the TVA handled the appraisals and allowed no price-trading or bargaining. If the people did not want to sell, their land was condemned and taken.

Family histories of the Proctor, Cable, Welch, Bradshaw, Jones, Hall, Cook, Laney, Brooks, Calhoun, Birchfield, Farley, Woodard, Martin, Myers, Higdon, Marcus, Culberson families are included.

Early pioneer life in the mountains becomes real for you. You'll wish every community had a family history such as Hazel Creek's. Included are thirty-six pictures of early settlers, schools, loggers, sawmills, and churches.

To cook dishes you've heard your great-grandparents talk about, you'll want to study Duane Oliver's publication, *Cooking on Hazel Creek*. Mr. Oliver compiled a cook book on Cherokee recipes, recipes that were cooked in a fireplace on Hazel Creek, and later southern cooking recipes.

Early settlers learned from the Cherokees how to cook corn, pumpkins, squash, plus learned how to make medicines from wild greens and herbs. Included in the "Cherokee Cooking" section are lye dumplings, ash cake, bear, and yellow jacket soup. The Hazel Creek recipes include leather-britches, gritted bread, cracklin' bread, poke salet, hominy, pickled beans and corn made in a crock with salt brine, souse meat, baked rabbit, quail, deer, persimmon pudding.

For more information on all three of the above books, write Duane Oliver, P. O. Box 394, Hazelwood, NC 28738.

Searching for birth and death records in North Caolina is not difficult if you are searching for people who were born or who died after October 1913. You just go the court house where the ancestor was born or died and look it up in the register of deed's office. Even a letter will usually get an answer and request you send a fee for a copy, usually three to five dollars.

But many people wish they could find these same records for those older family members. A family Bible may be your only hope. If you live in or around Macon County, North Carolina, you may have your wish come true. Because of his interest in family history, Lawrence Wood of Franklin, N. C., collected Bible records for many years. These have now been abstracted for births, deaths, and marriages by Charles Biddix and Wilma Muse, printed by the Old Buncombe County Genealogical Society. The publication, *Western North Carolina Bible Records*, contains 1,520 names.

The births go back to the late 1700s. The information included came from the following family Bibles: Patton, Connally, Arnold, Austin, A. H. Strain, W. H. Strain, Bryson. H. M. Weir, Burch-Crisp, John Burgin, Burgin, Burrell, McDowell, Cabe, Cathey, Chastain, Peek-Moss, VanHook, Moore, Henricks, Crisp, Cunningham, C. Russell, L. J. Kerlee, Sloan, Dills, Young, Walker, P. Gregory, Holland, Willson, Jones, Penland, Phillips, Reed, Rogers, Wood-Rogers, G. Williams. Many of these records cover much of Western North Carolina. Plus, the Old Buncombe Genealogical Society has files from these records which contain much more detailed information at its office in the Innsbruck Mall in Asheville.

Jean Warren and Willadean Boyd, whose ancestors were early settlers of Western North Carolina in the Upper Hominy section of Candler, compiled families' histories on this area, which is known as Big Cove.

The first settler was James Rutherford, who received his first land grant on August 23, 1799. Rutherford sold land in the early 1800s to Jays Belew and John Webb. Many of the early settlers, such as Daniel Williams, born in the early 1800s, who married Mary Joyce, still had in 1987 nine great-grandchildren living in the Big Cove area. Marriages into this family included Fletchers, Hyatts, and Rutherfords. Another early settler was Thomas Cathey, born 1797, who married Mary Ann Ingram. Marriages into this family included Longs, Burnetts, Singletons, Wrights, Taylors.

The history of Trull Chapel and cemetery is included along with the family of Rev. John Trull, born 1815, whose children married into the families of Jackson, Anderson, Sorrells, Pless. Other families discussed are Hodge A. Raburn, born 1759 in Rowan, sheriff of Burke, and in Buncombe County by 1831; John Perrin Joyce, born 1809; George Rhodes, born 1835; Washington Curtis, born 1837.

If members of your family ever lived in Big Cove, sometimes known as Webb Cove, you should find much family history in *The Big Cove History*. For more information write to Jean Warren, P. O. Box 533, Big Cove Rd., Candler, NC 28715.

Family historians, who buy copies of wills, deeds, marriage records, court records, Bible records, military records, know each item costs from $3 to $25, depending on the place written and the length. The money goes out as you hope for "that link" but many times for useless material to you since the records are obviously for another family with the same last name. Add the expense to the years of time plus costs for publication, and it is no wonder there are so few family histories available.

Families who can find a well-documented family history for one of their surnames are lucky, and the Brittains of Western North Carolina have one available. Shirley Cawyer compiled the *Genealogical Study of James Brittain*. James Brittain was a Revolutionary soldier who married Delilah Stringfield, made his home in Buncombe, and had fourteen children. Some of these stayed in Western North Carolina while others lived the story of settlers on the West, all documented by Ms. Cawyer. The early chapters prove that James's father was Joseph Brittain, Sr., born about 1723 in Virginia, whose will was probated in 1774 in Rowan County, gave the names of his children. Different existing family histories are discussed on earlier Brittains, particularly James Brittain who died about 1768 in Rowan and was possibly the father of Joseph, Sr. Ms. Cawyer discussed the obvious errors in some histories and then showed what is true from official documents.

Joseph Brittain, Sr., possibly had a wife Mary before the proven Jemima and had nine children. By 1777, the records for these nine children are in Burke County, which was formed from Rowan in that year. Three sons, Phillip, James, and William Brittain, received pensions for Revolutionary War service. Phillip moved to Bedford County, Tennessee, by 1818, while James and William stayed in Buncombe. William lived in the Reems Creek section in Weaverville, and his nine children are given.

The book is well-organized and easy to follow, even to the present generations, since each of the fourteen children of James and Delilah Brittain who lived near Mills River are discussed in separate chapters

Their oldest child, Mary Brittain, married Thomas Edwards in Buncombe County about 1800 They moved to Haywood, then about 1838 to Georgia and on into Alabama. Many references are made to the intermarriages into the families of Edwards, Howell, Johnson, Rees, Bryson, McCracken, Jarrett, and Sitton.

Second child Joseph Brittain, Jr., born about 1783, married Sallie McHenry and moved to Barren County, Kentucky. Third child, Amelia Brittain, born about 1785, married Ellis Edwards and died in Haywood County. Their eight children are discussed with many descendants listed through the present. Fourth child, Phillip, born about 1787, died in Henderson County, married Sophia Melinda Lewis. Fifth, Keziah Brittain born about 1789 married Jeremiah Pace, and both died in Dade County, Georgia. Many Davidsons intermarried with this family. Ms. Cawyer studied censuses, wills, newspapers, and Bible records from all involved states to be as accurate on children as possible.

Most of the early Western North Carolina families are mentioned. Son Benjamin Stringfield Brittain, born about 1793, married Celia Vance and moved to Cherokee County, N. C. The Georgia migration is shown in Nancy, born about 1794, who married Jacob Stuart and moved from

Buncombe to Gilmer County by 1840. A son was murdered by Confederate troops during the Civil War, even though he was a Confederate himself. Letters home from one of his sons who went on west to Harney County, Oregon, described that people lived in tents, and his wife wrote, "can't get a spool of thread. No, no running water but at the foot of Buttes, 4 miles east." Real facts are given on families spreading out from Buncombe across the United States.

Another daughter, Comfort Brittain born about 1796, married Montgomery Bell, and died in DeKalb County, Georgia. William Brittain, born about 1798, married Rachel Clayton and lived in Mills River. According to court records, William died before August 1867. Many Moores, Poseys, Johnsons, Joneses, Howells, Reids, and Israels intermarried with these Brittains.

Among the youngest five children were Susannah who married Alaph Wilson; James, Jr., who married Rachel Rebecca Smith; Lorenzo Don who married Arminta Russell, moved to Alabama and died in Missouri. Some of his descendants went to California in 1857 and kept detailed memoirs. Son Horatio Nelson married Elizabeth Morrow and lived in Haywood. The youngest child was Delilah Brittain.

Ms. Cawyer said it took twenty years to compile this history, but it must have been a continual task for the information that she has gathered. For more information write to Shirley Cawyer, 185 Brittain Circle, Stephenville, TX 76401.

An interesting family history was written by a local businessman, Robert D. Bunn, owner of an antique store established in the 1920s, now on Biltmore Avenue in Asheville. Mr. Bunn and Doris Ward published *The Life and Ancestry of Robert Dewey Bunn, born 1899, Asheville, North Carolina.*

Mr. Bunn knows about the changes in Asheville over the years since he is descended from brick makers, who came here in 1875, and has lived on Clayton Street all of his life. His grandfather, Albert C. Bunn, who was born in England and immigrated to New Jersey in the late 1860s, came to Asheville, bringing his son William Albert, born 1837, to set up brickworks for the new Buncombe County Courthouse. His business was established nearby at the corner of Charlotte and Clayton Streets. His son was also awarded the brickwork contracts for courthouses in Brevard in 1879 and Waynesville in 1882. (Pictures of the three old courthouses are included in this book.) These men also supplied brick for the Rumbough Hotel in Hot Springs, North Carolina.

William Albert Bunn's wife Martha was born in England and died in Asheville. He then married Katherine Dermid in 1889. Their children born in the late 1800s on Clayton Street included Robert D. Bunn. Robert, who married Fannie Darby, was a friend of nearby neighbor Thomas Wolfe.

Katherine Dermid descended from early Clear Creek settlers in present Henderson County. Her family is included with histories of Daniel Allen, born 1786, through his son George Allen of the Ebenezer Community, Merrimon Featherstone and wife Amelia Mills, with her well-known kin Ambrose and William Mills.

Family histories would be easier to trace and be more detailed if everyone would preserve his or her memories the way Robert Bunn did. For more information, write Robert D. Bunn, 15 Clayton Street, Asheville, NC 28804.

In the federal census of North Carolina in 1790, only two Burgins were listed. One was Benjamin Burgin of Burke County. A descendant of this Benjamin Burgin compiled a history with over 1,700 Burgins discussed in her *Echoes in the Mist, The Burgin Family 1677-1989*. The writer, Peggy Silvers, carefully documented her 476-page book, which contains 782 referenced to where she obtained her information.

Mrs. Silvers has that Benjamin Burgin was born in Kent County, Maryland, was the grandson of Phillip Burgin, born about 1658, who was transported to Maryland in January 1677. Phillip Burgin married Rosamond Sutton. His will was probated June 7, 1709, and listed his six children, including John, born September 14, 1704, who was the father of Benjamin, born December 25, 1741, left Maryland about 1765, settling on Yadkin River in Rowan County, before moving near present Old Fort, now McDowell County, by the 1780s. In addition to early censuses, civil war military records, deeds, inventories, wills, and documented stories are included. Multiple views of ancestors are seen from friends who wrote memoirs and official documents, such as wills. The facts are in Mrs. Silvers' book. You have to decide for yourself the many facets of your ancestors.

Major Ben Burgin, one son of Benjamin Burgin, and his house were described from memoirs of Flora Burgin Smith, living from 1862 to 1961, who was a granddaughter of Major Ben. His house was described as a "three-story house (on Crooked Creek in Old Fort) that was hewn out of logs. There were big fireplaces throughout the house. There were two big barns with stalls for dozens of horses . . .. He was a tall, good-looking man and walked with a cane. He died at the age of 96."

One story was told about a descendant, Samuel Davidson Burgin from Lincolnton, N. C., that visited Swannanoa in 1878, where his son John contracted diphtheria, died and was buried in Piney Grove Cemetery in Swannanoa. After they returned to their home in Lincolnton, four more children died within a month.

As so many others, some Burgins moved onward to Tennessee, Texas, Missouri, Louisiana, Alabama, Kentucky. One letter Mrs. Silvers shared which was written on March 22, 1876: Benjamin Mann wrote to a Burgin niece and nephew in Hendersonville, N. C., from Henderson, Kentucky, stating, "since our last correspondence till now, we have passed through a firey ordeial that swept away the lives of our dear children." He also wanted them to write and let him know about the Burgins, the Nesbitts, the Lytles, the Birds, and the Hemphills.

If you are related to the Burgins, you should have no trouble in finding out about your family history by studying Mrs. Silvers book. With over 1,700 Burgins "tied to" families, you may even find your own name. For more information write to Peggy Silvers, Route I, Box 796, Nebo, NC 28761.

A well-researched family history of one man and woman's decendants as they branched out across the United States is always interesting. *Descendants of David and Margaret (Carson) Byers*, compiled by Thurlo V. Byers, discusses the ones who kept going west plus the ones who stayed in Western North Carolina. This Byers family was in Chester County, Pennsylvania, by 1740 then moved to York County, Pennsylvania, before migrating down the Great Wagon Road into North Carolina and South Carolina.

(The Great Wagon Road ran from Pennsylvania through the Blue Ridge Mountains of Virginia through the Carolinas by way of Salisbury and Charlotte, N. C., Rock Hill and Chester, S. C., and on to Augusta, Georgia.)

David had bought land in Mecklenbury County, N. C., in 1764, but his land was later found to be in York County, S. C. The children of David

177

and Margaret were William, Samuel, Jeane/Jane, and Ann. After Margaret's death, David married Sarah Carson, and they had one daughter, Margaret. David's will was recorded March 27, 1795.

William, born April 6, 1747, in Pennsylvania, was a Patriot in the Revolution. He and his wife Jane moved from North Carolina in 1816 and went to Williamson County, Tennessee, where he died in 1832. Some of their children did not go to Tennessee.

One of David's daughters, Jane, who married David Porter, moved to Rutherford County, N. C., in 1794 as had her brother Samuel (born about 1749) with his wife and six sons about 1791. In 1803, Samuel moved into Buncombe on Mud Creek, but he kept moving. In 1834, he was in Lumpkin County, Georgia, with one son while the other sons stayed behind.

Samuel's son David, who was born in 1778, moved from Rutherford County to Haywood County where he married Rebecca McClain. Samuel's son Joseph Judson Byers, born January 17, 1780, in South Carolina, lived in Rutherford County and then moved to Buncombe in the early 1800s. He married Mary Kuykendall and first bought land from his father-in-law James Kuykendall on Mud Creek.

William, Samuel's son who was born about 1782, also moved to Buncombe, and another of Samuel's sons, Francis, born March 18, 1789, moved to Buncombe and bought land in present Henderson County in 1817. His wife was Judah Jones.

Descendants who moved into Missouri, Kentucky, Alabama, Illinois, and other parts westward are discussed. This 100-page book gives a detailed account of the Byers and includes various maps showing land ownership, interesting Civil War letters, and local families that married into the Byers' families. This book is available at the Old Buncombe County Genealogical Society.

In 1984, E. E. Corcoran, MD, of Asheville, wrote and published his family history. This tribute to the John Corcoran family of Charleston, S.C., and the Samuel Barnes Emmons family of Lancaster, S. C., is a good guide for readers who want to go into details of the direct lines back to great-great grandparents but want to avoid going into all the numerous branches which often makes a book end up as a lists of descendants. Included are early pictures, good insight into the Civil War situation, and interesting history about the house where the Corcorans lived for 130 years and which was still standing in 1984 on Orange Street in Charleston.

In 1993, Harry F. Dill compiled a family history, *Some Descendants and Kinsmen of William Dill, Sr., a Delaware Colonist*. William Dill died in Kent County, Delaware, in 1760, but his descendants moved into North Carolina, Tennessee, South Carolina, and Georgia. The 160-page soft-bound book includes official records and family data. Harry Dill has much information of William's son John Dill, Sr., who moved to Greenville County, South Carolina. For more information, write Harry F. Dill, 6019 Benjamin St., Alexandria, LA 71303-3816.

Brent Holcomb, a certified genealogist, wrote in 1987 a carefully documented history of the *Greer and Related Families of the Carolinas and Virginia*. This book discusses the ancestors and descendants of Jason Martin Greer, Sr. (1804-1891) and his wife Sarah Ann Sanders (1810-1879), both of whom lived and died in Union County, South Carolina. This Greer family migrated from North Carolina to Union County. The first Greer discussed is Thomas, born about 1710, emigrated from Ireland through the port of Wilmington and settled near Fayetteville, N. C. The related families of Sims, Glenn, Christmas, Smith, and Ferris were in Virginia, while the related Carver family was in eastern North Carolina. For more information, write to Brent H. Holcomb, Box 21766, Columbia, SC 29221.

Jean Pressley Warren compiled two booklets in 1984, including material from several contributors, on the Harris and Kirkpatrick families of Haywood County, North Carolina. One booklet concerns the direct descendants of James B. Harris, 1839-1925, and Martha Rachel Smart, 1833-1892. James Harris was the son of Toliver Harris and Nancy Hill. Martha Smart first married Leander Kirkpatrick, who was killed in the Civil War, after having four children by him.

The other booklet discusses the descendants of Leander Kirkpatrick and includes his war records. For more information, write Jean Warren, P. O. Box 533, Candler, NC 28715.

Over four-hundred pages related the family history of *The Hicks Families of Western North Carolina* from the Watauga River family of David Hicks. Compilers John and Mattie Hicks and Barnabas Hicks have included the ancestry of David Hicks, his children and children's children, with some to the tenth generation. The book, published in 1991, is a readable blend of the earliest history of the Watauga River area and its settlers, generation charts and stories about the Hicks' families, plus official documents.

Samuel Hicks, who was the ancestor of the Watauga line of the Hicks family, "appears to have arrived in Virginia in 1637" and was "an indentured servant." David, born 1719 in Goochland County, Virginia, was this Samuel's great-grandson. David with at least five grown children was one of the first settlers in the Watauga River area. He arrived about 1777 and claimed 300 acres at present Valle Crucis, North Carolina.

Most of the Hicks who stayed in Western North Carolina were descended from David's son Samuel, born 1753 and died in 1835, Ashe County, N. C., and David's son, David, Jr., who died near White Hall, Illinois, in 1840. The compilers state that David Hicks, Sr., had his property in Surry County, N. C., confiscated by Patriot militia officers since David was a Tory, and the Watauga settlement residents were "more tolerant toward Loyalists."

These remote settlers in the Watauga River area were often called "over the mountain men" and established a local government in 1771, the Watauga Association, although it was not recognized as such by North Carolina or Virginia. In 1776, North Carolina did set up the "Military District of Washington" in that area. By 1784, the Watauga Association members set themselves up as the "State of Franklin." In this area many families were not sure if they lived in North Carolina or Virginia, much less what county. The 1790 federal census showed the same people in both Wilkes and in Burke Counties.

David Hicks, Sr.'s, daughter Dinah/Diana, born 1758 in Caswell County, N. C., married Thomas Asher, and second Henry Heatley and lived in the Banner Elk community before returning to the Valle Crucis area. David's daughter Sarah married Charles Asher and lived on the Watauga River about 1785. Charles, according to the Hicks' book, was killed by Joseph White's Militia Unit "which still roamed the mountains in search of `outliers' and Tories." Sarah later married James D. Holzclaw. David's daughter Catherine married John Holzclaw.

"For reasons of safety, David Hicks established a second residence off the beaten path near what is now Banner Elk." He died in 1792/3 and his will was probated in Wilkes County.

A number of descendants moved to Haywood County. Samuel Sylvestor Hicks, born 1856, moved to Haywood County and later Swain County where he died in 1911. William Skyles Hicks, born 1874, who married Jennie Rathbone also moved to Haywood.

The Hicks' family descendants often married into the Harmon, Ward, Tester, and Presnell families in the Watauga area. The appendixes are informative, containing over forty pictures, readable copies of wills, grants, deeds, starting in 1778, relationships to Harmon, Bean, Holzclaw, Goulden, and Bates families. for more information write to John Henry Hicks, Route I, Box 102, Sugar Grove, NC 28767.

Frances Honeycutt's *The Ones Who Came Before* is an informative and well-written family history, published in 1986. The family names discussed in detail are Mills, Stepp, Lyda, Whiteside, Freeman, Whitaker, Harper, and Burgin. These families were in the Henderson/Buncombe area by the early 1800s.

Many family stories, most documented, are recreated, such as the one about a Grandmother, Polly Mills Stepp, who lived near Mills Spring and who in 1779 was scalped by Indians but survived. In addition to the family account, Mrs. Honeycutt quoted the Diary of Lt. Allair of Ferguson's Corps, Loyalist: "We then at that early hour moved on to one James Step's plantation, and halted. This man has been very unfortunate in his family; his wife, who is a very decent woman, was caught by the Indians. They scalped and tomahawked her several times in the head, treated the infant she had in her arms in a most inhuman and savage manner. They mashed its head in such a manner that its recovery is truly astonishing; but what this poor unhappy woman seems to regret is the loss of her oldest son, whom the savages took, and she now remains in a state of uncertainty, not having heard from him since."

As well as a family history, this book gives a view of early mountain customs, politics, and religious views.

Since her Freeman kin of Gerton were early gunsmiths, she related how guns were made by hand. She has included her own memoirs which give detailed insight into how life was very different not long ago on a farm in Henderson County. She remembered a farm with kerosine lamps and a spring house where churning, sheep-shearing, wheat threshings, corn shuckings, hog killings, and driving cattle to mountain pastures in the spring were all part of a yearly routine. She described molasses making and the "holeing up" process for preserving apples, potatoes, turnips, and cabbage.

Included are the memoirs of James Whitaker, born 1779, who moved into Buncombe in 1800 where he became a state congressman in 1818, moving to the Cherokee purchase on the Tennessee River in 1824 and finally, in 1835, moving into the Cherokee Nation on Valley River (now Andrews) where he helped create a Baptist church for Indians and whites. He wrote of the religious world's problems, particularly "The religion of the Bible against the traditions of men." As early as 1833, he was concerned about the "preservation of the Union" because of the high tariff that oppressed the southern states and the "annihilation" of states' rights.

Thirty pictures, some as early as 1860, are included in this book. For more information on this and the volume II of this book as described below, write Frances F. Honeycutt, Route 2, Box 366, Hendersonville, NC 28792.

In 1989, Frances Honeycutt published Volume II of *The Ones Who Came Before*. Her goal in family history has always been to better understand her ancestors, to know why they came to America, where and how they lived -- and she shares her information clearly. This is not just a book of lists of descendants but also descriptions of the countries from which ancestors came and countries which she has obviously visited. The early history of this country where ancestors settled is shown. Many stories of the Revolutionary War in Rutherford/Tryon County are included plus an account of the effects of the Civil War on the community of Edneyville in Henderson County. Inclusions of deeds, wills, petitions, early Bible records show the extent of her search.

The Mills's family history starts in England and a discussion is given for the ones who came to America, including William Mills who was born in 1699 in Derbyshire, England, married Mary Walton. His will was probated August 4, 1766, in Amherst County, Virginia, and included his sons Ambrose and William Henry Mills who were both Loyalists in the Revolution in Western North Carolina.

Frances Honeycutt found the Stepp/Stapp family first in Rappahannock (now Essex) County, Virginia. Again wills are used as proof of kinship for the Stepps who came into old Buncombe. Stories are included about their problems with the Indians and their lives as

Tories during the Revolution. A petition in Henderson County in 1857 gave the descendants of James Stepp and his wife Mary Polly Mills. The name of Jones is always a hard one to research, but Mrs. Honeycutt made a big find in the "daybook" of Solomon Jones, which proved he was born in Wales in 1725, moved to Virginia, then to Spartanburg, South Carolina, and had sons Thomas and John. Thomas and John Jones married sisters, Lucinda and Mary Jane Hicks, and have descendants still living in Henderson County.

The Lyda family moved into present Transylvania County from Virginia. Most of the children of Andrew Lyda, who was born in 1740, moved on, but two stayed in Western North Carolina and have many descendants, particularly from Andrew's son Jacob, whose will is included.

A detailed account of the Freeman family, that came from England to the Plymouth Colony in July 1635, includes what life was like for that group. Mrs. Honeycutt relates by public records how descendants came down through Virginia with Jesse Freeman moving into Rutherford County by 1790.

For the Whitakers, the Bible records of Joshua Whitaker born 1809 and wife Lydia Burgin list not only their children and births and deaths but also the children of Joshua's parents, James and Polly Whitaker, and the children of Benjamin and Elizabeth Brannon Burgin. Benjamin Burgin's will is also included. Other families discussed in detail are Whiteside, Flack, Reed, and Harper. For more information on Mrs. Honeycutt's books, see above.

You never know what family stories that have been handed down you should believe or those you should ignore. Dr. Kenneth Israel of Candler had been told thirty years ago that "Three Israel brothers were run out of Virginia for stealing horses." He spent years searching for his "horse thieves" that he did not find but did find enough to write a six-hundred page book on *The Children of Israel.* However, recently he and Willard Israel of Alabama discovered that their ancestor Michael Israel was a Revolutionary War soldier instead of a horse thief.

Many of the early settlers of Buncombe were men who had fought in the Revolutionary War against the Indians in these mountains. Much of the fighting consisted of small skirmished that only the local militia participated in. After the action, the militia men returned home, but they had seen new river valleys which were inviting for settlement. Many did return as soon as Buncombe was opened for settlement. The stories of these early skirmishes were told to family members and grew as folklore is prone to do, until later family members decided their ancestor must have been a well-known captain or colonel. Most were privates, but as Dr. Israel pointed out in his research: " The captains became generals, governor, and even kings. If the real truth were determined, many of the people of the mountain region could prove that there was not one, but perhaps as many as eight or more Revolutionary War soldiers in their family tree."

The mythical "general or king" theory can be dismissed with a few hours of research at Pack Library in Asheville, but the records of the regular soldiers are much more obscure and perhaps impossible to find. Dr. Israel had searched thousand of indexes and books pertaining to all Israels who had military service in all wars but had not found his Michael Israel. Michael Israel's Revolutionary War proof was finally found in a series of books compiled by John F. Dorman of Washington, D. C., *Virginia Revolutionary Pensions Applications.* Many of the Virginia Patriots received pensions for North Carolina service. Michael Israel died before the laws allowed him to apply for a pension, but his record of service at Kings Mountain was found in the records of William Carter in Volume 16.

After the Revolutionary War, all the members of Michael Israel's family moved from Wilkes County, North Carolina, and lived on the west bank of the French Broad River stretching from Hominy Creek up to Avery's Creek. Michael Israel died in 1819, and his widow Sarah died shortly afterwards. Finally, a Revolutionary War marker furnished by the Veteran's Administration and a Patriot marker furnished by the Sons of the American Revolution was dedicated at Michael Israel's grave site on the Lewis Johnson Farm, Glenn Bridge Road, at Avery's Creek. Keep searching, you may find, as Ken Israel did, that your information may turn out better than an ancestor's being a horse thief.

From all research now available, there were two families in the early 1800s in Buncombe County, North Carolina, now in the Edneyville section of Henderson County, that had similar last names: Justice and Justus.

Since no common ancestor was found for these but still a possibility, a 231-page, soft bound book was compiled on both families and was published in 1993. This compilation is based upon censuses, deeds, marriage and death records, Bible records, and family accounts. *Justis, Justus, Justice for All* extends back to mid-1600 records in Pennsylvania and Virginia and continues through about the 1850s, with about one-half of the book covering these families in Western North Carolina. This material was started about twenty years ago when the author was trying to continue what her father, Percy E. Justus, a descendant of John Justis and Thomas Justice, started before his death in 1965. She got back to her four-great grandfather, John Justis, who was born about 1741, and lived in Newberry, South Carolina, before moving to Clear Creek, then Buncombe County, North Carolina, now Henderson County, about 1800. She never found the parents of this John Justis, but in research of official records, she found more Justis, Justus, Justice people than imagined.

The book covers the early Swedish Gustafssons, two separate families, who both later used the name of Justis. Both Gustafsson families were in Pennsylvania and New Jersey by the mid-1600s. The English families of Justice were in Virginia in the mid-1600s. The Thomas Justice family of Henderson County seemed to be from the English. Thomas, a Revolutionary soldier, had Bible records that ended up in California and are included.

The index includes birth dates for the Justice and Justus names. For more information, write to Joyce Parris, 220 Northwest Avenue, Swannanoa, NC 28778.

If your name is Lance and you are from Buncombe County, you'll want to check the 1986 book, *Lentz Heritage*, compiled by J. Paul Lentz, who has researched records on the Lentz families for fifty years.

The records of early Buncombe settler Peter Lance show he was probably a brother to Bastian, Dewalt, and John Lentz, early German settlers of Rowan County. Peter and his family moved into Buncombe in the late 1700s and bought land in the Shoal Creek/French Broad River areas in the late 1700s. Peter Lance's children who left descendants in Buncombe and Henderson Counties include Flora, born about 1780 and married John Murray; Valentine, born about 1773 and had children Henry, Daniel, Lettie, Peter, Valentine, Jr., and Flora; John, born about 1758.

John Lance's children were born in the 1790s and early 1800s. Staying in Buncombe were sons John, Jr., Martin B. (married Jerusha Fletcher), Samuel J. (married Martha Fletcher), and William Riley, daughters Elizabeth (married Samuel Taylor), and Mary (married James Pressley). Moving to Gilmer County, Georgia, were sons Charles, Peter (married Rachel Greggs), and Thomas (married Catherine Starnes).

A descendant of Martin B. Lance in the late 1800s described a 240-acre Lance farm in Avery's Creek section: "Their log house sat up over the lush river dale on a rounded hill-the pastures, the wheat fields, the gardens all lay below, with a lovely view of the mountains. After the first killing frost, the round-up of the cattle, pigs, sheep from the mountain began half crop in the left."

For more information, write J. Paul Lentz, 2010 Trail 5, Burlington, NC 27215.

If you have an ancestor named McDowell, McDowall, MacDowell, you'll want to study *McDowells in America, a Genealogy* by Dorothy Kelly MacDowell. This 1981 book presents material Ms. MacDowell collected for over forty years from hundreds of sources and includes all the known McDowells in the United States. Kin is established only where it is know.

The characteristic the McDowells all have in common is their Scotish nationality; most were Scots-Irish from Northern Ireland. The McDowells emigrated into Pennsylvania in the early 1700s from where they moved southward and westward until they covered the country. Plentiful are the histories of the McDowell families in Western North Carolina, with much information on the families marrying into theirs.

Twenty pages cover the ancestors of "Hunting John" McDowell, born 1717 in Ireland, and Anne Edmiston. He was granted land in Burke County, 1748, died 1796, buried in Round Hill Cemetery near Pleasant Gardens, N. C. Members of their family married Asheville Pattons, Whitsons, Smiths. A grandson of "Hunting John," Major William McDowell, married Sarah Lucinda Smith in 1846, and they lived in the Smith-McDowell House on Victoria Road, Asheville; also nearby McDowell Street was named for him.

Colonel John Carson, who built the Carson House about 1810, married in 1778 Rachel Matilda McDowell, a daughter of "Hunting John"; therefore, many Carsons are included

The Greenlee family is included by Mary Elizabeth McDowell, born in 1709, marrying, in 1736 in Pennsylvania, James Greenlee. She was the daughter of Ephraim McDowell, born 1673 in Londonderry, Ireland, emigrating to America in 1729, married Margaret Irvine. One of Mary McDowell and James Greenlee's sons was James Greenlee, who married Mary Mitchell, then Ruth Howard, and lived in Morganton. From this family came the name Greenlee for the community a few miles east of Old Fort, where a son David Washington Greenlee, born 1787, married Mary Howard McEntire, and lived at "The Glades."

For more information about this book, write Dorothy K. MacDowell, 1700-42 Fifth Avenue, Hendersonville, NC 28739.

Sara H. Keller published the diary of her great-grandmother, Jane Duncan Todd Massey, who lived in Oconee County, South Carolina. The diary, covering 1900-1903, mentions her family members, neighbors, preachers, and farm life. For more information, write Sarah Keller, 3736 Chiara Drive, Titusville, FL 32796.

A thoroughly documented and interesting history of the Noland family was compiled in 1986 by J. Lynn Noland of Haywood County, North Carolina. The book discussed the Nolands from Ireland in the 1600s and focused on the ones who came into Haywood County by the early 1800s. The title of the book, *Milesian Mountaineers*, came from the Irish myth that the Noland family descended from Milesius, King of Spain. The Milesians from Spain went to Ireland about 1000 B. C. In 1000 A. D., the O'Nolans resided in County Carlow, Ireland. The history of Ireland is discussed though the 1640s during which time the Irish rebellion against the English caused tremendous retaliation by Oliver Cromwell's forces. Irish land was confiscated to pay the English soldiers, and by the 1660s, five-sixths of the Irish people "had perished or fled the land."

Many Nolans were on "Connaught Certificates, Trans-planters A. D. 1653-1654." The Nolands were in Maryland, then Virginia, with early ancestors of the Haywood County Nolands appearing in the land records of Cecil County, Maryland, in 1686. Pierce Noland's will was dated January 20, 1715, in Virginia from where his descendants moved into Granville County, North Carolina by the 1750s. Some moved into Wilkes County on the Brushy Mountains by the 1780s. Peter Noland's will of April 16, 1796, showed that he stayed in Wilkes County, but his descendants moved into the Pigeon Valley, Crabtree, Fines Creek, and Cataloochee sections of Haywood County.

Henry Nolan, his son Peter born 1786, William of Cataloochee who married Judith Allen, and William born 1803 of Fines Creek who married Frances Russell are each discussed in separate chapters with a follow-up chapter of genealogical listings through present generations.

The details on the children of William Noland illustrate the devastating results of the Civil War in Western North Carolina. On September 22, 1862, Sheriff Phillip Noland was ambushed and killed by an "outlier" while trying to enforce the Southern conscription law. Also, after being released from a Union prison, Allen Noland started home from Knoxville in 1865. Taking the Cataloochee Turnpike, he was seen entering the Pigeon River Gorge which had become a haven for renegades. He was never heard from again.

Since the "not-so-braggable" stories are included, these Nolands come across as real people. Some are "on the run" from the law, fleeing into Tennessee and on westward. Mr. Noland is candid about what is proven and what is speculation, but his facts are abundant. Each chapter contains detailed footnotes, and the 350-page book has a bibliography of 63 sources. Detailed census, will, and deed researches are obvious, with many of these official records being included in the appendixes. For more information, write J. Lynn Noland, 29 Noland Drive, Waynesville, NC 28786.

Ben F. Ormand, Jr., a resident of Brevard, North Carolina, wrote in 1983 the *Ormand History and Descendants of James Ormand, Sr., 1669-1766.* The background material briefly discusses five different families of Ormands in America; however, as described by the title, the main sections of the book discussed the family of James Ormand who settled in Mecklenburg County, North Carolina, to his current descendants. The book includes documentation with land grants first to James in 1754, deeds, and wills. Also included are interesting accounts of the family Bible which belonged to his son Benjamin (1745-1829) and the family reunions in Gaston County since 1897. Families who married into this Ormand family include the families of Froneberger, Goforth, Huffstetler, Price, Stacy. For more information write, Rev. Ben P. Ormand, 134 Hawthorne Drive, Brevard, NC 28712.

A 1983 book, *Kin Folks*, by Rose Pless Case is a bonanza for the Pless and related families of Western North Carolina. This book contains 463 pages with 92 photographs. The possible connection of the early Plesses of the Piedmont with the Plesses of Haywood County is briefly discussed. Mrs. Case has made a sincere attempt to preserve family information starting with Issac Pless, born in 1802, who was one of the earliest settlers of the East Fork of Pigeon River (Cruso area), and continuing to descendants to the present generations.

Issac Pless, who married Elizabeth Davis, was the only Pless on the 1830 and 1840 censuses in Western North Carolina. The marriages of Plesses into the Cogburn family, descendants of John Jefferson and Martha Spain Cogburn, are included along with the Allen, Burnette, Kuykendall, Trull, Watts, and other families.

Many proofs and explanations are cited in the book making it very understandable. Official Civil War documents for the Plesses plus material about the Sixty-Second Regiment with all companies from Western North Carolina are included along with details of the prisoner of war Camp Douglas in Illinois. The interesting sketches of individuals by family members along with pertinent news clippings and the Mrs. Case's informal comments on how this family material was put together are intermixed with the family listings. For more information, write Mrs. Wilma Holtzclaw, P. O. Box 1102, Canton, NC 28716.

Years of time, frustrating and conflicting research, hundreds of letters written, and much money go into writing and publishing a family history book. The end publication is basically a labor of love to honor ancestors. This labor of love shows in the interestingly and professionally written family history book by Millard Q. Plumblee, in 1984, *The Plumbly Family from Bucks to Buncombe , 1682-1982 and Allied Lines: Denton, Murray, Fletcher, Johnson, Gullick, Ballenger.* Mr. Plumblee of Caswell County spent many years as an educator and as a historian who had helped write books and contributed in the field of historic preservation in North Carolina. Therefore, it is not surprising that he included an informative review of English history to show the Quaker situation and to suggest possibilities about why the Plumleys left England for America in the late 1600s.

By 1680, six thousand Quakers were in Pennsylvania, which was established for them, and by August of 1682, Charles and Margery Plumley from Somerset, England, joined them in Bucks County. Many copies of legal documents are included, such as a will of Charles Plumley, son of earlier Charles, in 1708, which shows he left "To my bro. George Plumly my Norwester and my bro. John my leather jacket and britches and my courlored Holland Jacket and Breeches."

A William Plumlee who seems to be a descendant of these earlier Plumlys left Pennsylvania for the Shenandoah Valley in Virginia and married Phebe Denton there in 1762. She was the daughter of Abraham Denton II who was in Rowan County, North Carolina, by 1770. It seems William Plumblee was in Burke County by 1790. A possible son, Abraham Plumly, was granted land in 1789 near present Horse Shoe, North Carolina, then Rutherford County.

These Plumlees are traced through South Carolina, Tennessee, and then the focus turns to John Plumlee who was born September 26, 1790, to William Plumlee and Hester O'Neal in Greenville County, S. C. This John was in Buncombe County, North Carolina, before 1814 and married Mary Dugan Murray on September 1, 1814. She was the daughter of James and Margaret Dugan Murray of Buncombe County. They all lived near Fletcher. Much Murray family history is included along with John and Mary Plumlee's family.

A letter from their son William Plumblee, born 1829, Shufordsville address on March 12, 1855, tells his kin in Missouri that a bill had been passed for a "Rail Road from Greenville . . through Asheville . . to paint rock, Tennessee." He also described that "There is a great excitment in Henderson now about copper. There are several persons digging, none have found the mettle yet, though they think the prospects are good." He also told about Dr. Josiah Johnson from Mississippi bringing "the remains of Aunt Adeline Murray, at the request of her father, I suppose. I am told that her body is petrified as hard as a rock. Byers has not let anybody see it yet, he is at a loss to know what to do with it . . .."

The Fletcher family is also included by the marriage of Emma Rose Plumlee (1835-1905) who married Charles M. Fletcher, son of Dr. George W. Fletcher. Details are included of the William Pinkney Plumblee and Roxanna Gullick family that moved from Fletcher to Tigerville, S. C., in 1896. Much local history is included, such as the story of the beginning of the well-known Barber's photography shop in Hendersonville, a story of an all day trip from South Carolina to Hendersonville to sell peaches and staying at a campground and jockey lot near Main Street in the early 1900s.

Mr. Plumblee's well-researched 232-page book has pictures from the late 1800s, family charts, footnotes. For more information, write M. Q. Plumblee, Route 3, Box 259, Burlington, NC 27215.

A book published in 1987 was the memoirs of a former Asheville resident. Many people will remember the Rumboughs of Hot Springs and the Teddy Rumbough house in Asheville, Hopewell Hall, on Zillicoa Street, in the Montford section. Martha Baker, born July 12, 1867, in Philadelphia, met James Edwin (Teddy) Rumbough in 1888 in Hot Springs, North Carolina. They were married on October 23, 1890, in Philadelphia, and moved to Asheville. She and he both died in 1941.

The Rumbough's favorite winter retreats from the mountains included visiting Cuba, Key West, and Palm Beach where they often met people such as the Flaglers. The book is an interesting remembrance of a woman with a Victorian upbringing who described what she saw and heard, including tales of Teddy Roosevelt and old New York where the Waldorf Astoria stood instead of the Empire State Building.

The first part of her book included much about her childhood and family and her travels, which were worldwide in the late 1800s, such as in 1886 on a steamship to Europe. Lord Byron was a fellow passenger, but she was disappointed in the disparity between his poetry and his looks. Cruises in the early 1900s were described when she and her husband visited Jamaica, Cadez, Grenada, Algiers, Nice, Monte Carlo, Genoa, Malta, Cairo, Jerusalem, Paris.

The book includes the Rumbough family tree, starting with George Rumbough, "one of Woodstock, Virginia's first settlers, reportedly killed by Indians in the early 1800s." For more information, write John Rumbough, 816 N. E. 70th Street, Boca Raton, FL 33431.

A book published in 1983 on the Starnes family, *Of Them That Left a Name Behind,* by H. Gerald Starnes and Herman Starnes is interesting reading. The Starnes family, as usual in these books, is followed from their homeland to America, but the difference is the local and American history interestingly presented concerning each area in which the families settled. Extensive records were carefully researched but presented in a story-type form centering on the Starnes' participation in the early history plus a real look at the early customs and politics of the times, starting in the early 1700s. The book begins with the story of the Starnes' (German Starling) exodus from the Palatinate in Germany, giving details of camp life in England where many of our ancestors waited for their boat trip to America. Every reader will have a better understanding of the travails of their ancestors who came and became a part of these early settlements. The Starnes arrived in "New York City in the summer of 1710 to find themselves almost in a state of bondage to the colonial governor," making tar and pitch for the British Navy. The story continues to Pennsylvania, frontier Virginia, North Carolina, South Carolina, Tennessee, Louisiana, and Kentucky where "The Starnes first went to Boonesborough area in 1775 shortly after Boone chopped his trail." David Starnes (1758-1833), a great grandson of Frederick, Sr., immigrant from Germany, was in old Mecklenberg County, now Union County, North Carolina, in the late 1700s. "Captain John Starnes was said to have had two sons, Frederick and John, and a daughter, Christina. Family tradition is that son John (1779-1855), not mentioned in his father's will, was so angered by his receiving nothing from his father's estate that he moved away from Mecklenberg to now Starnes Cove."

The usual deeds, census records, tax lists, church records, court cases, etc., are included along with more than the usual number of maps and early family pictures. The authors discussed all Starnes' families, even though all are not proven kin. The authors did not try to guess how each family "fitted in," but gave thoughtful possibilities. Information should be requested from Now and Then Bookstore, 103 W. Franklin Street, Room 211, Monroe, NC 28110.

Western North Carolinians looking for the names of Cabe, Hall, Buchanan, Corbin, Crisp, Deitz, Frizzell, Bryson, Sutton, and Tatham will want to check a 1985 genealogical book *The Strain Family*. James Parker, Lawrence Wood (well-known local family historian of Macon County), Willard Strain have compiled the descendants of Andrew Strain, Sr., who was born before 1755, was on Buck Creek in Burke County by 1814, moved to Crabtree Creek, Haywood County about 1825 where he died in 1826.

Andrew Strain was married to Mary Reed, daughter of Robert and Nancy Cathey Reed. Andrew and Mary had thirteen children; the descendants of eight of their children were discussed.

Rachel Strain born 1773, married Richard Wilson, lived on Savannah Creek in Jackson County. Rozine Strain born 1776, married Matthew Russell, Sr., lived in Macon County. Mary Strain born 1782, married Rev. Moses Curtis, lived in McDowell County. John Frederick Strain born 1785, married Hannah Sharp, lived in Macon County. Sarah Strain born 17 October 1787, married James McClure, lived in Haywood and Macon Counties. Nancy Strain married William McClure and lived in Macon. Eleanor Strain born 1790, married William McGee, lived in Macon. Andrew Strain, Jr., born 16 June 1791, married Nancy Kidd, lived in Burke, Macon, and Lincoln Counties, N. C., then Anderson County, S. C.

This book includes numerous early pictures, well-documented proofs, newspaper obituaries, and a good addition of letters from individuals who remembered how the earlier Strains looked and lived. For more information about this book, write to Dr. James C. Parker, P. O. Box 11, Dahlonega, GA 30533.

The people in Europe who wanted to reap the benefits by establishing colonies in America may later have wished they'd come themselves. The long-term benefits were for the numerous poor people they had enticed to come; many indentured servants, after their servitude became more successful than the European speculators ever could have imagined.

Dorothy MacDowell did extensive research for four years on he descendants of "Commodore" Vanderbilt and his first wife Sophia Johnson. Mrs. MacDowell traveled the eastern seaboard, visiting libraries and historical societies to obtain information to write the book, *Commodore Vanderbilt and His Family*, which was published in 1990. The book is divided into four parts: the family background, the children of Commodore and Sophia Vanderbilt and descendants of his daughters, the descendants of his son William Henry Vanderbilt, and the descendants of William Henry's daughters and sons.

The family background section starts with Jan Aertsen Van Der Bilt, the three great-grandfather of Cornelius "The Commodore" Vanderbilt. Mrs. MacDowell states that "Jan Aetsen, born about 1620, was the first of the family to come to New Amsterdam, as New York was then called. He was from the village of Bilt in the province of Utrecct in the Netherlands." He was an indentured servant for three years before he

193

became a prosperous farmer and land owner on Staten Island, New York.

The father of the "Commodore" was Cornelius van Derbilt who "became a successful farmer and sailor who owned his own land and operated his own boat," and according to Mrs. MacDowell, the "founder of the Staten Island Ferry." The "Commodore" became the owner of two vessels which carried produce and passengers between Staten Island and New York. On November 19, 1818, he married Sophia Johnson. By the mid-1800s, he had become the leading steamboat owner in America; then, he started buying controlling interest in railroads. By the time of his death in 1877, he already had 63 descendants.

One of Cornelius's sons, William Henry Vanderbilt born 1821, was made vice-president of his father's railroad business and started purchasing real estate on the new Fifth Avenue in New York City. William's youngest son was George Washington Vanderbilt, born 1862, who owned homes on Fifth Avenue, in Bar Harbor, and in New Drop; however, Mrs. MacDowell noted, "When he saw the vista of the nearby mountains in Asheville, N. C., he decided that was where he wanted his real home to be. His first deed for property was dated June 10, 1890, when he acquired thirty-five acres. He eventually owned 125,000 acres "and had built a home with a floorspace of four-and-a-half acres," the Biltmore House. He married Elizabeth Stuyvesant Dresser. They had one child Cornelia, born at Biltmore House in 1900 who married Honourable James Francis Amherst Cecil in All Soul's Episcopal Church in Biltmore. They were the parents of George Henry Vanderbilt Cecil and William Amherst Vanderbilt Cecil.

The book is more that just a listing of genealogy and also includes early family memoirs with details on the intermarrying families. Much material has been added from newspaper articles. For more information write Dorothy MacDowell, 1700 - 42 Fifth Avenue, West, Hendersonville, NC 28739.

Many of you waited for this local family history by Bruce Whitaker since you knew his reputation for researching the Buncombe County families of Whitaker, Reed, Harper, and Wright. In 1989, Bruce Whitaker compiled these four families' histories into one, 520-page, hard-cover book reflecting his sixteen years of research.

Over 4,000 Whitaker descendants are discussed, starting with Joshua Whitaker, born about 1676 in England who died at the Isle of Man about 1715, and his wife Jane Parker of Lancashire, England, and then Dublin, Ireland, before her migration to Chester County, Pennsylvania. Quaker records prove the Whitaker's son William moved from Dublin to Pennsylvania in 1721. William married Elizabeth Carleton on February 13, 1722, in Pennsylvania and moved to Rowan County, North Carolina, by 1755 with seven of their nine children. Many of these descendants moved into Buncombe County about 1800.

Interesting accounts tell where individuals lived, their occupations, mannerisms, beliefs, their civil war letters, and how they died. There are also tales concerning the ones who moved on westward from Buncombe. The families of McCrary, Trantham, Rickman, Lanning, and Garren are discussed in detail because of their many marriages into the Whitaker families.

The Reed family started with John Reed who was born about 1715 in New Jersey and his wife Hannah Davis of New Jersey and Rowan County. About 1800, Eldad Reed and his wife Jane Whitaker moved into Buncombe with their children and settled on Cane Creek. Although many descendants settled on Gashes Creek and in the Riceville and Candler areas and in Henderson and Haywood Counties, many moved on into Tennessee, Missouri, Alabama, and Montana.

Lot Harper, who was born in 1781 in Pennsylvania and was the son of John and Barbara Struble Harper, moved into Buncombe by 1800 into the Fairview area. (His father John was a Revolutionary soldier who moved to Rowan County). Descendants of Lot Harper mainly lived in the Fairview area while some moved on into Indiana. Many Harpers married into the families of Stroup, Henry, Freeman, Sales, and Owenby.

Many of the Wright families of Buncombe had the ancestor Issac Wright of Rutherford County. Issac was born in 1788, and his wife Chaney/China, born about 1780 and an Indian. Their children moved to Broad River and Fairview areas. Many interesting tales of the Civil War, love and marriage, and death are included for these Wrights.

The book contains an interesting combination of factual record plus family tales and incidents. For more information, write to Bruce Whitaker, 333 Richmond Avenue, Swannanoa, NC 28778.

Publishing Your Family History Books

After all the years of work you put into creating your family history, a big question often arises. Should you publish it and offer it for sale? Since you hope someone else will be interested, you think that it could be lost by having one copy in one place. Plus, if others saw your work, they might have facts that could add to your information. Getting information was your purpose to begin with.

If you are thinking of turning what you have researched into a book that people will want to read, there is a guide: *Writing the Family Narrative* by Lawrence P. Gouldrup [Ancestry: Salt Lake City, 1988].

The writer suggests focusing the family narrative around a specific theme in order to write a "crafted family history." "The writer may begin with genealogical research, but he must augment that research with extensive local and general social, cultural, economic, scientific, and historical research if he expects to produce a successful exposition or narrative."

He explains that to plan the exposition, you start by analyzing your facts. What is the significance of the names, places, and dates on those pedigree charts and family group sheets? Why did the family migrate? Your land records, wills, and inventories should reveal how the family earned its money and how it spent it. What did the family value? You must get a perspective of life at a particular time from the history of the area. A study of the cultural and religious background will show moral values. Also, studying old newspapers for the area will give an idea of the community's values.

After this type of analyzing, you should be able to work out a thesis that makes some point about your ancestors so that you can create a plot for your real characters. At the end of each chapter in this book, Mr. Gouldrup further includes lists of books which may serve as guides, or at least as inspirations. Even though these ideas may not "fit" every type of genealogy, for a different idea on what you have the possibility of doing with your research notebooks, you may want to study this publication.

If you decide to publish, many publishing alternatives exist. The most professional copies result from sending your typed material to a publisher who would typeset, index put it in a hard cover. (Soft bound in this case is not much cheaper.) The cost would be about $20 per copy for 200 pages if you order 300 copies and have about 28 photographs. If you send your manuscript "camera ready" (which means copies would be made from exactly what you send), 300 copies with 5 photographs would be about $10.50 per book; only 100 copies, however, would be about $26 per book.

A local company which offers prices similar to these is Genealogy Publishing Service, 448 Ruby Mine Road, Franklin, NC 28734. This company also offers a 60-page booklet for about $10, "How To Write and Publish Your Family Book." This booklet is helpful regardless of where you decide to publish.

Another company you may want to check with is Gateway Press, Inc., 1001 N. Calvert St., Baltimore, MD 21202. This company only takes "camera ready" copies. Plus, many other companies are available for hard cover books. Just check genealogical publications you like the looks of in the library, and write to the company.

If you are more interested in getting the book published than in having a hard cover book, you may want to consider some alternatives. Dogwood Printing, P. O. Box 716, Ozark, MO 65721, will publish "camera ready" copies for 8 1/2 by 11, softbound books of 200 pages, 100 copies for about $1,000. Photographs are $13 per picture for the complete publication. Most publishing companies will not publish fewer that 100 books. Many people who publish a soft-cover book have a choice of a spiral bind or a regular bind. One thing you may want to consider, with a spiral bind, there is no title to be seen if the book is standing in a library shelf.

Using local copying printers, you could get your soft-bound, "camera ready" 200 pages copied with 100 copies for about $16, no extra for pictures. However, the picture quality is not the same as publishers who do "screened" prints for better results, often better than the originals. You would not have to have 100 copies printed. You could get more copies as needed.

Many considerations need to be thought through before publication. You must know how many copies, pages, and pictures before you can receive a price. While thinking of the number of copies you need, be realistic. The more books you order, the cheaper they will be, but think about how many you will sell. Also, what price will you have to charge for the book. These books are not easy to sell, and an overpriced book is really hard to sell. You need to get a contract price to decide the exact publication price. Then, you need to price mailers and get mailing costs. (Put a book about the size of yours into the mailer, go to the post office, find out the price for mailing it book rate. Book rate does not vary anyplace in the United States, even Hawaii.)

You will also need to add six percent sales tax for books sold in North Carolina. The tax form you need is available locally at 119 Tunnel Road, Suite E., Asheville. Tell the employee at the tax office what you are doing, and you will be given a simpler form than one in which you would have to go by the tax office every month with.

Additionally, consider the costs for advertising. Basically, this consists of giving a book so that a genealogical society will do a review of your book. Even newspaper reviews involve giving a free copy and hoping for a review. Very few newspapers will review this type book in a regular book section, and you have to depend upon newspapers that have a genealogical column. Plus, most libraries will appreciate a copy of your book if you donate it.

As you can tell, by careful planning, you can hope to get back the costs for publication, mailing, advertising, but you will never get paid for your hours, your travel, your paying for official records, etc.

Think carefully about your manuscript before those "camera ready" copies are sent. Study brochures that remind you odd-numbered pages should start chapters. Put in blank pages if necessary, but these do count for cost. Pictures can be interspersed most interestingly and almost as cheaply as "picture" pages. Study your material for clarity; you may need some type of family numbering system.

Put copies of original documents, if included, such as wills, Bible records, war records, in an appendix instead of interrupting the main text. Give where you received your information whether a person or an original document within the text or a footnote, such as "From Will Book B, p. 312, Buncombe County Court House, Asheville, N. C." If you are using family "Stories," say so and tell who told it to you. Also, no matter how time consuming, include a name index.

In the "Preface" tell what your purpose was in writing the book and explain the numbering system included. The "Introduction" is for background information of the family and the coverage of families you have included.

If all this sounds complicated and expensive, it is; but if you are really as devoted as most people are to what you have discovered, the effort is worthwhile. You may be the only one who can write this particular family history.

CHAPTER 7. MILITARY RECORDS

The "lure" of Western North Carolina probably came about by military expeditions against the Indians. Most people feel this lure of the mountains better than they can explain the attraction. Two gaps in the Blue Ridge Mountains, Hickory Nut Gorge to the south and Swannanoa Gap to the east, were the trails for the first white explorers into much of present Western North Carolina. In September 1776, General Griffith Rutherford and his troops in their expedition against the Cherokees came through Hickory Nut Gorge. Davidson's Fort, now Old Fort, had been built by his troops as an outpost, the "gate" before the Blue Ridge Mountains into Swannanoa Gap and Indian territory. Hunters and traders had tread into the mountains and many sat, waiting. The most adventurous settlers, the Davidsons, first started through Swannanoa Gap. Pennsylvania's loss was North Carolina's gain when the Davidsons decided to move south in the 1740s. John, George, and

Robert Davidson, Scottish immigrants from Northern Ireland, had settled in Pennsylvania. Robert died there at age 27, leaving a widow, Isabella Ramsay, and a son and daughter. The Davidsons may have been lured southward by a 435-mile "road" that ran from Philadelphia through Lancaster to Winchester in Virginia through the Shenandoah Valley, down Dan River into Yadkin and Catawba Rivers in North Carolina. Robert's widow and children settled on the Yadkin River while John and George settled with their families on what became Davidson Creek area in South Iredell County. John's survey for his Royal Grant was made November 26, 1748.

Robert and Isabella's son John became a delegate to the Provincial Legislation in 1773 and signed the Mecklenburg Declaration of Independence on May 20, 1775. His sister married Alexander Brevard.

George Davidson's youngest son, William Lee, was born about 1746. He married Mary Brevard, daughter of John Brevard and sister of Ephraim Brevard. Ephraim was the scribe for the Mecklenburg Declaration, and the town of Brevard was named for him. William Lee Davidson became a major in the Revolution, 4th N. C. Regiment which was assigned to the Continental Army. When General Rutherford was captured at Camden, S. C., Davidson was named Brigadier General by an act of the General Assembly on August 31, 1780. On February 1, 1781, while trying to prevent Cornwallis's troops from crossing the Catawba River at Cowan's Fort, General Davidson was shot, died, and buried at Hopewell Church. Davidson Counties in North Carolina and Tennessee were named for him as well as Davidson College.

General William Davidson's cousins, John's children, were the early Davidsons of Western North Carolina. Although John's residence was in Iredell County, he'd been to the Blue Ridge Mountains as pack horse master general with General Rutherford's expedition in 1775. Several of his children had gathered at the "gate" near the headwaters of the Catawba.

His son John married Nancy Brevard and lived near Old Fort. In an Indian raid in July of 1776, John, Nancy, and one child was killed. Their daughter Sarah was with her grandparents, the John Brevards. Sarah Davidson married Lambert Clayton on December 14, 1782. They became early Western North Carolina settlers.

Since the dangers from the Indians was well known to the Davidsons, it is hard to imagine the lure that would pull a man and woman with a child, servant, and belongings away from the protection of neighbors and the Fort. But Samuel Davidson, one of John's sons, did go through the Swannanoa Gap and to now Christian Creek near its influx into the Swannanoa River. "Vacant" land was all around for miles and miles where he built his cabin. His settlement, although the first in present Buncombe County, 1784, did last out the year since he was killed by Indians. His wife fled with the child and servant back to Old Fort.

Colonel Daniel Smith organized a group to find the body of Samuel and to avenge his death. Some in the group liked the land and went back to settle in 1785, creating the first permanent white settlement in present Buncombe, the "Swannanoa Settlement" near the influx of Bee Tree Creek with Swannanoa River, a few miles east of where Samuel was killed. The settlers included Samuel's twin brother Major William Davidson and his wife Margaret McConnell. This William, born about 1736, had participated in the Revolution. His family had lived in the "Glades" or Greenlee in present McDowell County. He lived the rest of his life on Bee Tree, dying May 16, 1814. A monument erected by the Daughters of the American Revolution is located at the Swannanoa Presbyterian Church near the location of this first settlement.

Standing on the knoll in the cemetery and looking at the mountains and into the valley toward the Swannanoa River, you can feel why many adventurers stopped and stayed here forever.

Revolutionary War

You often read that if you had a male ancestor in this country during the time of the Revolutionary War, there is a very good chance that he was involved in the war. However, your finding proof of this involvement is not always easy. He could have sold supplies to the army. He could have been in the state militia. He could have been in the continental forces.

The ones who served in the continental forces and were disabled were the ones who got the pensions from August 26, 1776, to 1806. (In 1832, pensions became available for many more Revolutionary servicemen, including the state forces.)

Copies of pension papers when available from the National Archives are valuable to family historians because the veterans' affidavits had to be very detailed. Most had date and place of birth, dates of service, military encounters, movements since the war, information from family Bibles, and sometimes a list of heirs. Fires in 1800 and 1814 destroyed most of the early applications, but since these applications were made to the federal government, at least a partial record of the earlier pensioners was included among reports to Congress in 1792, 1794, 1795. Murtie Clark compiled these existing early records, which are not available in the National Archives where most of the records are. *The Pension Lists of 1792-1795, with Other Revolutionary War Pension Records* was published in 1992 [Genealogical Publishing: Baltimore].

These earliest records are arranged by states, usually giving name, rank, regiment, description and circumstances of wounds incurred, and information regarding pension, place of residence, and physical fitness. Some pension applications were rejected; however, this does not necessarily mean the former soldier was lying. He probably could not supply the necessary information. Some early ones were rejected because they were in the state militia instead of the continental lines. The Congressional report stated that "in many cases no proof of service can be traced, owing to the imperfection or entire deficiency of the muster rolls."

Most of the men's disabilities in these early records were listed as "wounded . . . by musket ball," but many men "lost" the use of an eye from smallpox and several "lost sight in one eye from the smallpox inoculations" in 1777 and 1778. Some show disability from the extremely cold weather such as "feet frozen on a march from Oswego to Fort Rensselaer on the Mohawk River in Feb. 1783."

Many South Carolina soldiers are listed, dated 1792, plus a few other people who claimed "certificate of debt" which had accumulated interest since 1792. These amounts are for a few dollars to one over $7,500. Over three thousand veterans and a few surviving wives are listed in Ms. Clark's publication.

Another book, *The Pension List of 1820* was first published as a report by the Secretary of War on January 20, 1820. This has been republished and includes the pensioners who served nine months or more in the Revolutionary Army and were in "indigent or needy circumstances." Again, at this time, this was for the continental forces only. This book illustrated that by 1820 men from the continental forces from nearly every state had migrated to the new territories, including Ohio, Kentucky, Tennessee, Indiana, Illinois, Michigan territory. (This may have been the result of their being paid with bounty land in these frontier areas.) About 16,000 entries are included in this book. [Genealogical Publishing: Baltimore, 1992]

To order copies of military and/or pension records which you see listed in the 1820 book or if you just want to check on an ancestor, write Reference Services Branch, National Archives and Records Administration, 7th and Pennsylvania Ave., N.W., Washington, DC 20408. You must receive the correct form to fill out before you can request a search for the file. Send no money. After you fill out the form, you will be notified of the cost, about $10.

Many family historians have searched to prove their ancestors fought with the Patriotic Americans in the Revolution with no results. There is a possibility that they were for the British or Loyalists. At least thirty percent of our ancestors did not rush out with their muskets to fight for freedom from the British. In North Carolina, which probably contained a greater number of Loyalists in proportion to its population than any other colony did, three important factors influenced attitudes toward fighting for independence: religion, occupation, location of settlement.

The Moravians, Mennonites, Dunkards, and Quakers wanted to remain neutral. The Scottish people were bound by a religious oath to be good and faithful subjects of King George II of England. Most merchants, since they carried on trade directly with England, were not for war. Small farmers were not concerned about tariff acts. The clergy was basically made up of Loyalists. Many people did not live on the east coast but in the "back country" of North Carolina and remained loyal to the King because they resented the ruling class on the east coast which controlled the assembly and county offices, feeling their fellow North Carolinians did not do so much for them as the King of England. As many as two-thirds of the people were Loyalists in sections of Surry, Guilford, Orange, Rowan, Randolph, Chathum, Cumberland, Anson, Brunswick, and Montgomery Counties.

In May of 1776, the Patriots had the power, even though independence from England had not been declared, to enact laws against Loyalists or Tories, with some being put into prison ahd having to forfeit one-half of their estates. By 1777, all males over 16 years of age had to take an oath of allegiance to North Carolina or be banished from the state.

In January of 1778, Governor Josiah Martin reported from New York City, which was controlled by the British, that over one hundred and fifty people had come there from North Carolina in the last six months. N. C. Loyalists also went to the West Indies, Nova Scotia, England, Scotland, East Florida, and Ontario, Canada, (where 3,200,000 acres had been given to Loyalists by 1787.)

In 1779, all Loyalists' land was being seized and sold, and the jails were full of prisoners accused of treason. Many Loyalists who did not flee decided to change sides.

Few records are available for all the Loyalists who fought for England. More records are available for the ones who made claims, petitions, or pension requests from Great Britain. The complete official files of Loyalists' claims are in the Public Record Office in London. The British Record Collection in the North Carolina Archives has some "Loyalist transcripts" of the petitions of the N. C. claimants.

Several books available at Pack Library in Asheville give Loyalist lists and information. One is *Loyalists of the American Revolution* (two volumes) by Lorenzo Sabine. This contains biographical sketches of known Loyalists through- out the colonies. Sabine explained the lack of

205

knowledge about many Loyalists came about because they had to become exiles leaving personal papers behind. Another factor was for a generation or more, the ones who went to different American colonies to start over did not discuss the unpopular side they had taken during the Revolution.

Another helpful book at Pack is by Robert DeMond, *The Loyalists in North Carolina during the Revolution.* The appendixes list all the Loyalists he could trace through official records. For example, 102 names of Loyalists who were stationed on James' Island in 1782 plus about 1000 more in various regiments and prisons in Halifax and Wilmington are listed. Treasury papers list ones who received pay in the Bahamas, St. Augustine, Charleston. The appendixes also have records of land confiscated and sold in North Carolina, Loyalists' claims for loss of property, and the lists of N. C. Loyalists who received pensions from the British government from 1786-1831.

If you cannot imagine how many Loyalists were in this country, you probably have seen in too many history books that everyone was rushing off to fight the British, hollering, "Give me liberty or give me death." Also, perhaps, discovering that an ancestor was in the Revolution but a loyalist is not so exciting for most, but acceptable. Usually a plausible explanation is decided upon, such as "He'd just gotten off the boat from England," or "He was a Scot who had promised not to fight against England." However, some were in the Revolution who didn't fit as a patriot or a loyalist. Some, instead of feeling as Patrick Henry did, were described by Thomas Paine as "Summer soldiers .. who shrink from the service of their country."*Summer Soldiers: A Survey and Index of Revolutionary Courts Martial* by James C. Naegles, 1986, [Ancestry: Salt Lake City] may not be where you want to find your ancestor listed, but it contains excellent insight into the problems during the Revolution. The summarized 3,315 court martial records, which include 593 officers, contain a document number which refers to the original sources. The sources are from orderly books, published books, and on microfilm in the National Archives.

Neagles said that the two basic conditions for violations included the miserable camp life when the soldier felt he was needed at home and the opportunity to make money out of the situation, such as stealing military supplies, plunder- countrysides, and multiple enlistments. Enlisted men who deserted numbered 1,162. The book pointed out that many of the soldiers were "wary" when they left their own states and that if the camp life became too difficult, they would decide to go back home and not see anything wrong with doing so.

Included in the book are descriptions of the major battles in which desertions occurred, such as when General Benedict Arnold, to reach Quebec, "spent two months marching and boating through Maine in snow and bitter cold. Large numbers died of starvation or were frozen to death; others deserted en masse, stealing food and supplies." After being defeated, "hundreds more died of smallpox, malaria, dysentery, as well as murder at the hands of the Indians." At Long Island, 1,500 Americans died; 800 killed at Savannah; 700 killed at Brandywine; 5,000 taken prisoners at Charleston; 800-1,000 killed at Camden. Much detail is included on the deplorable living conditions: "During the two month trek to Quebec, soldiers were reduced to boiling and eating their shot pouches or any other scraps of leather they could find." During the Valley Forge encampment, 3,000 died of disease, smallpox being the primary killer. In addition to deserting to leave the living conditions, many left to reenlist for bonuses or to join the British who were paid high wages. If money were available for the patriots, the standard pay for a private was under $7 per month in fast-depreciating continental currency.

The penalties for a guilty verdict at a court-martial ranged from "floggings," being "drummed out of the service," (in which labels of Tory would be pinned upon the clothes of the man as he left camp with the troops assembled and a drum roll going), death by shooting or hanging, and confinements, sometimes on a war vessel. The penalties were similar for cowardice, fighting, gambling, excessive use of alcohol, and plundering. George Washington particularly disliked soldiers bothering the citizens in any way. One private from South Carolina was given "death by shooting" for deserting and attempting to go to the enemy. One captain from Pennsylvania was pardoned for being drunk during an attack and behaving "ridiculously, by frequently huzzaing during the approach to the enemy's works." One private from Massachusetts received 75 lashes for killing a cow and seven geese.

At Pack Library an interesting book is the 1984 *Revolutionary War Soldiers of Western North Carolina, Burke County*, Vol. I, by Emmett R.

White. This book has an excellent summary of the Revolution in Burke and present McDowell counties plus extensive biographical information for 165 soldiers. References are included with each entry.

For Robert Patton/Patten, who was born November 10, 1748, there is early information that he lived on a branch of Muddy Creek in Burke, son of Robert and Charity Patton who had earlier lived on Colwater Creek in Rowan County. A summary of his military service, which was mainly in Burke, included his being an Indian spy. His later data stated that he married Elizabeth Dysart in 1782, then gave a list of his children. His death date was March 18, 1813, in McDowell. Also, his land holdings and deed transactions are discussed.

War of 1812

Most family historians search diligently to see if an ancestor were in the Revolutionary War or the Civil War, but many overlook a war that happened in the early 1800s and may produce service, pension, or bounty land records: The War of 1812. Over 38,000 North Carolina men were involved as regulars or as attached state militia, including regiments from the Western North Carolina sections of Buncombe, Burke, Haywood, Rutherford.

The involvement of America in a second war with England came about for several reasons. First, American ships were trying to stay neutral during England's war against Napoleon and France. However, England not only prevented supplies from American ships going to France but also seized American sailors to run her own war vessels. President Jefferson ordered American ships to stay at home, but merchants, wanting to make profits, refused. However, the "impressionment" of Americans was one of the major reasons for the United States' entering this war.

Another cause was that many Americans felt that the British were arming and encouraging the Indians to fight the settlers. Western North Carolinians particularly in Haywood County feared this action. Great efforts were made to enlist volunteers into the fighting force; the government promised the volunteers a "rifle dress and give you your favorite weapon, and . . . you will cover yourself with glory." Plus the pay of $8 to $12 per month and $124 bounty for enlisting and 160 acres of free land when the war was over had to sound like a fortune. (Two volunteers from Buncombe and two widows of volunteers were still trying to obtain this promised 160 acres of free land in April of 1855.) Although these troops were raised for the federal government, money for pay, arms, and other supplies came from North Carolina. North Carolina was not repaid for these expenses by the federal government until one hundred years later.

The third reason had nothing to really do with the American people at this time: the American government wanted to obtain Canada and Florida to be part of America.

On June 18, 1812, when James Madison was President, the House and the Senate of the United States Congress declared "That War be and the same is hereby declared to exist between the United Kingdom of Great Britain and Ireland and the United States of America. . .." However, on April 10, 1812, "in pursuance of a Requisition of the President of the United States in virtue of an Act of Congress," troops in North Carolina had already been raised.

If Israel Pickens, who was a Congressman from Burke, Lincoln, Rutherford, Buncombe, and Haywood Counties, reflected indication of the Western North Carolina feeling, it is sure that they felt the war was a necessity. He called for patriotism against the English's capture of private citizens and its army of Indians. By July of 1813, the Creek Indians were ready to attack the western frontiers. They started at Fort Mims, Alabama. Many people feared the Cherokees would join them. However, General Andrew Jackson's troops, including volunteers from North Carolina and about five hundred Cherokees defeated the Creeks.

Some resistance occurred because of the state militia's being sent out of the home state to fight. Just as in the Revolution, there were two kinds of troops involved in the action, the regulars, who were volunteers, and the state militia, which originally was formed to fight only if the home area were attacked.

When the capitol of Washington was burned by the British in August of 1814, more troops were called for which took in many of the state militia. (This fire destroyed many Revolutionary War records.) *Muster Rolls of the Soldiers of 1812 Detached from the Militia of North Carolina in 1812 and 1814*, which lists the soldiers by county is available at Pack Library. In 1812, Rutherford County had four companies, Burke had two, and

Buncombe had a company of seventy men, including Thomas Rhodes, captain, Eli Merrill, lieutenant, Thomas Moore, ensign, and privates Thomas Justice, Cornelius Corn, Nathan Fletcher, William Murry, Andrew Garron, John Love. Haywood County had a company of seventy-three, including David Vance, Jr., William and James Welch, John and Issac Rice. By August 1814, Buncombe had 198 men in three regiments.

The town of Burnsville was named for Otway Burns, who was a seafaring privateer during this war. These privateers would attack and capture British merchant ships, robbing them of their supplies intended for the British fighting men. It is estimated Burns captured several million dollars worth of goods and ships from the English.

According to "War of 1812, Claims of Service" in film number 89 at the Buncombe County Archives in Asheville, a company of volunteers was being created in Buncombe in February of 1815.

Eighteen men from North Carolina were killed in action, and North Carolina pension rolls show that even in 1883, ninety-five North Carolina men, who were disabled in the war, were still drawing pensions, plus many widows. In 1835, several veterans appeared in Buncombe County courts to claim land for their serving nineteen days in this war. On April 14, 1855, Robert Brittain, "aged 67," stated that he volunteered in the county of Buncombe the 17th day of February 1815 for a six months period and was honorably discharged the 12th day of March 1815. He said he was in Capt. James Lowry's Co., Colonel Andrew Ervin. David Hughey, "aged 69," made a similar request with both requesting bounty land under the Act of March 3, 1855.

On March 27, 1855, Jemima Robards, who was 74, stated she was the widow of Thomas G. Robards who had served in this same volunteer company of Buncombe and had died in 1843. She stated that her maiden name was Chambers and that she and Thomas were married in Wilkes County August 13, 1805, had lived in Buncombe County about 43 years except for two years in Tennessee. She stated her husband first served under the Command of Captain Bailey, but "upon the receipt of marching orders Captain Bailey refused to assume command of his company" and that these "few soldiers" joined Captain Lowry's Company.

Elizabeth Casey, who was 75 and a Madison County resident also applied for bounty land as widow of Samuel Brittain, who was a private in Captain Lowry's Company and who died in May 1816. They were married in Buncombe in 1811, and her maiden name was Penland. In October 1816 she married Anthony Casey who died October 29, 1846.

Captain Lowry who was a resident of Buncombe and 72 in 1855 stated that these men were in his company about 24 or 25 days. The records do not state if any of these received their bounty land. It is doubtful since North Carolina did not receive the reimbursement from the federal government for the War of 1812 until 1916.

Also, strange is the date these men entered the War of 1812. The frontier threat from Indian violence ended in April of 1814 when the Creek Indians were crushed in Alabama with American troops getting much help from the Cherokee Indians. Therefore, this volunteer regiment in Buncombe was not raised to defend Western North Carolina but to defend the eastern seaboard. The peace treaty was signed on December 24, 1814, (before these men joined), at Ghent in Belgium; it was received in New York on February 11, 1815; six days before the Buncombe County volunteers were sworn into service for six months. News traveled slowly in the early 1800s.

The Civil War

War is never easy for anyone. The Revolutionary War was fought in order to establish the United States. Then, fewer than a hundred years after this country was the United States, the Civil War occurred, and no one was spared hardships and griefs. Who was on which side was almost like the toss of a coin. Some people came to America and landed in New England, some in Virginia. Many from Pennsylvania in the late 1700s and early 1800s came down the Great Wagon Road to North Carolina and South Carolina, while some stayed at home. During the Civil War, men with the same backgrounds and often the same fathers met on the battlefield on opposite sides.

Many immigrants came to America because of hopes for better lives. Their basic desires were to raise enough food and livestock to take care of their families. They really did not have time to march off to fight. There was strangeness of a man's being out at night and being stopped by troops, demanding him to say which "side" he favored. A wrong guess of the color of the uniform could mean quick death. People not really involved with either side could be killed just by visiting a known Union or Confederate family.

Any ancestor in the South between 1861 and 1865, whether wanting to be or not, was involved in one way or another in the Civil War. Not one man, woman, or child was exempt.

On December 20, 1860, South Carolina voted to secede from the Union. Mississippi, Florida, Alabama, Georgia, Louisiana, and Texas followed by February 1, 1861. Virginia, Tennessee, Arkansas were more reluctant, and, last of all was North Carolina that wanted to stay neutral. These eleven seceding states had a population of nine million with three and half-million being slaves. The twenty-three Northern states had twenty-two million people. Prolonged argumentation over which side to be for occurred in the slave states of Maryland, Delaware, Missouri, and Kentucky, but their governments decided to stay with the Union. West Virginia divided from Virginia and was for the Union.

North Carolinians just watched and waited back in 1860 and early 1861 while the more southern "cotton" states were hollering for and withdrawing from the Union. The North Carolina General Assembly did feel a crisis was coming and felt the state should prepare for war -- which side to fight with was not decided. A hundred page booklet by John Barrett, *North Carolina As a Civil War Background, 1861-1865*, gives details of these events. [1993, Historical Publications Section, Division of Archives and History: Raleigh]

North Carolinians were divided in their opinions. However, even with the Union meetings being held in the western section, the people for the most part against secession felt they could not fight against their "fellow southerners." The people of eastern North Carolina were for secession and in December 1860 even seized Forts Caswell and Johnston, near the mouth of the Cape Fear River, to protect the state from the Union.

As tensions grew, the people voted on February 28, 1861, to see if a convention should be held to decide what the majority of the people wanted. The ones against secession won for no convention. However, North Carolinians could not decide to watch and wait forever. After the April 13, 1861, battle at Fort Sumter in Charleston, President Lincoln called for 75,000 troops with two regiments to come from North Carolina. Governor Ellis answered, "You can get no troops from North

Carolina."

Secession was now favored by the people and was declared May 20 by a convention. Half of the members were excited and rejoiced; the others were quiet and depressed. Regardless of personal fears, "As members of the new family of States, North Carolina threw her entire strength behind the southern cause." During these early months, as troops were organized, "patriotism was at its height, as very few North Carolinians realized the tragedy of war. Young men left home for camps of instruction in the spirit of a holiday outing," stated Barrett, bringing with them bed- steads, violins, huge camp chests. War equipment was scarce and resulted in some soldiers being issued everything from old flintlock-type muskets dating back to the Revolution to carrying wooden poles with iron at the end as they headed for the Virginia front. With extreme conditions developing, excitement did not last long. The Conscription Act of April 1862 required all white males between 18 and 35 into service for three years. There were also taxes that required farmers to give one-tenth of all their produce to Richmond. Also, livestock, wagons, any provisions could be taken for the Confederate Army at the price it set. "For mountain folk, accustomed to individual freedom, these acts were especially galling."

By the fall of 1863, soldiers were deserting in large numbers. "In Western North Carolina a veritable civil war existed between the Confederate troops and the organized deserters and bushwackers," stated Barrett. Governor Vance estimated there were 1,200 deserters in the mountains by 1863. In the east, the Union had taken over, destroying homes and belongings. By the end of 1863, North Carolina was "at the mercy of the enemy."

By February of 1864, men from 17 years of age up to 55 were "conscripted" or drafted. Many more men hid out from the fighting while women and children were fighting starvation and the "outliers." Union General Grant's strategy was that winning was the prerequisite over suffering of the loss of lives, and people in some southern cities were starving. Also, in Western North Carolina in 1864 with only 500 Confederate soldiers and a "home guard," there were more problems. Colonel George Kirk easily went from east Tennessee to Morganton to destroy the railroad. The deserters continued to murder and steal without harm to themselves. Burnsville was raided by 75 men, and Henderson

County was described as in "a state of anarchy." Asheville was "thoroughly ransacked" on April 26 according to Barrett. Finally, on May 9 at Waynesville, "a small Confederate force under Colonel J. R. Love skirmished with a Union Cavalry detachment. These were the last shots of the war fired on North Carolina soil." In Barrett's book, there is a map of North Carolina with civil war engagements marked and fifty pictures and drawings of the generals and battle scenes.

Barrett presented the facts in the area of Western North Carolina; the feelings created by this war were worse. From Western North Carolina before the war was over about twenty thousand fought for the Confederacy and five thousand for the Union. The effects on the people were threefold: first, communities and families were torn apart by separate sympathies; next, the "outliers" terrified, robbed and murdered even children; finally, Stoneman's Union forces raided and occupied the countryside.

"Battlelines" were erected before the secession of North Carolina. Once agreeable families and communities had divided loyalties. A statewide vote was held on February 28, 1861, to determine if the people wanted the General Assembly to meet to secede. Sadie Patton in *The Story of Henderson County* told of the battle in the farming community of Edneyville where the Secessionists and Union men met at old Edney Store to vote on seceding from the Union. Politics were not friendly when, among the three hundred who met to vote, the Edney clan came armed with blacksmith-made bayonets to lead the community to secede. The election there carried for the Secessionists, but the bitter feelings were not resolved. This same type of situation was going on all over the area where many families and neighbors never considered themselves "true" family or "true" neighbors again.

Although North Carolina did not secede officially until May 20, 1861, troops were going out of Western North Carolina in April. William W. McDowell had organized the first volunteer company in North Carolina for the Confederacy, the Buncombe County Riflemen, which left April 18, 1861, while Zebulon Vance organized the Rough and Ready Guards. After the May vote, the Secessionists had the majority of the community plus the weight of the Confederate government behind them and often persecuted the known Union sympathizers. The Union Company F, 2nd N. C. Volunteers was composed of men from the mountains, familiar

214

place names such as Mills River, Crab Creek, Big Willow, Upper Mud Creek, Little River, with families left behind in those places to be persecuted.

Next, as the war and bitter feelings continued, many people not only in remote mountain coves but also in towns became fearful of "outliers." The "outliers" were not a phantom fear. Union sympathizers who were avoiding being drafted for the Confederacy were hiding in remote sections and robbing the countryside for provisions. Particularly the mountains bordering N. C. and S. C. in present Transylvania and Henderson Counties as well as the N. C. and Tenn. mountains were refuges for hundreds of men; most of these had to pillage for survival, but some degenerated into murderous gangs of renegades. Even people who earlier in the war had felt sympathy for their mistreated "Union" neighbors became repulsed and fearful as the groups of men became larger and ransacked homesteads as they pleased. The families were scared there would be no food left for them as well as for their own lives. They had no "protectors," since able-bodied men were writing from places such as Manassas and Murfreesbora.

Van Noppen in *Stoneman's Last Raid* reprinted a letter written February 14, 1865, in Rutherford City, N. C., to Governor Vance, telling about the atrocities of the "outliers," such as, "Alexander Grant had his house broken open and his daughter shot and killed in a bed, a considerable amount of other articles taken and himself nearly beaten to death." Some family Bibles listed sons as "killed by bushwackers while home on leave." Confederate soldiers coming home were killed during road ambushes or murdered in their homes. Even Confederate General Baylus M. Edney was assassinated in this manner. The bitterness continued and the constant threat of the "outliers" were preludes to when Stoneman's Union forces arrived. Most people survived, but families and neighbors were torn apart.

A November 28, 1863, letter, from which portions are quoted below, was saved by George Fletcher Frady of Asheville. (The letter was written to his great-grandfather.) Charles H. Lance, who was born in Buncombe County, wrote this letter to his brother Samuel J. Lance of Shufordsville, Henderson County. Charles H. Lance, living then in Gilmer County, Georgia, was about 67 in 1863 when he wrote the letter. He was not in the Civil War, but he was searching for his Western North Carolina nephews who were fighting for the Confederacy around Chattanooga, Tennessee.

"I have juste returned from Chattanooga, Tenn. I saw moore then I was expected to see. I saw thousands of Yankeys. I was in 100 yards of their picket guard and in 200 yards off the breste work . . . I saw 1000 upon 1000 of our soldiers all in good health. I hunted two days for Harvey Lance [son of his brother Martin B. and Jerusha Fletcher Lance of Buncombe]. I was in 100 yards of him and did not know it til I came back to Generals at Tunnel Hill. Harvey wrote to Nelson [Charles's son-in-law Nelson Israel of Western North Carolina] to send him some provisions. Nelson done so as the poore soldiers are suffering for victuals and all. I was all over the battleground. I saw Yankeys not buried. I saw hundreds of acres of land leveled between Ringgold and Chattanooga on both sides of the road stroud over with corn and wheat from 6 to 8 inches high that was destroyed by the two armies. Both our men and the Yankeys and not a cow or horse or sheep or hogg to speak of. I saw hundreds of acres of land lying waste. Plantations worth 1000 to 2000 dollars, not a person to be seen, all gone. I saw General Longstreet and General Breckinridge. I saw General Bragg's Headquarters. The soldiers told that Bragg was about my size and favored me very much. As I walked down our picket yard with a lieutenant, the soldiers took me for Bragg. I told them I was a better looking man than Bragg and created a heighte height. I saw more dead horses and mules all over the campment on both sides of the road for 18 miles. It is a continual scent. The creeks and branches are full of dead horses and mules. We had to drink the water and to make coffee with the water or do without. I can tell you the more when I see you . . .

"I may go all the way to Chattanooga as I suppose there have had hard fights this week. We heard the cannons all day Sunday, Monday, Tuesday, and Wednesday and Thursday. On yesterday we saw a gentleman from Ringgold. He said Bragg had cut up the Yankey army at a dreadful rate . . .

" Wheat is selling at $10 per bushel, corn from $8 to $10 per bushel, cabbage at $1 per head, apples $15 to $20 per bushel, cows and calves $150, horses from $300 to $600."

In this letter he says he supposes Burtin, son of Samuel J. Lance, was taken a prisoner at Chickamauga. (He was on September 20, 1863, and died in a Chicago prison of war.) He wants to know how many of his nephews from Western North Carolina are in the service.

Other letters were saved by family members. Letters during this time were not as common as letters are today; plus, the following are from two men who did not survive the Civil War.

On October 14, 1862, William Lance while with the 60th Regiment, N. C. Troops, wrote to his mother in Skyland from Murfreesboro, McDowell Camp. "Dear Mother, I hope you will continue to pray for me. Dear mother, I will do the best I can." He asked if she could send him a couple of pairs of socks and a blanket.

On October 22, 1862, he wrote to his father and mother, saying, "The health of our Regiment is tolerable good only we have plenty of mumps here at this time. . . .. You have no idea how bad I feel when I think of home, when I think of my little children. It nearly breaks my heart when I think of them but I will try to put it off the best I can."

William Whitaker wrote to his father in Edneyville from a "Camp near Berryville, Va., November 2, 1862." He said there was a "grate deal of talk about Small Pox" among the troops. He requested socks, a vest, a blanket, and a good pair of boots, woolen gloves.

The parents at home who received these letters had to hope for better times.

The state historical marker on old U. S. Highway 70 at Ridgecrest simply states, "Southern Troops turned back Stoneman's U. S. Cavalry raiding through Western North Carolina at Swannanoa Gap near here. April 20, 1865."

About four miles east of this marker, if you climbed down and up steep mountainous ridges, you may find another marker which is connected to this historical one. Resting on a slope beside large rhododendrons above a narrow valley and creek are a headstone and a footstone. The headstone only states in raised letters "U. S. Soldier." Standing at the stones and looking west up the narrow valley, you can easily imagine that even a small force could keep a large force from proceeding up Swannanoa Gap.

What his U. S. soldier's name was or who placed this gravemarker is a mystery. But it is a reminder that the effects of the Civil War were real in Western North Carolina. In the spring of 1865 in these mountains, instead of plowing the land and planting onions and potatoes, the able-bodied men were still fighting for the Confederacy, or being "Outliers" or a part of Stoneman's raiders who came.

Stoneman's Last Raid by Van Noppen gives a complete, documented account of Stoneman's activities from which portions are included here. General George Stoneman of Sherman's Union Cavalry had the assignment to raid North and South Carolina. He came out of Knoxville to tear up railroads (although WNC had none), kill livestock, and destroy property, not to fight battles. These "crippling" tactics resulted in starvation and misery.

Van Noppen stated that when Stoneman's raiders came through, resentments of Union sympathizers "Burst into sudden flame; and now that they [Union] had the upper hand those who had opposed or been lukewarm to the South had their revenge. Pillaging, burning, robbery, and every form of internecine warfare resulted, and the southern adherents reaped the whirlwind which they had sowed. For by far the worst depredations and crimes were committed by neighbors against neighbor and by the North Carolina and Tennessee soldiers in Stoneman's army. The latter were called `Home Yankees,' southerners fighting with the Yankees."

Stoneman left Knoxville in March 1865, through Boone, and was in Salisbury by April 11. He was hoping to release the Union prisoners there. The Union prisoners had grown to 10,000 after the exchange policy had been stopped by the federal government in 1864, hoping to cut down the number of available men for the Confederacy. As in other prisons, when the population grew, food, fuel, and clothing were scarce, and the prison conditions became the reason for many deaths. The surviving prisoners in Salisbury had been moved to Charlotte in February.

From Lenoir about April 15, Stoneman himself returned to Tennessee. Union Brigadier General Alvan C. Gillem was to march his troops toward Asheville. Gillem's forces were mainly "Home Yankees" made up of three Tennessee Regiments with colonels William Palmer, Brown, Miller, and Regan. The mountain people had only "Home Guards" to protect them, and these young boys and old men were no real threat to thousand of Union cavalrymen.

Gillem moved toward Morganton and found a surprising resistance put up by the "Home Guards." Perhaps in retribution, Morganton was severely plundered. Gillem moved west through Marion, and at Pleasant

Gardens they camped near Colonel Carson's home.

In Asheville when General J. G. Martin, commander of the Confederate forces in Western North Carolina, heard of the Union occupation at Pleasant Gardens, he commanded Palmer's Brigade and Love's Regiment of "Thomas's Legion" to the vicinity of Swannanoa Gap. (Thomas's Legion was made up of Qualla Indians who had William Thomas, as their agent and trustee, buy land with government money for them.)

The Swain papers state that on April 19, "They reached the Gap before Gillem did and after cutting down some trees and making some other arrangements to receive the raiders, waited their approach and when they advanced, repulsed them without any difficulty. The enemy spent two or three days at this Gap but were not able to effect a passage."

Although Union General Gillem's men were turned back on April 19, 1865, at Swannanoa Gap to prevent their coming through Asheville, Asheville had no cause for celebration. Asheville's plundering and pillaging were just prevented for a few days.

Asheville had succeeded remarkably well through the Civil War to keep from being ransacked. Asheville at this time had no railroads, no public water system, no public lights, no telegraph. In March of 1865, the court house did burn to the ground, with most records saved, but from all documented accounts, this was not the result of Union forces.

Asheville had no real organized protection, even though there was a small factory to manufacture Enfield rifles on Eagle Street and forts had been erected on the French Broad, Beaucatcher Mountain, and Stoney Hill, later called Battery Porter. The consistent defense came from the Silver Greys, the "Home Guard," composed of old men and young boys.

Late in 1863, Kirk's Union forces out of Tennessee were repelled from coming into Asheville. Then, on April 3, 1865, Colonel Issac Kirby, from the 101 Ohio, came out of Greenville, Tenn., with 900 soldiers. On April 6, they came up the French Broad into present Woodfin where Colonel George Clayton leading assorted troops stopped them after a five-hour resistance and started pursuit.

After Confederate General Lee had surrendered at Appomatox on April 9, 1865, on April 18, Union General Sherman and Confederate General Johnston had agreed not to fight until the terms of peace were worked out. Stoneman's command in Tennessee were ordered to quit also, but word traveled slowly. Therefore, after Union General Gillem was turned back at Swannanoa Gap, on April 19, he went to Rutherford County to continue destruction and moved through Henderson County toward Asheville. General Gillem intended to attack Asheville on April 23.

On April 22, Confederate General Martin in Asheville heard of the truce and set men on the two roads toward Hendersonville with flags of truce. On April 24, General Martin met General Gillem before he reached Asheville, and they agreed that in exchange for food and supplies, the Union forces could march on through to
Tennessee with no fighting. The Asheville citizens watched the peaceful march of General Gillem and his Union forces on April 25, 1865. General Gillem then left his troops outside of Asheville and proceeded to Tennessee.

Whether his men later received word that the truce had been broken on April 24 in Knoxville or whether they became undisciplined without his leadership is unknown, but regardless of why, two brigades under General Brown returned to Asheville during the night of April 26, captured Asheville and took from individuals what they pleased.

By May 15, 1865, the war itself was over when Jefferson Davis was captured in Irwin, Georgia. However, Asheville was more or less occupied for a year after the war.

Truth is elusive when one is studying the Civil War. The official records, books, and all accounts were written by people who had definite feelings one way or the other. The best you can do is to read both sides and decide that the truth lies someplace in between.

Regiment books give a day-by-day accounts of activities, battles, plus a general overview of the war itself, as seen by the adjutants of that particular regiment.

The account in 1903 by Captain Samuel W. Scott, G Company, and Samuel P. Angel, adjutant, in *History of the Thirteenth Regiment, Tennessee Volunteer Cavalry, U. S. A.*, gave the march through Asheville on April 25, 1865, under the flag of truce as "the enemy had stacked arms with accordance with the truce and rebel soldiers lined both sides of the streets, the soldiers on both sides guying each other." They marched peacefully through, since the armistice provided "hostilities should cease," and camped ten miles north of Asheville. They were overtaken on their way back to Tennessee when they were "overtaken by a courier with orders to return and join in the pursuit of President Davis." Their account is that General Martin, commander of Confederate forces in Asheville, refused to let them pass back through on April 28, 1865, and fighting occurred.

This account of the Battle of Swannanoa Gap stated that "on the 20th [April 1865] crossed the river and went to the Swannanoa Gap at the foot of the Blue Ridge which we found blockaded and held by a small force of rebels . . .. Our brigade remained here in front of the enemy who occupied a strong position with artillery in the gap, all day of the 21st . . . On the 22nd we marched at 2 a. m. over the same road we had passed over two days before ... "

Most regiment books have a roster of the regiment by companies. The dead of the 13th included two who were listed as having died at Swannanoa Gap.

"Daugherty, Elkana, Priv. 18, Co. I, Mar. 1, 1865, accidental, Swannanoa Gap, N. C." and "Dison, James, Priv. 18, Co. E. Jan. 15, 1865, captured; died at Swannanoa Gap."

However, copies of Daugherty's and Dison's military papers from the National Archives tell it differently: Elkanah Daugherty born in Ashe County, N. C., joined in Taylorsville, Tenn., 15 Oct. 1864, mustered in 15 March 1865 at Knoxville, "died in Johnson County at a private home 30 March 1865 by reason of an accidental discharge of his own gun."

James Dison born in Wilkes County, North Carolina, joined at Mossey Creek, Tenn., mustered into service 25 October 1864, missing in action by November 12, 1864, captured and taken prisoner at Morristown, Tenn., by Major General Breckenridge, and died in "Rebel prison at Danville, Va., on the 14th Jan. 1865. Cause of death - Rubeola." Neither Daugherty nor Dison is in the lone U. S. soldier's grave at Swannanoa Gap -- "facts" that are not true again.

The only truths for sure are the sad facts that each side felt its cause was right and acted accordingly regardless of the suffering, misery, and death of neighbors and that the United States people were ever reunited.

Storm in the Mountains by Vernon H. Crow illustrates the dilemma as he told of Thomas's Confederate Legion of Cherokee Indians and mountaineers. All skirmishes this Legion was involved with are described, including the dreaded raids of Union Colonel George W. Kirk and Asheville's occupation in May 1865. The Legion was raised and commanded by William H. Thomas, the Cherokees' agent who had made numerous land claims in Washington for the Indians.

The companies' men were mainly from Jackson, Haywood, Cherokee, Clay Counties in North Carolina; Blout, Sevier, Roane Counties in Tennessee. Second Companies A and B were mainly Indians. The two Indian companies were particularly feared since they were said to often scalp the wounded and the dead.

Thomas wanted his Legion to stay in the mountains to protect the local Confederate families from the Union soldiers and all the citizens from the bushwackers, who used the war and the mountains to become outlaws. Even Thomas's Lieutenant Colonel William Walker was murdered by bushwackers in his Cherokee County home.

Thomas was arrested in mid-September 1864 and sent to Goldsboro for not obeying orders in cooperating with Southern commanders and for his lenient treatment of deserters. (Many of his soldiers would run home to check on their families' welfare. He would forgive any deserters who wanted to join him.) Thomas was found guilty but took his case to President Davis who quickly exonerated him of all charges.

Mr. Crow used materials not only from archives and official documents but also from diaries and letters to relate the feelings of the men. Major William Stringfield from Strawberry Plains, Tennessee, became involved with the Legion when Thomas asked him to come to Cherokee County to muster in mountain troops. His endeavor resulted in 500 volunteers. After the war Stringfield married Marie Love, sister to Thomas's wife, and ran the White Sulfur Springs Hotel in Waynesville near the site where on May 6, 1865, the last skirmish of the Civil War in North Carolina was fought.

James Robert Love, Jr., whose cousin was married to Thomas and who was a grandson of Revolutionary Colonel Robert Love, became a colonel in Thomas's Legion. In the summer and fall of 1864, his troops were in the Shenandoah Valley and part of General Jubal Early's Valley Campaign. In Winchester, as the soldiers marched through, they were amazed by the cheering and the embracing of the citizens. In the "divided" mountains, they had never been openly welcomed. These soldiers marched onward to the outer fortifications of Washington, but

2,000 men had been lost in battles and the long march itself.

Captain Stephen Whitaker wrote to his father James in Cherokee County. "This has been the longest march of the war and was performed without rest. It has killed many good soldiers. I had to stop and wash the blood out of my socks more than once." William Stringfield wrote in his diary, "Our army is very anxious to enter Washington City. I fear for the people if they do enter there. So much misery has been brought upon our people by vile miscreants living there that they could not be restrained."

General Early studied Washington and the Union troops there from July 11-14, 1864, and was afraid the invasion would be a slaughter for his remaining troops. He withdrew into Virginia. Love's column started a long journey back home with fewer than 100 or its original 400. *Storm in the Mountains* was published by Press of the Museum of the Cherokee Indian, P. O. Box 770-A, Cherokee, NC 28719. Appendix II lists the companies' muster rolls.

Samuel J. Sloan, grandson of Colonel William W. Stringfield, gave Mr. Crow access to the collection of Stringfield papers which was the cornerstone for this book. The Stringfield collection is now in Hunter Library Archives at Western Carolina University, Cullowhee, N. C.

At Pack Library in Asheville, two different sets of books are valuable to check not only for the battles the Confederate troops fought in but also for lists of the Confederate troops' names.

One set of volumes compiled by Walter Clark *Volumes of North Carolina Regiments, 1861-1865*, discusses the battles of the seventy-eight regiments and about twenty battalions for the Confederacy. Mr. Clark gave background information in Volume I concerning the organization of the various regiments, the artillery, cavalry, infantry, before he discussed the particulars of the individual regiments.

He also explained that as state troops were organized they started being numbered Regiment 1, 2, 3, etc. At the same time volunteer Regiments were being numbered as 1, 2, 3, etc. also. This became confusing, so finally the state troops became 1-10 and the volunteers 11 and on. For example, the 16th Regiment N. C. troops started out at the 6th Regiment Volunteers. Very helpful for finding out which kinfolks were in the Confederate troops are the volumes of books compiled by Weymouth T. Jordan and published from the documents in the North

Carolina State Archives. Seventeen volumes of *North Carolina Troops, 1861-1865, A Roster*, have been planned with thirteen now published. These are organized by the soldiers' being in alphabetized order under his company and regiment.

Volume VI: Infantry 16th-18th and 20th-21st Regiments started with a history of the 16th regiment, which was organized in Raleigh for 12 months' service and composed originally of 12 companies from Western North Carolina, such as Company A, Jackson County, from the ones who enlisted at Webster on April 27, 1861; Company B, Madison; Company C, Yancey; Company D, Rutherford; Company E, Burke; Company F, Buncombe, Asheville, May 7, 1861; G, Rutherford; H, Macon; I, Henderson; K, Polk; L, Haywood. All of the men who entered this regiment were listed and described plus the dates where fighting were reported from the brigade's activities. The specific listings for each have information such as "Justus, Meridy D., Private. Born in Henderson County where he resided as a silversmith prior to enlisting in Henderson County at age 27, May 5, 1861. Present or accounted for until he died at Fredericksburg, Virginia, March 27, 1862, of disease."

Volume VII, which covers the 22nd through the 26th Infantry Regiments, discussed that the 25th Regiment was organized at Camp Clingman (located on French Broad Avenue, Asheville) on August 15, 1861. This regiment went to Morganton on September 18 where the men boarded trains, first for Raleigh and then for Wilmington. On November 5, these men were sent to Charleston, S.C. The exact dates and movements are given before the men were sent in the spring of 1865 to reinforce General Joseph Johnson's troops which were protecting Richmond, Virginia, from General George B. McClellans' troops -- then on to Petersburg on June 19.

The men of the 25th were at Malvern Hill on July 1 along with Zebulon Vance's 26th Regiment. Official records are quoted as saying the men "pushed forward under as fearful fire as the mind can conceive." "The fire was so fierce that three regiments were compelled to fall back under the crest of some intervening hills. About twilight the reassembled troops "raised a tremendous shout, and the enemy opened upon us a perfect sheet of fire from mustketry and the batteries. We steadily advanced to within 20 yards of the guns." The regiments involved had 22 men killed, 106 wounded, and 5 missing. The 25th was also involved in the Sharpsbury battle where two men were killed and thirteen wounded. In Fredericksburg, the men were involved in a battle on December 13. There 13 men were killed and 75 were wounded. More battles are described, until the regiment was "blocked off by Federal forces" on April 9, 1865. "Seventy-seven members of the 25th were present to receive their paroles" when General Lee surrendered at Appomatox Court House. The companies in the 25th included men from all over Western North Carolina, including Henderson, Buncombe, Jackson, Haywood, Transylvania Counties and Cane Creek and Pisgah sections.

In Volume IX, the 35th Regiment, Company G, also known as the "Henderson Rifles," is listed as organized October 5, 1861. Some of the men were discharged because of wounds, such as wounded in the leg at Swan Pines, Virginia, May 31, 1862, discharged July 10, 1862, by reason of wounds. Some deserted to the enemy; one Henry Garren, officer, was killed when he tried to take in a deserter from his company in Henderson County.

Volume XII, Infantry tells of the men in and the battles fought in the 49th, 50th, 51st, and 52nd Regiments, North Carolina troops. The 50th included companies called the "Rutherford Farmers," the "Green River Rifles," and the "Rutherford Regulators." Numerous sources are used in this volume, including diaries, letters, obituaries from early North Carolina newspapers, the 1860 federal census entries, cemeteries at Richmond, Winchester, Sharpsburg, Gettysburg, and Elmira. In the introduction, Mr. Jordan discussed the general belief that more North Carolinians deserted during the Civil War than men from other states. One explanation is that the men feared for the safety of their families since "near anarchy prevailed in the North Carolina mountains and much of the eastern third of the state was either Federally occupied or subject to destructive raids" because the state's troops had been sent to Virginia.

Preceding each regiment's roster is an account of the battles the companies were involved in. The 50th, for example, went to Virginia, then back into eastern North Carolina, South Carolina, and into Savannah to try to stop General Sherman's "march to the sea." The 10,000 to 18,000 Confederates were heavily outnumbered by Sherman's 62,000-man army and had to retreat "hundreds of miles, mainly on foot and in haste, through rain, mud, and water without tents and on scant rations." The Confederates would attempt to organize and fight such as at Bentonville, South Carolina, where they fought "hand-to-hand with clubbed muskets and ramrods, and the Federals fell back in disarray." However, they could not stop Sherman and his troops which pushed them back into North Carolina on their way to the Goldsboro railroad station for fresh troops and supplies. Confederate General Johnston surrendered to Sherman near Durham Station on April 26, 1865.

In reading the individuals' records, you can see that more men died from diseases than from battles. A typical entry from Company K, 50th Regiment: "Vedo Byas, private, born in Greenville District, South Carolina, and resided in Rutherford County where he was by occupation a day laborer prior to enlisting in Rutherford County at age 29, March 27, 1862. Hospitalized at Petersburg, Virginia, July 20, 1862, with chronic bronchitis. Returned to duty on August 8, 1862. Died in hospital at Petersburg on November 22, 1862, of typhoid fever."

In 1993, the North Carolina Archives continued its proposed seventeen volumes with Volume XIII. In this volume, battles and the men of the 53rd through 56th Regiments are discussed. Companies in the 54th and the 56th contained numerous men from Western North Carolina.

The 54th Regiment was organized May 16, 1862, with James Charles Sheffield McDowell, a Burke County planter, being elected as a lieutenant. By September, he was promoted to Colonel. He was wounded at Fredericksburg, Virginia, on May 4, 1863, and died four days later.

Company B was organized from Burke, Yancey, and McDowell Counties and Company I from Polk County. The 54th was assigned to the Army of Northern Virginia, commanded by General Robert E. Lee. On December 13, 1862, at Fredericksburg, 12,000 Union soldiers were killed, wounded, or missing. The Confederate figure was 5,000, with the 54th fighting in "homespun" uniforms with "very many" barefooted. Burnsides's Union forces were marching "division upon division" and advanced straight toward the prepared Confederates. "As the Federal dead piled up, seven, division-strength attacks had been methodically shot to pieces by the incredulous and increasingly sickened Confederates."

The individual soldiers are listed after a description of their war activities, such as from Company B, Issac Barnes gunshot wound at Petersburg, right leg amputated, died April 2, 1865, of wounds. Many died of "febris typhoides" and "diarrhoea chronic" in 1863.

The 56th Regiment included Company G, known as the "Henderson Blues," raised in Henderson County, April 1862. Private R. C. Love wrote a letter home on May 21 complaining the "pickled beef, ain't hardly fit to eat" and "bread so hard he could nock a bull down" with it. More serious problems faced Company G when they moved into Virginia in 1863. At Seven Pines, the 1862 battlefield was described with "the bones of the dead is lying all over the land." Most of their duties in the spring included the dangerous job of searching for deserters. The battles followed such as at Ware Bottom Church on May 20 where the 56th lost ninety men in less than an hour. By February, 1865, after men had lived in trenches for nine months, with little food and clothing and much filth, desertions had become the "most serious evil to contend against." In regular battles, many had been captured, such as John Kuykendall, born Buncombe, age 36, April 12, 1862, drummer, "captured at Five Forks, Virginia, April 1, 1865, confined at Point Lookout, Maryland, April 5, 1865, released about July 6, 1865." Only seventy-one members of the 56th were left when they were surrendered at Appomattox Court House on April 9, 1865. To purchase these books, write the North Carolina Archives.

The *Diary of Captain Henry A. Chambers* is a daily record showing how Chambers survived in the complex Civil War from January 1, 1862, to April 24, 1865. Chambers went from a carefree freshman at Davidson College to a Captain in C Company, 49th Regiment, North Carolina Troops, from a young man who was opposed to seceding to one who wrote on April 9, 1865., when General Robert E. Lee surrendered to General Grant, "Oh! God how can we bear this! Will not some terrible retribution yet come upon this motley crew who have waged upon us so unjust, so barbarous a warfare! upon this soldiery who have burned our houses, desecrated out altars, plundered our wealth. Can it be? that after so noble a struggle, after so many deeds of heroism and valor, after the shedding of so much precious blood we are to be subjugated! and by such people!"

Chambers did not dwell on the fighting of the previous day but tried to keep a semblance of the ordinary in his life by writing letters, reading books, going to church, and observing the weather.

On July 31, 1864, when with the 49th he participated in a battle near Petersburg, Virginia, with the 24th and 25th Regiments of North Carolina, plus troops from South Carolina, Georgia, and Alabama, he wrote: "A great pile of their dead were heaped up in the bottom of the mine where we were going to bury them. Many of our poor fellows had been dug out and many arms and legs and hands could yet be seen protruding from the different parts of the upheaved works." The next day he reported "nothing unusual" and the "company got out to wash today."

He had to believe the war was necessary to justify his part in it. He even drew "an instructive parallel between the course of the Papists and Jesuits" during the time of England's James II forcing the Roman Catholic religion on the English people and "the Northern fanatics of our time." He never wavered from the belief that the South was right once he joined its "Cause." Even during the best of times, however, for the South, he was only cautiously optimistic. On September 16, 1862, he commented on "Stonewall" Jackson's capturing 8,000 Yankees at Harper's Ferry: "Everything looks bright and cheering for our cause just now. Our arms are successful everywhere. Let us be prepared for any reverses however."

On October 9, 1862, after reporting " a sad reverse to our army at Corinth" with Van Dorn and Price defeated and a disorderly retreat, he added that he had received a letter from Miss M. E. S. He did not dwell on the horrors of war.

Many details are included such as the pay's being $11 per month and usually three months' behind. The meager value of $11 is shown when he mentioned cloth for a new uniform costing $50, a breakfast $10, and a bed for one night's sleep in Richmond $30.

"Stonewall" Jackson was described as an "ordinary looking" person, shabbily dressed, with a "mouth indicating firmness and decision."

On December 26, 1863, he related, "Last night the men fired off many guns about the camp in violation of orders and today suffered the penalty of their actions by being tied up by their thumbs and in carrying heavy logs of wood."

Near Kinston, North Carolina, he described camp: "As far as the eye could reach the camp fires flickered and glared in the murky darkness of the night. Around them were groups of men cooking, laughing, cursing, and singing. It was a wild and savage scene . . .." On December 31, 1864, he wrote, "Oh, God! How thankful to Thee ought those of us who survive, ought I, to be." Chambers survived the confusion of war and surrendered what was left of his troops at Appomattox. Appendixes in the book include a roster of the 101 men who served with Company C, 49th , and a sketch by Selby Daniels, giving biographical details of Henry A. Chambers, born near Statesville, a teacher in Morganton, an attorney, married Laura Lenior, a grand niece to Colonel Issac Avery. Chambers later moved to Tennessee and died in 1925.

This book was edited by T. H. Pearce and published in 1983 by Broadfoot Publishing Company, Route 3, Box 318, Wendell, NC 27591. Broadfoot specializes in Confederate and Southern history.

Tennessee was first settled by pioneers from Virginia who built forts along the Watauga River in 1769, thinking they were in Virginia. It was in North Carolina but later became Carter County, Tennessee. Trouble started for the people on these bordering land in April of 1861 when Lincoln ordered troops for the Union army. Even though the people's vote had opposed secession, the governor refused to send troops. By June 8, when the majority did vote for Tennessee's separation from the Union, representatives from Eastern Tennessee asked for a separate state. This was not allowed, although West Virginia was established for a similar reason, and loyalty to the Federal government was treason. The people of East Tennessee were not stopped, however, since it is estimated that between 30,000 and 40,000 men from Tennessee joined the Union army. Loyal Union men from Carter and Johnson Counties successfully burned railroad bridges on November 8, 1861, to cripple supply routes between Virginia and Alabama. These men expected troops to come from Kentucky to take over East Tennessee and to protect them. But help was long in coming, and many were killed or imprisoned while others fled to mountain hide-outs. Not until September of 1863 did Union forces come through.

A fifteen-year old proudly marched to join the Confederacy in his community while his brother sneaked out at night, hiding in the mountains and trying to find his way to Tennessee and perhaps be guided by Dan Ellis himself to join the Union forces. In reading the rosters, 18 was the age of the majority of the soldiers. Eighteen was the minimum age the men could join officially, but many were later found to be as young as 12. *The History of the Thirteenth Regiment, Tennessee Volunteer Cavalry* (Union) by Scott and Angel, 1902, told of Henry Lineback who was 15 and small for his age. "When taken to the mustering office, he stood on a small box that made him look as tall as the other boys." He later became a corporal, then after the War he lived in Mitchell County, North Carolina, and represented that county in the state legislature.

The Thrilling Adventures of Daniel Ellis by Himself published in 1867 told of the Union guide or "pilot" of East Tennessee during the "Great Southern Rebellion." He was born and lived in Carter County, Tenn.

He first became involved in the Civil War as a Tennessee "bridge burner" when in 1861 the United States government ordered the east Tennessee men for the Union to burn all the bridges and to destroy the railroad from Chattanooga. These "bridge-burners" had to flee to the mountains to hide, but Ellis led a group out in August of 1862 through the rebel lines to Cumberland Gap, Kentucky. Taking three weeks to hike there and back, he returned to take others who wanted to join the Union forces in Kentucky to escape conscription into the Confederacy. He related one journey from Tennessee with 75 men, including many from North Carolina. The rebels would often be on the roads below as Ellis led this through the high trails. He recalled crawling through sleet-covered bushes, swimming rivers with floating ice, clothes freezing to their bodies, and going without food for twenty-four hours. As Union sympathizers waited for him to guide them, he sometimes found them bunched together and massacred.

A steady trek of men, numbering in all about four thousand, were going northwest out of Tennessee and across the mountains into Kentucky. Then, in January of 1864, they were guided into Knoxville after it had been taken by Union forces. At that time many came from Madison County, North Carolina, southeast through the Smoky Mountains to Knoxville.

Daniel Ellis himself joined the 13th Regiment in January 1865. Being based near Waynesville, he took forty men with him to round up the rebel forces in Western North Carolina in May of 1865. The rebels would be turned over to various generals to be paroled. Often the men from both sides would have to travel about sixty miles with no food for themselves or their horses since so many troops had passed through that no provisions were available.

Daniel Ellis's book was republished in 1987 by Dan Crowe, 2361 Hiawassee Drive, Kingsport, TN 37644.

Perhaps the unbelievable is what causes the continued fascination with the Civil War. An upheaval no one wants again did happened; it is pondered over and over.

Another unusual incident happened in Roswell, Georgia, during the Civil War. Civilians, mainly women, numbering 350-400, were captured and charged as traitors while working in textile mills there. Not being content to hold these civilians temporarily, General William T. Sherman banished them north, away from families and homes. This puzzling and practically unknown story about Roswell in the Civil War was being researched in 1985 by Webb Garrison, writer and special correspondent for the *Atlanta Journal-Constitution*.

In July of 1864, Sherman, who was known to have a fierce temper, sent Ohio General Kenner Garrard to secure the bridge crossing the Chattahoochie River near Roswell, north of Atlanta, before the assault on Atlanta. Sherman not only recently suffered severe losses at Kennesaw Mountain but also had experienced trouble with resisting civilians in Northern Georgia all of June. In addition to these problems, when General Garrard arrived in Roswell, the bridge across the Chattahoochie had already been burned by the Confederates. Garrard captured the town and burned the three mills that had been making supplies for the Confederates. The workers at one mill had run up the French flag, perhaps hoping to spare the mill.

On July 7, after Garrard reported the flag incident to Sherman, Sherman sent a telegram stating that Garrard should "arrest all people, male and female connected with those factories, no matter what clamor, and let them foot it, under guard to Marietta, when I will send them by cars (rail) to the North. The poor women will make a howl. Let them take their children and clothing, provided they have the means of hauling or you can spare them." Garrard, perhaps feeling sorry for the weeping women, put them in 110 United States Army wagons instead of making them walk.

A *New York Tribune* reporter at the time wrote, "Four hundred weeping and terrified Ellens, Susans, and Maggies transported in the seatless and springless Army wagons, away from their lovers and brothers of the sunny South; and all this for the offense of weaving tent cloth and spinning stocking yarn." Newspaper reports also have the "traitors" going from Marietta to Nashville then to Louisville and into Indiana. A recent letter to Mr. Garrison told of one family: "Lucinda Elizabeth Wood, born 1846, was in Roswell where her father Robert and mother Margarette worked in the mill when it was destroyed. They were sent to the North or to Louisville as refugees. Margarette died en route, was buried in Louisville. Another family member, Mary Ann Sumner, died as she was being carried off the boat at Louisville and was also buried there. "The others were sent by way of steamboat up the Mississippi and Ohio Rivers, being taken care of until they could get employment and places to stay." Another letter tells of the refugees being dropped off from box cars across Indiana.

Probably most never got back to their homes and their loved ones in Georgia.

The strange stories of the Civil War never cease. In the *Wonderful West Virginia* magazine, an article, "Civil War Medals," by Carolyn Griffith, September, 1984, told of the State of West Virginia wanting to present 26,099 medals for the Union soldiers who fought with their regiments. "Many were to be claimed by men who had been mustered into West Virginia regiments" from surrounding states. Three types of copper and bronze medals were created, suspended on a piece of tri-colored ribbon, with the name of the individual soldier die-punched: Class I for officers and soldiers honorably discharged, Class II for officers and soldiers killed in battle, Class III for officers and soldiers who died from wounds or diseases during the service. These medals were waiting to be claimed at the state archives in Charleston, West Virginia, until April 1985.

Whether these were ever distributed or not is unknown. For more information write to Department of Culture and History, Cultural Center, State Capitol Complex, Charleston, West Virginia 25305.

The book, *Confederate Research Sources*, has not only the facts and history about the Civil War in the South but also state-by-state listings for where to search for information on individuals who were in the fighting plus on who were left widows. The author, James C. Neagles, states, "Medical care was primitive, and it has been estimated that two to three soldiers died of disease for every one killed in battle." [Ancestry, Inc.,: Salt Lake

He estimated six hundred thousand to more than one million fought for the Confederacy. North Carolina provided more men, approximately 125,000, for battles than any other Confederate state.

A history of each state's role and major battles in the war is included with such facts as "only Virginia saw more bloodshed than did Tennessee." For example, in the battle at Shiloh Church, Tennessee, on April 6, 1862, the Union suffered more than 13,000 casualties and the Confederates suffered more than 10,660 casualties.

Basically, the individual Southern states' archives have pension papers while the National Archives has the military records and the pension papers for the Union. For specific record sources in each state, this book is excellent.

Pictures of your ancestors who were in the Civil War may be available. No charge will be made by the army to check their collection. You will need to tell whether Union or Confederate, full name, what county, state, regiment, any other information you have. The army is also interested in adding pictures you may have to its collection. Write: Department of the Army, Special Collections Branch, U. S. Military History Institute, Carlisle Barracks, Carlisle, PA 17013-5008.

Confederate pension records are in the individual states' archives. The addresses of North Carolina plus adjoining states are North Carolina Division of Archives, 109 East Jones Street, Raleigh, NC 27611; South Carolina Department of Archives, Box 11669, Columbia, SC 29211-1669; Georgia Department of Archives, 330 Capitol Avenue, S. E., Atlanta, GA 30334; Tennessee State Archives, 403 Seventh Avenue, North, Nashville, TN 37219.

For the Union records, military or pension, or for the Confederate service records, write Reference Services Branch, National Archives and Records Service, 8th and Pennsylvania Ave., NW, Washington, DC 20408. You will have to first write and tell that you want the form to fill out for these records.

Spanish-American War

In 1898, volunteers from Western North Carolina heeded the "Remember the Maine" slogan when the country went to war with Spain.

In 1895, Cubans had started rebelling against the Spanish rule, and Americans sympathized with them. Plus, many politicians, including Theodore Roosevelt, felt we should fight Spain. President McKinley was hesitant. However, to protect American interests, on February 15, 1898, the United States battleship "Maine" was ordered to Havana harbor where it was destroyed by an explosion which killed 260 Americans. Regardless of not being able to determine who was responsible for the explosion, "Remember the Maine" became the cry that led President McKinley on April 11 to ask for war against Spain. This was adopted by Congress on April 20, with war formally declared April 21.

Since the regular army only had about thirty thousand men, on April 22 President McKinley asked for 125,000 volunteers, and the men from North Carolina, particularly Western North Carolina, responded immediately. *North Carolina's Role in the Spanish-American War* by Joseph Steelman gives the history of this brief war. [Historical Publications Section, North Carolina Archives, 1992]

In North Carolina three regiments of volunteer infantry were mobilized, one of which was composed of Black officers and enlisted men. Steelman stated, "The First Regiment was essentially a Western North Carolina unit. The mountain men in particular were in the vanguard of enlistees" with "surplus enlistees from Asheville, where 158 volunteered," being assigned to other companies.

Steelman described Camp Bryan Grmes near Raleigh where "294 tents were erected in rows" with bales of hay for the four men in each tent to sleep on. Sleeping on hay was the least of the worries the men had who marched into camp in "every kind and style of uniform" of the State Guard on the sixty percent who had uniforms. Only seventy percent had firearms. The $15 per month for privates was "long time" coming.

Worst problems awaited some companies, including men from Asheville and Waynesville who boarded a train on May 22 and went to Camp Cuba Libre near Jacksonville, Florida. Essential supplies such as shoes and rifles were still lacking; plus diseases such as typhoid fever, malaria, yellow fever struck the men. A large number of desertions took place, and Steelman stated, "Some who deserted the ranks were said to be walking back to North Carolina." Also, since the pay had become lost, it was said some "Tar Heels were observed begging in the streets of Jacksonville."

In the meantime, the well-trained regular navy had destroyed the Spanish fleet at the Battle of Manila Bay on May 1, 1898, and, by August 14, 1898, proclaimed military occupation of the Philippines. Moreover, in Cuba after successful naval blockades at Santiago, a land force including Roosevelt's "Rough Riders" on July 1, 1898, took San Juan Hill and from that point helped to destroy the Spanish fleet in Cuba. Feeling the war was over, the First Regiment thought it would be recalled but instead it went for guard duty in the Havana area. Steelman stated, "On the morning of December 7, 1898, the volunteers boarded a troop ship, the *Roumania*, and sailed for Cuba, a stint of some four months of occupation duty commenced without fanfare or publicity back home." However, "elaborate welcoming services were staged on April 24" when the troops arrived back home.

The Second Regiment of volunteers in North Carolina also contained many from Western North Carolina. This regiment served on the coastal areas of South Carolina, Georgia, and Florida and never reached Cuba or the Philippines The Third Regiment, made up of Black enlisted men and officers, went to Fort Macon, near Morehead City, also never left the United States. While the regiment was in Georgia in November, Steelman stated, "At least four members of the regiment were killed by white civilians."

Several pages of this booklet are devoted to the heroes of the war who were in the regular armed forces, including Captain Thad W. Jones of Asheville. Captain Jones was commanding Troop B of the Tenth cavalry regiment in the attack on San Juan Hill. Lieutenant William Shipp, born in Asheville, was killed in that battle.

For names of individuals who volunteered to serve in the Spanish-American War in North Carolina, three helpful books are available at Pack Library.

Hispano-American War, 1898-1899, First N. C. Volunteer Infantry gives a list of all who served in this regiment. Some from Western North Carolina were Major W. G. Smith of Asheville, born July 18, 1859, who volunteered April 27, 1898; Captain B. Alexander who was born in Swannanoa on November 23, 1869 and volunteered May 1898; Lieutenants Stringfield and Love from Waynesville; Corporal J. L. Justice; Privates A. L. and W. B. Whitaker from Asheville.

Another book available at Pack Library is *Roster of the N. C. Volunteers in the Spanish-American War 1898*-1899. This Adjutant-General's report stated that the First Regiment, arriving in Cuba on December 11, 1898, contained the "first American soldiers to arrive in Havana. Pen cannot describe the intense gladness, almost bordering frenzy, displayed by the Cuban people at the sight of their liberators." Most of the home addresses for Companies C through H show different towns in Western North Carolina. From the Third Regiment, composed of Black soldiers and officers, Private Zeb Patton, Company C, from Asheville was killed on November 21, 1898. (This would have been when this regiment was in Georgia.)

Another book, *History of the Negro Soldiers in the Spanish American War*, by Edward A. Johnson, published in 1899, discussed the Third Regiment of North Carolina.

If you would like to obtain actual copies of military records for an individual that you find listed, you may request this from the National Archives. You will need to have the complete name of the veteran, the branch of service, and preferably the regiment, company, ship, etc., and whether he was a volunteer or a regular. (You must obtain a form from the National Archives: General Reference Branch, National Archives and Records Administration, 7th and Pennsylvania Ave., NW, Washington, DC 20408.)

If you had a male ancestor who was in the United States and who was born between 1873 and 1900 that you wish you had more information about, try the World War I draft registration records. More than twenty-four million of these selective service records are on file at the National Archives, Southeast Region, 1557 St. Joseph Ave., East Point, GA 30344.

On June 5, 1917, all men between 21 and 31 years of age were required to register; by September 12, 1918, this age was extended for the ones who were not registered from ages 18 through 45.

To obtain these records, you must know the full name and the city or county and state where the registrant lived. Forms are available free upon request from the above address. After filling out the form, you must include $6 for each separate request for each selective service card.

Headstones and markers are available from the Veterans

Administration for unmarked graves for placement in private or local cemeteries of all soldiers honorably discharged. The headstones, the normal inscriptions, and the shipping are all free for qualifying individuals. The application form, VA 40-1330, must be completed and, if possible, a copy of the deceased veteran's last discharge certificate or other official documents
pertaining to his military service should be attached.

The applications may be picked up at the Veterans Service Office, Court House Annex, 189 College St. in Asheville, or may be ordered from Monument Service (42), Veterans Administration, 810 Vermont Avenue, NW, Washington, DC 20420. This application furnished all the needed information for how to apply for these free markers.

Service records after the Spanish-American War are not so easily available since they are restricted to immediate family members only. The ones remaining of these are at the National Personnel Records Center, 9700 Page Boulevard, St. Louis, MO 63132. A fire at this center in 1973 destroyed millions of these records.

However, you may be able to find some helpful information on these at your local court house. The military discharges at the Buncombe County Court House start about 1919 and continue through the present. Not all servicemen's discharges will be there since this is a voluntary procedure that is recommended by the service but not mandatory. There is an index to search which lists the name, branch of service, book and page.

The information on these discharges varies depending upon the date of the record. Basically, these tell the date of discharge, where, when enlisted, rank, date, where, physical descriptions, date of birth, where, occupation, battles and campaigns, medals, honors, wounds.

A typical World War II one showed at the Buncombe County Court House, Registrar of Deeds Office, that the person was a Staff Sergeant, 117th Engineers Division. He was separated from the service at Fort Bragg, N. C., 29 September 1945. He was born 24 October 1911, Black Mountain, N. C.; his eyes were blue, his hair was light brown, he was 5 feet 11 inches tall, and weighed 162 pounds. He was inducted on 28 July 1942 at Fort Jackson, S. C., and entered on 11 August 1942. He departed for "out of the continent" on 3 November 1942. His battles and campaigns were Luzon and the Northern Solomons; he received a Purple Heart on 16 December 1943; other medals included a Philippine Liberation Ribbon with one bronze star, Asiatic Pacific Theater Campaign with two bronze service stars, good conduct medal. He was wounded but no records were included. He was on foreign duty for two years, eight months, and twenty-six days.

APPENDIX A

The following inquiries to the "Family History" column, published in the *Asheville Citizen-Times*, are included for their genealogical information. These are alphabetized but are not included in the index.

The dates of these inquires are included and a big caution is on these because as you know from census study, during an eleven-year span, people move and people die. However, it is doubtful that they just lost interest. (If you write, be sure to include a pre-addressed, stamped envelope for ease of answering.)

Aderhold, Wm. Frederick, a Revolutionary soldier, and wife Mary Elizabeth who were in Lincoln County, N. C. Their children: Conrad, J. George, and Jacob born 1775 who married Elizabeth Sherrard. Judy Beebe, 907 Mansard Drive #208, Birmingham, AL 35209. [1986]

Alexander, Issac, Tyrrell County, will 25 March 1780 named John, Joseph, Abner, Jesse, Mary, Elizabeth Davenport, Ann, Sarah, Jamima, Zilphia, Millae, Clarca. Mrs. Virginia Jenson, Apt. 193, 600 Carolina Village Rd., Hendersonville, NC 28739. [1984]

Allen, Adoniram, born 1782 in North Carolina and on the 1840 Yancey County census. He was the son of Adoniram Allen who was born in 1734 in New Hampshire to David Allen, Sr., and was living in Surry County by 1772. Some of Adoniram's kin stayed in N. C. while some moved to Clay County, Kent. Am particularly interested in information on his son Nathaniel Allen who stayed in N. C. Also am interested in the ancestors of Philip Marion Allen of Yancey County. Mrs. Robert Allen, 1806 Maxwell Ave., Baltimore, MD 21222. [1990]

Allen, Col. Lawrence M., when and where he died? Allen from Madison County commanded the 64th N. C. Regiment (state troops) during the Civil War. James Hall, 1044 Douglass Dr., McLean, VA 22101. [1985]

Alley, Frederick, Rutherford County, sheriff from 1814-1820, married Susan Hampton in 1815. Would like names of children. Mrs. H. M. Hallenbeck, 50 Rumford St., West Hartford, Conneticutt 06107. [1984]

Arrowood, Soloman E., born February 21, 1848, died July 16, 1912, buried at Locust Grove Baptist Church, Buncombe, married Polly Roberts. Soloman's father was William Arrowood and his mother was

Nellie Buckner. Barbara Settle, 53 Capps Rd., Swannanoa, NC 28778. [1986]

Ashe family. My grandfather came from Dingle, County Kerry, Ireland. Do others know where their Ashe family came from? Walter F. Ashe, 40 Shorewood Dr., Asheville, NC 28804. [1989]

Ashton family. Three Ashton brothers, James, Samuel, and Thomas came from Scotland to the Asheville area in the mid-1800s. James Ashton married Agnes Scott (her mother was Mary Ann Scott, would like father), their son James Ashton married Kelly Magdaline Ramsey (daughter of William and Harriet Ramsey, born 1881) and had eight children. Wilma Craig, P. O. Box 1113, Black Mountain, NC 28711. [1984]

Avery, James, born about 1795, North Carolina, and in the 1820 Buncombe census. He was married to a Miss Gentry. Was she related to John N. Gentry? Was James Avery a son of Elizabeth Avery? All of these people lived in the Big Ivy section. The James Avery family lived later in Monroe County, Tenn., and then in Hart County, Kent. William A. Heady, Rt. 1, Box 143 A, Edinburg, TX 78539. [1986]

Baird, Joseph, died 1800 near Salisbury, married Hanna Lay of Buncombe. It is believed Joseph came to N. C. from Pennsylvania in the late 1700s. Would like name of parents. F. B. Davis, Rt. 6, Box 175, Franklin, NC 28734. [1984]

Bailey, Levi, from Madison County, would like to correspond with anyone working on this family. Polly Book, 641 Mag Sluder Rd., Alexander, NC 28701. [1984]

Baker, Jonathon, wife Susannah Coontz of Bakersville, N. C., in the late 1700s and early 1800s. Would particularly like to know if Belinda/Malinda, who was born May 1818 and married James Richardson, was Jonathan Baker's daughter. Belinda and James were married in Bakersville but left shortly afterward and moved to Ohio, then West Virginia. Jeanne Carter, 507 Blackburn Ave., Ashland, KY 41101. [1990]

Ballard, Steve, married Martha Guy and had children Liamon, Rome, Ellie, Newton, Posey, Riley (who married Mary Queen), Jerushia (Cricket), and Ollie or Ola. Joann Ballard Riddle, Rt. 8, Box 704-M, Morganton, NC 28655. [1987]

Ballard, W. S., pastor of Watauga Baptist Church 1887-1889. Would like information on the following ministers of this church: A. W. Davis 1892-1893, George A. Bartlett 1895-1897, T. C. King 1908-1910. Mattie B.

Fouts, 60 Brendle Rd., Franklin, NC 28734. [1986]

Ballew, Millie, born 1775, wife of Joseph Ballew of McDowell County. Would like maiden name. Lawrence E. Wood, 75 Peeks Creed Rd., Franklin, NC 28734. [1984]

Banks, John Riley, born June 9, 1846, died February 17, 1945, son of Henry Banks. John married Janey Josephine Dillingham 1865-1964, daughter of Tom Dillingham of Barnardsville. John and Janey Banks are buried in Maple Cemetery in Barnardsville. Would like more information on them and to know the name of the father of Henry Banks. Mrs. Robert Edmonds, 310 Stonewall Ave., Swannanoa, NC 28778. [1986]

Beck family of North Carolina, especially interested in Robert R. Beck, who was born in N. C. in 1820 and his brother James W. born 1808. Betty M. Dailey, P. O. Box 391, Bluffton, SC 29910. [1990]

Bell, Thomas and Rachel of Lincoln County, late 1700s and early 1800s. Was Rachel a Reed? Lawrence Wood, 75 Peeks Creek Rd., Franklin, NC 28734. [1986]

Benton, Joy Kime, who was an artist and a writer who lived in Hendersonville in the 1920s-1940s. Would like to hear from anyone who knew her. Mary Ingram, 28 Edgemont Rd., #1, Asheville, NC 28801. [1987]

Birdwell family. Would like information beginning with George Birdwell, mid 1700s in Virginia, and the family's migration to eastern Tennessee. Also would like to know if the main character of the book *Friendly Persuasion*, by Jessamyn West, was based upon a real Jesse Birdwell, a Quaker from Indiana. Jesse Walter Birdwell, 1014 S. W. 19 Street, Fort Lauderdale, FL 33315. [1988]

Black, Patrick born in North Carolina about 1803, married Emily (Milly) Bridges about 1830. Would like information on both of their parents. There children were James P., Telitha Jane, Montraville W., Nathan, Jesse, George W., William, and Jacob A. First three children may have been born in Tenn. All were raised in the Reems Creek/Flat Creek sections of Buncombe. James A. Black, Jr., 96 Spooks Branch Rd., Asheville, NC 28804. [1986]

Blackburn, William, fought in the Battle of Kings Mountain, from Lincoln County. He had a son Robert, born 1797. Would like more information. Bryte B. Whittener, 840 Gordon King Rd., Pisgah Forest, NC 28768. [1986]

Blanton, Alexander, born in Duplin County, N. C., about 1788. What was his relationship to John Blanton and Joshua Blanton who appear as heads of household on the 1790 census, Wilmington District, Duplin County. Sanford W. Blanton, 9993 Arcola St., Livonia, MI 48150-3203. [1988]

Boone, Lawrence Gold and brother Daniel VI from Burnsville. Both Lawrence and Daniel were blacksmiths who practices mainly in Western North Carolina in the 1940s and 1950s. Both were renowned for their iron work and were involved in the start of the restoration of Williamsburg, Virginia. Judy Boone, 137 Hedgewood Dr., Greenbelt, MD 20770. [1984]

Bradley, Richard, born about 1780, in 1830 in Monroe County with wife Edith. Children included Elizabeth, born Wilkes Co., 1818, and Linville, born July 7, 1823, Tennessee. By 1850, wife Edith with children was in Greene County, Missouri. Evelyn K. Freeman, 6515 Cumberland Place, Stockton, CA 95209. [1986]

Bramlett, Tolliver Robert, who was killed in Civil War. His widow went to Waynesville with their 13 children. His brother Melvin H. reportedly died of smallpox in Petersburg, Virginia. Would like to know parents, place of birth and death, wife and family. John E. Bramlett, Box 493, Clyde, NC 28721. [1988]

Brevard family. Would like any information. The inquirer's grandfather was David Franklin Brevard, born January 12, 1853; his parents were Susan Seline Harris and Thomas Ashworth Brevard, born Jan. 21, 1824. Mrs. Clyde Seay, 49 Turnpike Rd., Brevard, NC 28712. [1984]

Bridges, Helon Samantha, born 1871, Harnett County. Her father's name was Warren, and she married Neil Eric Wood in 1895. Would like information about her parents, brothers, and sisters. Carmen Wood, 6708 W. Clifton, Tampa, FL 33634. [1987]

Bridges, James, had a land grant in Buncombe in 1802. Is he the same James, born 1780, who moved to Greenville, S. C., and married second Frances Hannah Hitt, born 1808. Their children were Charles (1829), Benjamin F., Thomas Yancy (1808), Edmund, Henrietta, James, and Caroline. (James's children by his first wife were William, Emory, Samuel, and Julia Burns.) Martha Lawrence, 72 Riverside Estates, Brevard, NC 28712. [1986]

Brown, Silver, Mace, Briggs, and Chandler families from Yancey and Madison Counties. Would like to correspond with anyone searching these families. Mrs. Charles Chandler, 6500 Goodall Rd., Corunna, MI 48817. [1989]

Briggs, Leona, sister to Wilburn Briggs, Sr., and married John Edwards of Egypt, Yancey County, N. C. Would also be interested in any Briggs families in Yancey County. David Taylor, Route 8, 1457, Hickory, NC 28602. [1989]

Briggs, Howell Wilburn, Sr., born about 1827 and lived in Yancey County. His mother was Delothe (Dollie) Rhodes who lived with Charlotte Briggs Hensley, widow of Silas A. Hensley, before her death. Howell W. Briggs married Naomi Honeycutt. Who were her parents? Howell's second wife was Malinda Fox Hensley, a widow. Who was her first husband. David A. Taylor, Rt. 8, Box 1457, Hickory, NC 28602. [1990]

Brooks, Hiram, born in Buncombe County before moving to Madison County in the early 1820s. He was married to Plooy Summie, who was born in Lincoln County. Their children were James, Levi, Mark, Elizabeth, Sarah, and Mary. Would like to know the name of Hiram's parents. J. B. Brooks, 222 Tyler Heights, Marion, NC 28752. [1988]

Brooks, John Robert, married Elizabeth Jane Ensley, perhaps in Jackson County and lived in Haywood County in 1907. Would like to know parents of each. Also, would like to know if there are books or records available for the following families: McClure, Moody, Plott. Mrs. Will Jenkins, 372 East High Road, Apt. 1, Freeland, WA 98249. [1987]

Brown, Cornelius and Catherine, who lived in Hot House Township, Cherokee County, N. C., (near Murphy) in 1850. He was born in 1811, and Catherine was born in 1823. Would particularly like to know Catherine's maiden name. Renee Russell, 8 White Oak Road, Asheville, NC 28803. [1993]

Brown families, Warlick, Worley, Frisbee, Meadows, Ingle. Would like to correspond with members of all of these families in the Leicester area of Buncombe County. Mrs. Burma Warlick Harrold, 776 Missouri Ave., West Plains, MO 65775. [1988]

Brown, Milton, born about 1796, probably in Buncombe, married Kiziah Hooper in Haywood. They later lived in Macon and Cherokee

Counties. Was Milton related to Hugh or Robert Brown, both born 1770s and residents of Buncombe? Would like to know parents of Milton. Anne Goodwin, P. O. Box 2501, Cheyenne, WY 82003.[1985]

Brown, William, family buried in the Edward Family Cemetery, Beech Glen area of Madison County. Would like more information on these family members: William (April 16, 1786-March 13, 1851), Ruth Brown (Jan. 19, 1797-July 9, 1877), Rachel Brown (Jan. 1791-1858). Is the Nathaniel Kelsey (Feb. 21, 1799-May 19, 1877), buried nearby, kin to these Browns? Nancy Pope, 58 Bull Mt., Rd., Asheville, NC 28805. [1985]

Browning, Lockaby, or Nelson. During the Civil War, one of the ancestors from one of these families gave birth to twin girls. The father refused to leave his family, having no one to care for them and, being poor, no way to ensure that they could even survive. He then became a draft evader according to the family legend. They lived someplace near Flat Rock. A bounty was then placed on his head and he was forced to hide out in a cave near a creek. A neighbor named Donaldson followed the wife to the hiding place and shot the husband. Would like to know if anyone knows the name of the hiding family. Perry G. McCrary, 901 Jefferson Dr., Charlotte, NC 28226. [1985]

Bruton/Brewton, John, Benjamin, William, Joseph, Samuel, had land patents in 1763-1769 in Old Dobbs County, N. C. Perhaps were kin to the Fountain and Taylor families. Mrs. J. M. Hackma, 1815 Grant Rd., Wenatchee, WA 98801. [1986]

Bryant, James S., married Martha Ann Elizabeth Ellis before 1850. In 1850, they were in Surry County, N. C. Would like more information. Barbara White, 273 S. Dillwyn Rd., Newark, DE 19711. [1987]

Bryson, Hugh and Margaret McCall. Would like birth dates of children, this couple, and a picture of the Bryson home. This couple later lived with their daughter Mrs. William McCrary. Would also be interested in picture of William and Susannah Bogle Bryson from Mills River. Lawrence E. Wood, 75 Peeks Creek Rd., Franklin, NC 28734. [1993]

Bryson, Jonathon, born in Buncombe 1791, died in Webster, Jackson County, 1877, married Elizabeth Demaris Griffen. Would like to know Jonathon's parents. Maurine Cabe, Rt. 3, Box 1299, Asheville, NC 28806. [1984]

Buchanan family, Little Switzerland in 1800s. Joseph Buchanan and wife Elizabeth Hollifield, children William A. (in Civil War), Alfred, Robert, Daniel, George L. (Civil War, married Pittman), Jacob (married Pittman). Sophis Pittman Buchanan was buried in Bakersville in November 1922, wife of George L. Buchanan. Would like more information. Annabelle White, 5 Minot Place, Utica, NY 13502. [1986]

Burgess family, lived in Buncombe County during the late 1700s and 1800s. Mrs. D. R. Looney, 9208 South 93 East Ave., Tulsa, OK 74133. [1991]

Burgin, Bemjamin. Would like a copy of family records from his Bible which was sold in 1837 to Josia B. Burgin. Lawrence E. Wood, 75 Peeks Rd., Franklin, NC 28734. [1988]

Burnett, David, 1810-1904, wife Elizabeth Smith, born 1800. They are buried in Bethel Cemetery, Haywood County. Would like information about parents. Margaret Hannemann, 1314 Daly Rd., Ojai, CA 93023. [1983]

Burris family, born, lived, and died on the coast of North Carolina (Currituck, Hyde, Dare Counties). John Burrus born 1731; son, Zacheriah Burrus born 1786; son Allen Burris 1825-1881; son, Andrew Peele Burris, Sr., 1849-1932; son, Barney Columbus Burrus 1892-1923. Would like more information. Jack T. Burrus, 1027 East St., Waynesville, NC 28786. [1984]

Butcher, Susan, born in 1782 in North Carolina and was an Indian. She moved to Jefferson County, Mississippi and married Louis Blaube from France. Their children included Luminda, Sarah, Susan, James, and Mitchell. Dot Brown, 409 Fredrick, Monroe, LA 71201. [1990]

Byrd, George William, wife Annie Hutson, settled on Toe River Valley of North Carolina in the 1790s. Lloyd Bailey, 4122 Deepwood Circle, Durham, NC 27707. [1992]

Caldwell, Annie, born in Virginia about 1762, married William Hunter. Two known sons who were born to William and Annie Hunter were Robert Hunter, married in Buncombe County in 1807 to Susan Stice, and Samuel Hunter, born 1793, married Catherine Poteet in Rutherford County. Gwen Cody, 205 Cody Drive, Sevierville, TN 37862. [1988]

Calloway, John, born 1804, Madison County, N. C., married Elizabeth Ann about 1827. Would like to know his parents and the parents of his wife. They migrated to Hancock County, Tennessee, and later to Knox County, Kentucky, where John died about 1863 in the community of

Yellow Creek. Mrs. M. F. Calloway, 207 West Fairlane, Longview, TX 75604. [1986]

Camby, Maggie, daughter of Thomas Barney Camby and Theresa Jane Sumner. The other children of Thomas and Theresa Camby were Loy, Vic, Hattie, and Molly (born February 16, 1881). W. T. Connor, 361 Fairview Rd., Asheville, NC 28803. [1991]

Campbell, Alda Virginia, born in Newton, N. C., on May 25, 1850, and died in Hickory on February 6, 1921. She was the daughter of Milton Ogburn Campbell and Catherine Bost. Their other children included Rosa and James Campbell. Virginia married A. A. Shuford. David Mathews, Rt. 1, Box 530, Canton, NC 28716-9749. [1993]

Campbell, Samuel Armstrong, died May 1869 in Florence County, S. C., wife was Annie White, and they had four children: John Caldwell Calhoun Campbell born August 9, 1835, James Campbell born 1846, Mary who died at school in Raleigh, and Palmara who died at school in Raleigh. Samuel married his second wife Maartha Ann Thwing at Darlington, S. C., on July 17, 1849. Their two children were Southern Armstrong Campbell born in 1850 in Florence, S. C. and died in 1911. Would like to know the parents of Samuel. W. Allan Campbell, 1576 Utah Mountain Drive, Waynesville, NC 28786. [1989]

Candler College, near Acton in Candler. This college existed in the late 1800s and was established by William Gaston Candler in honor of his father and mother, George and Emaline Candler. George was the son of Zachariah Candler. Would like more information on this college. Robert C. Holbrook, 65 Hartshorn Rd., Candler, NC 28715. [1988]

Candler, James Madison, Madison County in the 1800s, had brothers George Washington Candler and Thomas Jefferson Candler.
His wife may have been Lucinda. Would like to know burial site of James Madison Candler. Would also like to hear from descendants of John Candler, brother of Zachariah Candler who lived in Alexander, N. C. John Candler settled near the Duck River in Tennessee. Eva C. Miller, 88 Patton Cemetery Rd., Swannanoa, NC 28778. [1988]

Carroll, William, Lincoln County in 1800. Nathaniel and William Carroll, Jr., were in Haywood County in 1820, 1830, then in Macon in 1840. Would also like information on Joseph Clements who lived in Rutherford County in 1820, 1830, and Macon in 1840. Janette Cain, Route 5, Box 301, Gainsville, GA 30501. [1986]

Carson family, Ellis, Peter, William J., John Springer, Leonard, Issace, Ella. Some or all moved about 1851 from Pennsylvania and would like to know the names of their parents. Lillian Carson Collins, Box 4, Webster, FL 33597. [1985]

Case, James Buchanan, married Catherine Parthenia Cook, daughter of Thomas Cook, 1815-1894, and Ann Galyean, lived in Case Cove in Candler. A grandson remembers attending a Case family reunion about 1930 at the log home of Will Case of Horseshoe where a brother Jim Case was also present. Both men had long beards and were Civil War veterans. Would like any information on any of these. Vernon Taylor, Rt. 2, Box 429-A, Candler, NC 28715. [1984]

Cathey families of Burke, Buncombe, and Haywood, particularly the family of William Cathey, Sr., in 1810 Haywood census. Was he the father of Andrew D. Cathey, died 1808, and Daniel Cathey, died in 1810? Lawrence E. Wood, 75 Peeks Road, Franklin, NC 28734. [1984]

Cauble family, particularly Jacob L. Cauble, who was born about 1803 in Rowan County and his relatives. Jacob is buried at Gashes Creek Church in Buncombe. He died in 1891 and is buried beside his second wife, Catherine Trexler. He moved into Buncombe about 1860 on Whitson's Creek. (Is this what is now known as Gashes Creek? Could Indian Branch have run from the Oakley area?) George Huntley, 173 Fairfax Ave., Asheville, NC 28806. [1992]

Chamber's Cemetery in the community of Beech near Reems Creek in Buncombe. Am particularly interested in the churches there in the 1890s, names of settlers, and records for this cemetery. Mrs. C. H. Smith, 685 Cedar St., Lander, WY 82520. [1984]

Chandler children who were born about 1857-1870 to George Washington Chandler and Elizabeth Boswell Chandler who were married in 1857 and were killed in an accident when the children were young. Catherine Miller, Rt. 7, Box 256, Fairview, NC 28730. [1983]

Chandler, John, wife Cela Wise Chandler of Haywood County in the mid-1800s. Frank E. Wise, P. O. Box 178, Nebo, NC 28761. [1987]

Chastain family. James Chastain, minister, who was born in 1740 in Goochland County, Virginia, died 1820, South Carolina; his son Obediah Chastain, who moved from South Carolina to Tennessee to North Carolina and Georgia; Obediah's don, David Chastain, born 1827, who married Lucinda Young, and moved to Georgia. Joyce S. Teeters, 3111

N. Marble Top Rd., Chickamauga, GA 30707. [1993]

Chunn family, particularly John Cicero Chunn, who came from Rowan County, and had a son Mathew Locke Chunn, who lived on S. French Broad, Asheville, until he died about 1954. Marjorie M. Cockran, 2611 Bayshore Blvd., PH-3, Tampa, FL 33629. [1985]

Clark, Abraham, a signer of the Declaration of Independence. Would like the names and dates of children and the address for the Society of Descendants of Abraham Clark. Mrs. M. C. Robbins, 164 Lynn Cove Rd., Asheville, NC 28804. [1986]

Clark, Ann, born 1785, married George W. Lytle (1785-1858). George was the son of Capt. Thomas Lytle and Susanna Petillo. Children of Ann Clark and George Lytle were Millington, born 1809, James P. born 1811, Littleton born 1812, Thomas B., John b. 1830, George Mills Lytle b. 1819, Rebecca b. 1807, and Susannah b. 1818. Martha Smart, Rt. 4, 54 Moss Drive, Rutherfordton, NC 28139. [1986]

Clark, John Hunter, married May 7, 1832, in Haywood County, N. C., Mary Polly Hood, daughter of Allen Hood. John died in 1848 in Cocke County, Tennessee, and Polly moved with the children to Burnet County, Texas, in 1874. Would like information about the parents of John. Jack Clark, Rt. 1, Box 428, Rockdale, TX 76567. [1991]

Clontz, Jacob, wife Susan, lived at Alexander, N. C., and had children Jeff, John, George, David, Sally, and Mary. Lee Clontz Gosnell, Watson Road, Arden, NC 28704. [1986]

Cockerham, William, born about 1777 in Halifax, Virginia, and wife Charity, born 1783 in Surry County, possibly the daughter of Charity Burch and James Jennings. The family was listed in the 1830 census of Macon County, N. C. The children Elizabeth C. Starnes Conley, John Burch Cockerham, and Alfred Newton Cockerham lived in Jackson and Swain Counties. Other children were Daniel Stewart, James, possibly William and Margaret. Would like any information on the parents or children. Ruth C. Shuler, 30 S. Country Club Drive, Cullowhee, NC 28723. [1990]

Cody family. Stephen Cody born about 1775, Thomas Cody born about 1750, Godfrey Cody born about 1755. All of these lived in Madison County in 1790. W. R. Cody, 3515 Longview St., Burlington, NC 27215. [1988]

Coffey, Daniel, born about 1806, North Carolina, and lived with first wife in Rockingham County in the 1830s. Married second to Nancy about 1839 and moved to McMinn County, Tennessee. Would like Daniel's parents and the names of his wives. Dorothy Shamblin, 662 Oxford Oaks Lane, Oxford, MI 48051. [1985]

Cogburn, James E. (Elijah?), born about 1801, probably in Tennessee, married first Polly Lance and had three children. He lived in Haywood in 1830-40 before he and Polly were divorced. He moved to Arkansas, and she married John Frady. Joyce Parris, 220 Northwest Avenue, Swannanoa, NC 28778. [1984]

Collins, David, born 1792, in War of 1812 from Duplin County, N. C., married Elizabeth Fussell from there in 1813. Would like to know the parents and family. Elmo Collins, Jr., Box 4, Webster, FL 33597. [1985]

Connelly, Nancy Ann, born 1778, North Carolina, died 1850-1860, possibly in Lawrence County, Indiana, who married William Connelly about 1790 in Wilkes County. William was born in 1768, son of John and Sarah Wilson Connelly, was a judge, moved to Indiana after 1820 from Little River area of Wilkes/Ashe County. Would like more on the family of Nancy Ann. Paula Conley Grant, 5160 Pawnee Drive, Silver Springs, Nevada 89429. [1986]

Conner, Desta Vastine, married John Patrick Casey, Wayne County, Georgia, about 1885, died in Polk County, Florida, in 1918. Two sons were Patrick and Thomas Casey. Two earlier sons were Jim and Will Conner. Desta Dyae, P. O. Box 324, Whittier, NC 28789. [1986]

Conner, George, born 1805, married Jane about 1828. Seven of their children were James A., Elvira, Obediah, Humphrey, Issac, Mary A., and Frances. The last record of George was in the 1850 census of McDowell County. Jane and children were on the 1860 census in Henderson County. Jo Ann Earwood Shepherd, P. O. Box 351, Christmas, FL 32709. [1986]

Conner, William (Billy), born in Cleveland County, wife Hannah Matthew. Would like ancestors of both. They had a son David Conner, born January 25, 1817, in Shelby, died January 16, 1896 in Balsam, N. C., who had married Neicie Branton also from Cleveland County. Would also like information on Neicie's father, William Branton who was buried in Cleveland County and had a son named John. Virginia Pursifull, 44 Balm Grove Ave., Asheville, NC 28806. [1986]

Cook, Hence M., born June 27, 1805, died February 10, 1885. One family tradition says that he and two brothers stole their way over from

Ireland on a potato boat about 1820 and settled in Buncombe. He married Elender (Nellie) Bryson and had seven children; they lived their last years in the Scott's Creek area of Jackson County. Dan Johnson, 505 S. Rietze St. #10, Concrete, WA 98237.

Cooper, William Hopplet, born 1822, died 1861, perhaps buried in northwest Georgia in Summerville. William L. Cooper, 214 Park Avenue, Marion, NC 28752. [1988]

Cordell, Rebecca Chadwick Allen, born March 3, 1827, Washington County, Tennessee, married John Henry Cordell in January 1856, Buncombe County. Would also like information on Louisa and Samuel Clayburn Cordell. Roberta Corn, 705 Christian Creek, Swannanoa, NC 28778. [1986]

Cox, William (1765-1849), wife Hannah Lamie (1767-1855), lived in Washington County, Virginia. Would like to hear from descendants. Mary Jane Cox, 2620 Lafayette Avenue, Richmond, VA 23228. [1992]

Coxey, Mary, born June 8, 1849, McDowell County, N. C. She married John Fortune and her parents were John A. and Mary Jane Whitesides Coxey. Would like more on her family. Emily F. Baldwin, 149 Mayberry Drive, Asheville, NC 28804. [1991]

Crane, Mary Elizabeth, born December 3, 1868, died December 10, 1936, Jackson County, N. C. She was in Quallatown community in 1910 and was married first to Severe Crowe, second to Will Green. One of her brothers was Anthony Crane, born about 1878. Her mother's name was Martha, born about 1847. Would like more information. Kirk Stephens, 16 Laurel Branch, Sylva, NC 28779. [1991]

Craig, James, wife Eliza of North Carolina. Their children were Sarah Elizabeth, Mary Jane, Margrett, Caroline, Robert, William, James Henry. Mrs. Ramona Schooley, P. O. Box 771363, Eagle River, Alaska 99577. [1992]

Creasman, Clarence Dixon. Is there a connection to the preacher Clarence Dixon? Would like to know if Adam Creasman, born 1790, was the son of Adam Creaseman lilsted in the 1790 census as living in Salisbury District, Rowan County. James Creasman, P. O. Box 1575, Pinetop, Arizona 85935. [1985]

Cresawn, Naomi, married Josiah Mace in 1808, Yancey County, N. C. Mrs. Walter Light, P. O. Box 173, Jonas Ridge, NC 28641. [1984]

Crook, Charlie Henry, wife Bessie May King, lived across the road from Sand Hill School, Enka, N. C. Their children were Margaret, Charles, Albert, Donald, Billy, George, Leonard, and Vernon. Betty Seals, 62 Beverly Rd., Asheville, NC 28806. [1986]

Cross family of Buncombe area, 1800 through 1860s. Some of these were Joseph Cross and Sarah Cogdill, William and Rebecca Cross, Rachel Cross and James D. Cobb, Anne Cross and William Davis, Matilda Cross and John H. Russell, Leander Cross and Elizabeth Arrington, Joseph Cross III and Mary Chatham. Richard E. Russell, 3635 N. Kercheval Dr., Indianapolis, IN 46226. [1990]

Crusius family. It is believed that four boys and their mother came from Lithuania or Germany; then after a few years two boys stayed and had families while the other two boys and their mother returned to their homeland. Donna Cruisius, P. O. Box 206, Canton, NC 28716. [1990]

Cunningham, Josiah B., born in North Carolina in 1828, married in 1847 Elizabeth Fails of Lancaster, S. C., died 1893 in Choctaw County, Alabama. Josiah had a sister, Martha Cunningham, who married George Washington Causey. Would like to know the parents of Josiah and Martha. The children of Josiah and Elizabeth included Thomas, born 1848, James, 1850, George 1852, and others born in Alabama. Betty LeBlanc, 8108 Moss Lane, Orange, TX 77630. [1990]

Curtis, James and Joseph, lived on or near Toms Creek in McDowell County. Was Polly Curtis who married Clark Bird a daughter of James Curtis? Did Johnathon Curtis, born 1747 and died 1834, have a daughter Lydia, born 1782, who married a William Martin and had daughters Betty and Cynthia? Lawrence E. Wood, 75 Peeks Creek Rd., Franklin, NC 28734. [1988]

Dale, Joseph Alexander, died in 1917, wife Mary Elizabeth Crawley, died in 1920. Am interested in their descendants. They were from Burke County, N. C. Their children were Sarah, William Theodore, Mary L., Charles Alexander (married Sallie Duckworth, 1895), Edward P., Nonnie, Odus N., and Otto Augustus. Terri Dale-Yates, P. O. Box 16294, Asheville, NC 28816. [1992]

Daugherty, Nelson, a Daugherty slave in the Black Mountain area, and wife Halley. Would like any information. Corrie Rutherford, Rt. 1, Box 102 B, Blue Ridge Rd., Black Mountain, NC 28711. [1986]

Davenport, George, lived at Altapass, N. C., in 1911, born in 1876, son of David Davenport. Samuel Wesley Davenport was his cousin and lived in McDowell County. Would like to hear from Davenport relatives. Jessie D. Orr, 119 Park St., Hendersonville, NC 28739. [1984]

Davidson, Margaret Nancy, born 1781 in Tennessee or North Carolina. Would like to know her maiden name. In 1850, she was living in DeKalb Co., Ala., with a son Paran Davidson. In 1860, she was living in Leake Co., Miss., with her daughter-in-law. Marie Davidson Hand, 800 Bostwick, Nacogdoches, TX 75961. [1986]

Davis, Ida Bell, married James Newton Ward and died in 1923. The children were William Fletcher, Robert, George Ernest, Fred, Lula. Would particularly like to know who her parents were and the names of her brothers and sisters. Dorothy Reece, Rt. 5, Box 412, Candler, NC 28715. [1988]

Davis, Peter, born 1825, married Mary Jane Angel, born 1826, lived in Franklin, N. C. One son was Leander "Lee" Davis, born June 19, 1852. Would like information on him and another Peter Davis who was born about 1818 in Buncombe and married Sarah Davis, daughter of David Davis of Black Mountain. Peter and Sarah lived in Macon County by 1850. Their children included John L, born 1840, Amanda born 1844, Robert born 1848, Leander G. born 1857. Fred Davis, Rt. 3, Box 509, Arden, NC 28704. [1987]

Davis, Rebecca, taught school in Moore County, near Cathage (perhaps Davis School), married John Martin Fry (born May13, 1824, died November 3, 1884), one child Clark Oscar Fry, born October 15, 1854. Would like to know names of Rebecca's parents, her birth and death dates. John Fry married, second, Lucy Stutts, daughter of Jacob and Elizabeth Barrett Stutts. Would also be interested if John Fry kin to Martins and of any Scottish ancestry. Robbie Frye Purser, Rt. I, Sunny South, Alabama 36780. [1984]

Dean/Deans, Reuben, born in North Carolina about 1791, also lived in Claiborn County, Tennessee. Betty Deans, Hwy. 71, Voca, TX 76887. [1988]

DeBord/DeBoard families. Have currently found the following members in North Carolina and would like to have more information: Reubin DeBord born 1756, James DeBord born 1774 and lived in Buncombe, Jacob born about 1770, William born 1769; Benjzmin, Ephraim, and Joseph DeBord were in North Carolina in the mid 1700s but moved to Kentucky. Also, would like any information on John

DeBord and wife Martha Edwards, both born about 1770, married January 13, 1795, in Surry County. One daughter was Priscilla DeBord who married John A. Sorrells on January 14, 1818, in Rutherford County. John Sorrells had a tavern on the road to Chimney Rock in the early 1800s. G. E. Burch, Rt. 2, Box 641, Huntsville, TX 77340. [1987]

Dempsey, Perry and Nettie, lived on School Road in the Oakley area, Asheville, during the 1930s and 1940s. Would like information about them. Marjorie Ramsey, 139 Jonestown Rd., Asheville, NC 28804. [1984]

Denman family of Surry, Rowan, Wilkes Counties from 1770-1791. First names included Moses, Hugh and wife Elizabeth, John, James, Christopher, and William and wife Hepsibah. A family of Denmans settled in Franklin County, Georgia in the late 1790s. Are these related? Would like any Denman information. Mary Gail Tutt, 405 North St., McGehee, AR 71654. [1986]

Diggs, Benjamin, born 1811, died 1876, son or grandson of Marshall Diggs of Anson County, moved to Mississippi in 1849. This name was often spelled Degge. Would like any information on these Diggs. Guy F. Taylor, 18 Archdale Rd., Columbia, SC 29209. [1986]

Dill family. Would like more information on the following. John Dill who born November 23, 1759, Kent County, Delaware, and died January 7, 1846, Carswell County, N. C. He married Mary Ann Fischer and had daughter Jane. Would like to know the other children's names and whom Jane married. Parents and birthplace of Jess Dill, born about 1888 in North Carolina. On the 1910 Greenville County, S. C., census he was listed with Batus Dill, born 1888, Brefort Dill age 2, and Benedict Dill age 1. Job Dill was on the North Carolina taxpayers' list for Bertie County, N. C., in 1759. Would like to know Job's place of birth, and names of parents, wife, and children. Joab Bruton Dill, born August 20, 1849, Greenville County, S. C., died June 14, 1928, Forest City, N. C., buried Pleasant Grove Cemetery, Forest City. Would like date of death and burial place of Joab's father, Charles Pinckney Dill. Harry F. Dill, 6019 Benjamin, Alexandria, LA 71303.

Dills, Peter, born 1720, died 1786, Rutherford County, N. C. He married Ann, born 1725, St. Andrews Parish, S. C. One child was Thomas Dills, born 1745, Rutherford County. Would like more information. Mrs. Mary Von Gerichten, 11501 Buckingham Rd., Austin, TX 78759. [1993]

Dillinger/Dellinger, Dr. John L., came from Buncombe County to Elijay, Gilmer County, Georgia, in the 1830s. He married Presha from South Carolina and was a stone mason and a herbal doctor. He was in Gilmer County until after 1860, then moved to north central Arkansas where he died in October of 1896. He had one son named Allen. Would like more information. Gladys S. Ryan, 1616 Richmond St., El Cerrito, CA 94530. [1989]

Donoho family, in North Carolina before 1814. Gaines Donoho married Bitsy Scriber, and had children Robert, Charlotte, William Harvey, and Gaines, Jr. Gaines Donoho's brother was William Carroll Donoho who married Frances Dade Davis. Would like more information on any Donohos. H. Lewis Sporl, 2512 Constance St., New Orleans, LA. [1992]

Dowdle, John and Oliver, buried between 1900 and 1910 in a cemetery in Whittier, N. C. Would like to know exactly where. These were infant sons of George and Sally Campbell Dowdle who moved from Whittier to Macon County. Nelle B. Green, Rt. 10, Box 359, Franklin, NC 28734. [1984]

Drake, Winnie, born about 1800, married Arthur Corn of Henderson County. Would like more information. Brenda Hudgins, 41 Mt. Carmel Dr., Asheville, NC 28806. [1987]

Driskall families. Would like information on any of these families. Dorothy Driskall Davis, 6 East Ecton Street, Asheville, NC 28806. [1986]

Durham, Joseph, by tradition from North Carolina, married Frances Waddell, March 31, 1803, in Fauquier County, Virginia, and by 1805 located in the part of Berkeley County, Virginia, that is now Morgan County, West Virginia. Would like any information. Fred T. Newbraugh, 6 Rockwell Circle, Berkeley Springs, WV 25411. [1988]

Edwards, Thomas and Elizabeth, lived in Rutherford County near Mountain Creek then on Turkey Creek in Buncombe County. His will was probated in 1811, Buncombe. Their children born between 1762 and 1779 were Martin, Nancy, William, Elizabeth (perhaps married John Wells), Charles (died in Haywood County), Thomas, Jr., (perhaps married Mary Brittain), John, S. P. Ellis (married Amelia Brittain, died in Haywood), Andrew (married Mary Woodfin). Would like to know if Bible records exist and if anyone has more information. Warren Stout,

P. O. Box 538, State University, AR 72467. [1988]

Ellenburg, James Henry, born about 1869, believed lived in Asheville, son of Adam Ellenburg, born 1813, South Carolina, married Matilda Taylor. Other known children besides James were William, Mary, John, Robert, Lorenza Dow (born October 15, 1860, lived in Greene County, Tenn.), Joe Sarah, and Idaa. Would like more information. Mrs. Frank Sauls, 205 Unaka St., Greeneville, TN 37743. [1984]

Eller, Jacob, Jr., in Buncombe by 1799. Most Ellers in this area trace their ancestry back to him. J. Gerald Eller edits "The Eller Chronicles," a family history newsletter and is compiling a history of Jacob's family and would like to hear from family members. J. Gerald Eller, Rt. 2, Box 145-D, Whittier, NC 28789. [1990]

Ellisor family, married into the Dubard/DeBord family that moved into Western North Carolina. The Ellisors and Dubards settled in South Carolina Dutch Fork area in the late 1700s. Is particularly interested in the parents of Philip T. Ellisor, born April 3, 1826, South Carolina, who married in Dallas County, Alabama, Laura Ann Elizabeth Dubard, born February 28, 1826, daughter of John G. Dubard, born 1804 in South Carolina. Philip and Laura Ellisor moved to Texas about 1850. Nancy Hargesheimer, P. O. Box 1901, Lubbock, TX 79408. [1991]

Ensley, James Elijah Lambert, born 1835, Buncombe or Henderson County. Possibly parents were Charles and Nancy Ensley. Would like more information. George D. Morris, 4847 Crown Ave., LaCanada, CA 91011. [1988]

Ensley, Rev. Wilson, married Mary Ann (Polly) Parris in 1845. Wilson was a son of William Ensley and was from a family of twelve, four of whom married into the Parris family. Would like more information. Marie W. Bostic, Rt. 1, Box 563-A, Clifton Forge, VA 24422. [1989]

Eskew family came into Western North Carolina from Georgia and Alabama. Would like more information. Lois M. Flynt, P. O. Box 241, Little Switzerland, NC 28749. [1984]

Evans, Myra Fox, lived in Marion, North Carolina, in 1940. Would like to contact relatives. Mrs. Robert W. Edmonds, 310 Stonewall Avenue, Swannanoa, NC 28778. [1985]

Farmer family from Cherokee and Asheville. Jessie Farmer, born 1874, married Jack or John Leverett and had three children: Nellie born 1908, married a Muncy and lived in Asheville and Maggie Valley, George born

1912, Clarence born 1916. Would like information about the Farmer and Leverett families. Judy Farmer, 826 Apache Trail, McMinnville, TN 37110. [1993]

Ferguson, William, born 1764, Amelia County, Virginia, married Judah Wood, daughter of Belfield Wood, March 1791, Greene County, Tennessee. He died December 9, 1834, Habersham County, Georgia. Their sons were Hugh born 1792, Henry Wood born 1793, William born 1794, John born 1797, James Hamilton born 1802, Belfield born 1804, Elijah born 1807, Ellis born 1807-1811. These were all born in South Carolina. Others sons were Champion born 1813, Edward born 1816, Andrew J. born 1820. These were born in Kentucky. Would like to hear from any Fergusons. Is the above Hugh Ferguson the one selling property on North Hominy Creek in Buncombe County in the 1820s? Leonard L. Damron, Rt. 1, Box 118, Sulphur Springs, AR 72768. [1989]

Fincher, Uriah, born about 1811 in North Carolina, probably Mecklenburg County. Was he the son of Jospeh Fincher born 1780 in North Carolina? Joseph married second in 1822 Mary Perry Horn, Mecklenburg. Would like any information on these Finchers. W. T. Horne, 2413 Oak Leaf Dr., Birmingham, AL 35217. [1986]

Foote, William, born in North Carolina in February 1821, possibly Surry County. Would like any information. Scott Hill, 801 Fifth St., Westwego, LA 70094. [1991]

Ford, Benjamin Jackson, born 1805, married Nancy Mantook, lived east of Newport, Tennessee, on Grassy Fork. Their children included Reuben, John Joseph, and James. Would like any information on this family. Jane Ford Taylor, Rt. 1, Box 313, Fincastle, VA 24090. [1987]

Fox, John, married Elizabeth about 1803-1810 in Yancey or Buncombe County. Would like any information. Mrs. Joseph Knopp, 2105 West 300 S., Marion, Indiana 46953. [1985]

Foxworthy, John, married Sarah Northcut on September 29, 1751, Stafford County, Virginia. Sarah was the daughter of William and Margery Page Northcut; William Foxworthy and Clarissa, daughter of William and Hannah Calvert married May 19, 1778 in Virginia; Alexander Foxworthy and Nancy, daughter of George and Frances Jackson Glascock married February 4, 1821 in Fleming County, Kentucky; Leroy Foxworthy and Mahali Jane, daughter of David and Anna Yeazle married April 10, 1851, in Fountain County, Indiana; Freeman Leroy Foxworthy and Serena Ellen, daughter of Marcus D. and Sarah A. Justus Furr, married August 23, 1879, in Fountain County, Indiana. Would like more information on any of these family members. Donald Foxworthy, 510 Overboork Rd., Baltimore, MD 21212. [1985]

Frady families in Western North Carolina. Would like any information. Betty Riddle, 442, Refuge Hill Road, Jasper, GA 30143. [1994]

Frady, Silas, born about 1837, son of Lewis Frady and grandson of Ephraim Frady. Silas married Laura J. Lindsey. Laura is buried at Hooper's Creek Baptist Church Cemetery. When did Silas die and where was he buried? James A. Black, Jr., 96 Spooks Branch Road, Asheville, NC 28804. [1990]

Freeman, Elizabeth, married Edward Doron in Rutherford County before 1781. They left Rutherford with five or six children in September of 1816, went to Tennessee, then to Kentucky. Would like to know the parents of Elizabeth Freeman and to correspond with members of the Doron/Doren/Doran family. Linda M. Wilson, 104 Chickadee Lane, Brevard, NC 28712. [1984]

Freeman, Rev. Humphrey P., born about 1824, probably in Madison County, married Lyia/Leah Eliza Rees, born February 13, 1822, Madison County. Children included Nancy, Moses Kelso, Talitha, Mary, William Posey, Samuel M., Sarah, Eliza, Daisy, Fremont, Nevade, and Laura. This family lived in Kentucky but were back in North Carolina by 1850 in Murphy, N. C. Later they moved to Missouri and then Nebraska. Rev. Freeman died August 3, 1889, buried in Auburn, Nebraska. Paternal grandfather believed to be Rev. Moses Freeman first pastor of Bull Creek Baptist Church in Mars Hill. Would like to know names of parents of Humphrey. Duane R. Freeman, 2168 I-50 Rd., Austin, CO 81410. [1988]

Fulk/Faulk/Volck family from Forsyth or Surry Counties. Would like any information. Kathie J. Smith, RR 2, Box 35, Coal City, IN 47427. [1992]

Gardner, Sarah, born about 1835, Yancey County, married Jasper Roland, then to a Ray of Yancey County. Would like more information. Brenda Hudgins, 41 Mt. Carmel Dr., Asheville, NC 28806. [1987]

Garland, William Alfred, born about 1868 in Rabun County, in Buncombe County in the late 1800s and living in Asheville after attending Wake Forest College. He was the oldest son of Jesse Lafayette and

Marinda Greenwood Garland. Would like to hear from descendants. Julia Anderson Garland, 2810 Georgia Highway, Otto, NC 28763. [1992]

Garren families of Western North Carolina. If you would like to share any Garren information or subscribe to "Garren Goodies," a family history newsletter, write to Garren Heritage Association, 380 Corbly Drive, #11, Hendersonville, NC 28739. The editor David Gilbert would like information on the descendants of Jospeh Garren, born about 1785, married to Eve, lived in Buncombe until after 1850, son of Andrew. Three of Joseph's four sons were William R., James, and Wiley. [1994]

Garren, Elizabeth, the first wife of Ephraim Garren, born 1822, Buncombe County. She was the mother of William L. Garren, born February 6, 1849, who married Alcy Lanning on March 11, 1869, in Henderson County. (Alcy was the daughter of James and Mary Vaughn Lanning.) Elizabeth also seemed to be the mother of James Thomas Garren, born March 1853, Buncombe, who married Mary Elizabeth Redmon on December 22, 1872. (Mary was the daughter of John William and Nancy Taylor Redmon.) Ephraim Garren married second Asabella Stroup on December 28, 1854, in Henderson County and had children Sarah, Anesta, Julius, Martha, Mary, and Arminta. Any information on these Garrens would be appreciated. Sarah Garren, 7004 Loch Commond, Austin, TX 78749. [1988]

Garrison, Katherine, born about 1800 in Buncombe and married David Merrell in Buncombe about 1824. Katherine died by 1834, and David Merrell then married her sister Elizabeth Garrison. They died in 1880 in Saba County, Texas. Were William, Absolum, and Comfort Garrison in Buncombe their kin. Would like to know the parents of Katherine and Elizabeth. Nela Daniel, 745 East 60 N., Orem, Utah 84057. [1986]

Would be very much interested in obtaining a picture of R. J. Gaston's General Store which was located in Hominey, N. C., in the early 1900s. This was the only store between Canton and Asheville for many years. Landry Thrash, P. O. Box 114, Candler, NC 28915.

Gaston, Martha Caroline, born August 4, 1822, in South Carolina. She was the daughter of William and Sarah Tindall Gaston and married George Winston Booth, son of Charles and lucy Abernathy Booth. Would like information on the family or ancestors. Sharon Johnson, 315 N. Bonner, Jacksonville, TX 75766.

Gibbs, Samuel Easmon, also known as Isam and Samuel Issac, married Jennie Evelyn Hollifield on March 19, 1922, Arcadia, S. C. He had two sons, Robert Alfred Gibbs and Talmadge Andrew Gibbs. He disappeared about 1934, possibly from Buncombe, Madison, or Henderson. Would like information on him. Patricia Gibbs White, 567 Paint Fork Rd., Barnardsville, NC 28709. [1984]

Gibens, Francis Marion, married to Georgia Ethelia Black in 1882. He left Benton, Arkansas, in 1903 by train for Tennessee and was never heard from again. Laurie Wharton, 3225 Milton, Dallas, TX. [1988]

Gibson, Odum, born about 1825, wife Carolyn M., born about 1822. They are listed on the 1850 McDowell Census. Their daughter Ann married William Silver in McDowell on January 13, 1878. Would like more information on all of these. Beth Silver, Rt. 5, Box 188, Marion, NC 28752. [1988]

Gilbert, Jesse, married Sarah Green in Edgecombe County on February 28, 1764. In 1767 he sold land (while buying in Johnston County) to John Green on both sides of Town Creek near Tarboro. Would like more information. Ileana Gilbert Drake, 358 Brevard Rd., Asheville, NC 28806. [1984]

Gilliam, Mark (Marcus), born 1796 in Franklin County, North Carolina, and died 1856 in Floyd County, Georgia. He married Rebecca Tucker of South Carolina. Mark is possibly the son of Sampson Gilliam and Drucilla Hill of Franklin County. Sampson died in Union County, S. c., in 1827. Would like to correspond with any Gilliam family researchers. Avis G. Holden, 1301 Tenth Ave., Albany, GA 31707.

Goins, Jane, wife of John Martin Goins, lived in Cleveland County, N. C., in 1900, married in 1898. By 1910, Jane was dead, and John was married to Lydia Tiddy. Children listed by 1910 census were Gertrude, Grace, Geneva, William, and Josephine. Would like more informa-tion. Peggy Lee Cox, Rt. 1, Box 778, Spruce Pine, NC 28777. [1989]

Goldsmith, William, born about 1812 in South Carolina. He moved to Buncombe County about 1840, later to Yancey and Madison Counties, married first Mary Buckner of Virginia, second to Mary Ann McMahon of Madison County. Would like to know about ancestors and descendants. Lynn Goldsmith, 11 King Circle, Pisgah Forest, NC 28768. [1986]

Goss family. Thomas Goss bought land in 1794 in Washington

District, now eastern Tennessee, and with him were Benjamin, John, and Matthew Goss. In 1822, they moved to South Carolina. Would like information on them. James A. Watson, 1750 Tower Drive, Ardmore, OK 73401. [1986]

Graham, Robert Lee, owned a mercantile store in Asheville about 1888 through 1892. Would like information on him. Robert Graham, 925 Parker St., Charlotte, NC 28216. [1988]

Grayson Family Assosciation is looking for people with Grayson family histories going back to the year 1800. Richard R. Grayson, M. D., Box 167, St. Charles, Illinois 60174. [1983]

Green, Daniel, was born in North Carolina about 1805, married Sophia Griggs in Hancock County, Georgia, in 1825. They later moved to Columbia County, Arkansas. Would like more information. Lynda Methvin, 3237 Schuler Drive, Bossier City, LA 71112. [1991]

Green, James, wife Mary Ann Morrow of Haywood County. They were married January 6, 1834 and moved to Sevier County, Tennessee, in the 1850s. Would like information about both of these. Gwen Cody, 205 Cody Drive, Sevierville, TN 37862. [1988]

Green, Rhody, married Thomas R. Brooks on November 23, 1837, Rutherford County. Would like to identify her parents. Frankie G. Brooks, 488 Mox Chehalis Rd., McCleary, Washington 98557. [1983]

Greenwood, George Washington, lived in Cherokee County in 1860, married Elizabeth Reece in Yadkin County. Their children were Sarah, Nancy, William M. Asburry, Celia, Noah E. J., James Franklin (who was a school teacher in the Connley School in Macon County), John D. W., and Harriett. Would like information about these and also James Franklin Greenwood who was living in Macon County in 1870. Irene Basey, 2984 East State St., Greenfield, IN 46140. [1988]

Griffin, Jonathon Griffin, born in Buncombe in 1791, died in Webster, Jackson County in 1877, married Elizabeth Demaris Thersa. Would like information about his parents. Margaret Hannemann, 1314 Daly Rd., Ojai, CA 93023. [1983]

Guthrie families. Would like information about the children of the following Guthries: children of John and Anne Guthrie -- Johnathan, Shadrack, Andrew, Abner, and Sally (married a Rutledge); children of Johnathan and Jamina Arrington Guthrie -- Mary (married Brown), Edwin, and Sarah/Sally (married Arrington). Kay G. Adams, 307 Barton

Rd., Asheville, NC 28804. [1991]

Guthrie, John, a Revolutionary soldier from Halifax County, North Carolina. Pension papers indicate he lived in Buncombe. Would be interested in more information and in knowing where he is buried. Margaret Longeteig, 3415 Tenth St., Lewiston, Idaho 83501. [1986]

Guyn, James (Dick). Name also spelled Gwynn, Gwin, Wyn, Wynne, lived near Cana, Carroll County, Virginia. He was born January 8, 1852. His children were James Jr., Susan, and George W. Gwynn born Carroll County, May 23, 1884 and died December 13, 1949, in Bristol, Tennessee. Would like more information. Lydia Jane Gwyn Burgess, Rt. 1, Box 231 B, Old Fort, NC 28762. [1985]

Haase, Jacob, Sr., born in Lincoln County, N. C., in 1770. He had children Jacob, Jr., Isaac born 1795, Henry born 1797, David, Sr., born 1801, John born 1807, Absalom born 1814, Ephraim born 1818, Noah born 1820, Polly born 1791. Would like more about these and the name of Jacob's wife. Norma Haase Crawford, Rt. 1, Box 490, Pierce City, MO 65723. [1989]

Hagan, Francis (Frank) Marion , born in North Carolina in 1860, married Harriet Elizabeth Bivins in 1878. Would like to know parents, brothers, and sisters. Betty Brown, 2541 Houghton Ave., Corning, CA 96021. [1990]

Halford, J. Fletcher, born March 13, 1818, possibly a school teacher from Rutherfordton, N. C., area. He was married first in 1839 and had children Hannah Jane born 1840, Betsey Ann born 1843, and Mary Janey. He married second Rosamond Burgin in 1845 and had children from 1845-1852: Martha, Alney Burgin Halford, Nancy Millisand, David, Eliza, and Malinda. J. Fletcher Halford left his wife Rosamond, and no records can be found for him. Would like any information about him. Nada Carroll, Rt. 2, Box 24, Old Fort, NC 28762. [1990]

Hall, Elizabeth Fox, lived in Burnsville, N. C., in 1940. Would like to hear from her relatives. Mrs. Robert W. Edmonds, 310 Stonewall Ave., Swannanoa, NC 28778. [1985]

Hall, Noracil Clementine, born about 1835, married Ernest Bright, and second, married Levi Thompson. Would like more information. Polly Harvey, 4489 Daugharty Rd., DeLand, FL 32724. [1989]

Hamilton, Andrew Wilson, Sr., born in middle Tennessee on October 30, 1816, married Elizabeth Phelps Silivan/Sullivan. A son Silas Monroe

Hamilton lived near Hope, Arkansas, and had eleven children. Would like more information. Mrs. D. P. Nave, 3634 Monessen Drive, Memphis, TN 38128. [1986]

Hampton, Col. Andrew, born 1720 and died 1805, came from England and fought in the Battle of Kings Mountain, in Rutherford County in 1780. He had three sons by his first wife: Ephraim, Ezekiel, and Zacharia; and fifteen children by his second wife, Mary Catherine Hyder. Would particularly like receiving information about Zacharia, but any information would be helpful. Rebecca H. Olsen, 3622 Citrus Trace, Fort Lauderdale, FL 33328. [1988]

Haney, Alfred J., born 1870 and died in 1966, married Anna Lou Ellen Mathis. Alfred was raised by Levi Haney but was really a Parris. He said he was from Little Rock and had brothers and sisters Sherman, Ben, John, Mel, Meg, and Alice. Would like more information on his Parris line and his brothers and sisters. Anna L. Thompson, Rt. 5, Box 164, Canton, NC 28716. [1984]

Haney, John, sometimes called Doc, was a Cherokee Indian, died December 20, 1916. He was the son of Jim and Carolyn Gear Haney and was at one time married to Laura Trammell. The family came from Haywood and Buncombe Counties. Would like more information. Rose Haney, Rt. I, Box 381-A, Topton, NC 28781. [1983]

Hardin, Herbert. Would like to know where his farm was located that was mentioned in a news account in the *Western Vindicator* (would also like to know where this was published) on June 15, 1898. "The Franklin Press": "Honor the Dead. Drury Allen, a Revolutionary soldier, lies buried at the old Herbert Hardin farm beyond Benick's Bridge, and his descendants and relatives propse to erect a monument . .." The names J. F. Flock, L. A. Allen, and Miss Mollie Carpenter of Macon County were listed as people who would be taking contributions. Thelma Welch Swanson, 19 Doraul St., Franklin, NC 28734. [1991]

Hargrove, William Whitney (Valentine), born January 4, 1816, in Western North Carolina. Would like to know exactly where born. His father was William Whitley Hargrove who served in the Revolutionary War. In 1822 the family moved to Tennessee. Son William married Dicy Carruthers in 1837. They later moved to Mississippi in 1839, Ozark, Arkansas, in 1852, and Lawrence County, Missouri, in 1854. One son was James Frank Hargrove. Kathleen H. Pitman, Pigeon Valley Rest Home,

Rt. 5, Box 102, Canton, NC 28716. [1990]

Harmon. Would like information on this family that came into Western North Carolina from Georgia and Alabama. Lois M. Flynt, P. O. Box 241, Little Switzerland, NC 28749. [1984]

Harkins, Daniel, Sr., lived in Madison County, Tennessee, at the time of the probating of his will, November 28, 1832. The heirs of his estate were James Deals, Salberry Sheffield, Rhoda Harkins Gary, Hiram Harkins, David Harkins, Daniel Harkins, Jr., and the heirs of Charles Harkins. Would like to hear from descendants. Mr. Arlyn Berthier, Rt. I, Box 524 AB, Hessmer, LA 71341. [1992]

Harkins, Martin and Martha. Martin was born about 1751 and died in 1823. One known son was Daniel, born about 1789 in South Carolina, married Melinda McCracken, daughter of David and Elizabeth Wilson McCracken of North Carolina. Daniel died in Lafayette County, Mississippi. Would like to know all of Martin and Martha's children. Mr. A. A. Berthier, Rt. I, Box 524 AB, Hessmer, LA 71314. [1991]

Harper, Lot, born in Pennsylvania, November 23, 1781, lived in Fairview section of Buncombe County, N. C. by the early 1800s. He married first Mariam Whitaker then her sister Susannah. Would like early information and his parents. Mrs. Earl Honeycutt, Rt. 2, Box 366, Hendersonville, NC 28739. [1983]

Harris, Toliver, born October 28, 1814, died November 1, 1894, married Nancy (1810-1905) and lived in Haywood County. Would like information on his parents. Supposedly, they had thirteen children, does anyone have names besides Henry, James B., Taylor, Sarah, Emaline? The son James B. Harris on October 31, 1865, married Martha Rachelle Smart Kirkpatrick (widow of Leander Kirkpatrick). Would like to -know the parents of Martha Smart. Jean Pressley Warren, P. O. Box 533, Candler, NC 28715. [1984]

Hart, Ephraim, born 1787 in Virginia, and died 1853, married Lucinda Freeman in 1813. Would like to know the name of Ephraim's father and if he had brothers in Burke, Henderson, and Rutherford Counties. Thelma Hart, 210 Lakeview Drive, Brevard, NC 28712. [1984]

Hart, Ephraim, born in Virginia in 1787 and died in 1853 in Henderson County. His and Lucinda's children were John Henry, James A., Andrew Jackson, Douglas Edward, Albert Adams, Mahuldia, George Washington, Elizabeth, Albert Webster, Meredith Lafayette, Sarah, and Abigail. Would like information on parents and other relatives. W. F. Hart, 677 Hart Rd., Pisgah Forest, NC 28768. [1984]

Hart family, lived in Guilford County, N. C., from the mid 1780s: Henry Hart, Sr., Adam Hart and wife Elizabeth Christman. Would also like information about Jacob Christman, Ludwick and Barbara Iseley. Jackie Hart Stegeman, 4219 Driftwood Drive, Colorado Springs, CO 80918.

Harvey, William Riley, born 1868 in North Carolina, married Laura Emma Scully and lived in Walnut, North Carolina, and Eastern Tennesee. Would particularly llilke the names of his parents. William's brothers and sisters were Sarah, James, John, Tom, Jaley, and Lizy. Malcolm Roger Harvey, 1103 Westwood Ave., High Point, NC 27262. [1991]

Hawkins, Benjamin, owned land in the 1790s and 1800s on the French Broad River near the present Biltmore Estate. His son John Hawkins settled in Hominey Valley. Would like information about his other children. Sidney Hawkins, 8 Leacroft Drive, Greenville, SC 29615-2234. [1992]

Hawkins, Naomi, born July 9, 1854, lived most of her life in Brevard, N. C. She had a sister Adaline Brannon, wife of Richard, in Henderson County and a brother Melvin (Pinkney). Another sister Serelia Merrill, wife of S. A., lived in Swannanoa. Was their father Allen Hawkins? Would like to contact the descendants of the children of Serelia Merrill: A. J., W. L., Fred, Rankin, Mrs. J. C. Burgin, Eulalah Merrill. Carol Cotter, P. O. Box 56, Skyland, NC 28776. [1991]

Haynes, William, born about 1750, father of William Haynes who married Elizabeth Hood, wife was Sarah Hill. Their daughter Sarah married David Shook of Haywood County. Would like information. Frank Morgan, 114 E. Church St., El Dorado, Arkansas 71730. [1984]

Helm/Helms, Eli, living in Cleveland, Tennessee, in 1900. Would like to hear from descendants. Lynda G. Methvin, 3237 Schuler Drive, Bossier City, LA 71112. [1990]

Hemphill, John Newlin, of the Whittier and Asheville areas. Would like any information and any descendants. Mrs. John S. Hemphill, Sr., 511 W. Midland, Winder, GA 30680. [1989]

Henderson County 1840 and 1850 censuses, booklet form, indexed. For more information, write Mrs. Lois Dorsey, Rt. 9, Box 252, Price Rd.,

Hendersonville, NC 28739.

Henderson, James, born in South Carolina in 1786 and died in Indiana in 1858. The family was living in North Carolina in 1815. Would like information. Robert F. Henderson, 479 N. Roosevelt St., Orleans, Indiana 47452. [1992]

Hendricson, Marion, born in January of 1855 in Lee County, Virginia, moved to Knox County, Kentucky, and married Alice Davis. Monica Wells, 1340 Caldwell Ridge, Knifey, KY 42753. [1989]

Hendricks/Hendrix, Hosea M., son of William Henricks. Hosea was born in Buncombe in 1849, and his parents were born in South Carolina. Would like information on his brothers and sisters. R. L. Hendricks, Rt. 1, Box 900, Lot 11, Waynesville, NC 28786 [1993]

Hensley family. Would particularly like information about Arsamus Hensley whose son was Bernard Monroe Hensley born about 1904 and married Elimina Murrney of Yancey County. Catherine Harrin, P. O. Box 475, Fletcher, NC 28732.

Henson, Rev. Thomas, buried at the Baptist Church Cemetery, Cullowhee, N. C. His son Phillip Henson married Empress Eugenia Lombard about 1906, daughter of Ora H. Lombard. Would like information about this family. Louise Henson, Skyland Rest Home, Sylvaa, NC 28779.

Hester, Joseph, born 1793 in Granville County, N. C., and died October 29, 1842, in Lincoln County, Tennessee. He left Granville County in 1837 and moved to Lincoln County. His children included Doctor Wilson W. Hester, Lt. Issac W. Hester born January 20, 1832, died 1859, Rev. Elijah L. Hester born 1841 and died May 12, 1907, married Mary Ingle in Lincoln County, and Ann B. Hester born 1840, married Rev. N. A. Bailey. Would like information on any descendants. Jackie O. Clark, 207 Hilton St., Murphy, NC 28906. [1989]

Hicks, Joseph, born April 14, 1797/98 in Georgia, married Margaret Shook on November 20, 1817, Haywood County, N. C. She was the daughter of Jacob Shook, born April 19, 1749, Northampton County, Pennsylvania, and Isabella Weitzell/Wysel. Would like any information. Mildred Hicks, 117 Russell St., Rayville, LA 71269. [1984]

Hill, Bryant and his brother David Hill, born in Western North Carolina between 1800 and 1809 in the present Haywood County area. Their father was probably Hinton A. Hill. Before 1832, they moved to

Habersham County, Georgia. Bryant married Ruth Daniel, daughter of Job Daniel of North Carolina. Would like any information. Mimi Jo Butler, 3812 Overlook Trail, Kennesaw, GA 30144. [1987]

Hill, Robert, Sr., died 1833 in Rutherford County, was married first to Margaret Johnson of Tryon County and second to Mary Eden. Is he related to William Hill who migrated from Scotland and was in Virginia in 1703 before coming to Tryon County in 1726? Would like any information on the ancestors. Cecil Hill, 200 Woodside Drive, Brevard, NC 28712. [1987]

Hills, Charles, died 1830, Rutherford County. Charles's brother, Zadock, married Rebekah Harvey; his sister Nance married Walter Sorrells. Charles Hills children were William (1799-1883) married Martha Patsy Deboard 1819 in Rutherford County, later moved to Asheville and in 1844 to Gilmer County, Georgia; Olive married Hiram Dunkin; Rachel married James Hall; Susannah married a Gregory. Would like information on descendants. Edwin Hill, 607 S. Jefferson, Kaufman, TX 75142. [1984]

Hoglen, John Western, born in Haywood County about 1863, married Dora Ann Milner and moved to north Arkansas-south Missouri about 1890. Known relatives, all of whom resided in Haywood County, were his brother William; sisters Rachel and Lottie; his parents James and Nancy Adaline Hoglen/Hogland; his paternal grandparents, Andrew J. and Agnes Woods Hoglen; and maternal grandparents, Stanford and Caroline Price Bradley. Would like more information, particularly on John Western Hoglen. Col. Hubert J. Hoglen, 1009 Dougherty Ferry Road, Kirkwood, MO 63122. [1985]

Holcomb, Delia, born 1858 in South Carolina, married in 1883 in Buncombe to James Albert McDowell, son of William Wallace McDowell and Sarah Smith of Asheville. Was her mother Martha Burnett of Greenville, SC. Clara B. Harris, Rt. 6, Box 204, Burnsville, NC 28714. [1986]

Holcombe, Issac and wife Lucretia McLain family, lived in Mars Hill, N. C., from the late 1800s until about 1935 or later. Their children were Lee, John, Daisy, Pansy, Nathaniel, and Jake. Would like to know birth and death dates of any or all of the above, the parents of Issac and Lucretia and where they were originally from. Lorraine Holcombe, 49 Pharr St., Canton, NC 28716.

Hollifield, Issac, born about 1804, probably in Burke County, later in Madison or Yancey Counties. Would like parents and information. Jay Hollifield, 205 Rowland Rd., Swannanoa, NC 28778. [1984]

Holman, Issac, born February 15, 1752, Rowan County, married Ellizabeth Johnson about 1772, enlisted in Revolutionary War in Surry County in 1775, then lived fourteen years in South Carolina, ten years in Georgia, remainder in Lincoln County, Tennessee, where he died August 25, 1834, widow then Hannah. Particularly interested in his children. Linda H. Swansson, 3359 E. Elm St., Brea, CA 92621. [1985]

Holt, Billie, born January 2, 1923, in Asheville. His mother was nineteen at the time of his birth, and he was given up for adoption to the Children's Home Society in November 1924. Would like the names of his parents. Terry Holt, 124 H., La Mancha Dr., Asheville, NC 28805.

Hood, Alfred, born about 1807 in Tennessee, married Nancy Harding, born about 1812 in South Carolina. Would like to know the names of parents, children, and marriage date. Margie Noe, 140 Trammell Rd., Marietta, SC 29661. [1990]

Hoodenpyle, Bill, last known address was Provo, Utah, possibly in Western North Carolina now. Would like to hear from him. Mrs. Arthur Painter, 12 Jones St., Sylva, NC 28779. [1983]

Hooker, Rev. James, a Baptist preacher in Barnardsville and Weaverville in the late 1800s. He had children Sara Lorella, William H., John A., Reese B., Lydia M. Would like the name of Rev. Hooker's wife. Would also like information on the availability of records for the Red Oak Presbyterian Church, Buncombe County, abandoned in the 1930s. Carolyn Young, Rt.3, Box 138, Candler, NC 28715. [1989]

Hooper family. Would like more information on the ones in Western North Carolina. Naomi Green, 233 East Harvard Avenue., Anchorage, Alaska 99501.

Hopkins, Samuel and Susan Sawyer, Tyrrell County, married April 8, 1831. Would like more information. Mrs. Virginia Jensen, Apt. 193, 600 Carolina Village Rd., Hendersonville, NC 28739. [1984]

Horne, Nancy, born July 2, 1775, married Jonathon Hicks, born February 11, 1772, in Charleston, S. C. Jonathon owned land in Buncombe County. Mildred Hicks, 117 Russell St., Bayville, LA 71269. [1984]

The Book of Hortons in America. Would like to purchase this book. Frank E. Horton, P. O. Box 755, Burnsville, NC 28714. [1993]

Decendants of John Houser, 1709-1763, was written in 1991 by E. A. Houser, P. O. Box 25872, Tamarac, FL 33321. This includes relatives in Rutherford and Cherokee Counties, N. C.

Howell, Garrett, settled in Buncombe County sometime in the latter part of the 1700s. He was one of three brothers who came from Scotland. One, James, settled in Mitchell County, and Thomas and Garrett settled in Buncombe County. Would like more information on these. Mrs. Grace P. Burgin, Rt. 2, Box 24, Old Fort, NC 28763. [1988]

Hudgins, William Miles, born about 1825, married Lucinda Searcy in Rutherford County in 1847, lived in the Broad River section. He married, second in 1898, Sarah Jane Taylor of Bald Mountain, (Broad River section) and died about 1899. Brenda Hudgins, 41 Mt. Carmel Dr., Asheville, NC 28806. [1987]

Huggins, Luke and Phillip, listed in the 1790 census in Burke County. In the 1800 census in Buncombe, there were Luke and two Phillip Huggins. These names do not appear in the N. C. census in 1810 census. Would like to know where they were after 1800, and are these the Philip Huggins from Virginia and the Luke Huggins from eastern North Carolina? Is the Phillip Huggins listed in the 1830 census of Lauderdale County, Alabama, the one from Buncombe? In 1830, Luke Huggins, born 1795, in Buncombe was in Crawford/Franklin County, Arkansas, living near Robert Huggins, born 1809 in North Carolina. Were Luke and Robert related. Jean Huggins Wingert, 79 La Prenda, Benicia, CA 94510. [1987]

Hughes, John, born 1805, married Rebecca, lived in Haywood County. Would like information. Rose Dean, Rt. 7, Box 226, Gainesville, GA 30506. [1984]

Humphrey, Elisha, married first Molly Perry on January 7, 1778. Molly died September 12, 1780; Elisha then married Betsey Jane Hardin. They had three children: William born 1806, Pelham born 1810, and Betsy Jane born 1812. Is there any information concerning another daughter Matilda, born in the early 1800s who later married Jacob Taylor and settled in Watauga County? Luther Franklin, Rt. 2, Box 508, Marion, NC 28752. [1986]

Humphries, Lewis, born 1778, and Elizabeth Humphries, born 1788, lived in Buncombe County from 1820-1840. Would like more information on these and also Elijah Humphries, born 1825, and Mitchell

Alexander Humphries, born 1846. Evelyn Rogers, Rt. 1, Box 591, Candler, NC 28715. [1988]

Hunter. An annual Hunter reunion is held in Blairsville, Georgia. These Hunters are descendants of John Hunter, born about 1775 in Virginia, and died in 1848 in Blairsville. He lived in the Arden area of Buncombe in the early 1800s and left about 1834 for Georgia. His children, some of whom remained in Buncombe included Andrew, Elizabeth born 1799, married Jospeh Lance, James W. born 1805, Martha born 1810, Rebecca born 1812, married Samuel Lance, William Johnson born 1813, Jason Henderson born 1818, Harriet born 1822. Wanda Gibson, Rt. 7, Box 7854, Blairsville, GA 30512.

Hunter, Wiley, born about 1815 in Buncombe and moved to Madison County. Were George W., Hiram, Philip, and William his brothers? Would like to know the names of his parents. He married first Mary Roberts about 1835. Their children were Thomas, Jane, Sarah, William, Harriet, James, Jerry, Nathaniel, Ellen, Katherine, Lydia, John, Louisa. Joan Long, 26 Ridgefield Place, Asheville, NC 28803. [1991]

Hunter, William, married Annie Caldwell. Would like to know more about her. She was born in Virginia about 1762. Two known sons were Robert Hunter, married in Buncombe County in 1807 to Susan Stice, and Samuel Hunter, born 1793 and married Catherine Poteet in Rutherford County. Also interested in Robert Hunter's daughter who married Jacob Hickman about 1841 in Madison County. Her name was Sarah or Sally. Sarah and Jacob's son was Robert Burton Hickman, born in Washington County, Tennessee, in 1844, and married Jane Plemmons on October 12, 1861, in Madison County. Gwen Cody, 205 Cody Drive, Sevierville, TN 37862. [1988]

Huntsinger, Boyd, born in Buncombe about 1903, adopted at the age of 7 and name changed to Fred Harold Lewis. He married Lavina McNabb in 1924 in Waynesville. Their children were George, Fred, Jr., Pearl, Raymond, and Ray. Mrs. George Lewis, P. O. Box 899, Merritt Island, FL 32952. [1984]

Hutcheson, Furny, born 1784, in Polk, Rutherford, or Cleveland Counties, N. C. He died in 1865 in Clayton County, Georgia. Would like to have more information. Also, would like the name of his first wife. They lived in Blount County, Tennessee, and had at least two sons, Roland born 1810 in South Carolina and Leander Caruth born 1820 in

Tennessee. Furny moved to Georgia about 1825 where he married Nancy Anthony in 1827. Furny's parents were Drury Hutcheson, born January 1, 1745, a Revolutionary soldier who moved to Spartanburg, S. C., and Mourning Southard/Southall; both born in Amelia County, Virginia. Randy Knight, Rt. 2, Box 98E, Robbinsville, NC 28771. [1990]

Hyatt, Robert and Martha Turner, were buried at Pleasant Hill Methodist Church Cemetery, Candler, NC. Would like to have exact birth and death dates for each so that a marker could be placed in this cemetery for them. He was born about 1801 and died about 1860; she was born about 1819 and died about 1870. Mrs. Willa Dean Boyd, Rt. 6, Box 808, Morristown, TN 37814. [1983]

Ingram family. Would like to exchange data with anyone researching this family. Mary Ruth Stultz, 5800 Swarthmore Dr., College Park, MD 20740. [1986]

Inman, Sarah, born in the early 1800s in North Carolina, married William Bennett, lived in Yancey County. Would like to know parents' names. Loren Ray, 2237 Woodland Blvd., Fort Myers, FL 33907. [1993]

Jack, Joshua, born in Eastern Tennessee in 1815, married Eliza O'Neal in Versailles, Indiana, in 1837. Sons included William Jack, Marion Jack, Robert Perry Jack. Was Joshua kin to Patrick Jack of Charlotte or Jeremiah Jack of Tennessee? Jacob Koehler, 526 N. Trenholm Rd., Columbia, SC 29206. [1987]

Janes, sometimes called Jeans, family from Lincoln and Rutherford Counties. Would like to contact anyone researching this family. John Janes died September 1826 in Rutherford County, wife Sarah, children Mary (Patton), Thomas, David, Jane, Nanny, John P., Sarah, Elizabeth, and Frances Curry. Billie Hardy, 2911 Kircaldy Court, Arlington, TX 76015. [1986]

Jarvis, Thomas, government official in North Carolina from 1691-1694. Would also like information about his daughter Ann. Mrs. David Francis, P. O. Box 326, Fairview, NC 28730. [1987]

Johnson/Johnston, Mastin, born 1807, North Carolina. Would like information on his parents. A sister Harriet Johnson, born 1797, married a Morris. A brother was William Johnson. Their mother Sarah was born in 1770 and in 1816 was a widow and married George Taylor in Huntsville, Alabama. Interested also in Jeremiah Mastin, who was in Craven County in 1790; John Mastin and Thomas Johnson in Stokes

County in 1790. Otho Johnson, 4003 Pinewood Drive, Jackson, MS 39211. [1986]

Jones, Mary Polly, born 1797, married Peter Corn (1792-1869). One son was Robert. Would like to know parents and other children. Louise Ward, Route 9, Box 504, Chestnut Gap Rd., Hendersonville, NC 28739. [1985]

Justice, Jasper Lawrence, born in Macon County in 1868 and died in 1921. Would like to know descendants. Mrs. Mary Johnson, P. O. Box 1015, Marion, NC 28752. [1983]

Justice, John, born about 1794 in Buncombe County, now Macon County, and died before 1850 in Macon County. He was married to Margaret Carpenter, born about 1797, in Lincoln county. Her father was indicated on census information to be foreign born. Would like any information about all of these. Bobby M. Edwards, Rt. 2, Box 56-C, Robbinsville, NC 28771. [1990]

Justice, William, also known as "Cublire" Bill," born December 3, 1835, died October 25, 1905. Veteran of CSA, married Elizabeth Largen (McDowell County) born December 7, 1834, died March 18, 1911. Would like information on the parents of William. The children of William and Elizabeth were John, William C. (1872-1958) married Lou Fowler, Sintha married John Seagle, Martha married Joe Plemmons, Maggie married a Green, Joseph Alexander (1859-1918) mar-ried Sarah Capps. Mary McCoy, 8 Pine Grove St., Marion, NC 28752. [1985]

Justus, Anna, born October 20, 1801, died February 29, 1848, buried at Edneyville Methodist Church Cemetery in Henderson County next to her husband William Lanning. One of their children was James Wilkerson Lanning. Would like to know the names of her parents. Joyce Parris, 220 Northwest Avenue, Swannanoa, NC 28778. [1994]

Keith, Cornelius, born 1715, Brunswick County, Virginia, married first in 1741 Juda Thompson, married second in 1743 Sarah/Mary Bohannon. He had ten children and lived in Surry, Stokes, Yadkin, Rowan Counties in the late 1700s. He died in Pickens, South Carolina. Would like more information about him and also William Keith II, born 1751, North Carolina, son of Cornelius Keith. He had six children in the 1790 census of Surry County, N. C. Later he moved to Pendleton, S. C., married Rachel Elrod, then moved to Jackson County, Georgia, after 1800. William Keith, 2160 Plum Lane, Austell, GA 30001. [1986]

Kerby, William R., married Frances Caroline Picklesimer on October 10, 1841, in present Clay County. Children were Leander, married Charity Queen; Jasper, Martha, Alfred, Anna, married John B. Howard in Hiawassee, Georgia; Luther, and Kandas/Candace. Would like information on William's parents. Jan Horn, 1690, Eaton #108, Lakewood, CA 80214. [1984]

King family of Henderson County. Would particularly like information about Judge Mitchell King, his children, brothers and sisters and their children. Mrs. W. E. Holder, Jr., 1037 Riverside Drive, Asheville, NC 28804. [1992]

King, Harrison (supposedly part-Cherokee Indian), born 1810-1815 in Western North Carolina, moved to Dale County, Alabama, in the 1830s and married Nancy Calloway. Their children were born between 1835 and 1842: Martha Ann, Elisha, Mary Elizabeth, John Mason. Would like any information on Harrison King and also on Henry Harrison King who was born in Henderson County and died about 1845, buried at Washington College, near Jonesboro, Tennessee. N. G. King, 4263 Bingham Ct., Stone Mountain, GA 30083. [1986]

King, John and wife Winnefred Williams (born in South Carolina about 1772). Would like more information about this couple who went from Anson County, N. C., about 1818 to Alabama, possibly with the Harris and Williams families of Anson. Two of John King's sons were named Drury King and Thomas King, born in the late 1700s. Pat Hoggle, 201 Oldfield Drive, Montgomery, AL 36117. [1988]

King, Samuel, Jr., born 1772, died February 2, 1849, son of Samuel King, Sr., and Elizabeth Underwood Davenport. Would like to know how many children he had. The known children were Jonathon, Jeremiah, Mary (married Glazner). According to the census, there were six more daughters and two more sons. They lived in Buncombe and the part of Henderson later formed into Transylvania. Stella Mace, 662 Crystal Drive, Hendersonville, NC 28739. [1984]

Kinsey, Absolem, Baptist minister, on 1790 census in Sampson County, N. C., died in 1827 in Culpepper County, Virginia. His wife was Phoebe Parks. Would like to have more information. Emit K. Ward, 4514 SE Woodward, Portland, OR 97206-2238. [1988]

Kirkpatrick, Milas Oliver, and Leander from Haywood County. Leander was killed in the Civil War. Would like more information about these. Ila Kirkpatrick Clement, 115 Cherrio Lane, Asheville, NC 28803. [1984]

Knight, Bethena, born 1818 in North Carolina, married Western Waterman in Bledsoe County, Tennessee, in 1825. In 1852, they moved to Laclede County, Missouri. Would like to know the parents. Marlene Wilkinson, 1200 French Ave., Lakewood, Ohio 44107. [1993]

Krykendall family, lived in the Pigeon River section of Haywood County and were descendants of Abraham Krykendall who is buried in Henderson County. Would like more information since John Krykendall was my grandfather and Issac who was born about 1816 and was in Henderson County in 1907 was my great-grandfather. Margaret Johnson, P. O. Box 8235, Asheville, NC 28804. [1983]

Kuykendall, Francis Marion, born about 1857, from Hendersonville, N. C. He was married to Sue Buckner. His father was believed to be Richard Kuykendall. Would like more information. Linda Hagan, 430 Haywood Rd., Asheville, NC 28806. [1988]

Kyle family, lived in Swannanoa Valley, Buncombe County in the early 1800s. Nancy Kyle married James Whitaker, Jr., (1804-1899) and moved to Andrews, N. C. Mrs. Ty Burnette, P. O. Box 190, Andrews, NC 28901. [1983]

Lance, James Jasper, born 1791, married Mary Prater, born 1794. Would like more information. James and Mary went to Warren County, Tennessee, from Buncombe County in the early 1800s. One son was Henry Lance, born 1816. Edwin C. Dodd, 2971 Coleridge Dr., Los Alamitos, CA 90720. [1987]

Lance, Mark, married Lillie Wallin, lived in Madison County in the late 1800s and early 1900s. He owned a business in Marshall, gave land on Big Laurel for the Mark Lance Memorial, and land for a teacher's home near the Presbyterian School. Would like to know his parents. Mrs. Arthur Painter, 12 Jones St., Sylva, NC 28779. [1987]

Landreth, William, died in 1801, Ashe County, N. C. Would like to have information on his descendants. His grandson Benjamin Landreth moved to Keokuk County, Iowa, in 1842. Would like to share Landreth information about the ones who went to Iowa and Kansas with the ones who stayed in North Carolina. Bonnie Martin, Rt. 2, Box 342, Neosho, MO 64850. [1990]

Lashley family, migrated from Virginia into North Carolina. Some of the surnames that intermarried into the Lashley family in Western North Carolina include Tatum and Welch. Would like more information. Jean Gilley, 1029 Cedar Crest Dr., Atlanta, TX 75551. [1990]

Laughter, John, Henderson County, married first Mourning Stepp born 1776, and second Nancy. Would like to have names of the children and the last name of John's second wife. Omega S. Scott, 3800 West Biddison St., Fort Worth, TX 76109. [1987]

Ledford, John Macon. Would like the name of an uncle that reared him in Macon County after his parents were killed in a storm near New Port, Tennessee about 1816. All members of the family were killed except John and possibly a sister. John was born in Burke County on March 15, 1814, and died in Buncombe on October 7, 1897. Carolyn Mills Griffee, 83 Appalachian Way, Asheville, NC 28806. [1984]

Leming/Lemons, George W., born in Haywood County about 1820, married Elizabeth Burchfield in January of 1856 in Jackson County, N. C. Would like more information. Elizabeth supposedly died young and George went to Blount County, Tennessee, during the Civil War. George married Maria Elizabeth Henry in Blount County in March of 1868. Gwen Cody, 205 Cody Crive, Sevierville, TN 37862. [1988]

Lewis, Benjamin, born 1764, entered the Revolutionary War from Lenoir County, N. C., and returned there after the war. In 1783 in Kinston, he married Celia Martin (born 1762, daughter of Highly Martin), and they had five sons and one daughter. In the early 1800s, they moved to Robeson County, N. C., where he died in November of 1821. Two of the sons, Quinnea and Lemuel moved to Mississippi in 1820. Would like information on family members who remained in North Carolina in addition to the ancestry of Highly Martin of Kinston. Harry W. Clark, 61 Terrapin Cove., Brandon, MS 39042. [1989]

Little, John, born 1803, Rowan County, moved to Lincoln County, Tennessee, as a young man, married Margaret Johnson. Their children were Martha Eliza, Benjamin F., Angus, Samuel, Mark, Rebecca, Permelia C., Nancy Matilda, Mary E., and Elizabeth. The majority of their children were born in Bedford County, Tennessee, moved to Washington County, Arizona, in 1850, where John died in 1874. Would like more information on this family. Peggy Jones, 608 N. Booth, Clinton, MO 64735. [1986]

Lockhart, Charles, married Jane Lufsey/Lifsey, who lived from

1795-1832. Would like proof of marriage of these. They had nine children born in Anson County. Would also like information on Emaline Bailey who was the second wife of Charles Lockhart; seven children were born to them, two in Anson County, five in Marshall County, Mississippi, where Emaline and Charles died. Mrs. Alan Babin, P. O. Box 236, Collierville, TN 38017. [1985]

Logan family. Would like information particularly on the parents and brothers and sisters of Freeman Logan, born 1806, North Carolina, died in 1874 in Tuscon County, Alabama, and the maiden name of his wife, Sabra, born 1801, South Carolina. Others who were in Tuscon County and may have been brothers of Freeman were Resin, born 1808, N. C.; Ben, born 1811, N. C.; Bryson, born 1816, N. C. Children of Freeman and Sabra Logan were Byrd, Rebecca, Nancy, Leander, Cynthia, Amanda, and Cornelia. Sara S. Nichols, 115-37th Street, Tuscaloosa, Al 35405. [1986]

Lonon, John, wife Martha Wisehonor. Would like to know where they were buried in Cherokee County, N. C. They lived in Valleytown Township, present Andrews, in 1870. Frank E. Wise, P. O. Box 178, Nebo, NC 28761. [1987]

Lonon, John, and wife Martha Wise. Would like to know where they are buried. They lived in McDowell County, N. C., then Cherokee County. In 1870, they were on the Cherokee County census, Valleytown Township. John died February 12, 1872. One son was William Wise Lonon who lived in Murphy. J. Purd Hays, 33 Woodmoor Ct., Leavenworth, Kansas 66048. [1988]

Lovingood, Viola. Would like information on her ancestors. One daughter was Edith Allan who married Allan McDonald, son of Minlinda Killian. Would also like to know about the Allan family. Wilma McDonald, P. O. Box 1038, Andrews, NC 28901.

Lumpkin, John, born June 2, 1762, Halifax, Virginia, and died 1834, Oglethorpe, Georgia, He was married to Lucy Hopson in 1780. Would like more information about them. The Lumpkins spent the summers in Buncombe County visiting relatives. Would like to hear from relatives of the Lumpkins. Dolores A. McCarty, 13532 Sagewood Drive, Poway, CA 92064-1730. [1993]

Luther Cemetery. Is there a Luther Cemetery in Buncombe County other than the Solomon Luther Family Cemetery in Candler, N. C.? Mrs. W. W. Case, Rt. I, Box 739, Candler, NC 28715. [1989]

Luther family. Would particularly like information on the descendants of Abraham Luther of Buncombe County and Julia Luther, born 1840, married Jeremiah Howell (1839-1916) in Haywood County. Their children were Ellen Howell Fowler born 1860, W. Albert Howell born 1862, and Victor Howell born 1870. Janice Hagan, 235 Hollow Ridge Dr., Athens, GA 30607. [1984]

Luther, Mary Caroline, born 1834, Buncombe, daughter of John Peter Luther (1806-1877), married 1852 James Reese/Reece. Would like more information on their descendants. In the 1850 Buncombe census, James Reese was listed as 21 with Daniel and Susanna Reese. Mrs. W. W. Case, Rt. 1, Box 739, Candler, NC 28715. [1984]

Lytle, Captain Thomas, Revolutionary soldier, born 1750, died 1835. He is buried at Bethel Cemetery in McDowell County, N. C. Would like to hear from any descendants. Dorothy B. Stephens, 214 Kelso Court, Cary, NC 27511. [1994]

Magee, Clemmons, born in North Carolina in 1829, married Rebecca Barham in Green County, Tennessee, on January 25, 1849. Would like information about his ancestors. Rebecca was the daughter of Herbert and Patsey Thomasson Barham, who were married in Stokes County, N. C., on October 27, 1813. Salette Latas, 104 Bryanwood Drive, Goldsboro, NC 27534. [1991]

Would like information on *Camp Martin* which was supposedly a hospital during the Civil War and near the Reems Creek area of North Carolina. Chris Morton, 33 Herron Cove Rd., Weaverville, NC 28787. [1986]

Mathews, Mary, born August 1799, married Daniel Knight Babcock in Cranston, Rhode Island about 1819. Would like her birthplace and the names of her parents. N. N. Babcock, P. O. Box 1088, Highlands, NC 28741. [1984]

Mathis/Matthews, Frederick, living in Burke County, N. C., in 1809 when his daughter Sarah was married to James Willie Belvin of Sumter County, S. C. One son was Shadrack Mathis who married Margaret Rogers. Would like more information. Leonard Boykin, Rt. 1, Box 127, Camden, SC 29020. [1986]

Maxwell family of Western North Carolina. Would like information particularly about James Maxwell whose daughter Mary "Polly" Maxwell, born in 1827 in North Carolina, married Thomas Cleveland Ballou of

Ashe County, and died about 1869 in Texas. James Maxwell also had a daughter Lucy Maxwell who married Baker Ballou in 1831. Phyllis Ballow DeFeo, 1142 Ashbourne Dr., Baton Rouge, LA 70815. [1993]

Meadow Fork Independent Baptist Church was established in 1884 in Joe, North Carolina. (Joe is a community in west Madison County on Meadow Fork.) The church property dates back to a 1852 deed from William Balding, born in Virginia on June 2, 1800, died 1889, wife Elizabeth Duckett, both buried in the church cemetery. Joe is named after William Balding's grandson Joseph Balding. Would particularly like more information on William Balding and trustees in the original deed: Joseph and Royal Cook, Fidilia Adolphus Balding, Jacob Duckett, L. H. W. Plemmons, Levi C. Hipps. Morris Haddock, Rt. 1, Box 203 A, Hot Springs, NC 28743. [1990]

Meadows, Samuel and Martha Wallis, who moved from Iredell County to Buncombe County in the 1820s. Their children included Cyrus, William Francis, Louisa, Robert G., John P., and James T. Meadows. Would like more information. B. Douglas Robinson, 331 Woodson St., Apr. 31, Salisbury, NC.

Messer, Solomon, born 1811-1812, married first Rosannah, second Sarah, and lived in Haywood County, N. C. Would like information about him and if he were a son of Solomon Messer on the 1820 census, Haywood. Would also like to know how the Sherrils and Hyatts are kin to the Messors. On January 22, 1907, Joseph Burton Sherril wrote that "my mother was a descendent of Richard and Betsy Walker. Solomon Messer whose affadavit connects us to the Walkers is dead. His affadavit was sent to the Dawes Commision." 0.[Dawes commission was a list of Cherokee Indians, most of whom went to Oklahoma.] In 1907 Manerva Stalcup Messer, born 1821, wife of Jack/John Messer sent to the Federal Government with other family history that her grandfather Hesekiah Hyatt was half Indian. Millie Stinnett, 82 Front St., Richwood, West Virginia 26261. [1985]

Middleton, Arthur, signer of the Declaration of Independence for South Carolina. Was he related to Joshua Middleton, born 1785, married Judity Risley in 1814, lived in Philadelphia, Pennsylvania. Beth Mueller, K-4 CrowfieldsLane, Asheville, NC 28803. [1986]

Miller family. Would like to know the nationality. Jerry Miller settled in the Starnes Cove area of Buncombe County, N. C., and raised ten children. Janette Miller Davis, 137 Holbrook Rd., Candler, NC 28715. [1987]

Miller, Harriet M., wife of Hiram Cordell who died in 1861. They were the parents of Zebulon Vance Cordell who was a Methodist Circuit preacher and born January 14, 1862, in Buncombe County. Would like more information about Harriet. She disappeared in 1862. Her father could have been Frederick Miller. Minnie Ownbey, Rt. 3, Box 3384, Blairsville, GA 30512. [1990]

Milner, Dell, married James Dotsun, August 10, 1886. Children were Maggie, married Joshua Chambers; Charles, married Harriet Mehaffey; Cora, married Ralph Davis; Ann, married Roy Palmer; Kaywood, marrieda Georgia Freeman; Homer; Horace. Would like information on Dell's family. Barbara Gaddy, 135 Keller St., Waynesville, NC 28786. [1984]

Mitchell, Charlie. Would like information on his family. His wife was Hazel Greer from Watauga County, N. C. Quita Mitchell, P. O. Box 534, Morganton, NC 28655. [1987]

Montgomery family. Would like information on these who came into Western North Carolina from Georgia and Alabama. Lois M. Flynt, P. O. Box 241, Little Switzerland, NC 28749. [1984]

Moody, John and Susan, lived in Caldwell and Yancey Counties, and Moody's Cove in Reems Creek, Buncombe County. They were married about 1855; John died after 1891. Would like any information about them. Would also like information on Mitilda Moody who married William Moses Fox in Yancey County in 1882. Mitilda died about 1897, and Moses Fox then married Lucinda Riddle Penland in 1897. He died in Weaverville in 1940. Mrs. R. W. Edwards, 310 Stonewall Ave., Swannanoa, NC 28778. [1984]

Moody, John. Would like information on parents and other relatives. He and his family moved to Yancey County about 1870. Among John Moody's known children were Mary Fox and Harrison Moody of Burnsville; Elizabeth Barnard, Benjamin Moody, Malinda Fox of Reems Creek area; Wilks, George W., and Calvin of Asheville. Doris Smith, P. O. Box 1071, Lander, Wyoming 82520. [1984]

Moore, Ella Lee, born June 2, 1868, died February 23, 1915, and was married to William McCame Worley, Buncombe County. Would like more information about Ella Lee. Frank M. Worley, 2204 River Ridge

Drive, Asheville, NC 28803. [1989]

Morgan, Perminter. Would like to correspond with any descendants of Morgan. Frank B. Morgan, 114 E. Church St., El Dorado, Arkansas 71730. [1984]

Morgan, Susanna, born in Rowan County about 1780, married Levi Truitt and was living in the household of her daughter Susannah Truitt Thomasson in Macon County in the 1850 census. Would like information on her parents. Mrs. M. F. Calloway, 207 West Fairlane, Longview, TX 75604. [1986]

Morrison, Johnathan and Susan "Patsy" Stepp, living in the Blue Ridge section of Henderson County, N. C., 1860-1880. Would like to hear from the descendants. Their children were Fanny, Epsey, Mary who married Drayton Randolph, Nancy who married M. L. Clark, Susan, John, Henry C., James B., and King. Lorraine Merrill, 36 Shuford Rd., Weaverville, NC 28787. [1991]

Morton, Ezekiel, born about 1775 and died in Albemarle, N. C., in 1834. Would like more information about him. His wife was Elizabeth Bromblow, born 1775 and died 1856 in Albemarle. Earline Hopkins, P. O. Box 423, Hartsville, SC 29550. [1991]

Mosley, Tartine/Tart, born Surry County, N. C., and died 1822 in Warren County, Tennessee. Would like more information on him. Heirs in 1829 were Gilly, Jr., and Sr., Elizabeth Woodall, Salley Mosley, Jessie W. Mosley, and Robert Tate. Would also like to correspond with any children or descendants of Richard Winfield Mosley, born 1850 in Surry County, married Zonie Lawson in 1908. Children were Harry born 1914, Lillie May born 1916, Harold, Martha born 1924. In 1930, Zonie and younger children were in Greenville, S. C. Mrs. Leonard Mosley, Route 2, Box 80, Clyde, TX 79510. [1988]

Morse/Moss, Joseph, born 1708 and died 1780. Would like to know the date that he married Sarah Shackelford from Carteret County, N. C. Would also like to know the name of Sarah's parents. Their children were Joseph, Joshua, James, and Theodore, who was born in 1730 and died in 1821. Edgar W. Morse, 1609 1/2 Baker St., San Francisco, CA 94115. [1991]

Murray, Samuel Jasper, born about 1850, married Betty Woodard, had eight children, lived in Flagstown, Tennessee. Would like more information about him. The father of Betty Woodard, John Woodard, settled in Jackson County, N. C., during the Civil War, on Cowee Mountain. Elizabeth Gibson, 192 Harrison Ave., Franklin, NC 28734. [1984]

Muse, William H., born 1822, died between 1870 and 1880, married Lila or Dicy born 1835. Would like more information on him. He possibly came into Western North Carolina from Moore or Craven Counties. One child was King Miles Muse, born 1855, died March 4, 1941, married Martha Ann Sharp. Wilma L. Muse, P. O. Box 272, Arden, NC 28704. [1985]

McCall, Alexander family. One daughter married Hugh Bryson who was born about 1798. This daughter, Margaret, lived in Mills River. Would like information about all Alexander's family. Lawrence Wood, 75 Peeks Creek Rd., Franklin, NC 28734. [1993]

McCollum, Martha, born in North Carolina about 1816, married about 1837 to Tom Tanner Sibley and settled in Russelville, Franklin County, Alabama. Would like to know her parents, brothers and sisters. With this couple on the 1860 census, seven children were listed: Milas 22, Colene A. 20, Wesley M. 17, Matthew C. 12, Martha Ann 10, Mary E. 6, Thomas T. nine months. K. D. Lyons, P. O. Box 1237, Black Mountain, NC 28711. [1994]

McConnell, James Harvey, Jr., born January 24, 1866, Mecklenburg County, N. C., died August 10, 1936, in Asheville. On March 24, 1896, in Asheville, he married Ella Narcissus McInturff. She was born in 1870 in Burnsville, N.C., and died in 1945 in Asheville. She was the daughter of Robert McInturff and Mary Jane Bradshaw, daughter of Robert Bradshaw and Myra Gibbs. Was Robert McInturff the son of John and Mary McInturff? H. Louis McConnell Sporl, 1002 Third St., New Orleans, LA 70130. [1990]

McCoy, Jim/James, perhaps from Kentucky, a trader who married a Cherokee Indian. Would like information on his father. Pembroke McCoy married Troy Avaline Waddle and had children Jesse, Andrew, Mary (married Zeb Comby), Lilly (married Jim Self), William Patterson (1889-1962) married Georgia Bailey. Mary K. McCoy, 8 Pine Grove St., Marion, NC 28752. [1985]

McCracken, Sarah Addie, and Henry Penland. Would like information on two daughters born in Haywood County to this couple. Tula, one daughter, married J. B. Bryson. Blonde, the other daughter, married W.

B. Cabe; both moved to Macon County. Mrs. Pearl J. Yates, Rt. 4, Box 104, Waynesville, NC 28786. [1984]

McCracken, Joseph and Sarah Vaughn, settled in the Crabtree community of Haywood County in the late 1700s. Would like information about their descendants. The burial site for Joseph and Sarah is in the Mount Zion United Methodist Church in Clyde. Peggy M. Briggs, Rt. 4, Box 92, Waynesville, NC 28786. [1987]

McCrimmon, John B., born 1812 in North Carolina, wife Maranda Adock of Anson County, N. C. They married about 1840 in North Carolina and died in Kemper County, Mississippi. His father was perhaps John McCrimmon, son of Angus McCrimmon of Cumberland County. Would like more information on either of these. Paul L. Kines, 9818 Edgecliffe Dr., Pascagoula, Mississippi 39467-9457. [1986]

McDonald family. Interested in information about parents of Allan McDonald, son of Minlinda Killian, who married Edith Allan. Wilma McDonald, P. O. Box 1038, Andrews, NC 28901. [1984]

McDonnell, Mary, born 1775 in Ireland, died 1853 in Macon County, married George Patton, brother to James Patton of Asheville, moved to Macon about 1820. Would like more information on her ancestors. Am also interested in purchasing the book *McDonnell and Allied Families* by Lina V. D. Cherry. John L. Waldroop, Rt. 68, Box 8, Tuckasegee, NC 28783. [1984]

McDuffee family of Rowan and Anson Counties. Would like to hear from anyone working on this family. How were the McDuffees connected to the Reed or Strain families. Lawrence Wood, 75 Peeks Creek Rd., Franklin, NC 28734. [1986]

McGehee/McGee Descendants, published in 1989, is Volume III of the lineal and collateral descendants of Thomas MackGehee, the colonist who settled in Virginia in the late 1600s. This book was published by Ethel W. Grider, 714 Third Ave., Winder, GA 30680.

McKee, Billy, lived in Mecklenburg County in the late 1800s, married to Laura Elizabeth Phillips, father of eight children. Would like date of death, marriage, and birth for Billy. Nash McKee, P. O. Box 1394, Weaverville, NC 28787. [1986]

McKinna/McKinney, Albert, born in Buncombe in 1812, married Martha Orr, daughter of Robert Orr of Buncombe. Would like to know his parents. They moved from Buncombe to Gilmer County, Georgia.

Leslee C. Fehlman, 3606 Peute Trail, Austin, TX 78739. [1986]

McLear/Malear family of North Carolina, originally from Cape Fear River area and of Scottish descent. Would like more information. William Miller, 13 Indian Trace, Lake Toxaway, NC 28747. [1984]

McPheeters/McPeters, Jonathan and Mary (McDowell). Would like the names of their children. Jonathan was born January 14, 1756, and was a Revolutionary War veteran, lived in Haywood County and died in Yancey County, N. C. Also would like information on Jonathan and Margaret (Reed) McPheeters of Yancey County and would like to know if this is the same Jonathan, born 1756, or his son. Loren S. Ray, 2237 Woodland Blvd., Fort Myers, FL 33907. [1993]

McLemores. Would like to correspond with anyone researching this family. John (Juan) Spell who died in 1795 in Louisiana married Francisca McLemore, perhaps daughter of Ephraim McLemore who settled in Surry County, and later Edgecombe County, N. C. Am also interested in Rogers, Sharp, Taylor, McIntyre, Goodberg, and Atkins families in North Carolina. Brenda Martina, Cedarcrest, Apt. 7, Waynesville, NC 28786. [1989]

Netherton, John. Would like to know whom he married about 1850 in Buncombe County. Virginia Warren, 4618 E. Ist Place, Gainesville, FL. [1983]

Newman, William, born at sea, March 1, 1782, landed in Charleston. Father believed to be Leon Newman. Would like any information on Leon and William Newman, such as if they settled in South Carolina and if later near Columbus and the Green River area of North Carolina. Carolyn N. Walker, Rt. 9, Box 510, Hendersonville, NC 28739. [1985]

Newsom, Ransom, born June 17, 1770, married Sarah Tippett in Rowan or Randolph County. Would like information on his family and also Bulla, Rollins families. Son of Ransom was Luke Newsom born December 15, 1802, married second Cynthia Bulla, daughter of John Bulla and Margaret Rollins. Betty Linenfelter, 1418 Oakwood Trails, Indianapolis, IN 46260. [1985]

Nicholson, John, born May 9, 1757, New Jersey, died August 2, 1838, Stokes County, N. C. Would like information on his parents and where he is buried. Would also like information on his first wife, Mary. Would like her maiden name and also the maiden name of his second wife, Cathrine (Caty), born September 15, 1766. Where born? Would also like information on Hiram Chandler who married Nancy Nicholson on December 29, 1846 in Stokes County. Also information on Anderson Nicholson, born November 11, 1801, who married Anna J. Jacqueline Cahoon, 738 Monte Vista Rd., Apt. 1, Candler, NC 28715. [1988]

Norville, John S., "Knifey John," moved from Cane Creek in Rutherford County to Asheville. Would like more information about his children. Tom/Thomas and Phil/Phillip Norville believed to have been shoe makers in Asheville; Cindy/Catherine may have married a Kerr/Karr/Carr; Martha may have married a Bowers. If anyone has information about these children, please write. Hicks E. Norville, Rt.6, Box 108, Robbins Drive, Forest City, NC 28043. [1989]

O'Kane family, moved to North Carolina from Northern Ireland in 1789. Two brothers were Henry and James who later moved to Rockingham County, Virginia. Would like any information on this family. Helen Woodruff, 806 S. State, Tahlequah, OK 74464. [1986]

Orr, Dr. Robert J., born about 1870 and married Sarah Reece of Haywood County, N. C., about 1889. Would like any information about his parents. At the time of his death in 1921, he was practicing medicine in Marfa, Texas. Mrs. Jeanna Jennings, 659 Hillside Terrace, Waynesville, NC 28786. [1991]

Osborne, Jonathan and Ephraim, early Haywood County settlers, came from Scotland. Would like more information. Jonathan owned land on the Pigeon River above Canton and Ephraim in present Clyde. Ephraim and his wife settled with eleven sons, one of whom was Judson. Thomas O. Isreal, Rockola Motel, Room 24, 1655 Patton Avenue, Asheville, NC 28806. [1988]

Osborn, Rev. Nicholas Robert, born in 1806 in Buncombe County, married Mary Johnson, daughter of James Johnson and Ann Cole. Both died in the 1890s in Gilmer County, Georgia. Leslee C. Fehlman, 3606 Peute Trail, Austin, TX 78739. [1986]

Parker. Would like to know what man named Parker was shot and killed by Hooper in Jackson County in the 1860s as stated in the *Asheville News*. Was it at a "mustering out" grounds during the Civil War? Edna Smith, Rt. 7, Box 53, Hendersonville, NC 28739. [1991]

Parker, George A., born November 17, 1856, Iredell County, wife Margaret E. Dishman, born July 2, 1858, Alexander County, near Taylorsville, N. C. They were married December 26, 1877, in Taylorsville.

Would like more information about him. He was employed as a carpenter for six years on the construction of the Biltmore Estate. B. F. Parker, Rt. 5, Box 160 B, Hendersonville, NC 28739. [1984]

Parker, Solomon, wife Lydia and father of Wilburn Booth Parker. Would like information on these and also on Alex and Decicy Houston, father of Parthena Houston. Both of these families were from Macon County and perhaps kin to George Parker. Anna L. Thompson, Rt. 5, Box 164, Canton, NC 28716. [1984]

Parris, James (1805-1847), married Amy McIntyre (1808-1890), lived in Haywood/Jackson Counties. Would like information on James and to know where he was buried. Their known children were William, James M., Alfred W., Polly (Mary) Ann, Martha, Elizabeth, Lucretia, Lucinda, Sarah. Would also like to know the connection between Rhoda (b. 1813), Alfred, Jacob, and Temperance Parris to the family of James and Amy Parris. Lucy P. Holcombe, 49 Pharr St., Canton, NC 28716. [1984]

Parton, William, born 1822, wife Nancy Sims, born 1824. They moved to South Carolina, Georgia, then Tennessee. Would like information on his parents. Roy Partain, Rt. 1, Box 242, Long Lane, MO 65590. [1990]

Pattons in the Buncombe County area. Would like more information, particularly the parents of William R. Patton, born 1844 in Greene County, Tennessee. His parents were from Buncombe. W. R. Patton in 1861 joined the CSA in Knoxville (Co. 0.F, 26th Tennessee Vols.), then settled back at Timber Ridge near Greeneville, Tennessee. In 1869, he married Mary Patton in Pilot Knob and moved to Bull's Gap, where his sons Joseph and John (Jack) were born. W. R. Patton died in 1884, and Mary took the boys to Buncombe and Haywood Counties where they finally llived at the headwaters of Crabtree Creek, near Mount Zion Baptist Church. The Patton family had cousins in the Black Mountain area, John and Jan Patton and their son Joe J. Patton, who married Mary E. Rhinehart of Haywood County. Jesse D. Patton, 28 Simon Street, Babylon, NY 11702. [1990]

Patton, Nancy, born in North Carolina, married George Britt, born in Tennessee. Would like more information on these, particularly the parents of Nancy. They were married in Washington County, Tennessee, in 1845 and lived in Buncombe by 1850. Hazel G. Jones, 302 Oak Hill Rd., Candler, NC 28715. [1984]

Payne, Jeptha, born 1816, in North Carolina, wife Rebecca Warren, born 1828, in North Carolina, lived at Deep Creek, Jackson County, then in 1880 in Swannanoa, Buncombe County. Would like more information. Their children included James, Benjamin, Susannah, John, Laura, Adeline, Henry, Sarah, and Harriet. Alberdean Payne, Rt. 3, Box 36 F, Omak, WA 98841-9754. [1993]

Pearson, John, a stone cutter, born in England. He cut tombstones in Henderson County, N. C. He was born approximately 1795. Would like information about him. Sarah G. Upchurch, 78 Rosewood Avenue, Asheville, NC 28801. [1992]

Pendry, Clanton Frances, born February 18, 1828, Yadkin County, N. C. She was married to Oliver Boyd and moved to Indiana. Would like information on her family. Anne Jensby, 714 Champion Court, Garland, TX 75043. [1991]

Petree, Jack Clayton, married Anna and was from Asheville. Would like more information about him. They were living in Sibley, Iowa, from 1920-1923. Kathy Petree Jacobson, 828 Eighth St., Bremerton, WA 98310. [1992]

Pertiller, Thomas, died about 1915 in Lytle Cove, near Swannanoa, N. C., wife Peggy. Would like more information about him. He had at least eight sons and six daughters and was a slave of Lytles in Fairview. Corrie Rutherford, Rt. 1, Box 102 B, Blue Ridge Road, Black Mountain, NC 28711. [1986]

Petillo, Polly, born 1782, married Millington Lytle (1789-1874), son of Captain Thomas Lytle and Susanna Petillo. Would like more information about Polly. Millington and Polly raised their family in the Swannanoa section of Buncombe and their children were Leander Perkins, Elizabeth born 1831, Alberti born 1825, Mary Martha born 1828, Millington, Jr., and Thomas twins born 1830, Susan born 1810, Elizabeth born 1823, Matilda, and Myra born 1811 and married John Smart. Martha Smart, Rt. 4, 54 Moss Drive, Rutherfordton, NC 28139. [1986]

"Phillips' Family News" was being published in 1993 by Dale F. Phillips, 1927 South 7th Street, Chickasha, Oklahoma 73018. This newsletter focuses on the family of George and Susanna Dyer Phillips (1725-1786) of Lunnenburg County, Virginia. Their children included Dyer, Mary, Elizabeth, Robert, and John.

Phillips, Charles, in Buncombe in 1800, moved to South Carolina about 1804, wife Jemima Hardy. Would like information on their families. Children were Mason born 1800, Hardy born 1804, Abraham born 1807, Bright born 1810, Mahulda born 1813, Elizabeth born 1815. Charles Phillips moved to east Tennessee on the Hiawassee River where children Clarissa born 1818 and Person born 1821 were born. Mary Jane Matz, 160 West 71st St., New York, NY 10023. [1986]

Phillips, George W., wife Mary E. Hughes. Would like information on their descendants. He was born in 1859 at Roane Mountain, Carter County, Tennessee, moved to Green Mountain, Yancey County, N. C., and then settled at Charleston Township, Swain County, N. C. Mary Phillips Shaw, 88 Grande Camino Way, Ft. Pierce, FL 34951. [1989]

Phillips, Joel, a Revolutionary soldier from Georgia. Would like information and the names of his parents. He was born in Virginia. He was in Anson County, N. C., by 1750 with two brothers, Zachariah and William. They moved to Wilkes County, Georgia, by 1772, where Joel died in 1792. Also, who were the parents of Joel's wife Elizabeth, whose will was recorded in Wilkes County in 1816. Mrs. Dan Wilson, 1617 Clear Brook, Henderson, TX 75652. [1990]

Pickle, Jacob, born about 1766 in North Carolina and died in Mississippi. Would like information about him. Were the following children who were born in North Carolina his? Robert born 1801, married Sarah Aldridge in Tuscaloosa, Alabama, and Henry born about 1807. George B. Pickle, P. O. Box 1181, Clinton, MS 39060-1181. [1992]

Pitmans, would like information on the following: McGilvery P. Pitman, moved to Cherokee County, Georgia, from North Carolina by 1832, married Mary Elizabeth Gwinn. They had sons Silvester, Radford (married Narcissa Bolton), and David McGilvery Gwinn of Hillsborough District, North Carolina, in 1790. John and Lila Pitman of Halifax District in 1790. Elizabeth Pitman who married Jeptha Baker in Mecklenburg County in 1797. Betsy Pitman who married Jonathon Fletcher in Rowan County in 1797. Kathleen Pitman, Pisgah Valley Rest Home, Rt. 5, Box 102, Canton, NC 28716. [1990]

Plemmons, Joseph Ignatius, born 1900 and died 1908. Was he buried in the Turkey Creek Baptist Church Cemetery? Gladys Plemmons, 375 Union Ave., S. E. #1, Renton, WA 98056. [1989]

Plemmons, Lee Anders, 1862-1928, wife Margaret McElrath, 1871-1912, buried at Green Hill Cemetery and probably from Madison County. Would like the names of the parents of both of these. Would also like any information on Canada Henderson, killed in the Civil War, married to Theresa Davies, 1831-1911, from Liverpool. Theresa later married J. J. Blyth of Henderson County. Louise Ward, Rt. 9, Box 504, Chestnut Gap Rd., Hendersonville, NC 28739. [1985]

Plunkett, Benjamin, born 1800, living in Burke County in 1830. Would like to know the names of his parents. Also would like information on parents and children of Nicholas Rough, Burke County. Emile J. Gex, Jr., 620 Stovall Ave., Picayune, MS 39466. [1984]

Poe, Jedithan, born 1780 in Virginia and was in Williamson County, Tennessee, by 1805, married Elizabeth (1788-1835), was in Franklin County, Tenn., when oldest son James Houge Poe was born in 1807. Would like information on parents and family. In 1829, he took his family (seven children) to Illinois. In 1838, he and two youngest sons went to Texas where he died in 1858. Was he kin to Simon or James Poe in North Carolina. Betty Poore, 136 N. Bend Dr., Biloxi, MS 39532. [1986]

Poer/Poore families. Would like to hear from others who are interested in the Edward and Jeremiah Poer/Poore families. They came from England, were children of Edward and Rebekah, settled in Guilford County about 1790. Marianne Webster, 10309 Ruckle St., Indianapolis, Indiana 46280. [1986]

Powers, Holloway, born in 1772, in Virginia, and died in 1852 in McMinn County, Tennessee. Would like more information. Lynn Burnett, 102 Olde Springs Rd., Columbia, SC 29223. [1993]

Proctor, Moses, born 1796 in Rutherford County, died 1864 in Macon County. Would like information on his ancestors. Moses left Rutherford with two brothers for north Georgia in the 1820s, married, had at least one son. Moses then moved to east Tennessee and married Patience Rustin. They were the first settlers of Hazel Creek, N. C. (Macon, now Swain County.) Duane Oliver, Box 394, Hazelwood, NC 28738. [1989]

Purcell, John, born 1773, died 1850, lived in Robeson County, North Carolina, most of his life. Would like to hear from descendants. Particularly interested in Malcolm Purcell (1790-1878), first child of John. I would like to buy a copy of *Lumber River Scots and Their Descendants: McLeans, Torreys, Purcells, McIntyres, and Gelchrists*, published in Virginia in 1942. Douglas Purcell, 633 North Randolph Ave., Eufaula, AL 36027. [1985]

Queen, Henson and Zelpha, lived in Cherokee County, now Clay, in 1850 and 1860. Would like more information. Their children were Isabella, Julius, David, Martha, John, Lucinda, and Franklin. Jan Horn, 1690 Eaton #108, Lakewood, CA 80214. [1984]

Queen, William, wife was listed as Elizabeth in the 1850 census of Macon County, N. C. Would like any information. He was born in Rutherford County about 1790 and moved to Macon County. Bill Queen, P. O. Box 1175, Waynesville,NC 28786. [1990]

Ragsdale, Lucinda. Would like any information. She was supposedly one-fourth Cherokee Indian, born in Hiwassee married Thomas Ray who came from Ireland. Marilyn Ciesielske, 2541 Little Rock Road, Plano, IL 60545. [1984]

Ramsey, Nancy, born about 1790, married Samuel Carter, born 1785, son of Edward and Mary Brown Carter of Buncombe County. Would like information about Nancy and also information about Solomon adn Lucinda Hensley Brigman, who died in 1885 and who lived near Stocksville, Buncombe County. Would also like a list of the children of Levi Buckner, born August 17, 1844, lived in Yancey-Madison area, and his three wives: Margaret Ray, Alice Roberts, Celia Wilson. Loren Ray, 2237 Woodland Blvd., Fort Myers, FL 33907. [1993]

Rathbun/Rathbone/Rathburn. Would like information from all people have records on this family. Most of this name throughout the United States are descended from John Rath-bone, who married Margaret Acres and came from England in 1654, first settling in Dorchester, Massachusetts. John and Margaret's children were John, Jr., born 1655, Thomas born 1657, Sarah born 1659, William born 1661, Margaret born 1663, Joseph born 1667, Elizabeth born 1670, and Samuel born 1672. Elizabeth H. Rathbun, 76 Forest Road, Asheville, NC 28803. [1987]

Ratliff/Ratcliff, Moses, of Rowan County, born 1733. Would like to know the name of his wife and any early information. Also need the name of the wife of Abraham Ratliff, son of Moses, who died March 31, 1836, in Haywood County. Would like to know parents of Richard Roberson who was in Haywood County early and married Mary Ratliff, daughter of Abraham Ratliff. Frank Morgan, 114 E. Church St., El Dorado, Arkansas 71730. [1984]

Ray, Henry and family, moved in 1904 from Todd on the

Ashe-Watauga County line. Would like information. Henry's wife was Cynthia, and their children included Charlie, married Frankie Tolliver; Robert, married Sylvia Halsey in Wyoming County, West Virginia; Laura married Frank Sheppard and lived in Ashe County; Sally; Minnie married Martin Houck of Wyoming County, West Virginia, and William. Would be particularly interested in Henry Ray's parents, brothers, and sisters. Rachel Conti, 9129 Barret Rd., Millington, TN 38053. [1986]

Ray, William Tryon. Would like the names of his parents and the parents of his wife, Millie Caroline Walker. They were married in 1846 in Surry County, North Carolina. Barbara White, 273 S. Dillwyn Rd., Newark, DE 19711. [1987]

Raye, William, born about 1935 in West Virginia and was married to Susie Vitatoe who had kin in Lafollett, Tennessee, and Kentucky. They were the parents of Don Vitatoe Ray who had a sister who died at birth. Would like any information. Don V. Raye, P. O. Box 8011, Roseville, MI 48066. [1991]

The Rays from Yancey County have a "Ray Family News Letter," which gives information on their reunions, census information for Rays, old church information. For more information, write Marie Brown, 7 Fern Glade Rd., Asheville, NC 28804. [1987]

Raburn, Hodge. Would like any information on parents or other relatives. The McDowell County census of 1870 has him as 56, living in Sugar Hill Township with Mary Raburn, 72. Could this be his mother? Was James M. Raburn on the same census who was listed as 50 be a brother? Clyde W. Rayburn, P. O. Box 278, Glenwood, NC 28737. [1984]

Rayburn, Hodge, born about 1759, died March 1, 1847. Would like to know where in the Candler area he was buried. He married first a Watkins and second Arminta Martin. He was a sheriff of Burke County, a member of the House of Representatives from Burke, a senator from both Burke and Buncombe. Jean Pressley Warren, P. O. Box 533, Candler, NC 28715. [1985]

Rector family. Would like information about Lewis Rector who married Frances Lunsford in 1788 and about Benjamin Rector who married first Martha Baker in 1780 and second Nancy Findley in 1806. The Rectors lived in Iredell, Catawba, Wilkes, Buncombe, Alexander, and Surry Counties. Jean Clerico, S. W. High, Topeka, KS 66604. [1984]

Reed, Mason, and Horton families of Western North Carolina. Would like information on the following. Ephraim Brevard Reed, born 1859 near Black Mountain, N. C., married in 1888 Martha Ella Elizabeth Mason, born 1866; both died in Greenwood, S. C. His father was J. C. Reed, born 1821, lived in Swannanoa; her parents were Andrew J. Mason, born 1825, lived in McDowell, and Mary Ann Elizabeth Horton, born 1837, died in Piney Flats, Tennessee. One son of Ephraim and Martha Reed was Alfred Ernest Reed, born 1901, Black Mountain, who married Maude Ethel Glenn. R. Wayne Matthews, 920 West Fischer Ave., Sherman, TX 75090. [1986]

Reed, James, born in North Carolina in 1784, married in 1810 Nancy McGee, both died after 1858. Would like more information. Their children were William born 1812, Daniel born 1815, Elizabeth born 1818 (married William McFee), James C. born 1820, Levi Quinn born 1822 (moved to Georgia in 1846), Nancy born 1824. Bertha F. Reid, Rt. 3, Box 397, Americus, GA 31709. [1988]

Reed, Robert, of Buncombe and Haywood Counties in the early 1800's. Would like more information. Was Nancy Stewman born 1798 in Buncombe and later moved to Macon a Reed before marrying? Need names of children of James Clark and Jean/Jane Reed of either Lincoln or Burke County in the early 1800s. Lawrence E. Wood, 75 Peeks Creek Rd., Franklin, NC 28734. [1984]

Reedy River in Greenville, South Carolina. Would like to know if this river were named for a particular person or if it were a geographical feature. Robert J. VonDeBur, 41 Applecross Rd., Weaverville, NC 28787. [1988]

Reems, Mary Ann, died about 1790, was the wife of Elisha Estes who died about 1782 in Franklin County, Virginia. Retha Ellison, Rt. 3, Box 270, Hull, GA 30646. [1986]

Rees, Enoch, born about 1795 in South Carolina and a brother Louis/Lewis who was a few years older and known to have been born in Pickens County, S. C. Louis was said to have been "half" Cherokee Indian and his wife Charity a "full" Cherokee Indian. Would like to know the names of their parents. Also looking for parents of Clinton Houston Moore, born in 1810 in North Carolina. Was there a Hightower connection? Frances M. Reese, 433 Hillcrest Circle, Hendersonville, NC 28739. [1985]

Rees/Reese, John, born 1813, South Carolina, died in 1899 in Etowah County, Alabama. Would like information on his parents and family. John married Narcissus Edwards (born 1819 in North Carolina) who was the daughter of Thomas and Mary Brittain Edwards, granddaughter of James Brittain of Mills River. A large number of families migrated to what is now Etowah County in the late 1830s. Reese City, Alabama, was named for John Rees who operated a mill on Little Wills Creek. Mrs. Tom Lolley, P. O. Box 910, Old Fort, NC 28762. [1984]

Rees/Reese/Reece, Thomas, lived in Henderson County from 1830-1860. He may have come from Pennsylvania. Would like more information. His known children are Alson E.; Elizabeth who married Abraham S. Lyday; Welborn. On the 1860 Henderson County census Thomas is shown as age 86, Mary 54, Welborn 40. Shirley Jenkins, 23 Vista Drive, Candler, NC 28715. [1991]

Reeves, Sarah Elizabeth, married William Camp, born 1773, son of John Camp and Mary Tarpley of Rutherford County area. Would like information on her parents. They moved from North Carolina to Greenville, South Carolina, then into Jackson County, Georgia, and, finally, into Jefferson County, Alabama. Also, would like parents of William Anderson Rice, born 1785, North Carolina, moved to Georgia and died in 1844, probably married Rebecca Redding. Camp Gilliam, 1709 Santa Maria, Kingsville, TX 78363. [1985]

Reeves, Melvin Hezikiah, III. Would like information on his descendants and the other following Reeves. Donna Fay Reeves and Donna Jane Reeves, children of Melvin Hezikiah Reeves, Jr., born May 20, 1909, died March 29, 1968, married Bobbie Glenn, buried Green Hill, Waynesville, N. C. Melvin Reeves, Jr., was the son of Melvin Reeves, born February 18, 1873, Madison County, who married Ernie Lucile Crymes in 1933. Janet Robeson Curphey, P. O. Box 916, Waynesville, NC 28786. [1989]

Reid, Samuel Wilkins, and wife, Jane Butler. Would like information on all families included. They lived in what is now upper Transylvania County. Samuel was the son of James William Reid and Lucretia Dillard. Samuel and Jane had ten children: Hester Ann Reid married Rufus Galloway, Mary Malinda Reid married James Fisher, Thomas Bryson Reid married Matilda Aiken, James Owen Reid married Hattie Siler, John Henry Reid married Sarah Breedlove, Thaddeus Dillard Reid married

Mary Louise Davis, William Massey Reid married Keturah Brooks, Samuel McDonald Reid married Lou Young, Lucretia Elizabeth Reid married W. Hampton Robinson, and Nancy Jane Reid married Lee F. Norton. Doris Reid Owen, Rt. 1, Box 187, Lake Toxaway, NC 28747. [1986]

Rhodes, Frank, married Mary Summer/Sumner whose children included Albert B. Rhodes, born 1856, married Cinthia E. Garren in 1877, and Elizabeth Jane Rhodes, born 1854, married Humphrey P. Conner in 1877. Jo Ann Earwood Shepherd, P. O. Box 351, Christmas, FL 32709. [1986]

Rhodes, Mary Polly, born 1796, in North or South Carolina, married John Hamilton about 1814, in Buncombe, lived in North Carolina until moving to Cherokee County, Alabama, in 1854. Would like to know the names of her parents. Their children were Nancy born 1815 married Tom Jordan; Robert born 1817, lived on Davidson River near Brevard; Alexander born 1821, moved to Alabama along with brothers, John born 1822 and William born 1825. Mrs. Hubert Akins, Rt. 6, Box 364, Fort Payne, AL 35967. [1986]

Rice, Wilson, married Emiline Watts, born 1848. Would like information on their family. Patricia Gibbs White, 567 Paint Fork Rd., Barnardsville, NC 28709. [1984]

Richards, George, born about 1727 and died in July of 1818, Franklin, N. C. Would like information on his parents. He married Tabitha Hudson in Virginia. Am also interested in the parents of Edward Branan born about 1798 in North Carolina. He married Rebecca Farr on January 4, 1825, in Newton County, Georgia. Would also like information on a Mr. Morrison who was married to Leodicy (born February 7, 1803) and had the following children: Andrew born 1827 in N. C., Lolena E. born 1829 in N. C., Lucinda A. born 1831 in N. C. Leodicy Morrison later married a Mr. Hyatt. Andrew A. Morrison, born 1827, married Rachel Turner in N. C., and by 1850 moved to Lumpkin County, Georgia. Fay B. Kitchens, 101 Jolly Roger, Monroe, LA 71203. [1988]

Riley, Walter Henry, wife Dora Virginia Garrett. Would like information on both of these. Dora's father was Samuel, probably from Sandy Mush, Buncombe County. The Rileys had four sons between 1910 and 1917 in the Asheville area: Oscar Bergen, Allen Walter, Frank, Raymone Lee. Walter Henry supposedly died when the baby was small, about 1917. Lana Henley, 8910 Bubbling Springs, Austin, TX 78729. [1988]

Roberts, Grant, born 1796 Buncombe, died 1886 in Georgia. He married first Frances Pass on August 14, 1825 in Clarke County, Georgia. Would like information on both their parents. His father may have been Josephus Roberts, and his mother was a Grant. Mrs. J. Paul Jones, 52 Chester Place, Asheville, NC 28806. [1984]

Roberts, John, born about 1829, Buncombe County. Were his parents John and Lucy Massey Roberts. He married Matilda Massey, and their children were Harriett born 1849, Cynthia born 1851, Laura born 1853 (married Nathaniel Hunter), and Burnet N. born 1856. Joan Long, Ridgefield Place, Asheville, NC 28803. [1991]

Roberts, John Wesley, born 1844 died 1924, Knox County, Tennessee. Would like to hear from his descendants. He married first Ellie Cake, who died in 1884. They had eight children from 1868-1884. He then married Rhoda Ann McCready, and they had eight children born between 1887 and 1904. John Wesley Kennedy, 1836 Gippy Lane, Charleston, SC 29407. [1992]

Roberts, Joshua, married Lydia Freeman, both buried at Flat Creek Baptist Church, Buncombe. Would like to hear from anyone connected to this family. Angie Graeber, 4838 Zephy Lane, Charlotte, NC 28209. [1985]

Roberts, Thomas Catlett, born 1831, died 1899, married Rachel Rebecca Davidson. Would like to know the names of his parents, brothers, and sisters. In 1850, he lived on Newfound and Turkey Creeks with David Roberts, then moved to Georgia. Dorothy Hyde, Rt. 2, Box 644, Candler, NC 28715. [1984]

Robertson, William, born 1824, Tennessee, married Elizabeth, had son Greenberry, moved into Yancey County. Brenda Hudgins, 41 Mt. Carmel Drive, Asheville, NC 28806. [1987]

Rogers/Rodgers, Hugh, born in North Carolina on October 30, 1822, was on the census of Dade County, Georgia, in 1850, and married to Elizabeth Amos and had two small sons. Would like to know the names of his parents. He moved to Tennessee in the late 1860s and to Texas in 1870, dying there on July 19, 1905. His father was born about 1800 in North Carolina, and his grandfather is said to have come from Ireland. Would also like information on Jesse William Rogers, son of Hugh

Rogers of Buncombe or Haywood Counties. When did he go and where in Tennessee? Did he have a son named Hugh Rogers born in 1822? Vivian Rogers Phillips, 27124 Underwood Avenue, Haywood, CA 94544. [1989]

Rogers, Martin, wife Adelia A. Hammett, lived in Buncombe County in the 1870s. Would like information. Delphine Miller 6727 Larmanda, Apt. 164, Dallas, TX 75231. [1986]

Rogers/Rodgers, Thomas who lived in Macon County, N. C., in the 1840s and 1850s. Am particularly interested in his death date, children's names, and birthdates. Vivian Rogers Phillips, 27124 Underwood Ave., Haywood, CA 94544. [1988]

Roland/Rowland, Mike, of Madison County, born July 29, 1836, and died February 19, 1918. Would like information about his parents. One son was William Roland who died in South Carolina. Carl Roland, 11 Edwards Rd., Nebo, NC 28761. [1988]

Rollins family, Randolph County, North Carolina. Am particularly interested in the parents of Margaret Rollins. She married John Bulla about 1807 and died March 1819. They 275 were Quakers and had the following known children: Cynthia born 1810 married Luke Newsom; Thomas born 1811; Betsey born 1812 married Joseph Wterole; Harrison born 1813; Patsy born 1815 married Frank Lytle; Andrew born 1816. Betty Lee Lingenfelter, 685 Winnetka St., Hernando, FL 32642. [1988]

Roper, James born about 1800. Would like information on him and descendants. He was born in Burke County and had a son William Roper, who was born in Burke in 1829. Mrs. Margaret Roper Mitchell, 4773 Hwy. 138, Stockbridge, GA 30281. [1988]

Ruddell/Ruddle, James, born 1790 in Tennessee, married Mary born about 1795 in South Carolina. Would like information about him. They lived in Macon County and had six children in 1830, then moved before 1838 to Gilmer County, Georgia. Names of the known children are David born 1823, James Neal born 1825, Mary born 1830, married John Sandlin. Perhaps Jesse in the 1840 Cherokee County, N. C., census and John in the 1850 Buncombe County census. Mrs. L. L. Presley, 4474 S. Cobb Drive, SE, Smyrna, GA 30080. [1986]

Ruff, Daniel, wife Delila, lived in Buncombe County 1850 through 1860. Would like any information on them and their two sons Hosea and Bedford Ruff. Would also like any information on John Carver and his wife Lizzie of Haywood/Buncombe or anything on their children George W., William, and Emmaline. John died in the Civil War, and Lizzie died shortly afterwards. Dianne Taylor, 6681 N. Montrose Rd., Tucson, AZ 85741. [1984]

Russell, James R., born Wythe County, Virginia, about 1823, settled in Madison County, N. C., with wife Sarah. Would like information on his family. Their children included Emilene, Andrew Jackson, Elbert, Noah, Lucille or Luther, Sarah. James was in the Confederate army, 29th Regiment, died May 7, 1862, Cumberland Gap, Tennessee. Ralph Russell, 23 Bevlyn Dr., Asheville, NC 28803. [1986]

Russell, John H., born 1817 in South Carolina, married Matilda Cross of Buncombe County in 1839, lived in the Turkey Creek area of Buncombe at least from 1840 through 1854. Would like information on him. Children were Mary Ann, Rachel, Leander Meret, Margaret, William, Harriet Jane, all born between 1841-1854. Richard Russell, 3635 N. Kercheval Drive, Indianapolis, IN 46226. [1990]

Russell, Matthew, born about 1740 in Ireland and married Jane McIntire. Would like to correspond with others interested in his descendants. Matthew died in 1812 in Pendleton, S. C. Son David was an early settler of Buncombe and Haywood Counties. Ruth Wynn, Rt. 1, Box 540, Iuda, MS 38852. [1986]

Sams, Alison Burton, died in 1904, wife Abigail Pressley, died 1920. Would like information on their descendants. One child was Leroy Sams, born 1878, who married Mabel Wells; Leroy worked for the Southern Railway and moved to Illinois. Other children were Bridgett Sams who married Marvin Nix and lived in Asheville; Rebecca who married Delphis Waldrop, moved to South Carolina; Vista who married Bascom Hunter. Steve Anderson, 660 Elam Forest Court, Stone Mountain, GA 30083. [1992]

Saxon, Pleasant, born Laurens County, S. C., about 1801, married Ethalinda Franks in 1830. Would like information on these. Both died in 1841 in Missouri. Orphaned were children Samuel, Joshua, William, John, Wesley, Mary Elizabeth, and Thomas who returned to South Carolina. Blanche Saxon Stein, 11027 Fernald Ave., Dallas, TX 75218. [1988]

Senf, John Christian. Would like information about the Hessian ancestry of John who supposedly left the Hession forces in Saratoga,

New York, in 1777, defecting to the American side in South Carolina. He became Colonel Engineer of South Carolina and was the second original member of the Society of the Cincinnati. He died in 1806 and is buried at Rocky Mount, S. C. Kenneth S. Jones, P. O. Box 782, Worchesster, MA 01613. [1989]

Shamblin, William, born about 1770 in Virginia, wife Susanna Hicks, born about 1778 in North Carolina. Would like to know parents of both. They were married November 12, 1799, in Stokes County, N. C. They moved to McMinn County, Tenn., in the early 1800s. Dorothy Shamblin, 662 Oxford Oaks Lane, Oxford, Michigan 48951. [1985]

Sheffield, John, Duplin, N. C., in the late 1700s. Would like information about him. His will was filed there in 1790. He mentioned children William, West, Wright, Bryant, Ephraim, Arthur, Isham, Nancy, Polly, Louisa, Catherine, and Tabitha. Some of his children moved to Georgia. Especially interested in William and his descendants. Mrs. Lamar Graham, 98 Belleview Park Rd., #7, Franklin, NC 28734. [1988]

Shook, George, born in Holland, came to America in 1740, married Elizabeth Grub/Grubb on August 8, 1748, in Pennsylvania. Would like information on him. They left Pennsylvania and came to Burke County, N. C. Mildred Hicks, 117 Russell St., Rayville, LA 71269. [1985]

Showalter family. Would like information on this family name. John Showalter, 701 Warren Wilson Rd., Swannanoa, NC 28778. [1989]

Shuford, Peter Monroe, born March 20, 1829, and died August 27, 1913. Would like information, particularly his parents. He lived in Burke County and married in Lincolnton. Martha S. Vance, Rt. 3, Box 20, Spruce Pine, NC 28777. [1984]

Silver family. Would like to hear from descendants of the following: Levi Dewise Silver, born September 16, 1836, married Jane Buchanan; Rosanna Silver born April 28, 1848, married John McGee; Martha Lucinda Silver born July 7, 1854, married Will Lintz. Gladys Gibbs, P. O. Box 248, Old Fort, NC 28762. [1984]

Simmons, Bell, born 1786, son of Jesse Simmons born 1760 in Stokes County, N. C., son of John Simmons born 1712 in Scotland. Would like information about descendants. William B. Howe, P. O. Box 565, Rolla, MO 65401. [1989]

Sims, Thomas B., wife Sarah Adaline Allison. Would like to contact relatives. Lillian Ledbetter Stumpp, 1819 East 12th St., Idaho Falls, Idaho

83404. [1991]

Sitton/Sutton family. Would like to exchange information on the following members. Joshua Hamilton Sitton, born July 23, 1836, Buncombe, married Hannah Elizabeth Cloninger. His brother Benjamin J. Sitton, born March 18, 1818, married Marando Olive Plemmons. John Bradley Sitton born May 28, 1829, Buncombe, married Elizabeth Mahulda Ivie. All married in Gilmer County, Georgia. About 1870 Joshua and Benjamin went to Searcy and Benton Counties, Arkansas. John never returned from the Civil War. Also interested in Samuel B. Sitton, born October 14, 1814, Greene County, Tennessee, married Nancy and was later in Smith County, Texas. Richard Bentley, 6541 Jaffe Ct., #12, San Diego, CA 92119. [1986]

Sitton, William, died in Haywood County in 1838 and was a vast landholder. Would like to know the connection between him and John H. Russell. On Christmas day of 1835, according to Sitton's records, when John Russell was 18 years old, Sitton loaned him $100 with no collateral or co-signer. Then, on Christmas day in 1836, Sitton again loaned him $100, even though the first $100 had not been repaid. John Russell obtained a marriage bond on December 2, 1839, to marry Matilda Cross of Buncombe County; co-bondsman was Marvel Sutton, who was married to Sally David of Rutherford County in 1829. R. E. Russell, 3635 North Kercheval Drive, Indianapolis, IN 46226. [1989]

Sitton, William, Haywood County, died about 1837, was State Senator in 1833. The name of his first wife is unknown. Children included Jacob born 1807, married Ann Ray; Moseph born 1809, married Jane; Samuel; Sara married Robert Penland; Elizabeth married Henry Stevens, Priscilla married William Ellis; Nancy married Lawson Bird. William Sitton married, second, Polly McClure, 1821. Would like name of first wife, names of other children, names of parents, places of burial. Mrs. Charles A. Bowers, P. O. Box 73, Montreat, NC 28757. [1984]

Slagle, Benjamin, married first Sarah A. Cox, second Nancy Hollifield. Would like more information. Would particularly like to know where they are buried and parents of Sarah Cox. Peggy Lee Cox, Rt. 1, Box 778, Spruce Pine, NC 28777. [1984]

Sloan, James C., born April 10, 1791, probably Rowan County, married December 1818 to Susan H. Bowers, died August 1853, probably Mecklenburg County. Would like to know the names of his parents. In

1850, they were in Iredell County with children Laura, Charlotte, Hiram D. C., Harriet B., and Thomas C. Juanita Reynolds, 1229 Lorie Circle, Brandon, FL 33511. [1985]

Slocum, William Henry, born February 1828, in North Carolina, married in 1851 to Elizabeth Roberts, born February 1829 in Tennessee. Would like information about him. They moved to Tilton, Cross County, Arkansas. He was in Company E, Gause's Regiment, 32 Ark. Infantry. Preston Slocum, Jr., P. O. Box 1879, Sylva, NC 28779. [1989]

Sluder, John Thomas, died 1845, wife Rebecca McAfee, lived in Buncombe. Would like information about them. They were in White County, Tennessee, in 1838, when son James Alexander Sluder was born. How was John kin to the Sluders who stayed in Buncombe? Col. Chester L. Sluder, 1025 Cuatro Cerros Tr., SE, Albuquerque, NM 87123. [1986]

Smathers, John, born December 17, 1773, married Mary Agner/Eigner, daughter of Henry Eigner, Jr. John died in Haywood County in 1805, buried in Locust Old Fields Cemetery. Would like to know the names of his parents. Frank Morgan, 114 E. Church St., El Dorado, Arkansas 71730. [1984]

Smith family. Would like more information on the Smith and Burgess families who lived in Buncombe County during the late 1700s and 1800s. Christopher R. Smith was born in Buncombe in 1804 and moved to Habersham County, Georgia. Rev. Burgess Smith, born in 1809 in Buncombe, possibly the brother of Christopher, moved to Elbert County, Georgia. Would like to know the names of their parents. Mrs. D. R. Looney, 9208 South 93 East Ave., Tulsa, OK 74133. [1991]

Smith, Henry E., wife Sarah Elizabeth Harris. Would like information on these. Their children included Minnie Ballard and Henry Ed Smith who lived in Buncombe County. Other children were Tom, John, and Will Smith, Mary Smith Brimer, Mandy Smith Bradley. Cindy Smith, Box 23, 1314 Tunnel Rd., Asheville, NC 28805. [1987]

Smith, John, received a grant in 1784 on Abotts Creek in the Rich Fork Community of Rowan County, N. C. Did he have sons John and Cornelius and later moved to Washington County, Greene County, Tennessee. Ms. Susie Thompson, 7110 Westway Circle, Knoxville, TN 37919. [1989]

Smith, John, lived in the Mars Hill area of Madison and married about

1843, Elizabeth Ammons, daughter of Rev. Jesse Ammons, one of the founders of Mars Hill College. Would like information on John's family. Their children were Rhoda Ann, Nancy Matilda, Rebecca, Jesse, Sallie, Avaline, William, Benjamin, Jack, Ambrose. Nancy L. Pope, 58 Bull Mountain Rd., Asheville, NC 28805. [1984]

Snauffer, George, settled in Clayborne County, Tennessee, in the late 1700s (from Bucks County, Pennsylvania), was Clayborne's Sheriff in the early 1800s. A son, George, fought in the War of 1812 and moved in the 1830s to what is now West Virginia. Would be interested in knowing the wife's name of Sheriff Snauffer and other children. (Name later spelled Snuffer.) Darry Snuffer, Box 428, Newland, NC 28657. [1986]

Snipes, Thomas, born about 1780, wife Elizabeth Hanks. Would like information on their parents. Their daughter, Rachel Nancy Snipes married John McPheeters/McPeters, son of Jonathan and Margaret. Loren S. Ray, 2237 Woodland Blvd., Fort Myers, FL 33907. [1993]

Snow, William, born Randolph County, N. C., 1769, English descent, wife Susan Myers, Dutch descent. Would like to correspond with anyone having information on these. The couple moved to Ohio and lived for several years before moving to Morgan and Roane Counties, Tennessee. W. J. Snow, 218 Sugar-fork Rd., Franklin, NC 28734. [1985]

Sparks family of Yancey County, N. C. Would like more information. Mrs. W. E. Holder, Jr., 1037 Riverside Drive, Asheville, NC 28804. [1992]

Sparks, James M., born in Mitchell County on December 27, 1843. Would like information about him. He was in Company C of the 13th Tennessee Cavalry as was his brother Charles Sparks. Lois A. Hoyle, Rt. 4, Slagle Rd., Bakersville, NC 28705. [1989]

Sparks, Jeremiah, born about 1846, married Lucinda Carolina Callahan, born June 15, 1842. Would like information about Jeremiah. Family stories say that they were from Yancey County and that Jeremiah was the son of Sam Sparks. Virginia H. Wilson, 1320 Allens Creek Road, Waynesville, NC 28786. [1992]

Spencer Historical and Genealogical Society was formed in 1990 by Virginia C. O'Bryan, 1326 East Lawrence Lane, Phoenix, AZ 85020-3034.

Stallons/Stallings/Stalons family, in North Carolina about 1805 through 1833, then moved to Western Kentucky. Would like more information. Ruebin Stallons of this family was born in Kentucky in 1833. Mrs. Richard Bearden, 126 W. Nova Scotia Dr., Port Richey, FL 33568. [1984]

Stanberry, Moses, born in North Carolina, married Elizabeth Snyder in Kentucky about 1820. Would like to know the names of his parents. Would also like to know the parents of Mary Jackson who married John Edwards about the time of the Revolutionary War. She is buried in Jackson County, Indiana. Virgie Starr, Rt. 1, Box 375, Stilwell, OK 74960. [1985]

Starnes, Millenium L., born 1851 in South Carolina, wife Mary Caroline, born 1855 in North Carolina. Their sons included Julius G., born 1884, S. C.; Jefferson Lee; Millenium, Jr.; Arthur Y., born 1900, S. C. Would like to know where this family lived in North Carolina after 1910 when they were in Mecklenburg County. Harry F. Dill, 6019 Benjamin St., Alexandria, LA 71303. [1991]

Stephens, Moses, born in the late 1700s in Buncombe County. He moved to Whitley County, Kentucky, about 1807. Would like more information. Will be happy to share information with North Carolina Stephens on the ones who went to Kentucky, Mississippi, and Louisiana. Velva Hall, 410 North State Street, Yates Center, Kansas 66783. [1990]

Stepp, Jessie, born about 1811 in the Black Mountain area, later lived in Yancey County, owning much land in the Mount Mitchell section. His grave is in our family plot, but the marker has no dates. Would like to know his date of birth and death. Joe Stepp, Aquone, NC 28703. [1989]

Stevens, William Oates, Sampson County, N. C. He was the son of Barnabus Stevens and Lydia Oates, who were married July 10, 1779, in Duplin County. Would like more information. Would also be interested in the relationship of Reddick Darden to the Stevens' family. Gail R. Lowe, 1003 Leycester Drive, Baton Rouge, LA 70808. [1993]

Stuart, Isam P., born September 5, 1804, and died March 1, 1888, married to Serenia, born February 10, 1815, and died April 15, 1887. Would be interested in her maiden name. Legend says that Serenia was related to Alexander Hamilton. The Stuarts are buried in the Stuart Cemetery located on the property of Howard McElrath off the David Whitaker Road in North Mills River, Henderson County, N. C. David Taylor, Rt. 8, Box 1457, Hickory, NC 28602. [1989]

Sumerline, born May 9, 1798, died in Memphis, Missouri, and his wife

Basheba Robards, born July 24, 1805. Would like more information about them. They lived on a farm located on Lewis Fork on the Yadkin River, Wilkes County, N. C. Their children were born between 1828 and 1849: Rufus, Edith, Hannah, Lorena, Lucinda, Elbert, Permelia, Mericcae, Catherine. Judy Johnson, 26061 Luzon Ct., Charlotte Harbor, FL 33983. [1992]

Summey family. Would like information on the Summey family and on the descendants of Elizabeth Corpening who married George Summey and lived near Flat Rock, N. C. Their three children were Albert Theodore Summey (1823-1906) married Sarah Rose Morrison; Langdon Cheves Summey (1826-1877); Ellen Summey married Julius Alonzo Corpening. Randy Gibson, P. O. Box 432, Rutherford College, NC 28670.

Swain, Samuel, wife Freelove George. Would like information. They were the parents of George Swain (born June 17, 1763, in Mass., and married Carolyn Lane Lory). These were the grandparents of David Lowry Swain and Matilda Swain. Would also like information on ancestors and brothers of Eli Barker Herrer, born November 18, 1807, Haywood County, died May 31, 1876, Waynesville, and ancestors of his wife Jane Yarborough, daughter of Elisha Yarborough. Jane was born January 9, 1811, Crabtree Creek, Haywood County, and died February 14, 1866, Waynesville. Virginia Pursifull, 44 Balm Grove Ave., Asheville, NC 28806. [1986]

Swainey/Sweeney, Elbert, born July 1, 1882, perhaps in Tennessee, died July 6, 1912, Buncombe County. Would like more information, particularly his parents. He was the son of Albert M. and Mary Wright Sweeney, who died after 1902 and is buried at Green Hills Cemetery. Elbert Sweeney was married to Minnie E. Ward, who died in 1955 and is buried at Riverside Cemetery. Minnie's parents were William and Elizabeth Ward. Elbert may have been killed in Asheville in 1915 or 1916. James A. Black, Jr., 96 Spooks Branch Rd., Asheville, NC 28804. [1993]

Swann family. Am particularly interested in the brothers and sisters of David Henry Swann born in Buncombe in 1846, married Nancy or Mary Clarke. Their son John Henry Swann was born near Asheville on October 12, 1872, in a small town named Lynne. Other children of David Swann inluded Oscar Stanley Swann, born Riceville, October 29, 1889, Willie, Alfred, Thula, Herman, Ellen, Inez, Mattie, Maud, Bonnie.

Carole West Lonergan, 1851 Cedar, Jacksonville, Illinois 62650. [1985]

Swann, William, wife Mary E. Capps. Would like information about their parents. Willliam and Mary both died about 1900 and lived in the Reems Creek area and in Swannanoa. Census records show he was born in South Carolina and his father in Virginia, and his mother in South Caroolina. Mary Capps Swann and parents were all born in North Carolina. W. H. Jones, 28 Garrison Rd., Weaverville, NC 28787. [1987]

Swann, William Francis, born about 1869 in Reems Creek or Ox Creek in Buncombe County, married Helena Westall about 1890. One son, Fred Ellsworth Swann, was born in June of 1893 in Elizabethton, Tennessee. Helena Westall's mother was a Clark; would like to know more about the Westall family. Ned Swann, 903 Parkwood Rd., Shelby, NC 28150. [1987]

Tabor family. Would like information about the following. Issac Tabor died in West Feliciana Parish, Louisiana, in 1830. His wife was Elizabeth. His brothers were Burl and Bevel Tabor who were also in Louisiana but were born in North Carolina in 1776 and 1777. Delbert McKnight, Rt. 6, Box 645, Gilmer, TX 75644. [1988]

Tate, R. T., wife Ellen. Would like information on their descendants. There were two boys, Jack and Ray, and one girl, name unknown. They lived in Asheville. Pansy Blalock, Rt. 4, Dutch Cove, Canton, NC 28716. [1987]

Tate, Col. William, in the North Carolina Confederate Cavalry, probably the 142nd. Would like information about him. W. N. Crawford, 1201 Dairy Ashford, Houston, TX 77079. [1987]

Taylor, Noah, born about 1829 in Henderson or Rutherford Counties. He went to Texas after 1860 and married Lenora. Would like to know the names of his parents. His and Lenora's children included Theresa born 1866, Albert T. born 1868, William H. born 1870, and Mattie Ophelia born 1873. He served as a Confederate in the Civil War. Shara Walerscheid, 2663 Pecos Highway, Carlsbad, NM 88220. [1990]

Taylor, Richard, son of James and Mary Gilbert Taylor. Would like information. Sadie Patton had in her book, *The Story of Henderson County*, that "Martha Barnett, daughter of David and Lavada Hamilton Barnett, married Richard Taylor and that they went to Texas." In 1880, they were still in Henderson County. When did they go to Texas, and where did they settle? David A. Taylor, Rt. 8, Box 1457, Hickory, NC 28602.

Thom, Alexander. Would like to correspond with anyone who has information about the 1753 Presbyterian Bible which belonged to Mr. Thom. Would also be interested in sharing knowledge about Francis Triplett from Virginia, John Rhodes from North Carolina, Parker and David Lucas from Virginia, and Ephraim Lyles from South Carolina. K. L. Schnabel, 616 Saxony Lane, Kenner, LA 70065-2636. [1992]

Thomas, Anthorite, born 1789, wife of James Dyer Justice. Her father was John Thomas of Henderson County. Would like to know the name of her mother. Mrs. Pat Verschoore, 3922 Brummel, Skokie, IL 60076. [1984]

Thomas, John, born 1792 in South Carolina, was in Buncombe about 1800, married Margaret Elizabeth Fain Wetzel (widow of Henry Wetzel and daughter of Ebenezer Fain and Mary Mercer, also Buncombe settlers in the early 1800s). Would like information on the parents, brothers, and sisters of John Thomas. Two children of John and Margaret were born in Buncombe, George Alerbury born 1819, and Elizabeth born 1823. John and Margaret moved to Union County, Georgia in 1832. Adelaide H. Williams, 2441 Breen Circle, Rock Hill, SC 29730. [1987]

Thomas, Robert, Sheriff of Henderson County, shot by Bushwackers on April 22, 1865. Would like more information on Robert. Mrs. Randal J. Lyday, 303 Gaston St., Brevard, NC 28712. [1983]

Thompson, Daniel, born in Buncombe County in 1793 or 1795. Would like more information. His parents were Samuel and Mary Thompson who had eleven children. Daniel and his father first filed on land in McMinn and Monroe Counties in Tennessee in 1825, and Daniel settled there are raised a family of eleven children. According to family tradition, this line of Thompsons came to South Carolina then to North Carolina and on to Tennessee. Daniel, Houston, and Mack Thompson were supposed to have emigrated from Buncombe County, and whether Samuel came with them or later is not known. Samuel and his son Daniel built a forge for making iron on the Thompson farm, utilizing the waters of the Conasauga, and it was later known as "Thompson's Iron Works." Mary Ann Thompson, 2721 Knollwood Court, Plano, TX 75075. [1989]

Thurston, James M., married Mariah Caroline Davis from Transylvania County. Would like information, particularly on his parents. He died at Fort Sumter, S. C., in 1865. Also, would like information about Benjamin Henderson, who lived in Transylvania County and had a child named James Edward Henderson. Would also like information about Rhoda Davidson who married Samuel Davis, born in Mecklenburg county about 1755. He was graduated from Princeton College and was a Presbyterian minister. Mildred Mims, 903 Shepard Square, Brevard, NC 28712. [1991]

Tilton family. Would like to correspond with any family member researching this family that was in Asheville during the 1920s through the 1930s. Particularly interested in Mrs. Jane Tilton. Helen Ingle, P. O. Box 367, Tuxedo, NC 28784. [1990]

Tolley family. Would like information on the following members. Daniel Tolley, born 1793, married Jane Howell and lived in Yancey County in the 1850s. Their son Swinfield Tolley who was born in 1842 maried Elizabeth Tolley, daughter of David Tolley and Susan Wilson. Swinfield and Elizabeth's son John W. Tolley was born in 1894. They also had a son William who married Laura Bailey, Are these Tolleys kin to Elias Tolley who was in Rutherford County in 1790 or Elhorah Tolley who was in Buncombe in 1810? Ruth Tolley McClure, Rt. 3, Box 408, Hendersonville, NC 28739. [1989]

Tolley, Robert Dyer, born about 1774. Would like information about his family. Margie Noe, 140 Trammell Rd., Marietta, SC 29661. [1990]

Tow/Towe, Thomas, born in the 1820s, married Martha Cogburn, born 1829, daughter of James Cogburn and Polly Lance. Would like more information on Thomas. He and Martha lived in Buncombe County and later Henderson. Thomas married, second, Hattie Pressley. Was he a son of William Towe who married Mary Fletcher? Were either of these kin to Reuben Tow? Joyce Parris, 220 Northwest Ave., Swannanoa, NC 28778. [1993]

Tow, William, born September 5, 1811, in North Carolina, married in Missouri, Mary Kelsey about 1833. Would like information about him. He died May 8, 1889, in Llano County, Texas. Were his parents part of the Tow family that migrated to Scandinavian Countries in the 16th and 17th centuries from Scotland? Katheryn Norton, 1625 E. Browning Avenue, Fresco, CA 93710. [1990]

Townsends of North and South Carolina. Would like information concerning their origins. Did they first settle in the Charleston area from

Massachusetts and with ancestral lineage going back to Raynham, England? James Walther, 83 Dogwood Drive, Weaverville, NC 28787. [1988]

Trewhitt/Truet, Judge Levi, born July 14, 1797, in Rowan, lived in Rutherford and Buncombe Counties before moving to Tennessee with his mother after his father died. Would like to know where his father died. Blair Trewitt, 7111 Factory Shoals Rd., S. W., Austell, GA 30001. [1992]

Truitt family. Would like information on the parents of Susanna Morgan who said she was born in Rowan County about 1780. She married Levi Truitt and was living in the household of her daughter Susannah Truitt Thomason in Macon County in the 1850 census. Would also like to know the names of the parents of Susan Ann Shearer who married Thomas Issac Truitt about 1825. Thomas and Susan went to Texas from Macon County about 1837, settling in Shelby County where they died before 1850. Would like to hear from descendants of James Madison Thomasson and wife Susannah Rebecca Truitt who lived near Bryson City. Mrs. M. F. Calloway, 207 West Fairlane, Longview, TX 75604. [1986]

Trosper family. Would like information on the following family members. Nicholas Trosper was in Burke in the late 1700s; Nichlas Trasper, probably son was on the Buncombe County census in 1820. Would particularly be interested in how this Trosper family was kin to the Hyatt family of Buncombe; Shadrack Hyatt and his wife Lucinda had a son born about 1846 named Nicholas Trosper Hyatt. Would like to get in touch with Lillian Bird Thomas, who wrote *Robert Patton, His Descendants and Brothers*,1961, Asheville, to find out more about the Peter Trosper who married Martha Carolina Patton, sister of Elizabeth Patton who married David Crockett. Gerald Brown, 111 Cumberland Ave., #7, Asheville, NC 28801. [1984]

Trosper, Peter, born 1779, received land grant on the Swannanoa in 1825, next to Robert Patton. He was supposedly married at least atwice and to Matilda Carolina Patton, daughter of Robert and Rebecca Patton. Would like more information about him. Did he have a daughter named Polly, born about 1823 or a son named Peter? How is he related to Peter Trosper who married Rebecca Logan and lived and died in Knox County, Kentucky? Also interested in Nickles Trosper who was in

Buncombe in 1820. Patricia H. Mellor, 5829 Riverside Lane, Fort Myers, FL 33907.

Truesdell/Truesdale/Trousdale family. Many Truesdell families were in North Carolina at various times. Would like more information about them. One family was that of John Trousdale who was born about 1703 and died in North Carolina. Diane T. Loy, 17990 Royal Crest Drive, Brookfield, WI 53045. [1991]

Turner, James, born in North Carolina on October 8, 1829, died in Livingston Parish, Louisiana, on August 19, 1892. Would like more information about his family. His parents were James Turner and Mary Harrell. Both parents were raised, married, and died in North Carolin. Would like to know the location. There were eight children in the family. One was James; one was Henry, born in N. C. on February 9, 1837, and died in Livingston Parish, August 22, 1912. Robert B. Craig, 8924 Gail Drive, Baton Rouge, LA 70809. [1990]

Underwood, James/Jim M., son of Bart Yancy Underwood from Wake County and Clayton, N. C. Would like more information. Some Underwoods came to Asheville. Marie Jordan, Rt. 2, Azalea Rd., Arden, NC 28704. [1988]

Vanderbilt, Susannah, born about 1797 in Tennessee, married in Tennessee about 1816 to Alexander Gray. Susannah's family may have lived in the area of North Carolina which was later Tennessee. Family tradition was that she was disinherited because she married Gray. Any help with her Vanderbilt line would be appreciated. Mrs. J. M. Setzler, 501 Lakeshore Rd., Jackson, MS 39212. [1986]

Vaughn, Sherwood, listed in the 1800 census of Burke County and the 1810 census of Lincoln County, N. C. Mrs. Granvil Vaughn, Rt. 1, Box 840, West Plains, MO 65775. [1986]

Wadlington, Thomas, Jr., born 1740 and died 1803, married Elizabeth Baskins. Would like more information about him. He moved from Newberry District to Rutherford County, N. C., in the late 1700s and was a Justice of the Peace. Would like the names of his father's and mother's parents. Thomas, Jr., was the son of Thomas, Sr., and Sarah Wyatt Wadlington. Dorothy W. Burd, P. O. Box 521, Maggie, NC 28751. [1990]

Waldrop family. Would like information about Will Waldrop who came to Buncombe or Madison County with his half-brother Noah Waldrop about 1870 or 1872 from Polk County. Will settled in the Sandy Mush section of Buncombe and Noah in Leicester. Who was the father of Will and Noah? Also, would like other information about them. Charlie Waldrop, 303 Charlotte Hwy., Asheville, NC 28803. [1989]

Waldrope/Wardrope, Edward, 1758-1844, served five tours of duty for a total of eighteen months in the Revolutionary War from Wake County. In 1780 he married Frances Roberts, and they had the following known children: Eli, Solomon, Polly, David, Tom, James, Elizabeth Underwood, Nancy McDaniel. The 1830 census of Buncombe shows Edward as head of household with one male 70-80 and one female 60-70. In 1834, he applied for a pension from Yancey County and was granted $40 per year. The list of polls for the 12th Congressional District showed Edward on Ivy in Jerves/Jarves precinct. In 1840 the census of Yancey County showed, in the household of Solomon Waldrope, a male 80-90. Edward is entitled to a marker at his grave for his service in the Revolution. Would very much like to know where he and Frances are buried so that a marker could be placed. John L. Waldroop, Rt. 68, Box 8, Tuckasegee, NC 28783. [1989]

Waldrup/Waldrop, Nancy, born in North Carolina about 1820. Would like to know the names of her parents. She married James Waldrup. They lived in Yancey County, N. C., and were in Madison County in 1860. They had the following children: John born 1841, Eli born 1844, William born 1846, Lucinda born 1839, Mary born 1842, Martha born 1844, Margaret born 1847, Sarah born 1850, Nancy born 1852. Linda Holder, 1037 Riverside Drive, Asheville, NC 28804. [1991]

Wall, Rev. Howell, Sr., born 1765 in Beaufort County, North Carolina, married Rebecca Varner in 1788 in South Carolina. Would like to know the name of his father. He was the grandson of Rev. Joseph Wall of Maryland who had sons James, Joseph, Howell, and Robert. Claude W. Wall, 8425 Kenilworth Ct., Baton Rouge, LA 70806. [1990]

Walton, Timothy J., born about 1801 in Georgia. Would like information about him. His first wife died young, and he moved to Western North Carolina where he married Emma Elvira Haren, daughter of Joshua Haren and Nancy Mackey, in Buncombe County, January 19, 1850. Timothy Walton died in Buncombe after 1880 and was at that time living with his daughter Mary and her husband, Issac Holcombe. Avery Parker, 181 Eller Cove Rd., Weaverville, NC 28787.

Warren, Alfred Martin, married Caroline Christine Fox. Would like information about both of these. Alfred Warren was from Buncombe County and born in 1843. He died in 1902. Christine, from Tennessee, died in 1903. One of their children was Eugene Leroy Warren who was born in 1883 and died in 1959. Would also like to know how Abner Eller was related to Christine Warren. James R. Warren, 4834 First Ave., North, Duluth, Minnesota 55803. [1993]

Washburn, Jane, born 1880, married John Martin Goins about 1897. They lived in Shelby, N. C., in 1900 and had four children. He married second to Lydia Tiddy about 1909. Am particularly interested in the parents of Jane Washburn. Peggy Lee Cox, Rt. 1, Box 778, Spruce Pine, NC 28777. [1988]

Watkins, James, born about 1860, Buncombe, married on November 18, 1875, Lucinda Murray, daughter of Samuel Murray and Addie Cannon. Would like information about him. They possibly lived in the Enka area. Would like to know where they are buried. Grace Watkins Pittman, Rt. 1, Box 404-B, Hendersonville, NC 28739. [1984]

Weaver. "The Tribe of Jacob, A Supplement, 1962-1984" was published in 1984. This book includes reprinted pages from Pearl Weaver's book on the John Weaver settlement in the Reems Creek Valley of Buncombe County. It also includes updated statistics on the descendants of Jacob Weaver, an overview of the family meetings from 1859-1983, poetry, and sketches. Wanda Teague, P. O. Box 341, Weaverville, NC 28787. Josephine Osborne, P. O. Box 291, Weaverville, NC 28787.

Weaver family, moved from North Carolina to Lancaster County, S. C. The brother and sisters in South Carolina included Fannie, Martha, Elizabeth, John Middleton, and Thomas P. Weaver. Mrs. Thomas P. Weaver was later listed on the 1850 census in Itawamba Coounty, Mississippi, with Ady (female) Weaver who was shown as born about 1780 in North Carolina. Francis Weaver Allen later lived in St. Francis County, Arkansas, and lived with Catherine Harrison, who was born about 1780 in North Carolina. Does anyone in Western North Carolina know how the Weavers and Harrisons were kin to the Middleton family. Mrs. Martha Bone, 1777 Pinewood Drive, Greenville, MS 38701.

Weaver, David, born in Anderson County, Tennessee, married Freeley Childrers about 1840. Would like information on him and any of their ten children. One of their ten children was Lorenzo Weaver who married Martha Bray. Marie King, 1812 South 8, Rogers, AZ 72756. [1990]

Webb, John Calvin, born in Buncombe in 1847, married Jane M. Hensley from Yancey County. Would like information on his father. The father's name was Henry Webb who lived in Buncombe in the early 1800s. Mrs. Ollie S. Henderson, 17 East Gilbert St., Hampton, VA 23669. [1984]

Wells, Henry Grady did research on the Wells family in Buncombe before the Civil War. This Henry Wells was a descendant of Larkin Wells, son of Thomas and Mary O'Bryan Wells of Buncombe in the early 1800s. Would like to know if anyone has a copy of this research. Thomas and Mary Wells had a son Henry Wells, who married Elizabeth Phillips, a daughter of Adam Phillips and Hannah Bailey. Henry Wells's son Hiram Phillips Wells was born about 1823 in Buncombe and was in Gilmer County, Georgia in 1850 when he married Susan Pence, daughter of Absolam and Frances Pence who were in Buncombe in 1815 and moved to Gilmer County by 1830. Leslee C. Fehlman, 3606 Peute Trail, Austin TX 78739. [1987]

West family. Would like information on the following. Silas West, October 24, 1818 - June 7, 1884, married Elizabeth Rogers, November 21, 1823-April 28, 1900, lived in Sandy Mush township, Leicester, N. C., raised fifteen children; William Posey, born 1846, married Milley Brinkley; James, born 1848; Andrew Newton, born 1851, married Sarah Bonham; Mary born 1854; Sarah, born 1855, married Gossett; Adaline, born 1857; Martha, born 1856; Charles Massey, born 1858, married Loni Henderson; Patrick, born 1860, married Sarah Mann; John S., born 1861; Hanna, born 1863; Eliza Jane, born 1864; Laura C., born 1867; Benjamin Frank, born 1868; Catherine, born 1871. Annie West Cookston, Rt. 2, Box 65, Franklin, NC 28734. [1984]

West, Julina Bryan, born 1816 and died 1857, married Job West. Her parents were Lewis Bryan and Judith Peek from Madison County. Afton W. Stanley, 2639 No 225 West, Sunset, Utah 84015. [1984]

West, Leonard, born about 1787. Would like to know where he and his wife are buried. Supposedly, they are buried on Walnut Creek, Madison County, but unable to find. Polly W. Book, 641 Mag Sluder Rd., Alexander, NC 28701. [1983]

Whitfield, Albert Liverett, born in North Carolina on July 24, 1852, married Jane Eliza Reid on December 21, 1876. Would like information about him. Jane was the daughter of Adam Patton Reid and Margaret Monteath who came from Scotland in 1853. Albert died on March 23, 1898, and is buried at Tweed's Chapel Cemetery. One son was named Adam Reid Liverett. Would especially like to know the name of Whitfield's parents. Patricia Liverett Loy, 1121 Northwest 185th St., Edmond, OK 73034. [1991]

Whitlow, John William, born about 1859 in Charlotte and died about 1891 or 1892 in Asheville. He had a sister Frances Whitlow Patterson who lived in Winston-Salem. John had been to the Asheville area hunting a job when he beccame ill of typhoid fever and died. His wife, Betty Jane Thomason Whitlow, stayed in Asheville and married a Dr. Gudger and was buried in the Gudger family cemetery in Candler. She was born August 16, 1862, and died February 11, 1925. Would particularly like to know where John Whitlow is buried. Betty W. Burke, 2407 S. Ponte Vedra, Ponte Vedra Beach, FL 32082. [1988]

Whittington Family History. Would like to know if anyone has a copy. This was prepared by Margaret Eller. Particularly interestsed in the family of Benjamin Whittington, born Drakes Creek, Warren, KY, on November 27, 1822, and died January 27, 1902, Yancey County, North Carolina. He first married Margaret Jane Ray in 1850, daughter of Henry and Elizabeth Wilson Ray; second married Harriet Angel. Margaret King, Rt. 2, Box 126, Burnsville, NC 28714. [1987]

Williams, Alfred A., born about 1822, married Elizabeth Brittain in Buncombe County in 1851. Elizabeth was the daughter of Robert Brittain and granddaughter of William Brittain. They lived in the Flat Creek section and raised a large family. Alfred Williams apparently died before 1870, when his wife was listed as head of household. Would like more information about him. W. H. Jones, 28 Garrison Rd., Weaverville, NC 28787. [1987]

Williams, John C., born about 1804 in North Carolina, living in Big Ivy section of Buncombe about 1850. Would like information about him and also information about his wife, Matilda Phillips, born about 1805 in North Carolina. Gerald Brown, Apt. 7, 111 Cumberland Ave., Asheville, NC 28801. [1984]

Williams, John L., of Chimney Rock and Fairview areas, born 1821 and died 1885. Would like information on his parents. He married first

Susannah E. Patton, and married second her sister Sarah Catherine Patton Byers. These were both daughters of Matthew Patton of Cane Creek. Would also like information on Nancy Williams, second child of John. Martha Brookshire, Rt. 4, 750 Old Leicester Hwy., Asheville, NC 28806. [1985]

Williams, William Withan, born 1800 in North Carolina, moved to Manleyville/Paris, Tennessee, married Elizabeth. Would like information about him. Would also like information about Nathan Winfield, born 1770 in North Carolina and died in Greene County, Georgia. Louise Williams, 943 Woodbourne Dr., S. W., Atlanta, GA 30310. [1986]

Williamson, Rev. Hill. Would like information concerning which Presbyterian Church had this minister in the Asheville area about 1888-1890. Would also like any information about him. Robert Graham, 925 Parker St., Charlotte, NC 28216. [1988]

Willis family. Would like information on the Willis family in Spartanburg, S. C., who were related to the Caldwells. Jane Caldwell Willis had children Ann-Pauline Rose, Andrew, and John Pinkney. Would also like information on the Gilbert family who came into Western North Carolina from Union, S. C., particularly John and wife Frances Gilbert. Mrs. T. A. Steele, 634 Monte Vista Rd., Candler, NC 28715. [1986]

Wills, Edward received a marriage bond in 1786 in Richmond County, N. C., to Sarah Vaughn. Would like information about him. She and Edward were in Wilkes County, Georgia, in 1801. Was she the daughter of Abner Vaughn of Richmond County? William R. Mills, M. D., P. O. Box 32, Doouglas, GA 31533. [1991]

Wilson, Joseph, lived on Buck Creek in present McDowell County, N. C. Would like information about his family. He possibly had sons Andrew, Jospeh and John. He died in 1909. Was he married to Mary Young, a daughter of Joseph Young, and was Captain Joseph Young of North Cove, old Burke County, a brother to Thomas Young, born 1747? Would also like information on the family of Thomas Gallion and wife Mary Young who married in Maryland in 1732 and moved to old Burke County, N. C. Lawrence Wood, 75 Peeks Creek Rd., Franklin, NC 28734. [1992]

Withrow, Thomas Jefferson, born about 1835, Rutherford County, died 1906, buried in Tanner Grove Cemetery, wife Priscilla, married in

1865. Would like more information about him. His ancestors migrated from Scotland and were in Virginia in 1746. Betty Mainer, P. O. Box 1663, Marion, NC 28752. [1987]

Wood, Neil Elic, born in 1866, Cumberland County, N. C. Would like information about his brothers and sisters. His parents were Goodman and Clarrissa Wood. Carmen Wood, 6708 W. Clifton, Tampa, FL 33634. [1987]

Woodard family. Would like information on the descendants of John Woodward who came into North Carolina from Tennessee at the close of the Civil War. Elizabeth Gibson, 192 Harrison Ave., Franklin, NC 28734. [1987]

Woodard, William, born about 1779, married Elisabeth, lived at Ivy, N. C., by 1800. Would like more information. One son was Isom Woodard who married Rebecca Webb of Tennessee. One son of Isom and Rebecca was Mountreville Woodard, born in Madison County, who married Elisabeth Ann Martin, and died in Searcy County, Arkansas. Connie Fields, 1028 Parkway Road, Salinas, CA 93905. [1989]

Woodfin, Denny. Would like information about her parents. She married Joseph Dennis Gash of Swannanoa about 1800. She later went to Missouri with several children. Would also like any Gash information that would relate to these. Ms. Willie Lou Jordan, P. O. Box 1817, Hendersonville, NC 28793. [1986]

Woody, John A., born about 1826, died in Macon County, N. C., on December 29, 1903. Would like to know the names of his parents, brothers, and sisters. His wife was Manerva Palestine Bradshaw, born April 30, 1827, died May 29, 1907. Christine Proctor, 510 Bryson Branch Rd., Bryson City, NC 28713. [1986]

Wright, W. Thomas, born 1859, and Thedore Wright, born sometime after 1862. Would like more information about them. Their parents were Jane Harris and George Washington Wright, Jr., of Haywood County, N. C. There were four children; the other two were Polly Anna, 1857-1901, unmarried, and Wesley Wright, born 1862. Jean Warren, P. O. Box 533, Candler, NC 28715. [1984]

York, John, and Rachel Lee, married January 25, 1805, in Rutherford County, N. C. Would like information about them. Would like to know if this John York appeared in Polk County, Tennessee, in the 1840 census and if Rachel York appeared in Monroe County, Tennesee, in the 1850 and 1860 censuses. Barbara Dooley, Rt. 67, Box 89-A, Cullowhee, NC 28723. [1984]

Young family. Would like family history on ancestors of this family. John Young was born in England in the early 1700s and married Martha Stuart, kin to the Stuart family of Scotland. John and Martha had thirteen children; several lived in the Hominy Creek area of Buncombe County, N. C. Stacy Young, a daughter, married John Webb who was an early settler in the Candler area. Am particularly interested in information of Columbus Hezekiah Young's daughters who lived in Candler, N. C. Mildred Young Smith, 314 Altamahaw Ave., Black Mountain, NC 28711. [1988]

Young, James, Buncombe County. Would like information about his parents. One son of James was William Jasper Young who was born in 1861 in Candler and married Lizzie Allen. Another son was Henry. Would like to know if Jack Young, whose mother was Jane Curtis Young was kin to James Young. Nellie Young Ammons, Rt. 3, Box 300, Candler, NC 28715. [1988]

CONCLUSION

From these inquiries from across the United States to just one column in Western North Carolina, you can see how many people are searching for their ancestors. You are not alone in this hobby or "obsession."

Even though you may not be sure why you want to know about all of your families, there must be a reason for why you work so hard. If you ever know, let me know why we are such "driven" people who holler, "I want to know." I have a feeling some ancestors do not want us to know everything, and we may never find out all the answers, but ---

Good luck!

APPENDIX B

PUBLISHERS' ADDRESSES

Ancestry Publishing Company
P. O. 476
Salt Lake City, UT 84110-0476

Clearfield Company
200 East Eager Street
Baltimore, MD 21202

Genealogical Publishing Company, Inc.
1001 N. Calvert Street
Baltimore, MD 21202

Historical Publications Section,
Division of Archives and History
109 East Jones Street
Raleigh, NC 27601-2807

INDEX

This index does not include names that are in the Appendix.

316